The Rights and Wrongs of Land Restitution

'Restoring What Was Ours'

The Rights and Wrongs of Land Restitution: 'Restoring What Was Ours' offers a critical, comparative ethnographic examination of land restitution programmes. Drawing on memories and histories of past dispossession, governments, NGOs, informal movements and individual claimants worldwide have attempted to restore and reclaim rights in land. Land restitution programmes link the past and the present, and may allow former landholders to reclaim lands which provided the basis of earlier identities and livelihoods. Restitution also has a moral weight that holds broad appeal; it is represented as righting injustice and healing the injuries of colonialism. Restitution may have unofficial purposes, like establishing the legitimacy of a new regime, quelling popular discontent or attracting donor funds. It may produce unintended consequences, transforming notions of property and ownership, entrenching local bureaucracies, or replicating segregated patterns of land use. It may also constitute new relations between states and their subjects. Land-claiming communities may make new claims on the state, but they may also find the state making unexpected claims on their land and livelihoods. Restitution may be a route to citizenship, but it may engender new or neo-traditional forms of subjection. This book explores these possibilities and pitfalls by examining cases from the Americas, Eastern Europe, Australia and South Africa. Addressing the practical and theoretical questions that arise, *The Rights and Wrongs of Land Restitution* thereby offers a critical rethinking of the links between land restitution and property, social transition, injustice, citizenship, the state and the market.

Derick Fay is Assistant Professor of Anthropology at the University of California, Riverside.

Deborah James is Professor of Anthropology at the London School of Economics.

The Rights and Wrongs of Land Restitution

'Restoring What Was Ours'

Edited by Derick Fay and
Deborah James

First published 2009 by Routledge-Cavendish
2 Park Square, Milton Park, Abingdon, Oxon OX14 4RN

Simultaneously published in the USA and Canada
by Routledge-Cavendish
270 Madison Ave, New York, NY 10016

Routledge-Cavendish is an imprint of the Taylor & Francis Group, an informa business

Transferred to Digital Printing 2009

© 2009 Derick Fay and Deborah James editorial matter and selection, individual chapters the contributors

Typeset in Sabon by
RefineCatch Limited, Bungay, Suffolk

All rights reserved. No part of this book may be reprinted or reproduced or utilized in any form or by any electronic, mechanical, or other means, now known or hereafter invented, including photocopying and recording, or in any information storage or retrieval system, without permission in writing from the publishers.

British Library Cataloguing in Publication Data
A catalogue record for this book is available from the British Library

Library of Congress Cataloging in Publication Data
The rights and wrongs of land restitution: 'restoring what was ours' /c Derick Fay and Deborah James.
  p. cm.
  Includes bibliographical references.
1. Indigenous peoples—Legal status, laws, etc. 2. Land titles.
3. Reparations for historical injustices. I. Fay, Derick. II. James, Deborah, Dr.
  K3248.L36R54 2008
  333.3′1—dc22
                                                              2007049627

ISBN10: 0-415-46108-1 (hbk)
ISBN10: 0-415-57449-8 (pbk)
ISBN10: 0-203-89549-5 (ebk)

ISBN13: 978-0-415-46108-5 (hbk)
ISBN13: 978-0-415-57449-5 (pbk)
ISBN13: 978-0-203-89549-8 (ebk)

Contents

Preface	xi
Acknowledgements	xiv
List of contributors	xv
List of Tables and Figures	xviii
List of abbreviations	xix

1 **'Restoring what was ours': An introduction** 1
   DERICK FAY AND DEBORAH JAMES

   The anthropology of restitution 2
   Restitution: a temporal process 6
   Property, community, government: citizen or subject? 11
       Community and governance: 'no nation within a nation' 12
       The institutionalization of property 14
       The rights and wrongs of restitution 17
   Conclusion 18
   References 19
   Notes 23

2 **Property, subjection and protected areas: The 'restitution' of Dwesa-Cwebe Nature Reserve, South Africa** 25
   DERICK FAY

   Abstract 25
   Grounding claims to land 27
   Bundles of duties, handfuls of rights 33
   The effectiveness of rights 35
   New forms of subjection 36
   Conclusion 38
   References 39
   Notes 41

3 'They should be killed': Forest restitution, ethnic groups and
   patronage in post-socialist Romania   43
   STEFAN DORONDEL

   Abstract 43
   Property, access and patronage in the post-socialist context 44
   Decollectivization and forest restitution 46
        Establishing new rights and duties en route to 'restitution' 49
        Rudari – a marginalized ethnic group 50
   Patronage, access and deforestation: mechanisms at work 51
   Conclusions 58
   References 60
   Notes 63

4 The lie of the land: Identity politics and the Canadian land claims
   process in Labrador   67
   EVIE PLAICE

   Abstract 67
   Introduction 67
   Interim 68
   Restitution 74
   The associations 76
        The Labrador Inuit Association 76
        The Innu nation 78
        The Labrador Metis Association 79
   Conclusion 81
   References 83
   Notes 84

5 The antithesis of restitution? A note on the dynamics of land
   negotiations in the Yukon, Canada   85
   PAUL NADASDY

   Abstract 85
   Giving land 88
   Competing conceptions of 'balance' in land selection 93
   References 95
   Notes 96

6   Enacting sovereignty in a colonized space: The Yolngu of Blue
    Mud Bay meet the native title process   99
    FRANCES MORPHY

    Abstract 99
    Introduction 99
    The Aboriginal Land Rights (Northern Territory) Act 1976 (Cwlth) 100
    The Native Title Act 1993 (Cwlth) 101
    Colonization and encapsulation: the Yolngu view 102
    Performance and enactment: the ritual space of the court 104
         The arena 105
         Who gets to speak, and how 105
    The witness statement – neither fish nor fowl? 108
    The Yolngu response 110
         The insertion of performance: sacred power made manifest 110
         The advantages of giving 'non-evidence' 111
         Ancestral forces insert their own performance 113
         The insistence on difference 114
    Conclusion 116
    References 118
    Notes 120

7   Ethnoracial land restitution: Finding Indians and fugitive slave
    descendants in the Brazilian Northeast   123
    JAN HOFFMAN FRENCH

    Abstract 123
    *Land restitution claims as spurred by the disappointment of
         development projects 125*
    'Discovery' of indigenous and black identities 127
    Multiple meanings of land and their impact on the value of restitution 129
    Factions and ruptures in the Mocambo 'community' 133
    Being black or Indian when land is at stake 136
    Conclusion 137
    References 137
    Notes 138

8   The will-to-community: Between loss and reclamation
     in Cape Town   141
     CHRISTIAAN BEYERS

     Abstract 141
     Introduction 141
     Background 142
     The question of community 144
     Racially differentiated citizenship 147
     The broken self 149
     Reconciling the old and the new 152
     Practical aspirations for a new District Six 155
     Apprehensions for a new District Six 157
     Conclusion 159
     References 160
     Notes 162

9   Through the prism: Local reworking of land restitution
     settlements in South Africa   163
     YVES VAN LEYNSEELE AND PAUL HEBINCK

     Abstract 163
     Introduction 163
     Competing discourses of land restitution 164
     Case study 1 – Cattle and the struggle for the city: Mandlazini 166
        Religion, land and politics 167
        Agri-village and settlement 168
        Reworking and fragmentation 170
     *Case study 2 – Seeking common ground, finding hidden claims:
        the Makhoba Community Project 172*
        The resettlement narrative 172
        Enter development values 175
     Emergent properties of land restitution 178
     Conclusions 180
     References 181
     Notes 183

10 *¿Dueños de todo y de nada!* (Owners of all and nothing):
    Restitution of Indian territories in the Central Andes of Peru   185
    MONIQUE NUIJTEN AND DAVID LORENZO

   Abstract 185
   Endowment versus restitution 185
        Indian highland communities: between haciendas and valley
            towns 186
        The law and 'the problem of the Indian' 187
        Usibamba: gaining ground and fighting for independence 188
   The Peruvian land reform: the SAIS as creature of the state 190
        Owing the state: 'gifts' and the Agrarian debt 192
        From restitution to endowment: from Indian to peasant 193
        Usibamba and the Túpac Amaru SAIS 193
        The remission of the Agrarian debt: the state's betrayal 197
        Sendero Luminoso (Shining Path) and Túpac Amaru 198
        Changed relationships: comuneros and the huacchis
            of the SAIS 201
   Restitution of land and indigenous rights in a new political climate 202
   Conclusion: rights, recognition and restitution 204
   References 205
   Notes 207

11 *Que sucede con PROCEDE?* (What is happening with
    PROCEDE?): The end of land restitution in rural Mexico   209
    KRISTINA TIEDJE

   Abstract 209
   Introduction 209
   Indigenous organizing and the state 212
   Background to restitution 213
   Land restitution and endowments 215
        Local memories 216
        Early twentieth-century nation-building 217
        Ejidos as material resource or site of autonomy? 219
        Indigenous campesinos 221
   Neo-liberalism and the end of land restitution 224
        The myth of the inefficient *ejido* 224
        Nahua *ejidatarios* mobilize against PROCEDE 226
        The multicultural challenge 228
        Claiming alternative modes of citizenship 229

Conclusion 229
References 230
Notes 232

12 'We'll never give in to the Indians': Opposition to restitution in New York State   235
BRIAN BLANCKE

Abstract 235
Introduction 235
Indian land claims (in the eastern US) 236
Public reaction to the 1979 Cayuga land claim settlement 238
Sources of public anger 242
    Hurt and risk 243
    Core beliefs and values 244
        The blame game – there are no guilty parties 244
        Whose land is it anyway? 245
        Reservations about reservations 247
    Weakness and lies 249
The Cayuga Work Group's response to the public opposition 251
Conclusion 253
References 254
Notes 256

Index 261

Preface

Throughout the world, land claims processes are under way to address dispossession that has taken place under colonialism and socialism. While many anthropologists have written on land restitution worldwide, from Cape Cod (James Clifford) to Romania (Katherine Verdery) to New Zealand (Michele Dominy), with a few exceptions authors have tended to stay within their cases and/or regions, rather than taking on the tasks of comparison and synthesis.

The chapters in this book begin the task of developing a comparative study of land restitution. Drawing on memories and histories of past loss, individual claimants and informal movements – and governments or non-governmental organizations (NGOs) working on their behalf – have attempted to restore and reclaim land rights. In the process, they have aimed to set right the injustices of colonial and post-colonial dispossession. This is not a simple task, especially where dispossession is deep in the past, and land may have changed hands many times. While restitution is an idea with an almost intuitive moral appeal, carrying it out inevitably forces lofty principles of justice and restoration to confront the messy practicalities of determining ownership, defining legitimate claimants, establishing evidence for claims and overcoming potential opposition by current landowners. Brian Blancke's account of the Cayuga Nation's land claim in New York tells vividly of some of these challenges, drawing its title from a song local landowners used to sing: 'we'll never give in to the Indians and we'll never give up our deeds'.

The negotiations involved in this process often require the submission of formal evidence. In the process, communities find themselves in interaction with outside actors. They may encounter both the stolid immovability of legal and bureaucratic process, and the more nuanced flexibility associated with less formal kinds of negotiation. But, as both Paul Nadasdy's chapter on the Yukon, Canada and Frances Morphy's chapter on Blue Mud Bay, Australia, demonstrate, in either event the results may be less than satisfactory to claimants.

In some settings, the (real and imagined) communities that held land may be geographically dispersed or long since passed away. The ways of life that they practised and living conditions that they enjoyed on their land may be undesirable or unfeasible by the time the possibility of restitution arises. Christiaan

Beyers writes of the 'will to community' among people removed from District Six, in central Cape Town, South Africa, recounting an informant's nostalgia and hope that restitution could restore a place free of urban violence: 'You could be outside late at night in District Six. Your children could be outside late [in the evening]. You don't have to be afraid. It shall all just be nice like it originally was there'.

Restitution is also a key context for reshaping relations between states and their subjects: as Katherine Verdery observed in *The Vanishing Hectare*, the state is often 'both playing the game and making the rules'. Land-claiming communities may make new claims on the state, but they may also find the state making unexpected claims on their land and livelihoods. As often, it is the state guided by, or in a complex interaction with, the demands of the market that results in the reshaping of claimants' original demands. Yves van Leynseele and Paul Hebinck tell of a case in South Africa where land restitution was accompanied by aggressive state demands that the claimants form an 'agri-village'; being 'traditional' had been compelling in staking and winning support for their claim, but once they received their land, they were told in effect that their agricultural practices had to be 'modernized'. Derick Fay, writing on the Eastern Cape, describes a process in which the state and its consultants impose a specific vision of restored forest as a tourist reserve. In Latin American cases featuring more than a century of struggle over land, its official restoration was similarly accompanied by its effective alienation from claimants. Monique Nuijten and David Lorenzo recount how in highland Peru the haciendas, although 'endowed' to communities of cultivators, were in fact run by the same groups of officers and administrators as before – although their grip was somewhat loosened by the impact of the revolutionary Shining Path movement. Kristina Tiedje tells of a situation in Mexico in which the state's radically free-market-oriented 'solution' of taking land out of communal (*ejido*) ownership and giving it to individual titleholders was fiercely resisted by those perceiving in this a threat of alienation or effective dispossession – that is, of 'the end of restitution'. Another form of effective dispossession is described by Stefan Dorondel in Romania, where state actors collaborate informally and illicitly with poor woodcutters to deprive newly restored landowners of their restituted forest. There are multiple means through which the impact of restitution may be reduced, even minimized.

Finally, in staking their claims, people often (re)define themselves as groups or communities, both feeding upon and stimulating assertions of cultural and political autonomy that may challenge the sovereignty of the state. In the Brazilian Northeast it was only the process of claiming that suggested the possibility of community orientation: Jan Hoffman French describes two groupings that commenced new forms of ethnic self-definition and imposed new kinds of community organization in order to stake their claim to land. Some bases for 'community', however, may prove more effective than others; Evelyn Plaice recounts a case from Labrador, Canada: attempting to build a claim based upon a hybrid identity and way of life, the Labrador Metis found their claim competing with apparently more publicly compelling ones based on 'native' status.

These authors and the others in this book highlight the way the study of land restitution intersects with key themes in political and legal anthropology. As claimants continue to organize, creating new forms of community and entering into new relations with the state in the process, restitution continues to offer a fruitful terrain for anthropologists seeking to understand the reworking of property and citizenship in contexts of political transformation, the politics of injustice and redress, the state and the market and the place of memory in the present.

The collection had its origins in conversations we had at a conference on land and landlessness at the Max Planck Institute in May 2002. Derick had just finished co-editing a book on a land claim in South Africa's Eastern Cape, while Deborah was in the midst of the fieldwork for her book on land reform in Mpumalanga. At that time we envisioned a workshop bringing together a range of social scientists working on land restitution in South Africa.

Stimulated in part by a reading of Katherine Verdery's account of restitution in Romania (2003), Paul Nadasdy's discussion of property in land claims in the Canadian Yukon (2002) and Hansen and Stepputat (2001)'s collection on the state and citizenship, we re-envisioned the project along more comparative lines. This resulted in a call for papers for the 2005 American Anthropological Association Annual Meetings. With the exception of the papers by Morphy and Fay (both written for this book), all of the contributions here resulted from that call for papers. Parker Shipton and Jake Kosek both served as discussants at the double panel, and we owe them and the other participants a debt of gratitude for their insights at an early stage of the process.

Derick Fay and Deborah James
November 2007

Acknowledgements

Figure 7.2 is reprinted with the kind permission of ITDG Publishing.

All the photographs in Chapter 3 were taken by Thomas Sikor and are reproduced with his permission.

Thanks to Daniel Müller who designed Figures 3.1 and 3.5.

Every effort has been made to trace and contact copyright holders prior to publication. If notified, the publisher will undertake to rectify any errors or omissions at the earliest opportunity.

Contributors

Christiaan Beyers is Assistant Professor in International Development Studies at Trent University. He has published on land restitution in *Journal of Southern African Studies*, *Anthropologica*, *Social Dynamics*, and the *South African Historical Journal*.

Brian Blancke holds a PhD in Social Science and a Certificate of Advanced Study in Conflict Resolution from Syracuse University. A mediator by profession, he is negotiation and difficult conversations trainer for Vantage Partners. He is also a research affiliate at the Program on Negotiation at Harvard Law School where he has published book chapters on the Third Side approach to conflict intervention through PON Books and Jossey-Bass.

Stefan Dorondel is a researcher at the Institute of Anthropology, Bucharest. He holds a PhD in History and Ethnology from the Lucian Blaga University in Sibiu, Romania.

Derick Fay is Assistant Professor of Anthropology at the University of California, Riverside. He holds a PhD in Sociocultural Anthropology from Boston University, and recently completed an SV Ciriacy-Wantrup Postdoctoral Fellow at the University of California, Berkeley. He is the co-editor of *From Conflict to Negotiation: Nature-based Development on South Africa's Wild Coast* (Pretoria, 2002), on the Dwesa-Cwebe restitution claim, and is currently finishing a manuscript on communal tenure and informal, locally organized land reform in South Africa's Transkei.

Paul Hebinck is Associate Professor in the Rural Sociology Development Group, Department of Social Sciences, Wageningen University, the Netherlands and Adjunct Professor in the Faculty of Science and Agriculture University of Fort Hare, South Afirca. His main research interests are in the field of land reform, agriculture and livelihoods in East and Southern Africa. Recent publications include an edited volume with Peter C Lent, *Livelihoods and Landscapes: The people of Guquka and Koloni and their resources* (Leiden/Boston: Brill Academic Publishers, 2007).

Jan Hoffman French is Assistant Professor of Anthropology at the University of Richmond. She holds a PhD in Anthropology from Duke University and a JD from the University of Connecticut Law School. Her post-doctoral fellowships include both the Kellogg Institute for International Studies and a Rockefeller Foundation fellowship at Northwestern University. A former practising attorney in Brazil and the US, her articles have appeared in the *American Ethnologist, American Anthropologist*, and *The Americas*.

Deborah James is Professor of Anthropology at the London School of Economics. Her research interests, focused on South Africa, include migration, ethnomusicology, ethnicity, property relations and the politics of land reform. She is author of *Songs of the Women Migrants: performance and identity in South Africa* (Edinburgh, 1999) and of *Gaining Ground? 'Rights' and 'Property' in South African Land Reform* (London, 2007).

David Lorenzo has an MSc as forestry engineer from the Universidad Complutense in Madrid. At present he is a PhD student at the Center of Development Studies of Roskilde University, Denmark. His research project is entitled 'Territorial Rule in the Central Highlands of Peru: Struggles over Power and Autonomy at the Margin of the State'.

Frances Morphy is Fellow at the Centre for Aboriginal Economic Policy Research, Australian National University, Canberra. She is co-author of *Macquarie Atlas of Indigenous Australia: Culture and Society through Space and Time* (Sydney: The Macquarie Library, Sydney); 'The spirit of the plains kangaroo', in T Bonyhady and T Griffiths (eds) *Words for Country: Landscape and Language in Australia* (Sydney: University of New South Wales Press 2001); and 'Tasting the waters: discriminating identities in the waters of Blue Mud Bay', *Journal of Material Culture* 11(1/2): 67–85, 2006.

Paul Nadasdy is Associate Professor of Anthropology and American Indian Studies at the University of Wisconsin – Madison. His publications include *Hunters and Bureaucrats: Power, Knowledge and Aboriginal-State Relation in the Southwest Yukon* (Vancouver, 2003) as well as articles in *American Anthropologist, Ethnohistory, Arctic Anthropology* and *Anthropologica*.

Monique Nuijten is Associate Professor at the Rural Sociology Group of Wageningen University, the Netherlands. In Mexico and Peru she conducted research on agrarian reform and communal land tenure institutions. A special focus in her work has been the law and relations between peasants and the state. She is author of the book *Power, Community and the State; the Political Anthropology of Organisation in Mexico* (London, 2003). Her last book is the volume co-edited with Gerhard Anders *Corruption and the Secret of Law: A Legal Anthropological Perspective* (Aldershot, 2007).

Evie Plaice is Associate Professor in both Anthropology and Education at the University of New Brunswick. Her research on the Labrador Metis (1978–91) focuses on land use and ethnic identity. She is author of *The Native Game: Indian/Settler Relations in Central Labrador* (St John's: 1990).

Kristina Tiedje (PhD, 2004 University of Oregon) is an Associate Professor (Maître de conférences titulaire) in Anthropology at the Université Lumière Lyon 2, France. Her articles have appeared in several journals and edited books in multiple languages. She is currently working on a book manuscript on the political ecology of the sacred in rural Mexico.

Yves van Leynseele is a PhD student at the department of Sociology of Rural Development, Wageningen University, The Netherlands. His PhD research involves the application of discourse analysis and ethnography to the competing claims on land in the Soutpansberg, South Africa.

Tables and Figures

Table

3.1	Population of Dragomirești commune	46

Figures

3.1	Participatory map	52
3.2	Illegal *Rudari* enclosure on the communal pasture	53
3.3	Wood trucks of the *Rudari* 'elite'	55
3.4	*Rudari* horse cart full of wood	56
3.5	Property rights over forest	58
5.1	Retained KFN settlement land	94
6.1	Problems of translation	109
7.1	Map of Sergipe with São Francisco River	126
7.2	Xocó Indian with Bishop	128
7.3	Quilombo supporter	129
7.4	Quilombo women of Mocambo dancing	130
7.5	Supporter of *Contra* opposition to Quilombo movement	134
10.1	The symbol of the Túpac Amaru SAIS	191
10.2	Illlustration from a training folder for SAIS *comuneros*	196
11.1	Map of the Huasteca	211
11.2	*Ejido* general assembly	221
11.3	Harvest Thanksgiving procession	222
11.4	Corn dolls on the altar at Harvest Thanksgiving	223
12.1	Map of original and proposed Cayuga Reservations	237

Abbreviations

ADC	Amatola District Council
ALRA	Aboriginal Land Rights (Northern Territory) Act 1976 (Commonwealth of Australia)
ANC	African National Congress
ARC	Agricultural Research Council
CBP	Consensus Building Processes
CEB	Church-based Ecclesiastical Community
CNC	National Peasant Confederation
CPA	Communal Property Association
CRLR	Commission on Restitution of Land Rights
CSPOA	Cayuga-Seneca Property Owners Association
D6BRT	District Six Beneficiary and Redevelopment Trust
D6M	District Six Museum
DAD	Decide-Announce-Defend public relations model
DEAT	Department of Economic Affairs and Tourism
DLA	Department of Land Affairs
DWAF	Department of Water Affairs and Forestry
ECDC	Eastern Cape Development Corporation
ECNC	Eastern Cape Nature Conservation
ECPB	Eastern Cape Parks Board
FLLPA	Finger Lakes Land Protection Association
HR	House Resolution
HLUA	Hector Land Use Area
ILO	International Labour Organization
IPS	Integrated Planning Services
ITC	Inuit Tapirisat of Canada
ITIA	Indian Trade and Intercourse Act
IUCN	International Union for the Conservation of Nature
KFN	Kluane First Nation
LIA	Labrador Inuit Association
LIDC	Labrador Inuit Development Corporation
LMA	Labrador Metis Association

MCT	Mandlazini Community Trust
MDC	Mandlazini Development Committee
MGA	Mutual Gains Approach to Negotiation
MPA	Marine Protected Area
MPG	Mokami Project Group
NAFTA	North American Free Trade Agreement
NANL	Native Association of Newfoundland and Labrador
NDF	National Department of the Forest
NGO	Non-Governmental Organization
NIMBY	Not in My Back Yard
NMIA	Naskapi-Montagnais Innu Association
NTA	Native Title Act 1993 (Commonwealth of Australia)
PFD	Private Forest Department
PILOTs	payments-in-lieu-of-taxes
PROCEDE	Programme of Certification of Individual Rights to Farm Plots, Common Land and Urban Lots
RBTLC	Richards Bay Transitional Local Council
RDP	Reconstruction and Development Programme
RLCC	Regional Land Claims Commission
SAIS	*Sociedad Agrícola de Interés Social* (Agrarian Association of Social Interest)
SCLO	Seneca County Liberation Organization
SDI	Spatial Development Initiative
SDP	Social Democratic Party
SFD	State Forest Department
SLAG	Settlement and Land Acquisition Grant
SSP	Sampson State Park
Tralso	Transkei Land Service Organization
TVP	The Village Planner
UFA	Yukon Umbrella Final Agreement
YTG	Yukon Territorial Government

Chapter 1

'Restoring what was ours'
An introduction

Derick Fay and Deborah James

Land dispossession is seen by some as the central political-economic issue of colonialism and as central to the creation of modern capitalism. It has rested not only on force but also on new forms of property and discipline; it has instantiated and affirmed Lockean notions of property and civilization and constructions of racial and ethnic difference. If land bridges material and symbolic concerns, as both a factor of production and a site of belonging and identity (Shipton 1994), then the loss of land is likewise simultaneously material and symbolic. Land restitution promises the redress of such loss. It is aimed at enabling former landholders to reclaim spaces and territories which formed the basis of earlier identities and livelihoods. Drawing on memories and histories of past loss, individual claimants and informal movements – and governments or non-governmental organizations (NGOs) working on their behalf – have attempted to restore and reclaim their rights. Land restitution thus brings the past into the present.

They have aimed, in the process, to set right associated injustices and violations. Land restitution thus forces the moral principles of restoration and justice to confront the difficult practices of determining ownership, defining legitimate claimants and establishing evidence for claims. It is an arena for state formation and nation-building, but also one where alternative forms of governance and counter-national identities may emerge. Particularly, in practice, restitution may draw both on modernity's romantic aspect, a nostalgia for the lost rootedness of landed identity and *gemeinschaft*, and on its technicist aspect, as restitution is implemented through state bureaucracies and often tied to plans for 'development'.

Land restitution may also have unofficial purposes: establishing the legitimacy of a new regime, quelling popular discontent, or attracting donor funds. Likewise, it may produce unintended consequences. Notions of property and ownership may be transformed, local bureaucracies may be entrenched, spatial patterns of land use that replicate older patterns of racial and economic segregation may be reinstated or consolidated. Moral discourses about righting past injustice through restitution may obscure its exclusionary aspects or its tendency to reinforce existing forms of social differentiation.

Land restitution arises from and relies upon key social relationships. Community belonging, often framed in terms of ethnicity or autochthony, may enhance the claims of certain dispossessed people but can also exclude others. Restitution frequently involves brokerage, as NGO representatives and others mediate between land claimants, landowners and the state. It also creates new relationships between states and their subjects: land-claiming communities may make new demands on the state, but they may also find the state attempting unexpectedly to control their land and livelihoods. It may be a route to full citizenship, or lead to new or neo-traditional forms of subjection. Thus land restitution contradictorily invokes the two visions of nationhood and political order: 'one based on a liberal ethos of universal human rights, of free, autonomous citizenship, of individual entitlement; the other assertive of group rights, of ethnic sovereignty, or primordial cultural connection' (Comaroff 1998: 346; cf. Mamdani 1996). These take many forms, ranging from debates over the acceptability of sub-national sovereignties to those about whether restitution and neo-liberal notions of property are compatible.

The paragraphs above, adapted from a call for papers for a panel of the 2005 conference of the American Anthropological Association, highlight some key issues relating to land restitution. The papers delivered at that panel (with two additions) and now published in this book examine cases of land restitution worldwide. They aim, through ethnographic detail and with analytical precision, to illuminate theoretical questions and address some policy implications. In the process they intend to establish land restitution as a legitimate and fertile topic for investigation.

The anthropology of restitution

How can land restitution – in all of its national and local variations – be considered a coherent object of social or anthropological analysis *sui generis*? A study of restitution arises out of, and contributes to, a series of recent theoretical debates. But rather than simply elaborating upon established fields of enquiry, restitution brings these together in a unique and unexpected way. It requires us to think about property, social transition, injustice and redress, citizenship and community, the state and the market. In finding points of convergence between these diverse topics, the study of restitution prompts us to rethink each of them in turn.

A key topic of recent interest among anthropologists, and scholars of law and society, is that of property. Given recent bold attempts to take studies of property beyond their earlier limitations and, in particular, to question its 'thingness' or materiality (Verdery and Humphrey 2004; F and K von Benda Beckman and Wiber 2006; Strathern 2005), our focus on land might appear restrictive. Such studies show that it is not only land but many other things – water, wild game, ideas, intellectual contributions, cultural products and processes – that can be 'owned'. Indeed, in settings of late industrial capitalism with transnational labour flows, land might be considered of little material importance. It can even be a liability rather than a productive resource (Verdery 2004). But it is precisely land on which restitution, as conceptualized in the present book, is centred. By emphasizing the restoring of *land*, we investigate how the return of territory at once promises the freedom of autonomy and self-governance, but may accompany this with the disadvantages of paternalism and even a second-class status in society, or may deny it by reinstating existing power inequalities and property relations. Landed property is the site where the promise of citizenship in the modern state is held out. In cases of restitution, such enjoyment is promised, but its realization may be fiercely contested and endlessly delayed. Citizenship in a specific territorial setting is thus both a poignant possibility and a frustratingly unachievable dream.

Looking at the restoration of landed property to its former owners thus allows us to examine the character of specific socio-legal and political contexts within which this is deemed possible, or desirable. Doing so enables us to make fruitful and instructive comparisons between such contexts, beyond merely showing how far they may have progressed in institutionalizing Western-style concepts of ownership, or mapping where the societies in question may be placed on the onward march towards the commodified relationships of global capitalism.

The political and legal contexts of restitution are those of disjuncture. Typically, restitution occurs to set right some earlier breaking apart of the social fabric. Equally, it may be at a present moment of social rupture that such redress is deemed possible. This may be the hiatus of a rapid transition between an old regime and a new, not-yet-established social order. Societies emerging after the end of the Cold War and the fall of the iron curtain, such as those of post-apartheid and post-socialism, are the most obvious examples here (see Burawoy and Verdery 1999; Comaroff and Comaroff 2000): both are represented in this book (see Chapters 2, Fay; 9, Leynseele and Hebinck; 8, Beyers; 3, Dorondel, in this book).

The rupture may, however, be less total, less far-reaching. Restitution also appears at moments of generalized social turmoil, as in North America in the context of the civil rights movement and anti-Vietnam protest. The late 1960s and early 1970s saw the rise of the American Indian Movement in the US, highlighted by the seizure of Alcatraz in 1971 and the protest at Wounded Knee in 1973. In Canada, around the same time, the Trudeau government's proposal to repeal the Indian Act was met with a range of critical counter-proposals by Native activist groups. In this context, by 1974, both the US and Canadian governments had established land restitution policies for native peoples. Such policies walk a cautious line, promising to set right the past injustice of land loss without positing any major transformation to or reform of the social fabric as a whole (see Chapters 4, Plaice; 12, Blancke, in this book).

Other settings of more gradual transition may also provide the setting for restitution as states roll out new policies on land and its ownership and use, often as solutions to earlier failures which were themselves originally conceptualized as 'solutions' (see Crush 1995). In much of Latin America, especially in countries with long histories of land reform, new policies concerning indigenous rights and multiculturalism have emerged in the wake of the rise of human rights discourse, '[coinciding] with the 500-year anniversary of the European "discovery" of America, peace processes in several countries, the decline of the socialist alternative, and significant indigenous uprisings' (Speed and Sierra 2005: 3). In the Brazilian Northeast, new opportunities to self-identify as 'indigenous' or as 'African-descended' provided a means for groups to frame their desire to get land back (see Chapter 7, French, in this book).

But these 'solutions', although concerned with changes to land tenure, have not necessarily favoured its restitution. In the early twentieth century, Mexico had set in place restitution and redistribution policies in which land was allocated to communal groups, but in the 1990s, the state began bringing an 'end to restitution' by allocating land to individuals in an attempt to integrate its landholders into market-based relationships, despite considerable resistance (see Chapter 11, Tiedje, in this book). In the Peruvian example, the language of 'indigeneity' had currency in the early twentieth century, but restitution came in the 1960s to be linked to a language of 'peasants' or '*campesinos*'.[1] From the late nineteenth century to the present, landholders have engaged with power-holders, whether the recognized government or the revolutionary Shining Path, in attempts to procure independent ownership of the lands they work (see Chapter 10, Nuijten and Lorenzo, in this book).

In all these contexts, however varied, it is the experience of social disjuncture which gives restitution its promise of a liberatory, more equitable future. It is, in many cases, a keenly felt past injustice which leads to claims for redress. Those who once suffered the loss of a material, territorial basis of identity and livelihood demand that past wrongs are set right. Deriving from the experience of being wronged and from the gravity of things long past, restitution claims acquire a moral weight. The right to have the land restored is claimed on the basis both of grievance and of a shared memory of that grievance (Rowlands 2004; Feuchtwang 2000, 2003). Injustice, grievance, shared memory and community are thus closely linked ingredients in the restitution package.

In addition to the matter of social disjuncture, a further definitive feature concerns the role of the state. Restitution contexts are often those in which the state is a key actor, often 'both playing the game and making the rules' (Verdery 2003: 81). It intervenes, in part, to protect the beneficiaries of the process – at least temporarily – from the ravages of the market. But state sovereignty in the 'transnational' contexts of global capitalism is on the wane (Hansen and Stepputat 2001; Trouillot 2001). State-planned economies are dwindling, 'state capitalism' (Hart 2001) is a thing of the past, and the market has been deemed a more effective midwife for development than the state. Returning land to its former owners, however, is often deemed to be a matter which cannot be left to the market. The state is required to act as nursemaid, although it may be preparing eventually to set its charges loose in the world.

A further peculiarity of restitution contexts is that they bring the state into relation with its citizens in something rather different from the classic interaction between 'people and the state' (Robertson 1984). Here the study of restitution makes a definitive contribution to our understanding of citizenship. The state as part-protagonist of, and part-participant in, restitution does not so much attempt to turn an 'unreliable citizenry' with its multiple views 'into a structured, readily accessible public', by laying out a single path to progress and thus creating homogeneity (Robertson 1984). Instead, restitution establishes the ground for a distinct *kind* of citizenship by constituting people as members of communities or groups, often in response to these groups' own insistence that they be seen in this way. Such communities may be coterminous with those thought of as native, indigenous or autochthonous (see Chapters 12, Blancke; 7, French; 10, Nuijten and Lorenzo; 6, Morphy; 11, Tiedje, in this book).

Restitution thus promises to restore land to specific groups within the broader fabric of society which are understood as having earlier been unfairly dispossessed. It often represents a stage – but not necessarily the final stage – in a long-term set of struggles waged by such groups. When we study restitution it becomes clear that property, rights and underlying conceptualizations of law are understood in sharply different ways (see Chapter 6, Morphy, in this book): not only cross-culturally or across different societies but also *within* particular social settings. The very fact that restitution is feasible in a specific setting reveals that a part of this intra-social struggle has already been 'won'. But this may be only the first step on a long road, with the nature of property relations – and indeed of the entire social fabric – being contested at every point along that road. By promising to make concrete the past, to make viable what had become mere 'history', by reinstating whole social orders from a past era, restitution represents a poignant prospect: a new set of ownership rights might be installed, predicated upon those which are said to have existed at some point in the past. As one of our authors puts it elsewhere, restitution is a 'particular socio-legal context' within which unusually boundless possibilities for social and political agency may crystallize (Beyers 2005: 10). In making such promises it may also pose threats to those with a stake in the dominant order of property relations. Even if the particular pieces of land in question are not of great value in and of themselves, the symbolic weight attached to their return, and the extent to which sets of social linkages may be unravelled in the process, are such as to generate fear. Here, the materiality of land encompasses immaterial significance. But the implications of bringing the past into the present through land restitution are more than just symbolic or ethereal.

Perhaps because of the threats posed to dominant property regimes, restitution turns out in many – even most – cases to be unachieveable. Or it is so narrowly circumscribed that it fulfils none but the most symbolic purposes, as many of our authors demonstrate here.

Restitution: a temporal process

Land issues are, of course, spatial: they are concerned with the creation of meaningful ties between people and places, and with the production of particular kinds of space (cf. Lefebvre 1991). Land restitution, however, focuses attention on the *temporal* aspects of land. As Berry has observed, property rights can be understood as a social *process* (Berry 1993). To elaborate further, we propose here a processual framework which will allow us to situate the accounts that follow in terms of where they fit in the restitution story.

The first moment is that of loss: of dispossession itself, whether through conquest, treaty, expropriation, eviction, sale etc. (or transactions differently understood by the two sides involved; cf. Chapter 6, Morphy, in this book; Bourassa and Strong 2002). Although this is arguably the most important phase of all, in that it sets up very the necessity of restoration, it is of significance for the communities discussed here primarily inasmuch as it is remembered through narratives, physical traces and memorabilia, and inasmuch as this memory inspires action in the present day. The means of dispossession matter in several ways. First, they affect the endurance of ties between dispossessed people and their land. In temperate regions of North America, or in South African cases of apartheid 'forced removal', dispossession often meant the relocation of people to remote reservations or racially defined separate areas. In other parts of South and southern Africa, Australia, or South America, by contrast, Europeans often acquired title over land which cultivators continued to occupy as tenants or farm workers. Dispossession on paper might take decades to translate into actual evictions. Second, the way dispossession occurred will affect the kinds of evidence (titles, other archival records, physical traces of occupation etc.) that will be available, and whether such evidence is deemed necessary at all.

After dispossession, time passes. This interim period may be counted as a second formative temporality in restitution, and another key point of variability: is the lost land the home of one's childhood or youth imbued with nostalgia for a happier, better time (see Chapter 8, Beyers, in this book)? Or did it belong to some distant ancestors, with a connection that may have been forgotten – or unimagined – prior to the land claim (see Chapter 7, French, in this book)? In either case, with the passage of time, land is sold and bought in transactions where the cleansing magic of the market may be imagined as washing away the guilt of dispossession; new owners may claim they bought land in a morally neutral transaction, arguing that restitution will simply create new injustices (see Chapter 12, Blancke, in this book; cf. Bourassa and Strong 2002).

The third formative moment in restitution is the creation of a restitution policy. It is here that one must inquire into the political and economic conditions of possibility of restitution.[2] There has been no restitution, for example, for the descendants of the English peasants dispossessed of their land during the process of enclosure. Likewise, there are many post-colonial states which have not undertaken a programme of restitution. As we argued above, regime changes are often the enabling conditions for the formation of restitution policy. Social movements, whether or not prompting such regime changes, may also form part of the enabling environment.

Where restitution programmes exist, they may make claims to be comprehensive, even transformative. But they are inevitably limited in their scope, in terms of who may claim and of where restitution fits in national policy priorities. Creating a restitution policy entails identifying categories of potential claimants, whether on the basis of history, ethnicity, indigeneity, treaty status or other markers. As Verdery has shown, in Eastern Europe, this meant asking 'which pre-communist property order should restitution recreate?' (Verdery 2003: 83). Simultaneously, of course, this entails exclusions: by defining those who are not eligible for restitution, policy may also define those who may be *vulnerable* to it (see Chapter 12, Blancke, in this book).

Typically, this also means that certain kinds of claims, judged to be 'in the broader national interest', may be seen to trump the claims of bounded groups who formerly lost their land. Which kinds of broader claim are deemed to be of superior moral, economic, political or environmental status to those of restitution will depend upon the larger policy context. This in turn will relate to political considerations, and be in part determined by the government's accountability to particular constituencies. In Canada, military, industrial and tourism development may go ahead on land that is subject to claims. Claims may appear as a strategy to preempt further land loss (see Chapter 4, Plaice, in this book), even when the 'claimants' are technically the 'owners', who are then conceived of as 'ceding' rights to the state (see Chapter 5, Nadasdy, in this book). In South Africa, by contrast, where restitution is enshrined in the post-apartheid constitution and is linked to a larger narrative of national liberation (du Toit 2000: 80–1), the presence of a land claim is thought to be in line with the 'political demand for land' which informed that country's new constitution (Dolny 2001). Restitution thus imposes a moratorium on any market transactions involving the land concerned (James 2007).

In practice, however, the question of whether restitution claims form part of, or are trumped by, notions of the broader national interest, is more complex. There are gaps between the place of restitution in principle and in policy, on one hand, and in practice, on the other. In the case of New York State, the gap becomes evident in the lengthy negotiations between the federal government and the white settler citizens who are reluctant to allow an Indian reservation in their 'back yard' (see Chapter 12, Blancke, in this book; Mackey 2005). As long as the negotiations continue unresolved, the principle of restitution is unrealized. In the South African case, the gap is evident in the contrast between the 'constitutional priority' of land restitution in South Africa and the unrealistically small budgets available to put it into practice (Walker 2000). So long as there are insufficient funds to administer and settle the thousands of land claims, the 'promise of the constitution' will remain unfulfilled as high-minded principles of justice founder upon the rocks of hard-nosed practicality.

The fourth formative moment is that of making particular land claims. While restitution policies may define eligible categories, actual land claims typically entail another round of boundary-drawing, wherein concrete groups of people constitute themselves as claimants, or are constituted as claimants, through the brokerage of NGOs, activists and benevolent – if paternalistic – state agencies. In effect, restitution requires the establishment of new forms of 'imagined community' (Anderson 1983), backed up by the experience of shared loss and variously based upon grounds of geography, genealogy, language, ethnicity, culture, way of life or race. Some of these grounds may prove more effective than others in actually securing land rights and mobilizing communities (see Chapter 4, Plaice, in this book); others may alienate potential claimants, who refuse to identify with previously stigmatized categories and hence refuse to 'join up' (see Chapter 7, French, in this book).

The claimant groups then enter into processes of negotiation and litigation. These may involve a range of 'stakeholders', but the state is typically central. As a result, land claims may provide political opportunities, but they may also create new forms of dependency and opportunities for state control. Leynseele and Hebinck (see Chapter 9, in this book) tell how the transfer of land to claimants in South Africa triggered developmentalist state planning-processes that had parallels to apartheid-era interventions in rural society. In her earlier work, Nuijten has written of land claims in Mexico as part of the state's role as a 'hope-generating machine' (Nuijten 2003); in her co-authored article in this book, she and Lorenzo show another possible outcome in Peru, where restitution led to the transfer of land to a state-managed institution hence resulting, decades later, in disappointment and in renewed demands for restitution (see Chapter 10, Nuijten and Lorenzo, in this book).

Such negotiations may also reveal communities' weaknesses and de facto vulnerability. Nadasdy (see Chapter 5, in this book) vividly recounts the uncomfortable joking among negotiators that appeared at moments when the unequal power relations between Canadian and Kluane First Nation negotiators came to the fore. Fay (2001) has shown how communities were primarily dependent upon state representatives for access to archival evidence regarding their claim; They mistakenly perceived that, without such evidence, the claim would be unlikely to succeed if pressed in court. Ultimately, the need for fulfilling state sanctioned definitions of community might exclude potentially valid claims. Myers retells Ian Keen's account of the Alligator River II land claim, in Arnhem Land, Australia:

> Much of the claim was rejected because the claimants did not appear to be a 'local descent group' as that term was being defined judicially by the Land Commissioner. The irony is that the claimants ... were denied their claim because it did not conform to the anthropological model of Aboriginal

land tenure incorporated into the Land Rights Act, which is essentially Radcliffe-Brown's 'orthodox' patrilineal, patrilocal horde model.

(Myers 1986: 147)

In similar vein, those petitioning the court to have their rights recognized in Australia's Blue Mud Bay claim gave performative accounts of aboriginal law which the court refused to recognize as germane to its proceedings (see Chapter 6, Morphy, in this book).

Successful land claims, one would expect, require evidence: on what basis does *this* group of claimants actually have a right to *this* piece of land? Demonstrations of historical continuity and ways of proving entitlement tend to be of key importance where there is active opposition to a claim (see Chapter 12, Blancke, in this book).[3] As du Toit has observed, there was in South Africa an early 'vision of the restitution process that was profoundly litigious and adversarial in its emphasis' (du Toit 2000: 80), a description that would be equally applicable to Blancke's account of a land claim in New York State, US (see Chapter 12, in this book). But concerns about evidence are not of great significance in the present group of chapters, suggesting that in certain contexts the specifics of territory are less in dispute than the principle of restitution itself. Where there is contestation, it is not so much over particular spaces and areas as over whether restitution ought to be allowed at all.

In South Africa, however, du Toit continues, 'the main problem in the restitution process has turned out to be, not a state or current landowners who are intent on opportunistically challenging the claimants' right to claim, but the practical problems that follow after that right has been assented to' (du Toit 2000: 88). The post-transfer phase thus constitutes our fifth formative moment. After the land claim has been 'won', the hard work begins. Then-Vice-President of South Africa Jacob Zuma told an audience at the Dwesa-Cwebe handover ceremony in 2001, 'prepare yourselves people of Dwesa and Cwebe – development is coming your way!' (Palmer *et al.* 2002b: 275), but four years later virtually none had arrived. Transfer ceremonies may be full of pomp and circumstance, but after the dust has cleared and the politicians have all gone home, claimants are confronted with the question of what to do with the land. This may engender what Žižek calls 'the loss of the loss' (cited in du Toit 2000: 82), as the experience or memory of dispossession loses its salience as a rallying point for unity, and the imagined past is confronted with the practical realities of the present (see Chapter 9, Leynseele and Hebinck, in this book). Beyers (see Chapter 8, in this book) depicts tensions in the land claim on Cape Town's District Six between owners and tenants, and between coloured and African claimants, about how (and whether) the past 'community' should be reconstituted.

Despite the nominal transfer of ownership, the demands of the state often weigh heavily upon the post-transfer process. In the extreme cases described by Nuijten and Lorenzo in Peru and by Fay in South Africa (see Chapters 10 and 2, in this book), restitution transferred land to state-run institutions, effectively failing to address demands for local ownership and control. In Brazil's Northeast, claimants collectivized production on previously individually farmed land in order to meet the state's expectations of 'communal' use as a condition of restitution (see Chapter 7, French, in this book). In South Africa, a discourse of 'tradition' and 'custom' that was an asset in staking a land claim became a liability when state planners demanded that claimants undertake 'modern' and 'progressive' activities on their newly acquired land (see Chapter 9, Leynseele and Hebinck, in this book).

The post-transfer phase of land restitution often entails resettlement, with all of the pitfalls that process entails (see Scudder and Colson 1982; de Wet 1994).[4] For some claimants, like many of the African former residents of District Six described by Beyers (see Chapter 8, in this book), the prospect of returning to their former homes may hold little of the appeal anticipated by the framers of restitution policy. There may also be fierce opposition to resettlement and property transfer from those affected, as happened in New York State (see Chapter 12, Blancke, in this book; Mackey 2005).

Sixth, and finally, there is the time 'beyond restitution'. This may or may not entail the possibility of a formalized 'end of land restitution'. Tiedje's chapter (see Chapter 11, in this book) describes the termination in the 1990s of Mexico's longstanding land restitution programme. Even as Mexico saw a growing movement for indigenous rights, the *ejidos* which had been created to allow communities to receive land earlier in the century were subject to a programme of neo-liberal privatization. With individual title comes the possibility of a new 'time of disintegration' (Cotroneo and Dozier 1974), as in the US in the late nineteenth century: sales of newly individually titled land under the Dawes Act among the Coeur d'Alene Indians led to 'the irrevocable loss of approximately 84 per cent of the tribal holdings, a total economic and political destruction of the tribal entity and an almost complete loss of individual initiative' (Cotroneo and Dozier 1974: 405–6). Granting title that does not allow sale, however, may be perceived as paternalistic and a denial of full property rights (cf. Ntsebeza 2005; James 2007).[5] In cases where restituted land may be sold, dispossession through the market may continue even though (legal-political) restitution has taken place. If such dispossession is little documented, this may be because the ravages of the market have not yet been experienced to their fullest extent. It may also be because the formal process of restitution is one defined and undertaken by the state, whereas its aftermath may not be. Once it has been accomplished, the claimants tend to be lost from view. If they later lose their land because of market forces, this is not a matter typically designated as part of the restitution process.

By drawing attention to these defining moments in the restitution process – dispossession, policy formation, community formation, claim-staking, transfer, post-transfer and 'post-restitution' – we have attempted to set out a framework to encompass the accounts that follow. Documenting the temporalities of restitution allows the reader to position the present book's case studies in relation to the process overall, and stimulates comparative reflection about that process. Some of these begin early in the story, with the formation of claimant communities in response to the promises of restitution, while others take a retrospective look at the process.

Property, community, government: citizen or subject?

In following this step-by-step sequence, it should be borne in mind that the expectations placed upon restitution, together with the practical difficulties of fulfilling these, are such that its final phases may never occur. It is not simply that the process drags on because of bureaucratic delays or the need for extended negotiations between contesting parties. There are other factors, intrinsic to the exercise, which make for a sense of incompleteness. Here we return to the question of the materiality or 'thingness' of property, and to the way anthropologists have recently questioned the 'persons-things-relations nexus' through which property is commonly understood (Strathern 2005; Verdery and Humphrey 2004). Restitution juxtaposes the most concrete of objects – land – with abstractions about the past social relationships which it nurtured and with vague promises to restore these in the future. It also conjoins pragmatic action in the here and now with invocations of justice and principle, asserting that the latter can only be achieved through the former. But in the process of making the property promise come true, restitution often translates into a far narrower achievement. It may restore a hierarchical status quo ante rather than a liberatory alternative (see Chapters 8, Beyers; 3, Dorondel; 10, Nuijten and Lorenzo, in this book). It may yield up an unwieldy and unusable asset which is more like a 'liability' (Verdery 2004). Thus, even those to whom the state *has* delivered upon its promises may feel they have been cheated: they thus require a further, more complete form of restoration. How far-reachingly can restitution address the issues it claims to be able to resolve? It may have been charged with too broad a range of tasks; too burdensome a symbolic and material load.

The restitution of land, our chapters demonstrate, is typically associated with certain assumptions. Special types of people who have set themselves off from the broader social fabric by living on these lands are often presumed to require separate forms of governance. They appear to embody a particular – and separate – approach to community living and communal property ownership. But at the same time these same property relationships are assimilated to – or blended with – those which predominate round about (see Chapter 6, Morphy, in this book). They are subjected to institutionalization, and/or yield to the market forces which permeate the rest of society. Thus, although the 'persons-things-relations nexus', for restitution claimants, is presented as a separate and distinct one, it is undergoing continual transformation. Claimants' ideas about property originate in a complex dialogue between themselves and the broader legal discourse used within the state. They assert, contest or modify these ideas (and, with them, their right to be recognized, hold property, be accommodated, be governed) in their interactions with the broader social world. In the process, restrictions on the extent of restitution become clear. At the same time, a certain resentfulness may appear among those outside of the process who are made to 'bear the burden' of whatever claims do materialize.

Community and governance: 'no nation within a nation'

Restitution involves morally laden expectations that it is as communities – especially 'indigenous' ones – rather than as individuals that people will lay claim to land. This is not necessarily a timeless feature of restitution. The Mexican *ejiditarios* of Tiedje's chapter, for example, were earlier seen as being able to achieve citizenship of a homogenized nation through their individual access to land (see Chapter 11, Tiedje, in this book; see also Lomnitz 1999). Rather, the emergence of such discourses appears to be a recent phenomenon: a manifestation of what Kuper calls the 'return of the native' (Kuper 2003; see also Kuper 2004; Heinen 2004; Kenrick and Lewis 2004a and b). But not all those concerned are willing to frame their expectations in these terms. Dissenters may disparage discourses of indigeneity and the communal landholding which it implies, as occurred among some of the people of the Brazilian Northeast discussed by French (see Chapter 7, in this book). In Labrador, although some groups self-identified in the exclusivist 'native' idiom, others, although equally committed to gaining land and recognition, were less ready to be seen as native (see Chapter 4, Plaice, in this book).

Restitution's communities may then be premised upon other kinds of groupings. Some of the earliest restitution cases in South Africa were in so-called 'black spots', areas where mission-educated 'progressive' Africans had bought land under individual freehold title (James et al. 2005; Harley 1999). Their members, in some cases, had earlier separated themselves from the ranks of those deemed to be 'traditional', precisely in order to begin participating in market- or commodity-relationships, and often through the purchase of 'private property'. In such settings, private property and market relations may pull people towards more individualized identities and more direct relationships between citizens and the state. They are 'owners', seen as distinct from the 'tenants' who have no formal basis for the return of property (see Chapter 8, Beyers, in this book; James et al. 2005). But their experience of dispossession which led 'black spot' owners to seek restitution counteracted this: it pulled them together and consolidated them as communities in order to facilitate their participation in the claims process.

Even where native or indigenous discourses are not readily embraced, expectations of community tend to remain. This was the case in the Brazilian

Northeast, where the Quilombo Clause awarding land to slave descendants laid down that such land could only be held collectively, by an association, and where this assumption of communal ownership led to many initial difficulties in organizing production (see Chapter 7, French, in this book). It has also been the case in South Africa's highly development-oriented restitution process, where there have been many misunderstandings over the nature of community identity and community ownership. The state and its agents, basing their approach on a 'communalist discourse' (James 2000), imagined community to be egalitarian and inclusive. Claimants, in contrast, often thought of it as exclusive and definitively bounded. Or, as in the case of District Six, exclusivist and inclusivist versions of community coexisted and were in contention within the ranks of claimants themselves (see Chapter 8, Beyers, in this book). In any event, the state's suppositions about the communal character of African landholding arrangements led to attempts to transfer ownership of farms to groups. The effect of this was to privatize responsibility for development, social services and the adjudication of disputes. The result has been lack of clarity on the nature of rights and responsibilities, on how disputes between communal owners are to be resolved, and on exactly who is entitled to make decisions about land use. Many rural land restitution cases were thus wrecked because of this failure to specify precise rights and obligations after properties were given back (James 2006; Pienaar 2000). In short, the exigencies of communal ownership meant that restituted property became 'fuzzy' in South Africa, as it had in Romania a few years beforehand (Verdery 1999; see Chapter 3, Dorondel, in this book).

In this case, and others in this book, the 'special rights' in terms of which restitution claimants demand their entitlement to land (see Chapters 6, Morphy; 11, Tiedje, in this book) form the basis of a series of tensions around citizenship, sovereignty and nationhood. If claimants contend that they are members of a distinct group (or if the state is construing them in this way) it seems likely that they will occupy – if successful – domains separate from the broader body politic: in effect, 'little republics' (Carstens 1999). If land is something exclusively owned by a group, this expression of autonomy and independence precludes integration with others, vis-à-vis matters of authority, law and order and the provision of services. But alongside autonomy comes, perhaps, a second-class status: claimants are assigned the character of subjects rather than citizens (Mamdani 1996).

Even as they constitute themselves as groups, claimants may make claims to national citizenship. Claimants in the Brazilian Northeast flew the national flag even at the moment that they became Indian (see Chapter 7, French, in this book). But claimants may also assert a degree of autonomy and separation from the nation. Mexican *ejidos* were established through restitution as a space of political and ritual autonomy (see Chapter 11, Tiedje, in this book). Such claims to autonomy become more controversial when they strike against deeply held national values of political equality. As Blancke explains in respect of the Seneca County Liberation Organization, a group formed to oppose the Cayuga

Nation's land claim, 'On reservations, Indian nations exercise their inherent sovereignty as "domestic, dependent nations". This struck many citizens and politicians as unfair. Why did Indians have "special rights" when other Americans did not?' (see Chapter 12, Blancke, in this book; see also Mackey 2005). Those opposed to the claim expressed their protests with billboards proclaiming 'no nation within a nation'. They made frequent reference to dimensions of their citizenship such as the 'tax base' to show that *their* landownership was not tied to 'special rights' but reflected obligations incumbent upon all citizens.

In this case special pleading generated new forms of special pleading in response. Restitution had a knock-on effect, causing the forming of new autonomies in protest against it. Restitution's opponents used equally localist and anti-governmental discourses. They organized on a local basis (as residents of Seneca County rather than as citizens of the US or of New York State), and their reference to the tax base asserted a local Lockean claim to state parks in opposition to the equally localist claims asserted by Indian nations. All-in-all, they claimed to have been politically disenfranchised by a *federal* legal process which marginalized the input of *local* residents.

In these and other cases, the citizenship of restitution is being claimed on the basis of being distinct from, rather than being part of, the nation as a whole. Interestingly, there are two cases depicted here in which people tried to frame their 'special rights' in a manner sufficiently broad as to include rather than exclude others. These are the District Six Beneficiary Trust and the Labrador Metis Association (see Chapters 8, Beyers; 4, Plaice, in this book). Given the state's tendency to privilege more 'nativist' claims, these groupings' discourse of adaptability, breadth and inclusivity did not necessarily enjoy great success. But, in the Canadian case, the more 'nativist' associations ultimately found it equally difficult to make headway.

The institutionalization of property

Because the state acts as the arbiter and implementer of land claims, land restitution is a site where both the authority of the state and the language and notion of property gain currency. Nadasdy (2002) has illustrated this point clearly, showing how participation in the Canadian land claims process has forced Kluane First Nation representatives to stake their claims in the language of property, despite radically different conceptions of the relationship between people and things. As he explains, the very act of defending against loss of land to outsiders has required an uncomfortable engagement with the notion of property:

> Just to engage in land claim negotiations, KFN people have had to learn a very different way of thinking about land and animals, a way of thinking that to this day many Kluane people continue to regard with disapproval. Despite this, many of them have put aside their discomfort with the idea of

'owning' land and animals, electing to participate in the land claim process because they see it as the only realistic chance they have to preserve their way of life against increasing encroachment by Euro-Canadians.

(Nadasdy 2002: 258)

Likewise, Myers has noted in Australia that 'certain features of Aboriginal land tenure became "fetishized" in the claims process . . . The problem is that land claims are not indigenous processes, although they attempt to somehow reproduce traditional rights and claims' (Myers 1986: 148; see also Povinelli 2004). To claim land requires an acceptance or at least a strategic embrace of the notion that land is a 'thing' with definable boundaries that can be 'owned' with some degree of exclusion of others (cf. Bohannan 1963). In this respect, restitution may 'make places into territories' (Peluso 2008, forthcoming). But some claimants continue vehemently to resist such a switch of legal register (see Chapter 6, Morphy, in this book).

Staking claims in the language of property does not mean, however, that property-holders are conceived as unmarked rights-holding individuals. An abstract 'owner', devoid of any personal or collective history, would not be able to invoke the story of past dispossession that restitution requires. Such stories not only lay down a record of claims, they also strengthen the claimants' 'resolve as to the legitimacy of their claims', and may strategically position the claimants in a wider social discourse as Fortmann has shown (1995: 1060–1). In the context of restitution, a successful claim requires being able to tell compelling stories of loss that can enlist the sympathy of powerful outsiders (du Toit 2000).

Such stories position claimants as particular kinds of persons or groups of people, able to fit into the categories of eligibility of a particular restitution policy. But stories of dispossession are, on their own, seldom enough. Restitution processes, typically modelled on or taking place through courts, often require 'evidence' beyond the stories of claimants, and are dependent on documents: title deeds, archival records, and the like. These documents are often produced and possessed by those potentially opposed to claims. Occasionally, claimants may be able to introduce non-textual forms of evidence. Grave sites are a common example, but evidence takes other forms. At Dwesa-Cwebe, South Africa, claimants led representatives of the Land Claims Commission to deep pits where their ancestors had stored maize. Braun (2002) tells how land claimants and their NGO allies identified 'culturally modified trees' in the forests of British Columbia; as he explains, to stake their claim, they then 'had to educate the court on how to properly read the forest' (Braun 2002: 99). But the Blue Mud Bay aboriginal claimants were unable to have their ritual performance admitted as evidence in court (see Chapter 6, Morphy, in this book).

Stories and documentation may not be enough, for prior occupation and descent are not the only bases for ownership. Lockean claims to property based on labour and 'improvement' come into play in restitution. Such arguments were commonplace as justifications for European colonists' seizure of land from colonized peoples worldwide (Verdery and Humphrey 2004: 4). They find echoes among the local residents opposed to the land claim in Blancke's account of New York State: they opposed the transfer of a state park because they had contributed their tax dollars to the 'improvement' of the area, creating a locally specific claim on a nominally state-owned public asset (see Chapter 12, Blancke, in this book). Likewise, French describes an opponent to a land claim who 'saw the land as representative of her father's hard work and ambition' (see Chapter 7, French, in this book). At the same time, the promise of 'improvement' can contribute to the viability of a land claim. Willingness to participate in 'development' positioned the Northeast Brazil slave descendants of French's account as suitable recipients (see Chapter 7, French, in this book). Likewise, land reform beneficiaries and policymakers in South Africa face pressure to show evidence that restitution is leading to 'development' and 'economically beneficial' land use (see Chapter 9, Leynseele and Hebinck, in this book), particularly in the light of declining productivity following the forcible takeover of commercial farms in neighbouring Zimbabwe.

Environmental discourse also enters into restitution, both for and against. One form this takes is the notion of the 'environmentally noble savage' (Redford 1991) that has been deployed by movements for indigenous rights (along with romantic notions of community resource management; cf. Li 1996). But concerns about conservation have also been used to limit the land uses available to claimants where their claims involved protected areas (see Chapters 12, Blancke; 2, Fay, in this book; Palmer *et al.* 2002a; Steenkamp 2001; Wynberg and Kepe 1999). They also provide a counter-argument for those opposed to claims. Writing of New Zealand, Dominy (1995) describes 'white settler assertions of native status': settlers made claims to a distinct culture and way of life grounded in knowledge of a particular landscape as a counter to a Maori land claim on their grazing land. But they also invoked an environmental discourse, arguing that they possessed 'a form of cultural and ecological adaptation that ... enables them to maintain the balance between agricultural production and environmental conservation on a particular property for generations' (Dominy 1995: 365).

There are various kinds of justifications which, in the eyes of the state, can form a valid basis for restitution. Although these may take as much account of future potential as they do of past entitlement, it often seems to be taken for granted that some form of indigenous identity constitutes necessary grounds for eligibility. It may not be sufficient – urban Maori in New Zealand who are clearly 'indigenous' but do not have membership in a 'tribe' (*iwi*) have been excluded from claims (Bourassa and Strong 2002: 258). But it is typically compelling. Plaice's account of attempted restitution in Labrador shows the strength of indigeneity and the weakness of an alternative strategy. Three rival native organizations formed and employed markedly different moral and political strategies to press their respective claim to both land and an enduring local, land-based identity. Of these the Metis, a group of mixed race with settler-native origins, was the group least fixed on notions of native ancestry. Instead, its members saw their claim as validated by a way of life lived on the land. Their interest lay not in being 'different' from normal Labradorians but rather in being 'typically of Labrador'. Part of this involved a wish to continue participating in general market-based enterprise within the area overall, rather than in doing something specifically 'native'. In short, they were hybrid Canadians much like any other: 'independent, individualistic and adaptable' to new environments, and capable of using 'a range of traits and qualities', but with a strong sense of local connection. But their chosen method of identification, partly forced upon them by the more 'native' versions adopted by their two rival associations, appeared to carry less moral weight than these (see Chapter 4, Plaice, in this book).

The rights and wrongs of restitution

Restitution is often thought of as a 'right' to rectify earlier 'wrongs'. In South Africa, for example, restitution was thought of by many as similar to the Truth and Reconciliation Commission, as a way of setting right the record and achieving justice for the victims of apartheid. But such an idea implies that there is or was a perpetrator of the acts of dispossession that are being righted. While it is not always made explicit, the question lurks in the background of who is to be blamed and who must be held responsible for whatever wrongs restitution is aiming to set right. Put in concrete terms: if land is to be reclaimed, who has to lose it as a result?

Sometimes it is the nation as a whole which takes responsibility, and then negotiates its way out of the dilemma. In Canada (see Chapters 5, Nadasdy; 4, Plaice, in this book), the state has created claims processes that might appear to be privileging restitution while in practice it is finding a way to circumvent troublesome land claims in the interests of the broader nation and its 'development'. Land claims, however morally weighty, have not precluded military and industrial projects on claimed land. Thus although there was lip service paid to the importance of restitution, it was still judged secondary to matters of broader national interest, particularly when this concerned matters of 'the environment' (see Chapters 4, Plaice; 12, Blancke, in this book). Here, 'the environment' became a trope invoking the broader public good and outclassing the nationally less significant project of 'restitution'. Similar processes occurred when the Dwesa-Cwebe reserve was restored to its claimants in South Africa (see Chapter 2, Fay, in this book).

The criteria of eligibility for restitution may also deliberately exclude certain categories of past dispossession, indirectly defining the nation and excluding others who might appear to have legitimate claims. As Verdery explains, restitution in Czechoslovakia and Hungary was defined in a way that set de facto limits on the categories of people who might claim land: the policies set the dates for eligible restitution claims at points that post-dated the expropriation of land from Jews and Germans. Throughout Eastern Europe, 'politicians in all countries ... tried to select baseline dates that left out significant ethnonational others, who could be sacrificed because they had little electoral weight' (Verdery 2003: 84).

In other cases, specific groups of landowners may perceive that they, rather than the 'nation', are being singled out to carry the costs of restitution (see Chapter 12, Blancke, in this book). In response to the fears of the white majority, New Zealand eventually explicitly excluded private land from restitution claims, and resolved not to purchase private land for purposes of restitution (Bourassa and Strong 2002: 238–40); this had the unintended effect of making high country farmers, who *lease* state-owned pastoral land, particularly vulnerable to restitution claims (Dominy 1995). White Zimbabwean farmers have been singled out more violently; they have been 'haunted by the specter of racialized dispossession' (Moore 2005: ix) and see themselves as being forced to bear the brunt of it. White South African farmers have made similar complaints, but if they perceive the general political drift to be against them they may hide this. 'I know how they feel, I too love the land' said one man whose farm had been sold to the state so that it could be restored to its original owners. Such sentiments display a mixture of genuine feeling with opportunistic relief at having their land bought from them in conditions of neo-liberalism where making a living on the land has become precarious (James 2007).

In these cases moral equivalence is asserted: one group of 'chosen people' displaces another whose members may feel equally 'chosen' and hence experience themselves as discriminated against if it is they who are being made to bear the cost of what should be broader projects of social justice. These costs reflect the broader political and socio-legal climate and context, which shapes how far restitution claims are allowed to occupy the moral high ground.

Conclusion

The work of restitution remains unfinished, a reminder of histories of colonial and socialist dispossession. To give a few examples, in Canada in 2003, 13 'comprehensive' land claims had been settled (encompassing about 40 per cent of Canadian territory) while more than 70 remained under negotiation, while 251 'specific' claims had been settled of 1,185 submissions (Minister of Indian Affairs and Northern Development 2003: 8–11). New Zealand's Waitangi Tribunal had received 779 claims in 1999, and planned to entertain new claims through 2010 (Bourassa and Strong 2002: 243). In South Africa, some 63,455 claims were lodged before the December 1998 deadline for submission (Hall 2003: 1). Romania is perhaps the most extreme example: following Law 18 of 1991, providing for liquidation of collective farms and restitution to prior owners, there were about 6,200,000 claims, and 'in a 1998 interview, the

Romanian Minister of Justice stated that Law 18 had produced the largest number of court cases in the history of Romanian jurisprudence' (Verdery 2003: 97).

Diverse experiences have shown that restitution is no panacea for rural poverty or underdevelopment; claimants are all too likely to face disappointment without other kinds of support to make land rights *effective* for production and livelihoods (see Chapter 3, Dorondel, in this book; Verdery 2003: 20). That restitution may disappoint seems almost inevitable, given the symbolic weight ascribed to it by claimants and activists alike. Nevertheless, as the figures above show, it is a persistent source of *hope*, a hope that may entrench a state bureaucracy's 'hope-generating machine' (Nuijten 2003), but may also promise political and economic autonomy and self-determination (see Chapter 7, French, in this book). Legacies of dispossession persist: loss of land is not a one-off event, but an *ongoing process* insofar as it continues to shape the life chances of those affected and their descendants (Hart 2002: 39). Likewise, demands for restitution seem unlikely to cease as states and citizens around the world confront legacies of colonialism and socialism. As claimants continue to organize, creating new forms of community and entering into new relations with the state in the process, restitution will continue to offer a fruitful terrain for scholars seeking to understand the reworking of property and citizenship in contexts of political transformation, the politics of injustice and redress, the state and the market, and the place of memory in the present.

References

Anderson, Benedict (1983) *Imagined Communities: Reflections on the Origins and Spread of Nationalism*, London: Verso.

Berry, Sara (1993) *No Condition is Permanent: the social dynamics of agrarian change in sub-Saharan Africa*, Madison, WI: University of Wisconsin Press.

Beyers, Christiaan (2005) *Land Restitution in District Six, Cape Town: Community, citizenship and social exclusion*, DPhil dissertation, Sussex University.

Bohannan, Paul, (1963) ' "Land", "Tenure", and Land Tenure', in Daniel Biebuyck (ed.) *African Agrarian Systems*, London: Oxford University Press.

Bourassa, Steven and Ann Louise Strong (2002) 'Restitution of Land to New Zealand Maori: The Role of Social Structure', *Pacific Affairs* 75(2): 227–60.

Braun, Bruce (2002) *The Intemperate Rainforest: Nature, Culture, and Power on Canada's West Coast*, Minneapolis, MN: University of Minnesota Press.

Burawoy, M and K Verdery (1999) 'Introduction', in M Burawoy and K Verdery (eds) *Uncertain Transition: ethnographies of change in the post-socialist world*, Oxford: Rowman and Littlefield.

Carstens, Peter (1999) 'Restructuring Souls: Missions To The Nama (C1800–C1950)', paper presented at workshop on An Apartheid of Souls, London School of Economics.

Comaroff, John L (1998) 'Reflections on the Colonial State, in South Africa and Elsewhere: fragments, factions, facts and fictions', *Social Identities* 4(3): 321–61.

Comaroff, Jean and John L (2000) 'Millennial Capitalism: first thoughts on a second coming' (introduction to special issue 'Millennial capitalism and the culture of neoliberalism'), *Public Culture* 12(2): 291–343.

Cotroneo, R and J Dozier (1974) 'A Time of Disintegration: The Coeur D'Alene and the Dawes Act', in *The Western Historical Quarterly* 5(4): 405–19.

Crush, Jonathan (1995) *Power of Development*, London: Routledge.

De Wet, Chris (1994) 'Resettlement and Land Reform in South Africa', in *Review of African Political Economy* 21(61): 359–73.

Dolny, Helena (2001) *Banking on Change*, Johannesburg: Viking Books.

Dominy, Michelle (1995) 'White Settler Assertions of Native Status', *American Ethnologist* 22(2): 358–74.

Du Toit, A (2000) 'The End of Restitution: getting real about land claims', in B Cousins (ed.) *At the Crossroads: Land and Agrarian Reform in South Africa into the 21st Century*, Cape Town and Johannesburg: University of the Western Cape and National Land Committee.

Fay, Derick (2001) 'Oral and Written Evidence in South Africa's Land Claims Process: the Case of Dwesa-Cwebe Nature Reserve', unpublished paper presented at Oral History Association Annual Meeting, October 2001.

Fay, Derick and Robin Palmer (2000) 'Prospects for Redistribution of Wealth through Land Reform at Dwesa-Cwebe', in B Cousins (ed.) *At the Crossroads: Land and Agrarian Reform in South Africa into the 21st Century*, Cape Town and Johannesburg: University of the Western Cape and National Land Committee, pp 194–210.

Feuchtwang, Stephan (2000) 'Reinscriptions: commemoration, restoration and the interpersonal transmission of histories and memories', in S Radstone (ed) *Memory and Methodology*, Oxford: Berg.

—— (2003) 'The Transmission of Loss and the Demand for Recognition', in K Hodgkin and S Radstone (eds) *Regimes of Memory*, London: Routledge.

Fortmann, Louise (1995) 'Talking Claims: Discursive Strategies in Contesting Property', *World Development* 23(6): 1053–63.

Hall, Ruth (2003) 'Rural Restitution: Evaluating land and agrarian reform in South Africa occasional paper series no. 2', Bellville: University of the Western Cape Programme for Land and Agrarian Studies.

Hansen, TB and F Stepputat (2001) 'Introduction', in TB Hansen and F Stepputat (eds) *States of Imagination: Ethnographic Explorations of the Postcolonial State*, Durham, NC: Duke University Press.

Harley, Anne (1999) *AFRA: 20 years in the land rights struggle, 1979–1999*, Pietermaritzburg: Association for Rural Advancement.

Hart, G (2002) *Disabling Globalization: Places of Power in Post-Apartheid South Africa*, Berkeley, CA: University of California Press.

Hart, Keith (2001) *Money in an Unequal World: Keith Hart and his Memory Bank*, London: Texere.

Heinen, Dieter (2004) 'Discussion: on the return of the native', *Current Anthropology* 45(2): 262.

James, Deborah (2000) ' "After years in the wilderness": development and the discourse of land claims in the new South Africa', *Journal of Peasant Studies* 27(3): 142–61.

—— (2006) 'The Tragedy of the Private: owners, communities and the state in South Africa' in F and K von Benda-Beckmann and M Wiber (eds) *Changing Properties of Property*, Oxford: Berghahn.

—— (2007) *Gaining Ground? 'Rights' and 'Property' in South African land reform*, London: Routledge.
James, Deborah, Alex Xola Ngonini and Geoffrey Mphahle Nkadimeng (2005) '(Re)constituting Class?: Owners, Tenants and the Politics of Land Reform in Mpumalanga', *Journal of Southern African Studies*, special issue J Beall and S Hassim (eds) 'Fragile Stability: State and Society in Democratic South Africa', 31(4): 825–44.
Kenrick, Justin and Jerome Lewis (2004a) 'Discussion: on the return of the native', *Current Anthropology* 45(2): 263.
—— (2004b) 'Indigenous Peoples' Rights and the Politics of the Term "Indigenous" ', *Anthropology Today* 20(2): 4–9.
Kuper, Adam (2003) 'Return of the Native', *Current Anthropology* 44(3): 389–402.
—— (2004) 'On the return of the native', *Current Anthropology* 45: 265–7.
Lefebvre, H (1991) [1974] *The Production of Space*, tr. Donald Nicholson-Smith, Oxford: Blackwell.
Li, Tania Murray (1996) 'Images of Community: Discourse and strategy in property relations', *Development and Change* 27(3): 501–27.
Lomnitz, C (1999) 'Modes of Citizenship in Mexico' *Public Culture* 11(1): 269–93.
Mackey, Eva (2005) 'Universal Rights in Conflict: "Backlash" and "benevolent resistance" to indigenous land rights', *Anthropology Today* 21(2): 14–20.
Mamdani, Mahmood (1996) *Citizen and Subject: Contemporary Africa and the Legacy of Late Colonialism*, Princeton, NJ: Princeton University Press.
Minister of Indian Affairs and Northern Development (2003) *Resolving Aboriginal Claims: A Practical Guide to Canadian Experiences*, Ottawa: Minister of Public Works and Government Services Canada.
Moore, Donald (2005) *Suffering for Territory: Race, Place, and Power in Zimbabwe*, Durham, NC: Duke University Press.
Myers, Fred (1986) 'The Politics of Representation: Anthropological Discourse and Australian Aborigines', *American Ethnologist* 13(1): 138–53.
Nadasdy, Paul (2002) 'Property and Aboriginal Land Claims in the Canadian Subarctic: some theoretical considerations', *American Anthropologist* 104(1): 247–61.
Ntsebeza, Lungisile (2005) *Democracy Compromised: chiefs and the politics of the land in South Africa*, Leiden: Brill.
Nuijten, Monique (2003) *Power, Community and the State: the political anthropology of organisation in Mexico*, London: Pluto Press.
Palmer, Robin, Herman Timmermans and Derick Fay (eds) (2002a) *From Confrontation to Negotiation on South Africa's Wild Coast: Conservation, Land Reform and Tourism Development at Dwesa-Cwebe Nature Reserve*, Pretoria: Human Sciences Research Council.
Palmer, Robin, Derick Fay, Herman Timmermans and Christo Fabricius (2002b) 'A Development Vision for Dwesa-Cwebe', in Robin Palmer, Herman Timmermans and Derick Fay (eds) *From Confrontation to Negotiation on South Africa's Wild Coast: Conservation, Land Reform and Tourism Development at Dwesa-Cwebe Nature Reserve*, Pretoria: Human Sciences Research Council.
Peluso, Nancy (2008, forthcoming) 'From Common Property Resources to Territorializations: Resource Management in the Twenty-first Century', in Peter Cuasay, and Chayan Vaddhanaphuti (eds) *Commonplaces and Comparisons: Dynamics in Regional Eco-politics of Asia*, Chiang Mai: Faculty of Social Sciences, Regional

Center for Social Science and Sustainable Development Monograph Series, Chiang Mai University.
Pienaar, Kobus (2000) ' "Communal" Property Institutional Arrangements: a second bite', in B Cousins (ed.) *At the Crossroads: Land and agrarian reform in South Africa into the 21st century*, Cape Town and Johannesburg: University of the Western Cape and National Land Committee.
Povinelli, E (2004) 'At Home in the Violence of Recognition', in Katherine Verdery and Caroline Humphrey (eds) *Property in Question: value transformation in the global economy*, Berg: Oxford.
Redford, K (1991) 'The Ecologically Noble Savage', *Cultural Survival Quarterly* 15(1): 46–8.
Robertson, AF (1984) *People and the State: an anthropology of planned development*, Cambridge: Cambridge University Press.
Rowlands, M (2004) 'Cultural Rights and Wrongs: uses of the concept of property', in Katherine Verdery and Caroline Humphrey (eds) *Property in Question: value transformation in the global economy*, Berg: Oxford.
Scudder, Thayer and Elizabeth Colson (1982) 'From Welfare To Development: A Conceptual Framework for the analysis of Dislocated People', in A Hansen and A Oliver Smith (eds) *Involuntary Migration and Resettlement: The Problems and Responses of Dislocated People*, Boulder, CO: Westview Press.
Shipton, Parker (1994) 'Land and Culture in Tropical Africa: Soils, Symbols and the Metaphysics of the Mundane', *Annual Review of Anthropology* 23: 347–77.
Speed, Shannon and María Teresa Sierra (2005) 'Introduction', *Political and Legal Anthropology Review* 28(1): 1–9.
Steenkamp, Conrad (2001) *The Makuleke Land Claim: An environmental conflict*, unpublished PhD dissertation, University of the Witwatersrand.
Strathern, Marilyn (2005) 'Land: tangible or intangible property', Amnesty International lecture, Oxford.
Trouillot, M (2001) 'The anthropology of the state in the age of globalization', *Current Anthropology* 42(1): 125–38.
Turner, Victor (1969) *The Ritual Process: Structure and Anti-Structure*, Chicago, IL: Aldine.
Van Gennep, A (1960) *The Rites of Passage*, Chicago, IL: University of Chicago Press.
Verdery, Katherine (1996) *What Was Socialism and What Comes Next?*, Princeton, NJ: Princeton University Press.
—— (1999) 'Fuzzy Property: rights, power and identity in Transylvania's Decollectivization', in M Burawoy and K Verdery (eds) *Uncertain Transition: ethnographies of change in the post-socialist world*, Oxford: Rowman and Littlefield.
—— (2003) *The Vanishing Hectare: property and value in post-socialist Romania*, Ithaca, NY: Cornell University Press.
—— (2004) 'The Obligations of Ownership: restoring rights to land in postsocialist Transylvania', in Katherine Verdery and Caroline Humphrey (eds) *Property in Question: value transformation in the global economy*, Berg: Oxford.
Verdery, Katherine and Caroline Humphrey (2004) 'Introduction: raising questions about property', in Katherine Verdery and Caroline Humphrey (eds) *Property in Question: value transformation in the global economy*, Berg: Oxford.
von Benda-Beckmann, Franz and Keebet and Melanie Wiber (2006) 'Properties of

Property', in F and K von Benda-Beckmann and M Wiber (eds) *Changing Properties of Property*, Oxford: Berghahn.

Walker, C (2000) 'Relocating Restitution', *Transformation* 44: 1–16.

Wynberg, Rachel and Thembela Kepe (1999) *Land Reform and Conservation Areas in South Africa: Towards a Mutually Beneficial Approach*, Pretoria: IUCN South Africa.

Yashar, Deborah (2005) *Contesting Citizenship In Latin America: The Rise of Indigenous Movements and the Postliberal Challenge*, Cambridge: Cambridge University Press.

Notes

1 As Deborah Yashar has noted, Peru is unique among the countries in Latin America with the five largest indigenous populations in that it did not see the emergence of a significant indigenous movement in the 1990s (Yashar 2005).
2 This was pointed out by Jake Kosek in his comments as a panel discussant.
3 Anthropological notions of identity and community as fluid and constructed may stand in tension with the strict boundaries required by the legal process. James Clifford describes the failure of anthropological notions of identity to convince a Massachusetts court of the validity of their land claim (1988). More recently, a lawyer opposed to the Richtersveld land claim in South Africa argued that anthropologist Suzanne Berzborn's description of community as 'constructed' undermined the claim. Identity of Richtersvelders under scrutiny, *Sunday Times*, 4 May 2005, available at www.suntimes.co.za/zones/sundaytimesnew/newsst/ newsst1115212706.aspx. See also Myers (1986: 146–52) for a related discussion of anthropological research on Australian Aboriginal land claims.
4 Parker Shipton reminded the authors of this in his discussion at the conference.
5 The state may also constrain sale where 'higher' national priorities would be threatened, as in the Dwesa-Cwebe and Makuleke claims on state-owned conservation areas in South Africa; the terms of these settlements give the state the 'right of first refusal' in the event that the land were ever put up for sale.

Chapter 2

Property, subjection and protected areas
The 'restitution' of Dwesa-Cwebe Nature Reserve, South Africa

Derick Fay

Abstract

This chapter examines the themes of property and subjection in the land claim on Dwesa-Cwebe Nature Reserve, South Africa. The context of a claim on a protected area gave rise to complex bases for claims: the claimants merged descent with participation in struggle, while their opponents drew on a diverse mix of discourses under the rubric of conservation. Although the claimants won the claim, the form of property they received may be characterized as 'a bundle of duties and a handful of rights'. In addition to maintaining the pre-restitution land use, the restitution claim was the vehicle for the formalization of obligations to a number of 'secondary stakeholders'. While the duties associated with landownership expanded considerably, the rights being secured by the claimants were quite limited; they did not include forest products and grazing, and were limited to rental income, a one-time cash payment and access to government grants. The effectiveness of the rights that were transferred in turn depend on a set of ambient conditions that is highly contingent upon factors beyond the control of the claimants. Finally, the institutional arrangements that have been created to administer the restitution funds appear to be leading to new forms of subjection; they have become a vehicle for an emergent local government to assert unprecedented control and influence in the region.

A visitor to Dwesa-Cwebe Nature Reserve, in South Africa's Eastern Cape Province, in late 2005 would be hard-pressed to recognize that the reserve had been the subject of a successful land claim in 2001. Land uses had remained unchanged: the reserve was still fenced, and local residents had no access to forest produce or grazing. People who had spoken optimistically in the late 1990s about renewed forest access now made statements like 'Nature [Eastern Cape Nature Conservation] is too strong. We have given up hope'. The Haven Hotel continued to operate within the reserve, and several dozen white-owned cottages remained, still exclusively occupied by families who had been coming there since the early twentieth century. While the land claim settlement agreement had resulted in the transfer of R14 million, and lease agreements with the hotel and cottages, the proceeds remained within the coffers of local government rather than having been transferred to the newly established landowning trust (Palmer 2005).

This chapter does not attempt to be an exhaustive account of the Dwesa-Cwebe land claim;[1] rather I approach the Dwesa-Cwebe case through the lens of the anthropology of land restitution, focusing on ways in which the transfer of land rights and creation of new forms of property has created new obligations and forms of subjection. Here, as Verdery observed of Romania, restitution has created a situation where the 'state [is] both playing the game and making the rules' (Verdery 2003: 81). But at Dwesa-Cwebe, at least, this concise phrase may suggest a too-monolithic image of the state; many different agencies of the state have been involved, both in playing games and making rules, sometimes at odds with one another. The outcome has been a situation where land restitution has resulted in few tangible changes on the ground.

The first section of the chapter examines the bases for the community's claims and the conservation authority's counterclaims to the Nature Reserves. Rather than grounding community membership in the descendants of people removed from the reserves, the claimants defined community here in relation to participation in the land struggle. The claim thus fused discourses of prior occupation and use with accounts of the more recent protests in the reserves. The conservation authority, in contrast, invoked a hybrid of scientific, nationalist and internationalist discourses under the rubric of conservation, de-emphasizing the commercial rationales invoked at the initial establishment of the reserve in the 1890s.

In the second part of the chapter, I examine the form of property that was actually transferred to the claimants, characterizing it as 'a bundle of duties and a handful of rights'. The duties associated with landownership expanded considerably: in addition to maintaining the pre-restitution land use of Dwesa-Cwebe Nature Reserve as a protected area, under the continued control of Eastern Cape Nature Conservation, the restitution claim was the vehicle for the formalization of obligations to a number of 'secondary stakeholders'. On the other hand, the rights being secured by the claimants were quite limited; contrary to popular demands, they did not incorporate rights to forest products and grazing, and were limited to rental income, a one-time cash payment, and access to government grants.

The third part of the chapter considers the question that Katherine Verdery has poignantly raised in her study of restitution in Romania: what 'ambient conditions' are necessary to make land rights *effective* (Verdery 2003: 18–20)? I show here that the effectiveness of new rights of ownership of tourism facilities that the claimants have received are in practice highly contingent upon factors beyond their control.

In the fourth part of the chapter, I address the question of whether restitution creates new forms of subjection by examining the institutional arrangements that have been created to administer the restitution funds. The claimants have successfully avoided control by chiefs and Tribal Authorities, but they have instead been subordinated to local government. The restitution funds have been transferred to the Amatole District Municipality, rather than to the newly created landowning trust. Restitution has thus become a vehicle for an emergent local government body to assert its control and influence. This new subjection, however, has taken place in a democratic context, and has stimulated the involvement of the land claim's leaders in local electoral politics.

Grounding claims to land

In the introduction to this book, we drew attention to the important role played by stories of prior occupation and descent in forming communities and staking restitution claims. At Dwesa-Cwebe, claims based on descent and prior occupation were invoked in order to produce narratives that fit the requirements of South Africa's 1994 Restitution Act: that dispossession took place after 1913 for the purposes of racially discriminatory legislation or practices.[2] At the same time, however, the experience of struggling for the land is, in itself, seen by the claimants as grounds for membership in a 'community' and access to the benefits of restitution.

The Dwesa and Cwebe forests surround the Mbashe River as it meets the Indian Ocean, on the southeast coast of South Africa. The forests span approximately 18 km of coastline, and extend inward for 3 to 5 km, encompassing over 5,700 ha. The river itself is a natural, political and cultural boundary, separating the two forests, the districts of Willowvale and Elliotdale, and two historically distinct populations of Xhosa-speakers. Between the 1890s and 1930s, many of their ancestors, and a few people still alive in 1999, were forcibly removed from their homesteads in the grassland within the forests and between the forest and the coast. Over the same period, they saw whites establish the Haven Hotel and several dozen holiday cottages in the same areas. In the late 1970s, the administration of the black 'homeland'[3] of the Republic of Transkei fenced the forests and created the Dwesa-Cwebe Nature Reserve, sealing off local access to building materials, medicinal plants and grazing in the forest clearings, while allowing tourism facilities to remain in place on the Cwebe side.

As Robin Palmer and I have argued, Dwesa-Cwebe does not meet definitions of community in spatial, economic or cultural terms (cf. Kepe, 1998): it spans the geographic and administrative borders of Willowvale and Elliotdale districts, and encompasses the territories of multiple Administrative Areas.[4] Moreover, it encompasses diverse categories of 'stakeholders ... with disparate economic positions and livelihood strategies, and ... diverse ethnic, religious and associational groupings' (Fay and Palmer 2000: 196). The division between Dwesa and Cwebe somewhat resembles that between 'school' and 'red' people once described by the Mayers (1971). Adjoining the Dwesa forest in Willowvale are five communities where schools have operated since the 1890s, with thriving churches. Labour migrants from these communities often take their spouses and children along with them to town, in order to further their children's education in urban schools. Many of their ancestors were placed there by the colonial state, to form a buffer zone between the defeated Xhosa Chief Sarhili and his troops. Adjoining the Cwebe forest in Elliotdale are two communities made up partly of the descendants of Chief Sarhili's forces, people who rejected *izinto zabelungu*, 'white people's things'. Schools here were established in the 1960s, and people have depended overwhelmingly on male migration to the mines, favouring forms of employment and housing that discourage expenditure on urban temptations. People from Dwesa stereotype those of Cwebe as unsophisticated: 'they did not know how to drink tea until we taught it to them'. People from Cwebe counter that *abafundileyo*, educated people, cheat the uneducated: 'the teachers will say, we need money for *ihistori* (history). We don't know what this thing, *ihistori*, is; we only know that it is something at school. Then they eat our money'.[5]

Despite these cultural, historical and economic differences, Dwesa-Cwebe formed as a 'community' through a struggle for land rights, initiated in a locally driven process that has come to be supported by the state and non-governmental organizations (NGOs). The state's initial role was entirely indirect: by removing people and closing the reserves, the state contributed to the eventual constitution of Dwesa-Cwebe as a socio-political entity and imagined community. No official designated Dwesa-Cwebe as a 'community' or sought to create an administrative structure for the region; rather, state actions created a population of dispossessed people with a shared experience of exclusion and a basis for future solidarity.

In the transformed political climate of the early 1990s, local residents began a protracted struggle to restore their rights to the forests. The initial leaders came from two villages on opposite sides of the river. Working independently, they sought out the assistance of the then-opposition African National Congress (ANC), and were referred to the Umtata-based activist NGO Transkei Land Service Organization (Tralso).

The early 1990s were marked by conflict, culminating in a co-ordinated mass protest inside the reserves in the midst of a severe drought in 1993–4. Immediately afterwards, the reserve management opened negotiations with locally elected Village Conservation Committees to establish a permit-based system for use of forest products on a temporary basis, and made the grasslands within the reserves available for grazing, on a temporary basis, until drought conditions abated. Both of these concessions, as well as staff changes when Eastern Cape Nature Conservation (ECNC) took over from the Department of Agriculture and Forestry, served to improve relations between the reserve management and the neighbouring local residents.

At the same time, local leaders worked with Tralso and a related NGO, the Village Planner (TVP),[6] to prepare to submit a formal land claim under the incoming ANC government's land reform policies. Tralso had not sought out the 'communities'; rather, local leaders had sought Tralso's assistance in a locally driven struggle. This process nonetheless contributed to the constitution of Dwesa-Cwebe as a community: local leaders recognized the value of an alliance, and began to co-ordinate their protest activities and negotiations; at the same time, Tralso began to handle 'Dwesa-Cwebe' as a single 'case'.

Many of the same local leaders were involved in the negotiations with the reserve management and the preparation of the land claim, and they form the core of the current leadership of the elected body – the Dwesa-Cwebe Land – that was created in the land reform process to represent the claimants and to take ownership of the land. Institutionally, the Trust incorporates trustees from all seven of the villages adjoining the reserves, elected by communal property associations (CPAs). The CPAs themselves are headed by elected committees that represent the residents of their defined territories.[7]

The definition of 'community' at Dwesa-Cwebe reflects 'a *denial of diversity* ... organised around a common goal of access to natural resources and the benefits accruing from land ownership' (Fay and Palmer 2000: 196). The members of the Dwesa-Cwebe Land Trust have defined the boundaries of Dwesa-Cwebe in terms of past participation towards the goal of restoring access. The claimants generally explain the composition of the Dwesa-Cwebe Land Trust in terms of the common experience of those whom it represents. They see their shared past struggle both as a basis for unity and for exclusion of those who did not participate. For them, the Dwesa-Cwebe 'community' is conceived as '[encompassing] the residents of the areas ... that took an active role in the protest actions of 1994' (Fay and Palmer 2000: 196). Some also justified this inclusivity in relation to a national political vision. To quote Waphi Siyaleko of Hobeni, 'just as Mandela combined the homelands and South Africa, so we are combining Dwesa-Cwebe as one place, and not speaking of Hobeni or Mendwane [two of the constituent communities] separately'.

This commitment to an inclusive definition of community has important implications for the ability of the land claim to fulfill local aspirations of 'development' – the 'community' encompasses nearly 15,000 residents in over 2,200 households (Fay and Palmer 2002: 28). On the one hand, this has increased the scale of the funds the claimants have received from various government grants, allocated on a household basis. On the other, it means that the overall population is vastly more than could expect a viable income from the only land-based development option acceptable under the terms of the land claim agreement: tourism, centered on the Nature Reserves, which remain a protected area.

In contrast to the claimants' attempts to establish ownership based on prior occupation, descent and struggle, other parties make arguments that the reserves should remain a protected area. These are grounded in a conservationist discourse, with three dimensions: assertions of scientific value, national heritage and a relational notion of place. This discourse has largely effaced the historical justification for the creation of the reserves. The vision behind the establishment of the reserves in the 1890s was conservationist, but it was also racist and commercial: CC Henkel, the Chief Forester of the Transkei who oversaw the establishment of the forests in the 1890s explicitly focused on commercial exploitation by whites, aiming to reserve the forests to the crown, rather than relinquishing them to the teams of roving woodcutters who had been active in inland forests (cf. Tropp 2002). He reported on the removal of African residents with pride, stating that 'the Government has thus acquired most valuable areas, suitable for the cultivation of sugar-cane, coffee, tea, mangos, bananas, pineapples, &c.'. Likewise, he stressed the fact that most trees in Dwesa and Cwebe forests were of a few commercially valuable species (Henkel 1893: 136).

Nearly a century later, Dwesa-Cwebe remained a protected area, but the justifications for its status had shifted. Later conservationists did not abandon the call for protection of the area, but changed the framing of their arguments from a focus on its potential revenues for the state to one justified by the apparent neutrality of science. From about 1969, the Wildlife Protection and Conservation Society of South Africa took a strong interest in the forests of the Transkei coast (Wildlife Society 1976), and commissioned a study of the Dwesa forest in 1974 (Moll 1974). Moll recommended increasing conservation measures on the basis of the 'scientific value' of the forest, the increasing threat posed by the surrounding communities, its position as the southern limit of a great many species of fauna and flora and its importance in the light of forest destruction throughout South Africa. Acting on these recommendations, the Transkei authorities proclaimed the area a Nature Reserve in 1975 and commissioned ecologist Ken Tinley to compile a reserve management plan.[8]

In late 1977, based on the calls by Moll and Tinley for further scientific research, a group of scientists from the University of Cape Town led by biologist Roy Siegfried visited the area with the aims of inventorying plants and animals occurring at Dwesa. Rather than emphasize the presence of a few species of particular commercial value, as Henkel had in the 1890s, Siegfried and later conservationists stressed the *range* of species found. Siegfried envisioned the reserve as a 'reference point for assessing the consequences of exploitation of natural resources elsewhere on the Transkei coast' (Siegfried 1977: 3). These documents have remained the central body of scientific knowledge of the biophysical properties of these forests, in the absence of more recent research. In the 1990s, ECNC officials tended to rely on the content and justifications from these studies, in part because little research on the coastal forests had taken place since then.[9]

These authors also set out a construction of Dwesa-Cwebe that remained salient in conservationists' arguments in the 1990s. While their data-gathering focused on Dwesa-Cwebe, they also emphasized its *relational* properties as part of a larger ecological-political system. They envisioned the forests' value in relation to the larger picture of protected areas in the Transkei and in South Africa more generally: they noted that the reserve was the largest protected area on the Transkei coastline, and represented it as deserving protection because of its place in the larger spatial distributions of plant and animal species, and because of the possibility that it could be used comparatively, as a 'control' to assess the effects of environmental degradation in unprotected areas.

Related arguments, asserting Dwesa-Cwebe's place as part of a specifically South African natural endowment, appeared among the opponents of the land claim in the 1990s. Arthur Dye, a zoologist at the University of Transkei who had studied marine resources at Dwesa-Cwebe, made the case in a letter urging ECNC to oppose the land claim: 'Dwesa [is] part of the heritage of the entire nation and not just for the benefit of local communities. Dwesa has local, regional, national and international importance'.[10] A similar argument was made by a representative from the Department of Sea Fisheries in a November 1998 workshop held to discuss the draft Master Plan for the management of the reserves, when he argued against the opening of the coastline for subsistence harvesting. In his statement, he invoked the idea that the value of the reserve extended to parties far beyond the local area. Deploying a rhetorically forceful populist discourse associated with the country's multi-racial elections, he reconfigured it as an argument for the exclusion of local people from resources, stating that the coast must be preserved 'for all South Africans'.

Ironically, while the end of apartheid created the possibility for land restitution, it also opened new arguments for potential opponents to the Dwesa-Cwebe land claim. Freed from its status as a pariah nation, South Africa became a member of and signatory to a range of international conservation bodies and agreements. This meant that the network of relations that was used to justify the significance of Dwesa-Cwebe was expanded to include comparisons between South Africa's protected area network and international standards. With the nation's re-entry into the international community, conservationists argued, South Africa was now obligated to live up to global standards of conservation.

The Wildlife Society of South Africa renewed their long-standing interest in the Dwesa and Cwebe forests, now drawing upon international justifications. Arguing against the Dwesa-Cwebe land claim in May 1996, Keith Cooper of the Wildlife Society wrote to Peter Mayende, Regional Land Claims Commissioner, that:

> In terms of South Africa's recent ratification (December 1995) of the International Convention on the Protection of Biodiversity, we have an international obligation to protect and conserve our rich variety of genetic resources. Since our Country's Protected Area network only comprises six percent of our total surface area, this figure is very low in terms of world standards.[11]

These perspectives were incorporated into the official position of Eastern Cape Nature Conservation, as represented in their 22 October 1998 submission to the

Land Claims Court, which noted that Dwesa was one of the few Category II protected areas in South Africa, citing the United Nations Convention on Biological Diversity and South Africa's shortfall in terms of international standards for the proportion of land that should be protected:

> The International Union for the Conservation of Nature (IUCN), of which South Africa is a country member, has set a guideline of 10% of total land surface area as the minimum for a representative protected area system. The total surface area of South Africa's protected area system presently encompasses less than 6% of the total land surface area.

In interviews, ECNC officials also emphasized Dwesa-Cwebe's place within the boundaries of the Province of the Eastern Cape. These institutionalized territorial and bureaucratic boundaries provided another frame of reference within which to highlight the significance of Dwesa-Cwebe. At a meeting with Gerry Pienaar of ECNC in June 1998, he drew my attention to a map indicating the location of the protected areas of the Eastern Cape. The overwhelming majority of these were situated in the western half of the province (that is outside the former Transkei), where the state had been able to buy up white-owned farms. While the protected areas in the western half of the province were roughly 10 per cent of the area, in the eastern half (where areas of high rainfall and endemic biodiversity are concentrated), only about 2 per cent of the land area was protected. While conservationists outside the state framed their argument primarily with reference to larger networks, Pienaar emphasized the forests' significance with reference to an administratively and territorially defined portfolio of professional responsibility.

Despite their case for maintaining the protected area, within a year-and-a-half of the protest action ECNC recognized the local political unfeasibility of opposing the claim. They insisted, however, on restricting the rights to be transferred to the claimants; they agreed not to challenge the restitution claim, provided that the reserves continued to remain a protected area under a joint management system. In a position paper in April 1996, ECNC stated that it '[recognized] and accept[ed] the *moral* grounds for a restitution claim' (emphasis in original), and accepted that some form of restitution was appropriate, with the content of this restitution to be negotiated among 'all the stakeholders'. While ECNC conceded the issue of legal title, it still sought to limit the content of the rights and duties that would accompany the transfer of title. It also conveyed an implicit threat; following an opinion provided to the Land Claims Commission by the Legal Resources Centre,[12] it stated that 'our understanding of the documented evidence is that a strictly legal restitution claim could be difficult to substantiate'.[13]

Bundles of duties, handfuls of rights

Property has long been conceived in the social sciences as a social relationship between owners and non-owners entailing rights and duties with respect to things (for example, Gluckman 1943, 1965; Hallowell 1943), with these rights analyzable in terms of discrete 'bundles' rather than in terms of sweeping and universally applicable categories of 'private', 'public', and the like. In this section, I consider the form of property actually transferred to the Dwesa-Cwebe claimants, illustrating how the duties associated with landownership expanded considerably while the rights proved to be far less than what the claimants had expected.

Early in the negotiation process, in late 1995, swayed by – or at least willing to entertain – the argument that tourism development in a protected area offered the best hope for improving local livelihoods, the claimants agreed to maintaining the protected status of the land, under a system of joint management (Palmer *et al.* 2002). This concession was an early step in the process of narrowing the rights to be transferred to the claimants.

Even as the Dwesa-Cwebe claimants received new rights, they also received new duties. Obligations to maintain the conservation status of the land to meet national and international expectations were merely the first step. For Dwesa-Cwebe residents, prior to the land claim, the duties involved in land tenure were primarily to their neighbours, sub-headmen and headmen, and perhaps secondarily to the Magistrate in Elliotdale and the Forest Reserve management (Fay 2005). With the land claim they have now been asked to take into account a variety of new 'stakeholders.' In structuring the land claim negotiations, the Land Claims Commission recognized a number of 'secondary stakeholders', including the holiday cottage owners, the Haven Hotel, the Eastern Cape Development Corporation, a parastatal that held the existing lease to the Haven), tribal authorities, Transitional Rural Councils (a temporary local government structure), ECNC, the Nature Reserve management, adjacent communities, the Department of Land Affairs (DLA), the Department of Water Affairs and Forestry (DWAF), the Department of Economic Affairs and Tourism (DEAT) and the Wild Coast Spatial Development Initiative (SDI). The interests of each of these parties was expected to be taken into account in the restitution process. The process of sorting out the claimants' obligations to these various parties – what to do with existing leases on cottages and tourism facilities, how to settle the jurisdictional claims of different state conservation agencies, whether the claimants had to give priority to the SDI's development plans, and so on, delayed the settlement agreement – agreed in principle in 1996 – until mid-2001.[14]

Early on, officials within the Land Claims Commission wrestled with the question of how to create a form of property that could transfer 'ownership' while qualifying the claimants' land-use options. In a March 1996 memorandum on tenure issues relevant to the claim, Harald Winkler of the Regional Land

Claims Commission pointed out that 'if a restitution award is made to the Dwesa-Cwebe communities, it would – under current tenure options – be an award of a title deed'. Title deeds, he continued, conflated a bundle of rights which might better be separated. He elaborated that, 'in the Dwesa-Cwebe case, it might be desirable for the community to hold rights to use natural resources, water rights, mineral rights, and grazing and arable rights. However, it might be argued that, given the societal importance of the land as a former reserve, the community should not have the right to establish residential sites on the land, nor to buy or sell the land'.[15]

The hypothetical set of rights discussed by Winkler here was far more inclusive than that incorporated in the initial deed of settlement a few months later, in June 1996. The claimants eventually agreed that their rights would not include residential, agricultural or regular grazing use; the land would continue to be used for conservation purposes, as the cornerstone of a tourism-based local development programme, with the reserves to be managed under a system of joint management, which was expected to include access to forest produce under a permit-based system and emergency grazing when necessary under drought conditions.

The final settlement agreement, reached in 2001, added a range of financial grants to the claimants' package. These included a R2.1 million consideration to cover lease in perpetuity, R1.6 million as compensation for giving up residential rights and maintaining the conservation status of the land, and access to additional state development grants totaling some R14 million. This substantial figure looks less impressive on a per household basis; it is about R940 (or US$150) per household in the 'community'. The grants accompanied the claimants' nominal ownership of the reserve, including the Haven Hotel and holiday cottages. In a separate agreement, the cottage owners entered into three-year renewable leases at the generous price of R1750 per year.

As the financial 'bundle' grew, however, the claimants' rights to *land* contracted; moreover, the funds came with a new set of obligations to outsiders in terms of what claimants could *not* do with the land. Land uses other than conservation and limited tourism development (subject to a range of environmental regulations) were prohibited. Ownership did not include any management rights or responsibilities: ECNC would continue to manage the protected area and ECDC would continue to manage the Haven. Perhaps the greatest blow to the claimants' aspirations to autonomy came with the decision that the Amatole District Municipality, not the Dwesa-Cwebe Land Trust, would manage all of the settlement funds, with responsibility for investing the money in local development and commissioning a development plan. As in the cases described by Leynseele and Hebinck (see Chapter 9, in this book), the post-transfer phase of restitution became an opportunity for developmentalist agencies within the state to assert their authority.

The effectiveness of rights

Katherine Verdery has drawn attention to the relation of land restitution to the 'ambient conditions' that make property rights effective or ineffective (Verdery 2003: 20; cf. Chapter 7, French, in this book). The ability to translate abstract rights into material gains may depend upon a number of other factors of production and enabling conditions. Rights do not necessarily translate to the ability to benefit (cf. Ribot and Peluso 2003: 153–514; Leach *et al.* 1999: 233–4). In the case of Dwesa-Cwebe, the 'effectiveness' of the rights being transferred to the Dwesa-Cwebe land claimants is highly contingent upon factors that are largely beyond the control of the claimants. In this section, I focus on the lease payments and hotel employment which are envisioned to be the main source of benefits from the land claim in the long term. In the one that follows, I consider the implications of the fact that these funds are being channeled through local government.

From the outset, tourism, grounded in but not limited to the protected area, was presented to the land claimants as the basis for improvements to their livelihoods. Even before the claim was resolved, the risks of this approach were becoming evident. Largely independently of the land claim process, the Wild Coast SDI, a politically important regional development plan, had included Dwesa-Cwebe as one of its 'nodal clusters' for tourism development (cf. Kepe 2001). An extended bidding process ultimately failed to attract investors, after casting uncertainty on and delaying the claimants' negotiations with the Haven and cottage owners. A subsequent attempt with European Union funding to revitalize the SDI with smaller-scale projects resulted in impressive planning documents, but internal management problems prevented the project from being implemented in the southern half of the Transkei (André Terblanche, personal communication).

The reluctance of investors to bid in the SDI programme reflects some of the constraints on tourism in the region. In contrast to the Makuleke land claimants, who have a piece of land directly adjoining Kruger National Park, in the hub of ecotourism activity in southern Africa (Steenkamp 2001), the Dwesa-Cwebe claimants have acquired a piece of land in an out-of-the-way corner of the country; the reserve is several hours' drive off a main highway, half of this on an unpaved and ill-maintained gravel road, and more than four hours from the nearest major urban centre (East London). At the time of the SDI bidding process in 1999, the parastatal Eskom had promised to deliver electricity in 2003, although by 2005 this still had not taken place. In the meantime, the Haven Hotel has continued to spend more than R200,000 per year to provide limited hours of electricity with two unreliable diesel generators (Palmer and Viljoen 2002: 201).

Even an unprecedentedly successful tourism venture would be unlikely to provide significant local employment. Household surveys in 1998 revealed that in Hobeni, the adjoining village closest to the Haven, one in four households had had a family member employed at the hotel at some point, but this figure was skewed by the fact that many of the respondents were Haven employees who had acquired sites in Hobeni *after* being employed by the hotel. In the other surveyed villages (Cwebe and Ntubeni), only one of the 130 households surveyed had a family member who had worked at the hotel (Palmer and Viljoen 2002: 216).

Although a programme of renovation and electricity provision was getting underway at the Haven at the end of 2005, recent events revealed the hotel's vulnerability even further. Despite the complaints of the claimants, their land claim was only for the *land*, not for the totality of resources to which they had lost access; it did not affect the status of the Dwesa-Cwebe Marine Protected Area (MPA; established in 1991, in the final days of the Transkei homeland regime). In the second half of 2005, the Department of Marine and Coastal Management began aggressively enforcing a total ban on fishing in the MPA, effectively eliminating the appeal of the Haven to many of its guests, who came both to fish on their own and for the occasional tournaments organized by local angling clubs. The hotel manager reported precipitous drops in occupancy rates, and community members who had worked as guides and assistants to fishermen staying at the hotel found themselves without even this casual employment.

The rights of ownership of tourism facilities, job opportunities and lease incomes were all presented to the claimants from the outset of their restitution claim. Ten years after the communities agreed to maintain the protected status of the reserves, tourism had offered them very little. These rights were deeply compromised by a set of infrastructural, market and regulatory constraints that made it nearly impossible to render them 'effective'. If, as Verdery suggested, the state was 'playing the game and making the rules' (Verdery 2003: 81), it was doing so in contradictory ways. The rights granted by one arm of the state (DLA) were being undermined by the limited support and regulatory policies of others. But even state programmes like the SDI, aimed to attract tourism to the region, had exposed the limitations of these rights.

New forms of subjection

In the introduction to this book, we discussed the possibility that the creation of enclaves for land claimants, separate from the larger civic realm, might involve new forms of subjection: 'if claimants contend that they are members of a distinct group (or if the state is construing them in this way) it seems likely that they will occupy – if successful – domains separate from the broader body politic'. At Dwesa-Cwebe, in the heart of a region central to Mamdani's study of how indirect rule in Africa divided citizens from subjects (1996), the claimants have succeeded in avoiding being 're-subjected' to the rule of chiefs. They have become more citizens, participants in national politics, than subjects.

The construction of community described in the first section of this chapter is significant here; the Dwesa-Cwebe claim is *not* based on indigeneity or tribal identity, but on common experience of dispossession and struggle. Local traditional authorities had a history of collaborating with the homeland regime on the closure of the reserves and in the implementation of unpopular 'betterment' villagization policies, and some were initially hostile to the land claim; none played any leadership role in it (cf. Timmermans 2004: 127; Fay 2005). As one Tralso staff member stated in 1998, 'the only power they have is to disrupt'. Because the traditional authorities were not involved in the land struggle, they were marginal to the process in the late 1990s when institutional structures for ownership were being established. The land is owned by an elected community Trust, which itself represents elected CPAs. While some of the CPAs have chosen to incorporate headmen as *ex officio* members, headmen have no special privileges, none of these associations incorporate Tribal Authority structures. Members of the Dwesa-Cwebe Land Trust have also contributed to public testimony arguing against the controversial Communal Land Rights Act of 2004, expressing their concerns that their land might be handed over to Tribal Authorities (Dwesa-Cwebe Community Representatives 2003: 2).[16]

While land restitution at Dwesa-Cwebe has not entailed subjection to chiefs, it has been the vehicle for the creation of new relations between the claimants and local government. Throughout the claim process, NGOs and state officials alike led the members of the Dwesa-Cwebe Land Trust to expect that they would receive control of resources acquired through the land claim. Instead, the claimants have experienced what might be described as 'civic subjection', a form of subordination that may be prove to be a catalyst for democratic participation. Restitution has not meant community control over any new resources; rather, the funds from the settlement agreement and the leases on tourism facilities have been transferred to the Amatola District Council (ADC), a local government body (Palmer 2005). While incorporation into the ADC puts the Dwesa-Cwebe region under a relatively well-funded and technically competent branch of local government, it also places any planned development in the area under the purview of the ADC's Integrated Development Planning process (Palmer 2005: 14).

Relations with the ADC were particularly tense shortly after the transfer of the restitution funds to the ADC. In June 2002, the claimants discovered that the ADC had been deducting the costs of meetings with the Trust from the restitution funds, without the permission of the Trustees. When in September 2002 they requested funds (a modest R75,000) to cover their own expenses, the establishment of an office and the hiring of an administrator, they were turned down. After undergoing training, they eventually received this support in 2004 (Palmer 2005). While the ADC's concerns about the management capacity of the trustees may have some validity, there are also echoes of paternalism in the refusal to allow the claimants access to the resources for which they had struggled.

The aggressive role of local government may not necessarily be a negative outcome in the longer-term, however. In contrast to the subjection to unelected chiefs highlighted by Mamdani (1996), the local government bodies that have taken control of the Dwesa-Cwebe restitution funds are democratically elected. By late 2005, the Dwesa-Cwebe trustees had come to accept that an ongoing collaborative relationship with local government was going to be a necessity if they were to establish control over the restitution funds. Restitution here stimulated new political participation: 2005 saw several of the trustees returning to local politics; they had been active in the ANC in the early 1990s but had dropped out to focus on the land claim. Trustees were attending ANC local party caucuses to select a slate of candidates for the next local government elections, scheduled for March 2006. This effort proved successful; as of January 2006, the Chair of the Dwesa-Cwebe Land Trust was a strong candidate for a seat as local councillor in a ward which encompasses the Dwesa-Cwebe communities. Although his candidacy did not succeed, the trustees were able to bring their concerns to the local ANC and continue to see the party structure and local government as an important arena in which to continue their struggle to derive benefits from the legal rights they hold.

Conclusion

Land claims on protected areas make the possibility that restitution may 'right' the 'wrongs' of dispossession more problematic. As we argued in the introduction to this volume, the prospect of restitution raises an implicit question: 'if land is to be reclaimed, who has to lose it as a result?'. State conservation agencies face the immediate prospect of losing land in claims on protected areas, but at least according to the arguments of conservationists, the broader losers would be the nation and the international community. These arguments have proven compelling, and considerable effort has gone into finding ways to maintain the protected status of claimed land while providing some modicum of restitution (for example, Wynberg and Kepe 1999; Steenkamp 2001).

Certainly there is the legal appearance of restitution at Dwesa-Cwebe; the claimants have successfully won a land claim, but as I argued in the introduction, little appears to have changed on the ground. The claimants have received a limited bundle of rights, accompanied by many obligations, and have been incorporated into a forum for new state intervention. Moreover, many of the original grievances of the claimants have remained unaddressed: despite ongoing negotiations over joint management of the reserves, and a pledge by the reserve management (in 1999) to reopen the permit-based system for access to forest products, since the restitution agreement in 2001 local residents have had no access to building materials, medicinal plants, grazing or other resources from the reserve. The transfer of management in 2006 from ECNC to the newly-established Eastern Cape Parks Board (ECPB) appears unlikely to restore local access; staff of the newly established board had reputations for hard-line approaches to protected area management (H Timmermans, personal communication).

In the meantime, the frustrations of residents of the areas adjoining the reserves have grown. By 2005, residents who had initially co-operated with the conservation authority and left reserve fences intact, had joined their less co-operative neighbours in the practice of fence-cutting in order to gain access to the forest. Residents of Hobeni had also renewed the strategy of direct protest within the reserves, acting independently of the Trust and of the land claim leadership. They staged a protest inside the reserves in late 2004, cutting trees and harvesting shellfish, but were summarily arrested and some sentenced to prison terms. They were attempting to claim the rights they had expected to receive at the outset of the land claim, but which had been gradually sacrificed during the long negotiation process. While most of the trustees were sympathetic to the protesters' complaints, the trustees refused to intervene on their behalf, insisting that such protests take place through established negotiation channels with reserve management.

While restitution may have promised a measure of autonomy and self-determination as the introduction suggests, this has been continually compromised by the actions of diverse arms of the state, which have acted both to support and to undermine the transfer of effective rights through the restitution process. Many residents' original grievances remain outstanding, while the Trust has seen the fruits of its labour pass into the control of local government — in which it now aims to intervene, through the electoral process. For ordinary residents, and for the members of the Dwesa-Cwebe Land Trust, the success of their land restitution claim has been but one step in an ongoing struggle for the restoration of land rights.

References

Department of Land Affairs (2001) *The Dwesa-Cwebe Community Land Restitution Claim. Settlement agreement in terms of section 42D of the Restitution of Land Rights Act No. 22 of 1994*, unpublished report, East London: Regional Land Claims Commission.

Dwesa-Cwebe Community Representatives (2003) 'Dwesa-Cwebe Community Consultation', available at www.lrc.org.za/Docs/Papers/2003_Nov10_DWESA_Community_Submission.doc (accessed 13 January 2006).

Fay, Derick (2001) 'Oral and Written Evidence in South Africa's Land Claims Process: the Case of Dwesa-Cwebe Nature Reserve', unpublished paper presented at Oral History Association Annual Meeting, October 2001.

—— (2005) 'Kinship and Access to Land in the Eastern Cape: Implications for Land Tenure Reform', *Social Dynamics* 31(1): 182–207.

—— (2007) 'Mutual Gains and Distributive Ideologies in South Africa: Theorizing Negotiations between Communities and Protected Areas', *Human Ecology* 35(1): 81–95.

Fay, D and R Palmer (2000) 'Prospects for Redistribution of Wealth through Land Reform at Dwesa-Cwebe', in B Cousins (ed.) *At the Crossroads: Land and agrarian reform in South Africa into the 21st century*, Bellville: University of the Western Cape Programme for Land and Agrarian Studies and the National Land Committee, pp 194–210.

Fay, Derick, Herman Timmermans and Robin Palmer (2002) 'Closing the forests: segregation, exclusion and their consequences from 1936 to 1994', in Robin Palmer, Herman Timmermans and Derick Fay (eds) *From Confrontation to Negotiation on South Africa's Wild Coast: Conservation, Land Reform and Tourism Development at Dwesa-Cwebe Nature Reserve*, Pretoria: Human Sciences Research Council.

Gluckman, M (1943) *Essays on Lozi Land and Royal Property*, Rhodes Livingstone Paper No. 10, Livingstone: Rhodes-Livingstone Institute.

—— (1965) *The Ideas in Barotse Jurisprudence*, New Haven, CT: Yale University Press.

Hallowell, AI (1943) 'The Nature and Function of Property as a Social Institution', *Journal of Legal and Political Sociology* 1: 115–38.

Henkel, CC (1893) 'Report of the Conservator of Forests Transkeian Conservancy for the Year 1893', in *Reports of the Conservators of Forests, for the Year 1893*, Department of Agriculture, Cape of Good Hope Government.

—— (1894) *Report of the Conservator of Forests and District Forest Officers for the Year 1894 (With Appendices)*, Cape Town: WA Richards & Sons.

—— (1903) *History, Resources and Productions of the Country between Cape Colony and Natal, or Kaffraria Proper Now Called the Native or Transkeian Territories*, Hamburg: Hamburg Press.

James, Deborah (2006) 'The Tragedy of the Private: owners, communities and the state in South Africa', in F and K von Benda-Beckmann and M Wiber (eds) *Changing Properties of Property*, Oxford: Berghahn.

Kepe, T (1998) 'The Problem of Defining "Community": Challenges for the Land Reform Programme in Rural South Africa', paper presented at the International Conference on Land Tenure in the Developing World, University of Cape Town.

—— (2001) *Waking Up from the Dream: the Wild Coast SDI and the pitfalls of 'fast track' development*, Research Report No. 8, Cape Town: Programme for Land and Agrarian Studies, School of Government, University of the Western Cape.

Kepe, T, R Wynberg and W Ellis (2005) 'Land Reform and Biodiversity Conservation in South Africa: complementary or in conflict?', *The International Journal of Biodiversity Science and Management* 1(1): 3–16.

Leach, M, R Mearns, and I Scoones (1999) 'Environmental Entitlements: dynamics and institutions in community-based natural resources management', *World Development* 27: 225–47.

Mamdani, Mahmood (1996) *Citizen and Subject: Contemporary Africa and the Legacy of Late Colonialism*, Princeton, NJ: Princeton University Press.

Mayer, P and I Mayer (1971) *Townsmen or Tribesmen*, Cape Town: Oxford University Press.

Moll, E J (1974) *A Preliminary Report on the Dwesa Forest Reserve, Transkei*, Cape Town: Wildlife Society of Southern Africa and University of Cape Town.

Palmer, R (2005) 'A Luta Continua: The Struggles for Survival and Control at Dwesa-Cwebe, a Rural Area on South Africa's Wild Coast', unpublished manuscript.

Palmer, R, H Timmermans and D Fay (eds) (2002) *From Confrontation to Negotiation on South Africa's Wild Coast: Conservation, Land Reform and Tourism Development at Dwesa-Cwebe Nature Reserve*, Pretoria: Human Sciences Research Council.

Palmer, R, H Timmermans, K Kralo, D Lieberman, R Fox, D Hughes, K Sami, N Motteux and U Van Harmelen (1997) *Indigenous Knowledge, Conservation Reform, Natural Resource Management and Rural Development in the Dwesa and*

Cwebe Nature Reserves and Neighbouring Village Settlements, Grahamstown: ISER, Rhodes University.

Palmer, Robin and Johan Viljoen (2002) 'South Africa and the New Tourism', in Robin Palmer, Herman Timmermans and Derick Fay (eds) *From Confrontation to Negotiation on South Africa's Wild Coast: Conservation, Land Reform and Tourism Development at Dwesa-Cwebe Nature Reserve*, Pretoria: Human Sciences Research Council.

Ribot, J and N Peluso (2003) 'A Theory of Access', *Rural Sociology* 68(2): 153–81.

Siegfried, WR (1977) *A Report on Preliminary Surveys of Selected Communities of Plants and Animals at Dwesa Nature Reserve*, Cape Town: Fitzpatrick Institute, University of Cape Town.

Steenkamp, C (2001) 'The Makuleke Land Claim: An environmental conflict', unpublished PhD dissertation, University of the Witwatersrand.

Terblanche, A and M Kraai (1996) *Dwesa and Cwebe: Enduring, democratic conservation after apartheid's abuses*, unpublished report commissioned by Tralso, Umtata.

Timmermans, Herman Gerald (2004) 'Rural Livelihoods at Dwesa/Cwebe: poverty, development and natural resource use on the Wild Coast, South Africa', Masters thesis, Rhodes University.

Tropp, J (2002) 'Roots and Rights in the Transkei: Colonialism, Natural Resources and Social Change, 1880–1940', unpublished PhD dissertation, University of Minnesota.

Vaughan, A (1997) *Beyond Policies and Politics: Options for Conservation and Development in Dwesa and Cwebe: A Diagnostic Study for the Land and Agriculture Policy Centre*, unpublished report, Pretoria: Land and Agricultural Policy Centre.

Verdery, Katherine (2003) *The Vanishing Hectare: property and value in post-socialist Romania*, Ithaca, NY: Cornell University Press.

Vermaak, M and B Peckham, B (1996) *Towards Integrated Natural Resource Management At Dwesa-Cwebe Reserve & Adjacent Communal Land: A Preliminary Survey of the Legal History of the Reserve, Current Legislation, & the Legal Rights & Obligations of Interested Parties*, unpublished report, Grahamstown: Rhodes University.

Wildlife Society (1976) 'The Wildlife Society at Work in the Homelands', *African Wildlife* 30(5): 51.

Wynberg, R and T Kepe (1999) *Land Reform and Conservation Areas in South Africa: Towards a Mutually Beneficial Approach*, Pretoria: IUCN South Africa.

Notes

The Research Institute for the Study of Man (New York, US) in 1998 and the Wenner-Gren Foundation for Anthropological Research (New York, US; Grant #6329) in 1999 provided funding for this research. Additional fieldwork in 2005 was funded as part of an S.V. Ciriacy-Wantrup Post-doctoral Fellowship at the University of California, Berkeley. Thanks are especially due to Kuzile Juza and Waphi Siyaleko of Hobeni, Makuthiweni Mangakeva and Mxolisi Nombona of Cwebe, the other members of the Dwesa-Cwebe Land Trust, and numerous Hobeni and Cwebe residents. At Rhodes University, long-term collaboration with Robin Palmer and Herman Timmermans has been invaluable, while the Institute for Social and Economic Research provided me support as a Visiting Scholar. André Terblanche and Mcebisi Kraai of the Village Planner and Tralso provided me with information, documents and hospitality.

1 Much has been written on the history of the Dwesa-Cwebe land claim (Vermaak and

Peckham 1996; Terblanche and Kraai 1996; Palmer *et al.* 1997; Vaughan 1997; Palmer *et al.* 2002; Fay 2007; Palmer 2005) and the policy issues around land claims on protected areas (Wynberg and Kepe 1999; Kepe *et al.* 2005).

2 Following is a typical account, collected by the activist non-governmental organization, Tralso: Nogxiya, born around 1911, told them that 'when I was born our cattle grazed everywhere, until we were chased out of the forest. I was born in Madakeni close to the sea. When the government chased us out they also took everything from us ... There were houses along the coast up to the Haven. The cottages were inside our villages' (in Terblanche and Kraai 1996: 10).

3 'Homelands' were political entities created by the South African government from the old 'Native Reserves' in order to create the appearance of political devolution within the context of apartheid; the Transkei homeland was granted 'self-government' in 1963 and 'independence' in 1976.

4 An 'Administrative Area' refers to the territory under a single headman, the smallest unit of administration in the Transkei.

5 These differences, and their relation to economic differentiation, are discussed in detail in Fay and Palmer (2000).

6 The change in the NGOs hides continuity in personnel. André Terblanche worked for Tralso on the Dwesa-Cwebe case in 1992, and subsequently founded The Village Planner. The two organizations collaborate regularly.

7 The CPA model was created early in South Africa's land reform process as a model for group ownership of land; it was developed locally through the state's tenure reform process, implemented by the Village Planner through meetings and workshops with elected leaders and their constituents in 1996–7. It was through this process that local people came to define the precise spatial and social boundaries of the units represented in the Trust. See James (2006).

8 This paragraph and the one following are adapted from Fay *et al.* (2002: 90–6), wherein Timmermans discusses Moll and Tinley's reports and recommendations in great detail.

9 On the state of the literature, see Timmermans' exhaustive review of the literature in Fay *et al.* (2002). A more contemporary literature exists on coastal marine resources at Dwesa-Cwebe, which have been the focus of ongoing research by researchers at the University of Transkei (now Walter Sisulu University).

10 A Dye to G Pienaar letter of 10 June 1997, personal files of A Terblanche, Umtata.

11 K Cooper, Director of Conservation, the Wildlife Society, fax to Peter Mayende, Regional Land Claims Commissioner, of 16 May 1996, in files compiled by the Land Claims Commission and made available to the claimants (LCC files).

12 B Sephton, Legal Resources Center, memorandum of 5 July 1996 to P Mayende, Regional Land Claims Commissioner, East London (LCC files). Sephton described the situation to me in similar terms in an interview at the LRC offices, Grahamstown, on 30 July 1996.

13 'Land Claim against the Dwesa and Cwebe Nature Reserves: Position Statement by Eastern Cape Nature Conservation', 24 April 1996 (LCC files). Gerry Pienaar of ECNC, the author of the statement, made both of these points to me in an interview at the ECNC offices, East London, 10 June 1998.

14 Some of the many details of these various processes can be found in Fay (2001); Palmer (2005); and Palmer *et al.* (2002).

15 In personal files of Kuzile Juza, Hobeni.

16 The Dwesa-Cwebe claimants' success in keeping traditional authorities at arms' length contrasts with the situation in KwaZulu-Natal, where Tribal Authorities have taken control of the restitution process, effectively using it as a 'land acquisition scheme' (Charles Chavunduka, personal communication).

Chapter 3

'They should be killed'
Forest restitution, ethnic groups and patronage in post-socialist Romania[1]

Stefan Dorondel

Abstract

It is claimed by some development experts that private property both brings economic benefits for the owners, and enables the sustainable exploitation of a natural resource. This chapter explores a contrasting case where the private ownership of forest led to deforestation. Engaging the concepts of property rights, access and patronage, the chapter shows how a historically deprived ethnic group in post-socialist Romania has been engaged in a patron–client relationship by those who have access to the post-socialist state. Here, land restitution has re-created older forms of inequality and injustice.

> 'Property is a trifle'.
> (Ion Iliescu, the President of Romania 1990–6, 2000–4)

The 1989 upheaval brought important social, political and economic changes in Central and South-eastern Europe. Of these, perhaps the most urgently requested – and subsequently the most minutely scrutinized and analyzed – has been the transformation of property rights. Such a transformation has led scholars to question what has often been viewed as axiomatic: the 'golden rule' that private property rights work better than common ones to preserve natural resources, and that private property creates, 'through internalisation of benefits, incentives to productive activity' (Radin 1993: 7). This chapter explores a case in post-socialist Romania in which private property rights to forests, restored through land restitution, not only failed to conserve a natural resource but actually led to its depletion. I explore the way in which people with access to the state, such as the local policeman, the state forest guards and the employees of the village mayor's office, manipulate a deprived ethnic group through patron–client relationships, in order to benefit from the forest. Property rights over the forest provide scarcely any benefit to the owners. Benefits accrue, instead, to the elite of that village and other persons from outside the village with access to state positions. This chapter contributes to a growing body of work (Acheson 2000; Sowerwine 2004) which suggests that theories of property rights which emphasize the effectiveness of private property for sustainable and productive use need to be considerably revised.

Property, access and patronage in the post-socialist context

Theories on property and access have rarely been discussed in relation to patronage in post-socialist contexts. It is my argument that property, access and patronage are closely related in the context of post-socialism. The restitution or redistribution of land and forest in post-socialist times opened the opportunity for differentiated access to natural resources, depending less on formal rights to property than on the political position, or connections to those in power, of the owner. In post-socialist Romania, although forest restitution was a right of former owners, many had no access to labour, capital or the market. This restricted their opportunities to benefit from their newly restored property rights over the forest. In this setting it is not ownership but rather access to political position or to the state that has become the most important factor in the exploitation of a natural resource. The resulting inequalities of access find expression through, and serve to strengthen, pre-existing ethnic identities. Patronage, as an unbalanced form of social and economic relationship between two groups, is the mechanism through which those who have access to the state are able to draw economic benefits from the forest, irrespective of their ownership of this resource.

Property has been defined as a social relation between people regarding a 'thing' or 'things' (for example, Gluckman 1943, 1965; Hallowell 1943; MacPherson 1992, 1978). When an owner considers how to use the 'thing' over which he has property rights, he is faced with a number of limitations concerning its use, some deriving from his obligations towards other people (Verdery 2004). His duty is not to harm others by exercising his right. The duty of others, reciprocally, is to respect the owner's rights, which should be enforced by the state or by law (customary or formal). In post-socialist Romania, as I will show, great emphasis is placed on rights in the popular imagination, often resulting in a neglect of the duties attached to these rights.

To add to this relational definition, one can usefully conceive of property as Verdery does: as a social, cultural and political system. As a social and cultural system, property is also linked to social identity (Verdery 2005) and is a matter of political arrangements in which local-level power and control are of crucial importance. After 1989, people with political positions at the local level managed to appropriate different 'things' of value: land, land-related assets and forests (Verdery 1994, 1996, 2003). People having access to local political positions and charged with the implementation of reform at the local level were able to control and, very often, to hijack access to natural resources: mainly land (Verdery 2002). The devolution of power from central to local level gave great power – especially to the employees of the mayor's office. Like many other authors (Rabinowicz and Swinnen 1997; Verdery 2002) I suggest that land reform and local-level land reform implementation must be understood as somewhat distinct actions: while the former represents a legislative action of national government the latter represents the way in which the local administration puts this into practice. At local level people with political power succeeded in avoiding, changing or hijacking the law in their own interest.

All in all, as Verdery suggests (1998), property should be defined as a bundle of powers rather than a bundle of rights. One can observe in post-socialist villages the incomplete power of owners to draw economic benefits from the assets they own (ibid). At this point the concept of access becomes crucial.

'Access', following Ribot and Peluso (2003) is the 'ability to benefit from things – including material objects, persons, institutions and symbols'. The difference between the definitions of 'property' and 'access' is that the former is defined in terms of rights, while the latter is defined in terms of the various ways people derive benefits from resources. The key distinction between 'property' and 'access', then, lies in the difference between 'right' and 'ability' (Ribot and Peluso 2003: 156). Ribot and Peluso emphasize that ability is akin to power, defined as 'the capacity of some actors to affect practices and ideas of others' (Ribot and Peluso 2003: 155–6). Drawing on Ribot and Peluso's way of mapping access I consider three interrelated mechanisms: one is based on non-legal means, the second draws upon factors such as labour, authority and social identity; the third depends on social networks.

The first mechanism of access is based simply on theft. When owners neglect to protect their property because of inconvenience, lack of capacity or because they consider the associated duties (for example, hiring forest guards) to be illegitimate, theft – that is, appropriation by those who are *not* owners – is the main way of getting access to the forest. Those who have access through this mechanism – a gypsy-like group of woodcutters known as the *Rudari* (see below, n 4) – consider theft as legitimate as it is the only way of surviving. Their historical cultural traits are strictly linked to the forest which makes them the perfect, and most readily exploitable, labour force for those who hold state authority.

Further mechanisms of access concern authority and social relations (Ribot and Peluso 2003: 172). Whereas those forest owners with no local state-derived authority are unable to extract a benefit despite having received the right to the forest through restitution, those who occupy a position as representatives of the state at local level are able to draw considerable economic benefit from the forest. In partial contrast to the African case, where diverse social ties enable access to land and other resources (Berry 1989, 1993), the primary route to such access in post-socialist countries is via links to state agencies.

The phenomenon of patronage is of key importance in analyzing these relationships. Patron–client relationships use the language of kinship (Gellner 1977) to express a kind of exchange relationship. The patron assures protection for the client in return for a flow of services such as cheap labour or various goods (Scott 1977), but this reciprocity is skewed by power imbalances between patron and client (Littlewood 1980). In cases such as the present one, the patron–client relationship is an inter-ethnic one (see Rassam 1977). A weak state, and in particular the absence of an effective bureaucracy, creates the conditions for patron–client relations at the local level (Hart 1989, 1991; Berry 1985). In the post-socialist case, the weakness of the state offers the possibility to certain of its employees to use it in pursuit of their own interests. The patron–client relationship in the case I will describe below was premised on the use of the state as an essential element of bargaining by the 'patrons' – local office-holders – for their own interest. The policeman, the mayor's office employees or the state forest guard represent the state at the local level and are responsible for implementing its laws. But they use the powers bestowed upon them by the law in their own interest.[2] I suggest that we are witnessing a 'privatization' of the post-socialist state in the interests of its local representatives.

In this particular case of patron–client relations, both parties derive economic benefits from the exchange, but in starkly differentiated manner. While the state representatives gain important economic benefits by acquiring cheap forest land, the 'clients' – the *Rudari* – do little more than ensure their survival through this exchange. Apart from their illegal activities in the forest, they have no means of subsistence other than a meagre social benefit. Both *Rudari* and state representatives gain at the expense of private forest owners who derive virtually no advantages from their ownership.

Decollectivization and forest restitution

Driving from Pitesti, the capital of the county, on the national road, after about 20 km a wonderful landscape opens up before one's eyes: a hilly region crossed by the Argesel River and dotted with forests, crop fields and pastures. After another 6 km one arrives in Dragomireşti,[3] the commune of 2,852 people where I carried out my fieldwork in 2004. The commune comprises three villages: Vâlceni, Dragomireşti and Costeşti, and three ethnic groups: Romanians, which are the majority, Roma people (*ţigani*) and *Rudari*.[4] The last census (2002) gives the figures shown in Table 3.1.

The social structure of Dragomireşti commune at the beginning of the twentieth century comprised smallholders (owning private and collective agricultural land as well as private and collective forest), noblemen (owning private

Table 3.1 Population of Dragomireşti commune

Villages	Total	Romanians	Roma (including Rudari)	Other ethnic groups
Dragomireşti	656	645	11	
Vâlceni	571	517	54	
Costeşti	1625	933	593	99

(*Source:* The County Department of Statistics Pitesti)

land and forest) and bondsmen[5] (living on the noblemen's land, doing corvée and eventually receiving small plots of agricultural land and in some cases small areas of forest as well). Most inhabitants of Dragomireşti village and many of those in Vâlceni were free smallholders (*moşneni*), with each such family having its own small agricultural and forest plots. Villagers from Costeşti, on the other hand, lived on noblemen's land (*clăcaşi*) and had no land or forest of their own. This pre-socialist scenario is important for the present property relations in the village for two reasons. First, given that Costeşti villagers have no historic claim to forest ownership, the village has become an important market in which *Rudari* can sell timber and firewood. Second, the heirs of noblemen each received 10 hectares of forest under the state's post-socialist restitution programme. They were the forest owners who were to be most 'targeted' by both *Rudari* and local state representatives in the course of their attempts to gain access to forest resources.

In 1945, 4000 ha of forest and 500 ha of arable land were expropriated by the state from the noblemen of Vâlceni and Costeşti and distributed to around 300 families from all three villages (Pârnuţă *et al.* 2003: 221). Under the state's land reform programme, compensation was given for these expropriations at the time. The end of the Second World War saw Moscow gain extensive influence over Romania. The project of collectivization, a soviet blueprint for the countries under its influence, started in Romania in 1949 and continued for a period of 13 years. In 1962 the communist regime announced that collectivization had been accomplished throughout the country. What this meant at the local level was the collectivization of agricultural land and the nationalization, in 1948, of the forest. Forest owners had to give up their property rights without compensation of any kind.

After the 1989 breakdown of the Communist regime, one of the first tasks the new government had to fulfil was that of changing the property regime. Central among its tasks was the restitution of land and forest to the pre-1948 owners. Forest restitution laws were intended to establish rights and duties for the forest owners and the conditions under which a forest could be exploited. Through law 18/1991, former forest owners receive no more than 1 ha of forest, regardless of how much they owned before 1948. Former owners have to produce documents to prove their pre-1948 ownership of forest, while heirs of former owners, in addition to submitting documents, are required to prove their relationship with the owner.

Law 26/1996, also called the 'Code of Forestry', establishes the rules of management and exploitation of the forest, private and public; that is, it sets out an array of duties that forest owners are obligated to uphold. It specifies the protection and monitoring of the forest, the terms under which it can be utilized, and sanctions for the breaking of this code. It lays down the maximum area that can be cleared (5 ha, expanded to 10 ha in 2000) and specifies which products may be exploited (wood and non-timber products such as wild fruit or mushrooms). It stipulates that the public forest be managed by the National

Department of the Forest (NDF)[6] and the private forest be administered by its owners: individually or in associations. The owners are obliged to regenerate the forest within two years of its being cleared. The NDF will also assist the owners to clean and maintain the health of the forest at the owner's expense. The owners have to provide for monitoring of private forests (Art 70), through contractual agreements with the NDF. They are obliged to cut only those trees marked by the forest guards (*padurari*), and they require permits in order to transport felled trees out of the forest. Regulations may be enforced by the forest guards, the chief of forestry district, and the forester engineer (Art 105). The foresters also carry firearms which could be used when required

These rules proved very onerous for private forest owners, in part because of the excessively bureaucratic character of the procedures involved. An owner wanting to use his or her forest is required to commission and pay for a survey. The first step is to make a written request at the mayor's office. The office, after verifying the property rights of the owner, will send this request to the Local Forestry Department which verifies the property rights of the owner and the characteristics of the forest (the type, age and growth rate of the trees), and then establishes the amount and precise location of the timber to be extracted, up to one cubic metre per hectare of forest. More importantly, it establishes the type of cutting. This might, as in the case of commercial firms, involve 'clear-cutting' or, as is more usual for private owners, be restricted to 'cleaning a dense forest' (*răritură*). The result of the study is sent to the owner and the forest guard responsible for *state forest* in that particular village.[7] The owner then waits until the forest guard has marked the trees which he considers are ready to be cut, such as the diseased ones or those which impede the growth of young trees.

But there are multiple opportunities to overlook the law, and loopholes in the bureaucracy are readily exploited. Delays prior to surveying, for example, may extend or reduce depending on the position of the owner within the village or his personal relationship with the mayor or the secretary of the mayor's office. Once the survey has been completed, most forest guards depart after having marked the trees which may be cut rather than remaining to see their instructions carried out. Few of my informants restricted themselves to cutting only the trees noted in the survey and marked by the guard.[8]

All-in-all, state control coupled with state weakness has had two major results in the case of forest restitution. First, the laws give power to the local representatives of the state: the policeman, the forest guard and the mayor's office representatives. The prerogatives of the national state are checked by its local representatives who are able to manipulate or hijack the law in their own interest. It is these office-holders who have become the patrons in the village. Second, private forest owners suffer the greatest restrictions. If they had followed the law, several owners assured me, they would have frozen during the winter, since one cubic metre of firewood – the amount permitted – is enough for only about one month's heating, and thus only about one-fifth of the total amount required.[9] The remainder, in the official view, ought to be purchased. But, as one villager put it, 'buying firewood when the forest is plenty in the area and when I have my own forest would be really stupid'.

Establishing new rights and duties en route to 'restitution'

Out of 4,181 ha, the total surface of Dragomireşti, 2,553 ha is covered with forest. The forest represents the most valuable natural resource in the whole area. There are several reasons for its high value. First, all households in the village use wood for heating as well as for household construction (barns, stables, fences are all built with wood). Second, wood is a very good source of income and a very quickly tradable commodity. Third, there is a good market within the village since there are people who own no forest at all but who still need to build and/or heat their houses.

The restoring and privatizing of forest was a gradual process rather than a sudden switch of relationships and obligations. The law regarding forest restitution was passed in 1991, and forest restitution became effective in 1993 when the State Forest Department (SFD) gave back 172 ha of forest in one single plot. However, until 1997, when people received the deeds according to measurements made by the mayor's office for each individual plot, the forest was still considered to be collectively owned (*in devălmăşie*).

Between 1993 and 1997 the forest guard, paid by the mayor's office, was responsible for monitoring this common forest. The forester was respected and feared and no deforestation occurred during this period. The forester required owners to observe forestry laws and insisted on approving every case of tree-felling. A household was allowed to fell trees in accordance with the surface its members had claimed. The owners protested, feeling that as long as they could not exploit the forest according to their wishes they were not its true owners. Finally, the local council caved in and decided that there was no need for a forest guard, and he was dismissed. Despite the law which requires that every owner should monitor his or her own forest or request the SFD to do so on a contractual basis, the private forest remained without any watch at all.

Other scholars studying Eastern Europe have pointed to similar situations in which owners tend to separate their ownership rights from the obligations attached to these, especially if these are conceived of as obligations to the state (Howarth 1998; Sikor 2006). After experiencing almost 50 years of state regulations intruding brutally into their lives, people reject all state regulations concerning property rights. Although the shift of ownership from state to private hands should not change the duties an owner has regarding the object of ownership, people strongly reject the idea that any such duties exist. Very often I have heard in the village: 'it is my forest, why does the state regulate how forest should be used when it belongs to *me*?'. It seems that the new language of ownership creates false expectations which confuse people. Private property, from the villagers' standpoint, means total independence from the state: no external regulations are accepted over their desired use of private natural resources.

Although, during this interim period after the guard's dismissal, forest owners were able to assert some independence, this did not last for long. But this time it was not merely their obligations to the state that intruded upon what they felt was their right to autonomous ownership. More forest restitution soon occurred, with villagers from Dragomirești receiving another 428 ha of forest under law 1/2000. Every entitled villager could receive up to 10 ha of forest.[10] This was the situation in the village in 2003: large areas of forest had recently been transferred to private ownership. While they had nominal rights to property, however, the forest owners did not acquire effective access to their forests. Instead, patron–client relationships between government officials and *Rudari* undermined the position of private owners and buttressed the power of local state officials. The convergence of these various factors led to significant deforestation in the period after 2003.

Rudari – *a marginalized ethnic group*

Dragomirești houses a substantial community of *Rudari*: an ethnic group which historically owned neither land nor forest but which traditionally made a living by working with wood, as manual labourers, builders or crafters of baskets and household tools. Their social and economic identity is closely linked to their occupation. There is a legend explaining the economic and ecological niche which *Rudari* have occupied. When Jesus Christ was crucified nobody wanted to build the cross. Somebody from the *Rudari* offered to do it. Consequently, God punished them by forever making them work with wood and never allowing them to do anything else.

Before 1948 (the year of forest nationalization) they worked as labourers in the noblemen's forest. While men felled trees and chopped wood, women made wooden baskets and wooden barns, brooms and pitchforks. Their cottages (*bordeie*) were built in the forest: 'We used to live in the wood' an informant told me. This echoed a statement made by an informant to Ion Chelcea, the ethnographer who studied them during the inter-war period more than 60 years ago:[11] 'we have no country of our own. We settle wherever we find forest' (1940: 76). They never rented land because they had no animals to work with, never pursued animal husbandry, and had no agricultural skills. Moreover, although the younger *Rudari* fought as soldiers in both world wars, unlike other Romanians they did not receive land in compensation.

Since *Rudari* made their living from wood they needed to procure it somehow. Chelcea describes two ways of doing this in the 1940s: one was purchase, the other was theft from the private forests. In the latter case, they would go into the wood, wrap up the trunk of the tree in order to muffle the noise of the saw, and cut it. Sometimes this required bribing the forest guard: 'for half a kilo of *rachiu*[12] the forest guards turn a blind eye', said an informant (Chelcea 1944: 120). But more often they were in conflict with these guards, as indicated by the statement 'the forest guards are as bad as dogs are' (*pădurari-s ca cîinii*).[13]

As with many landless people, the relationships of *Rudari* with their land-holding neighbours combined discord with close interdependence. On the one hand there were conflicts between Romanians and *Rudari* over incidents of forest trespassing and settlement on communal grazing lands. On the other, almost all household wooden tools were made by *Rudari*. They exchanged these tools for maize flour, food or clothes or – when selling their products at the fairs – for money. The only need *Rudari* expressed when Chelcea did research among them (1928–38) was to have their own forest in order to be able to collect wood for their work: this, they claimed, would enable them to subsist without stealing. An informant complained to Chelcea: 'you can't go into the forest because they [the forest guards], catch you; if you go to the market to trade your wooden stuff they [police] ask you for a permit. I don't understand this law . . .' (1944: 124). When they were found illegally in the wood they were fined. But, as Chelcea pointed out, since they were too poor to pay any fine and had no property of their own to be confiscated, they were usually released.

Under the communist regime the *Rudari* continued their forest work. The forest guards employed the men as an informal labour force; they were considered ideal for this job, being very skilled and requiring few returns. Instead of being paid, they asked in return only the right to gather dried boughs for firewood. This job was not official: *Rudari* were never formally hired by the forest guards to do labouring but negotiated an agreement with them informally.[14] When *Rudari* had no work to do for the forest guards they worked as day labourers in agriculture in or, more often outside, the village.

In 1990 a few *Rudari* families received small plots of land of 0.4 ha per household.[15] When, in 1991, law 18 requested the land to be given back to its former owners, the mayor's office took back the land that had been previously distributed to *Rudari* and gave it to the former owners. The *Rudari* then started to illegally build their houses on communal land (*izlaz*). After 1989, with the general decline of Romanian industry, the Dacia car factory started to restructure[16] and the very first workers laid off were those from the lowest positions. *Rudari* were among them. The only choice for them was to continue – or return – to work in the forest, for the forest guards, and/or to enter into patronage arrangements with state employees.

Patronage, access and deforestation: mechanisms at work

Land reform created three types of forest ownership: private, state, and in some parts of Romania, collective. On the participatory map (see Figure 3.1)[17] one can see that deforestation (represented by the shaded area) occurred on the private plots rather than on the 600 ha under the surveillance of the state forest

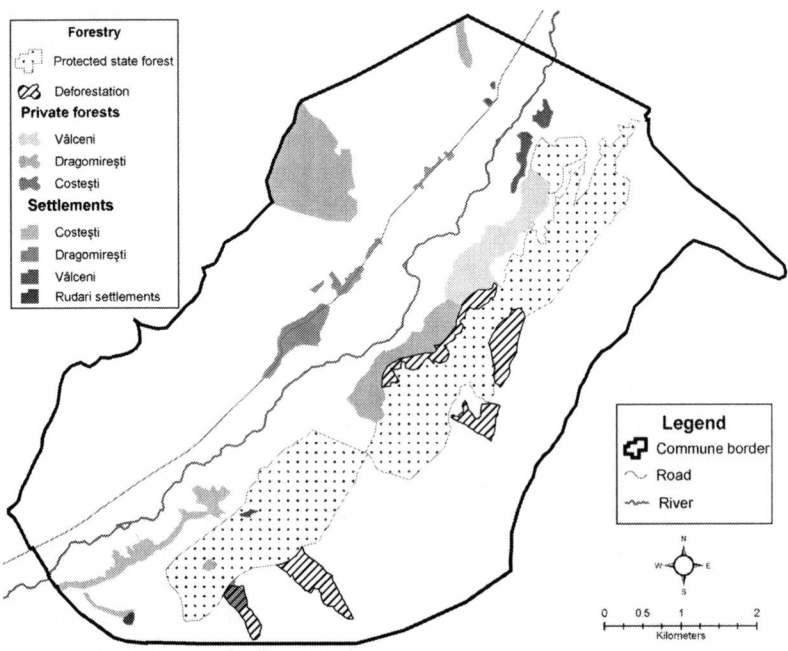

Figure 3.1 Participatory map.

guard (represented by black points on the map). Deforestation, that is, occurred in private forest areas beyond state forest guard control.

What restricts deforestation to these areas of private forest is a series of tacit agreements between forest guards and the Rudari who do the illegal tree-cutting. As mentioned earlier, it is easy to fell trees on state property without fear of being caught especially in an area as large as 600 ha. The difficulties of forest surveillance are exacerbated by the fact that foresters and forest guards, restricted to the use of their slow-moving city cars, are often forced to operate on foot. But even without such difficulties, forest guards show little interest in policing state-owned forest areas. 'They won't dare to cut trees in the state forest' I was told. Forest guards did not seem perturbed by the fact that the forest is evaluated every year by a national commission, and that every tree that is cut illegally has to be paid for by them out of their meagre salaries, around €100 per month. How were they able to retain their calm attitude in the fact of these harsh sanctions on misconduct? And why was it, conversely, only in private, from restituted forest, that trees were being stolen in Dragomireşti? While villagers blame the *Rudari* for the theft, using the words from the title of this chapter: 'they should be killed since they are not good for anything else but stealing our forest', the truth is more complex. *Rudari* are used as scapegoats and as a cheap labour force by state employees like policeman, forest guards and some people from the mayor's office. It is they, via their patron–client relations with these woodcutters, who are behind the theft of trees from privately owned and restituted forest. The mechanism of patronage in this village is as follows. *Rudari* obtain information chiefly from the state forest guards as to which particular private plots may be cut in order to avoid making the 'mistake' of cutting the state forest trees for which those guards are responsible. If a forest guard does catch *Rudari* thieves with a cartful of wood they will bribe him – the amount of money most often mentioned was about 500,000 lei (about €15)[18] – as well as providing his family with a 'gift' of high quality wood.

People from the mayor's office also have leverage on *Rudari*. As most *Rudari* have neither pensions nor salaries, they receive social benefits from the state (around €20 per month). The employees of the mayor's office are those who 'give them money'.[19] The mayor's office employees allow *Rudari* to graze their horses on the communal pasture, and to build their houses illegally on the communal pasture in Costești (see Figure 3.2), without paying any fees. There is no documentation of this arrangement: as the mayor's office employees told me, they do not ask for money from *Rudari* since they are too poor to pay.

Another important service the mayor's office employees provide for *Rudari* – particularly the *Rudari* elite – concerns the evasion of road tax. Officers should normally ensure that those who have cars, tractors and trucks in the village pay taxes to the state, but they turn a blind eye to multiple vehicle ownership within

Figure 3.2 Illegal *Rudari* enclosure on the communal pasture.

the *Rudari* elite. At least three *Rudari* families own two or three unregistered trucks and at least one unregistered off-road car.

The illegality of these arrangements is threefold: first, the grazing ought by rights to be paid to the mayor's office since it is the legal administrator of communal pastures; secondly, building houses on communal pasture involves a change of land use which should be approved by several commissions at the regional and even national level; thirdly, vehicular tax ought by rights to be levied on all vehicle owners irrespective of their ethnic origins.

Another state agent who provides services to *Rudari* is the village policeman. He offers protection against the law. He mostly protects the few families owning trucks, who, in turn, provide him with a very large quantity of wood and money. Those who *were* fined were mostly those caught with cartfuls rather than truckloads of wood, the fine for which was relatively small. Although he issued fines to these people he knew that this was, in fact, a pointless measure: because most *Rudari* are very poor, the court never validates these fines.[20] He thus selected these poorer people for a fine because, on the one hand, their services as providers to state officials of wood (or bribes) are not very consistent. On the other hand, he needs some activity to report to his superiors. He once, for example, arrested and fined a young man, owning a small horse cart, from the lowest class among the *Rudari*.

Such selectivity allowed policemen to report some success in crime prevention to their superiors while enabling them to continue protecting the larger operators – the truck owners – by allowing them to circulate with unregistered trucks. Police collusion with large-scale truck-owning *Rudari* tree thieves went still further. On several occasions forest owners (those who own a larger area of forest) complained to the County Police that there was theft in their forests. The Police Special Forces came in the middle of the night in order to catch the thief but were unable to make any arrests. These owners complained that somebody who knew about the police raid had warned *Rudari* to stay home that night. They suspect that the warning had been given either by the local policeman or the forest guard.

Although these relationships serve to produce and reproduce internal differentiation among *Rudari*, those in the different strata depend upon each other occupationally: they are literally 'partners in crime'. Social stratification within the community is based on ownership of the means of production: chain saws, horse carts and trucks for wood transportation. There are three categories of *Rudari*: the poorest, who have only their hands and who help to load the horse carts, those who own a chain saw and a cart; and a few families who own one or more trucks. The middle group – those with a cart – are the most numerous. In the Agrarian Register (*Registrul Agricol*), which lists all the houses and the ownership status and means of production for every household in the village, more than half of *Rudari* families are listed as owning a horse cart. The horse carts are important not only because their owners are less likely to be fined large amounts of money but also because the slopes with good forest do not allow any other means of transportation. It is impossible for a truck, I was told, to go where a horse cart would penetrate without difficulty. All felled trees and cut wood are transported from the hills to the *Rudari* settlement by cart. From here, those owning a truck buy the better wood which they then transport to the southern part of the county, to forest-less lowland villages. Such transportation and sale is exclusively the business of a few better-off families among the *Rudari*.

There are two mechanisms of 'forest loss' at work. The first simply involves illegal deforestation. *Rudari* with horses and carts, and their poorer companions who have nothing to offer but their labour, go into the forest and cut trees on private plots. Then, the cart's owner sells the wood either to *Rudari* truck owners or directly to villagers in Costeşti who own no forest at all. Villagers prefer to buy fire-wood from *Rudari* (although they know very well how this wood is obtained) because it is less expensive than the wood sold by the SFD.[21]

Second, purchasers of wood – officials from the mayor's office, forest guards, village policeman or outsiders – 'buy the forest' very cheaply, threatening the owners that 'if they do not sell now for a lower amount of money they will lose their forest, because *Rudari* will cut it anyway'. The most advantageous business for the buyer and the most disadvantageous for the seller is the buying of 'standing trees' (*pe picioare*); buyers negotiate additional discounts by arguing that they must pay for the cutting and transport of the trees. Owners here are

Figure 3.3 Wood trucks of the *Rudari* 'elite'.

Figure 3.4 Rudari horse cart full of wood.

doubly disadvantaged since, despite their lamenting that they have 'sold the forest', they are still registered as its formal owners and forest land will be a taxable asset from 2006. The agricultural officer and the former vice-mayor of the commune have bought large numbers of standing trees through the use of just such threats. They pay about 10 million lei (around €300) for 1 ha of forest: about 10 per cent of the market price.

Caught between the untenable alternatives of losing their forest to the 'thieving *Rudari*' or selling it for an intolerably low price, forest owners choose the latter, considered the 'lesser of two evils'. In patron–client relationships between the buyers in state employ and the illegal *Rudari* woodcutters, the *Rudari* feature as a symbolic weapon in the rhetorical armoury of the wood-buyer/patrons. The 'traditional occupation' of the *Rudari* becomes a threat to be used by local state officials in their own pursuit of forest purchase through this second route mentioned above.

The patronage relations I have described so far invest the forest with political significance. First, the local chief of forest guards, the agricultural officer and the policeman support the Social Democratic Party (SDP), which was in power at the time of my fieldwork. The forest guard is allowed to be a member of a political party (he is also an officer in the local government) but the agricultural officer and the policeman are public servants. For them affiliation to a political party is forbidden by law.[22] Although they are not formally members of the party they visibly support the SDP by campaigning for it during elections.

Neither the former nor the current mayor attempted to prevent deforestation by the *Rudari*. While they did not benefit materially from forest exploitation, they did benefit politically. An episode which occurred during the electoral campaign clarifies the relationship between politics, patronage and deforestation. One of the candidates promised the *Rudari* elite that he would never bother them with 'forest problems' if they would not trespass on his forest land (he owns 1 ha of forest). All candidates promised that they would promote the interest of the *Rudari* at county level.[23] On a local television talk show, the two finalists for the office of mayor were asked what they thought about deforestation. Both of them denied that it was really occurring, beyond some petty *Rudari* theft of branches from the wood. Next morning I met the mayoral candidates and I asked the same question. They told me that it would have been pointless to tackle this problem, since *Rudari* would in any case continue to cut the forest as the only economic alternative for them. By being evasive in their answers they were keeping open the possibility of being voted in by *Rudari*.

A commodity chain analysis of forest resources (Ribot 1998) shows that those who are at the end of the 'illegal commodity chain' earn a good amount of money, while the actual owners of the forest are mostly losers. Among *Rudari* those who load the carts receive about 60,000 lei/day (less than €2), plus food and alcoholic drink (*tuica*). Those with carts receive about two cubic metres of wood daily – which can be sold for between 600,000 lei (€17) and 500,000 lei (€14), depending on quality. The rich *Rudari*, belonging to those few families protected by policemen, declared to me that for the transportation of one loaded truck they receive at least 3 million lei (€90); but everybody else agreed that the figure was closer to 10 million (€300). As mentioned earlier, not only does the forest owner derive no benefit but his/her forest is transformed from an 'asset' into a 'liability' (see Verdery 2004). S/he retains an unproductive plot of land which, since it is still registered as forest in the official papers at the mayor's office, is taxable.

There is also a second, legal commodity chain.[24] This links owners, who gain 10–30 million lei (€300–€900) for 1 ha of forest, to the buyers of 'cheap forest'. If they export their timber, they receive between €150 per cubic metre and €800 per cubic metre, depending on the type and the quality of the timber.[25] The legal commodity chain is based on the illegal one; without the illegal cutting there would be no pressure on the forest owners who would thus be in a position to sell forest at the market price (between 500 million and 1 billion lei, around €12,300–€24,600).

The actual property rights over forest are illustrated in Figure 3.5. Those who benefit mostly from the forest have no significant holdings compared with the village average. The head of the local police, for example, has no forest or land since he was not born in this village. He was invested as chief of the local police but he has no property rights in Dragomireşti. The local chief of the state forest

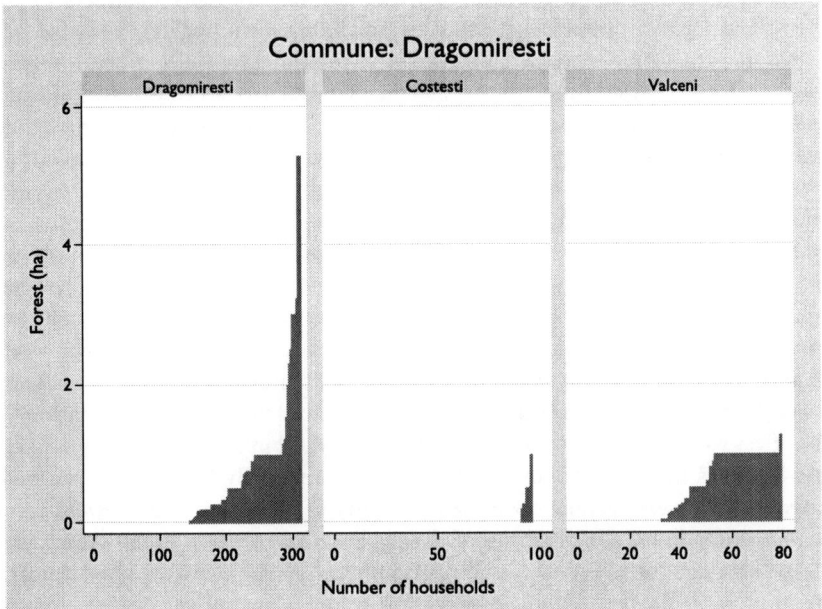

Figure 3.5 Property rights over forest.

guards, another villager drawing benefits from his position as a state agent, has only around 2 ha of forest. Another state forest guard owns officially less than 1 ha of forest. Being from Costeşti and from a quite poor family, he inherited little land or forest. The agricultural officer was not born in this village so she has no land or forest at all. Her husband has around 3 ha of forest, shared with his brothers. It can be seen from this that those who succeeded in gaining access to the forest are those who hold little or no acreage. In contrast are those who have property rights but are not able to draw significant economic benefits from it. Few families who hold more than 5 ha of restituted forest were able to use their rights to good effect. The forest is an asset with potential economic importance, but one which is nearly useless without access to state agencies.

Conclusions

As other authors have pointed out (Kaneff 1998; Giordano and Kostova 2002; Sikor 2004) land reform – and particularly land restitution – has attempted to restore a historical situation which existed before 1948. This has certainly been true for the *Rudari*, members of an ethnic group that was deprived of the forest before nationalization and that has again been deprived by the post-socialist state. Given this situation, *Rudari* are easily exploitable as clients by the local elite. The relationship between the two groups has all the classic hallmarks of clientelism. While the patrons have access to state positions, the *Rudari* are impoverished, having no land or forest of their own and living from meagre social welfare grants. They are skilled woodsmen for whom stealing and smuggling wood represents the only way to survive in a tough economic environment. There is an obvious imbalance of power between the two groups. While the patrons have the power of the state behind them, the *Rudari* find themselves at the margins of society, both at a local and national level. Where those who have access to state positions also have the support, explicitly or tacitly expressed, of the local politicians, the *Rudari* have little or no political representation. *Rudari*, as clients, offer knowledge about forest exploitation, cheap labour force, timber for free and a symbolic motivation: they are the scapegoats held responsible for deforestation.

While Ribot and Peluso, speaking of the importance of 'access', refer to benefits mainly in their material sense (2003), I argue here that it is necessary to recognize the importance of symbolic benefits. The fact that *Rudari* are used as a threat and as a symbol of deforestation by the local elite brings important economic benefits for the latter. Manipulating this symbol, patrons put themselves in a powerful position vis-à-vis private forest owners. The value of the forest is negotiated by the patrons and owners from different, unequal positions. 'Instrumentalizing' the symbol of 'thieving' or 'clear cutting *Rudari*', patrons establish the economic value of the forest in their own interest.

In post-socialist Romania those who have access to state jobs (especially as representatives of the state at local level) have access to natural resources and they draw benefits from this. Ownership per se seems not to play an important role in Dragomireşti, where most villagers hold forest but are unable to make substantial profits from doing so. Owners' difficulty in excluding others, an important feature in property rights, also affects their right to alienate property: it makes transactions of forest land between owners and buyers inequitable since they take place in a very unsafe social environment. It is the pressure put on these owners (by threatening them with the strong possibility that *Rudari* will fell their trees) that influences the outcome of these transactions. Forest owners cannot aspire to acquiring 'market value' for their forest; they must simply accept whatever price the local state officials offer them. Moreover, deforestation is produced by precisely those state agents who are supposed to protect the forest and the landscape and to implement the provisions of the law.

This patron–client relationship is made possible by the existence of a market. Only when wood became marketable – that is, when the Romanian government adopted a neo-liberal policy, liberalizing wood commerce in the post-socialist context – were those in privileged positions able to draw economic benefits from the forest. During the socialist period people constructed wood houses which were also heated with wood. But it was when post-socialist governments created a market for wood and thus the opportunity for private firms to export wood that deforestation occurred. Economic global interconnectedness created the chance for certain post-socialist actors to exploit the natural resources at local level, in their own interests but at the legal owner's expense.

This study contests the claim that the restitution of private property rights necessarily leads to sustainable management. Instead, in the case explored here, the restitution of forests as private property led to insecurity and deforestation. Local state actors, although excluded from restitution per se, benefited from the devolution of power to the local level and hence derived economic benefit from land they did not own.

References

Acheson, J (2000) 'Clearcutting Maine: Implications for the Theory of Common Property Resources', *Human Ecology* 28(2): 145–69.
Anderson, TL and FS McChesney (2003) 'The Evolution of Property Rights', in TL Anderson and FS McChesney (eds) *Property Rights: Cooperation, Conflict, and Law*, Princeton, NJ and Oxford: Princeton University Press.
Benda-Beckmann, von, K and F (2000) [1994] 'Coping with Insecurity', in F and K von Benda-Beckmann and H Marks (eds) *Coping with Insecurity: An 'Underall' Perspective on Social Security in the Third World*, Indonesia and The Netherlands: Pustaka Pelajar & Focaal Foundation.
Berry, S (1982) *Oil and the Disappearing Peasantry: Accumulation, Differentiation and Underdevelopment in Western Nigeria*, Working Paper No. 66, Boston, MA: Boston University, African Studies Center.
—— (1985) *Fathers Work for their Sons: Accumulation, Mobility, and Class Formation in an Extended Yorùbá Community*, Berkeley, Los Angeles, CA, London: University of California Press.
—— (1989) 'Social Institutions and Access to Resources', *Africa* 59: 41–55.
—— (1993) *No Condition is Permanent: The Social Dynamics of Agrarian Change in Sub-Saharan Africa*, Madison, WI: University of Wisconsin.
Blaikie, P and H Brookfield (1987) *Land Degradation and Society*, London: Methuen.
Bromley, WD (1991) *Environment and Economy: Property Rights and Public Policy*, Oxford, Cambridge, MA: Blackwell.
Bulgaru, V (2003) *Reforma agrară din 1921 – fundamente economice* [The Economic Foundations of the 1921 Agrarian Reform], Timişoara: Editura de Vest.
Chelcea, I (1940) Originea *Rudarilor* [The Origins of *Rudari*], *Pagini de etnografie si folclor*, Bucuresti: Atelierele 'Imprimeria' S A.
—— (1944) *Ţiganii din Romania. Monografie etnografică* [The Gypsies from Romania. Ethnographical Monographs], Bucuresti: Editura Institutului Central de Statistică.
de Waal, Clarissa (2004) 'Post-socialist Property Rights and Wrongs in Albania: An Ethnography of Agrarian Change', *Conservation and Society* 2(1): 19–50.
Fortmann, L and WJ Bruce (1988) *Whose Trees? Proprietary Dimensions of Forestry*, Boulder, CO, London: Westview Press.
Fortmann, L and C Nhira (1992) *Local Management of Trees and Woodland Resources in Zimbabwe: A Tenurial Niche Approach*, Harare: University of Zimbabwe, Centre for Applied Social Sciences.
Fortmann, L and J Ridell (1985) *Tree and Tenure. An Annotated Bibliography for*

Agroforesters and Others, Madison, WI, Nairobi: Land Tenure Center and International Council for Research in Agroforestry.

Gellner, E (1977) 'Patrons and Clients', in E Gellner and J Waterbury (eds) *Patrons and Clients in Mediterranean Societies*, London: Duckworth.

Giordano, C and D Kostova (2002) 'The Social Production of Mistrust', in CM Hann (ed.) *Postsocialism: Ideals, Ideologies and Practices in Eurasia*, London, New York: Routledge.

Gluckman, Max (1943) *Essays on Lozi Land and Royal Property*, Rhodes Livingstone Paper No. 10, Livingstone: Rhodes-Livingstone Institute.

—— (1965) *The Ideas in Barotse Jurisprudence*, New Haven, CT: Yale University Press.

Hallowell, A Irving (1943) 'The Nature and Function of Property as a Social Institution', *Journal of Legal and Political Sociology* 1: 115–38.

Hammel, AE (1968) *Alternative Social Structures and Ritual Relations in the Balkans*, Englewood Cliffs, NJ: Prentice-Hall, Inc.

Hann, CM (1993a) 'Property Relations in the New Eastern Europe: The Case of Specialist Cooperatives in Hungary', in H De Soto G and DG Anderson (eds) *The Curtain Rises: Rethinking Culture, Ideology, and the State in Eastern Europe*, Highlands, NJ: Humanities Press.

—— (1993b) 'From Production to Property: Decollectivization and the Family-Land Relationship in Contemporary Hungary', *Man* 28: 299–320.

—— (1998) 'Introduction: the embeddedness of property', in CM Hann (ed.) *Property Relations: Renewing the anthropological tradition*, Cambridge: Cambridge University Press.

Hann, CM, C Humphrey and K Verdery (2002) 'Postsocialism as a topic of anthropological investigation', in CM Hann (ed.) *Postsocialism: Ideals, ideologies and practices in Eurasia*, London, New York: Routledge.

Hart, G (1989) 'Agrarian Change in the Context of State Patronage', in G Hart, A Turton and B White with B Fegan and LT Ghee (eds) *Agrarian Transformations. Local Processes and the State in Southeast Asia*, Berkeley, Los Angeles, CA, Oxford: University of California Press.

—— (1991) 'Engendering Everyday Resistance: Gender, Patronage and Production Politics in Rural Malaysia', *Journal of Peasant Studies* 19(1): 93–121.

Howarth, W (1998) 'Property Rights, Regulation and Environmental Protection: some Anglo-Romanian Contrasts', in CM Hann (ed.) *Property Relations: Renewing the anthropological tradition*, Cambridge: Cambridge University Press, pp. 181–200.

Kaneff, D (1998) 'When land becomes "territory": Land privatization and ethnicity in rural Bulgaria', in S Bridger and F Pine (eds) *Surviving Post-Socialism: Local strategies and regional responses in Eastern Europe and the former Soviet Union*, London: Routledge.

Littlewood, P (1980) 'Patronage, Ideology, and Reproduction', *Critique of Anthropology* 15: 29–45.

MacPherson, CB (1992) [1978] *Property: Mainstream and Critical Position* (edited, with an introductory and concluding essay by CB MacPherson), Toronto, Buffalo, NY, London: University of Toronto Press.

Mathijs, E and JFM Swinnen (1998) 'The Economics of Agricultural Decollectivization in East Central Europe and the Former Soviet Union', *Economic Development and Cultural Change* 47(1): 1–26.

Mungiu-Pippidi, A (2005) 'Reinventing the Peasants: Local State Capture in Post-Communist Europe', in Ş Dorondel and S Şerban (eds) *Between East and West. Studies in Anthropology and Social History*, București: Editura Institutului Cultural Român.

Müller, D, B Wode and C Wehr (2003) *Manual on Participatory Village Mapping Using Photomaps: A Trainer Guide*, Social Forestry Development Project (SFDP) Song Da, available at http://amor.cms.hu-berlin.de/~muelleda/publications.htm. Accessed 24 March 2008.

Ostrom, E (2001) 'The Puzzle of Counterproductive Property Rights Reforms: A Conceptual Analysis', in A de Janvry, G Gordillo, J-P Platteau and E Sadoulet (eds) *Access to Land, Rural property, and Public Action*, Oxford: Oxford University Press.

Paulson, S, LL Gezon and M Watts (2003) ' "Locating the Political in Political Ecology" An Introduction', *Human Organization* 62(3): 205–15.

Pârnuță, G, M Gorgoi and S Trâmbaciu (2003) *Monografia satelor Contesti, Davidesti si Voroveni* [The Monograph of Contesti, Davidesti and Voroveni Villages], Craiova: Scrisul Românesc.

Rabinowicz, E and JFM Swinnen (1997) 'Political economy of privatisation and decollectivization of Central and East European agriculture: definitions, issues and methodology', in JFM Swinnen (ed.) *Political Economy of Agrarian Reform in Central and Eastern Europe*, Aldershot, Brookfield, VT, Singapore, Sydney: Ashgate.

Radin, MJ (1993) *Reinterpreting Property*, Chicago, IL: Chicago University Press.

Rassam, A (1977) 'Al-tabaïyya: Power, patronage and marginal groups in northern Iraq', in E Gellner and J Waterbury (eds) *Patrons and Clients in Mediterranean Societies*, London: Duckworth, pp 157–66.

Ribot, CJ (1998) 'Theorizing Access: Forest Profits along Senegal's Charcoal Commodity Chain', *Development and Change* 29: 307–41.

Ribot, CJ, and NL Peluso (2003) 'A Theory of Access', *Rural Sociology* 62(2): 153–81.

Rose, MC (1994) *Property and Persuasion: Essays on the History, Theory, and Rhetoric of Ownership*, Boulder, CO, San Francisco, CA, Oxford: Westview Press.

Scott, CJ (1977) 'Patronage or exploitation?', in E Gellner and J Waterbury (eds) *Patrons and Clients in Mediterranean Societies*, London: Duckworth.

Sikor, T (2004) 'Conflicting Concepts: Contested Land Relations in North-western Vietnam', *Conservation and Society* 2(1): 59–79.

—— (2006) 'Land as Asset, Land as Liability: Property Politics in Rural Central and Eastern Europe', in F von Benda-Beckmann, K von Benda-Beckmann and M Wiber (eds) *Changing Properties of Property*, New York: Berghahn.

Singer, JW (2002) *Entitlement. The Paradoxes of Property*, New Haven, CT, London: Yale University Press.

Sowerwine, J (2004) 'Territorialisation and the Politics of Highland Landscapes in Vietnam: Negotiating Property Relations in Policy, Meaning and Practice', *Conservation and Society* 2(1): 97–136.

Stewart, M (2002) 'Deprivation, the Roma and "the Underclass" ', in CM Hann (ed.) *Postsocialism: Ideals, Ideologies and Practices in Eurasia*, London, New York: Routledge.

Verdery, K (1994) 'The Elasticity of Land. Problems of Property Restitution in Transylvania', *Slavic Review* 53(4): 1071–109.

—— (1996) *What was Socialism and What Comes Next?*, Princeton, NJ: Princeton University Press.

—— (1998) 'Property and Power in Transylvania's Decollectivization', in CM Hann (ed.) *Property Relations: Renewing the anthropological tradition*, Cambridge: Cambridge University Press.
—— (2002) 'Seeing like a mayor. Or, how local officials obstructed Romanian land restitution', *Ethnography* 3(1): 5–33.
—— (2003) *The Vanishing Hectare: Property and Value in Postsocialist Transylvania*, Ithaca, NY, London: Cornell University Press.
—— (2004) 'The Obligations of Ownership: Restoring Rights to Land in Postsocialist Transylvania', in K Verdery and C Humphrey (eds) *Property in Question: Value Transformation in the Global Economy*, Oxford, New York: Berg.
—— (2005) ' "Possessive identities" in post-socialist Transylvania', in Ş Dorondel and S Serban (eds) *Between East and West: Studies in Anthropology and Social History*, Bucuresti: Editura Institutului Cultural Roman.

Notes

1 I thank Derick Fay for reading an early draft of this chapter. His comments helped me to sharpen my analysis. He and Deborah James also assisted in editing later versions. I also thank Barbara Cellarius, Andrew Cartwright, Thomas Basset and Jeff Romm, for their helpful comments. My appreciation goes to Anamaria Ross for a careful reading and feedback. I gratefully acknowledge Emmy Noether Program of Deutsche Forschungsgemeinschaft which funded my research at Yale University and at Humboldt University Berlin. I am alone responsible for the analysis presented here. I presented a shorter version of this chapter at the Conference of the European Association of Rural Sociology, Kezstehely August 2005.

2 There is an entire literature on the weakness of the post-socialist state which I am not going to explore in detail here. However, the post-socialist state has been labelled as 'captured' (Mungiu-Pippidi 2005), 'vanished' (Verdery 2002), or 'predatory' (de Waal 2004). In all circumstances, the post-socialist state is used by local elite in its own interests.

3 This is not the real name of the commune or of the villages composing the commune. Some of my informants asked me not to use their real names. Since this chapter, like many papers dealing with post-socialism, presents some phenomena which can be construed as bending or breaking the law I preferred to anonymize my informants' names as well as those of the villages.

4 I will not here explore the debate as to whether *Rudari* are or are not a part of the Roma people. Very often, the scientific debate over their ethnic group, apart from the fact that it took place in the inter-war period at a moment when Romania was very close to Nazi ideology and politics, ended up with racial considerations (see for instance Chelcea 1940). I should only say that they do not consider themselves either as a Roma minority group or as Romanians. However, the Romanian state registered them within the 2002 census, as Roma people. The Romanian population also distinguishes between Roma, 'gypsy singers' (*ţigani lăutari*) and *Rudari*. An expert on Roma ethnic groups in south-eastern Europe, Stewart (2002) considers them as a part of the Roma people, even if they do not speak Romani language and they do not consider themselves as such. At the political level *Rudari* are represented by the Partida Romilor (The Roma Party) but only in a formal way since they do not recognize themselves as Roma. What *Rudari* have in common with Roma people is that they never owned land or forest.

5 Formally, corvée was abolished in 1864. But as most Romanian agricultural economists and historians point out the land reforms from 1864, 1921 and 1945 meant only

changes in ownership structure. Labour remained 'feudal' as poor peasants received land without any mean of production. The relationship between noblemen and peasant remained the same, in a process which has been labelled *neoiobagie* (neo-bondage). See for instance Bulgaru (2003).
6   Regia Națională a Pădurilor Romsilva in Romanian.
7   This is the case in those villages, such as Dragomirești, where there is no Private Forest Department (PFD). In the cases where there exist a PFD, as in Dragova, this is the duty of the private forest guard.
8   The only danger faced by the owner is the possibility of meeting a police patrol or forest guard. If he has more trees than permitted he is liable to a huge fine (up to 20 million lei – around €300) or even imprisonment.
9   As the average size of private forest in the village is 0.4 ha in Dragomirești and Vâlceni and under 0.1 ha in Costești, the law allows forest owners to cut less than 1 cubic metre of forest every year. The estimation is based on my personal survey of land and forest in the village.
10 Whereas in Dragomirești few families had owned more than 10 ha, in Vâlceni and Costești there were several noblemen who had owned large tracts of forest. Their heirs, however, received only 10 ha each. In this case, then, restitution levelled the inequalities of earlier ownership patterns rather than reinstating these.
11 The next short historical account is based on Chelcea's ethnographical work on Rudari, the only historical source I can count on pertaining to *Rudari* history (Chelcea 1940, 1944). I set aside his racist suggestions and take into account only his very accurate ethnographic descriptions.
12 *Rachiu* or țuică is a plum brandy. Arges County is very famous for this drink all over the country.
13 During my stay in their settlement I have often heard it said that '*pădurarii sunt mai răi ca câinii*' ('the forest guards are worse than dogs').
14 In an economy found deeply in crisis as the socialist Romanian economy was, 'voluntary work' represented an option for the state. Of course, nobody was willing to do that so the forest guards had to manage somehow.
15 The local council under the pressure of *Rudari* decided to give every *Rudari* family a small plot for the construction of the house. They based their decision on the decree 42 issued in January 1990 through which every family can receive a small plot of maximum 5000 sq metres.
16 The restructuring of a plant in post-socialist times often means the downsizing of the number of workers. During communist times, employment had nothing to do with the rationality of a market economy, very often being dictated by political reasons: there were no unemployed workers in a socialist country.
17 Besides the classical methods engaged by an anthropologist (interviews, participant and direct observation, archive work) I also employed participatory mapping as a way of grasping more detailed information about land and forest relationship at local level. The objective of a participatory map is to enable villagers to carry out the interpretation of some aspect of their land resources and to point out what is important for them. After taking several GPS points on the edges of the commune, a satellite image of the entire area was ordered. A transparency was put on that image and a group of five people from the village was asked to take part in discussions. In the second session, held in one farmer's household, three farmers mapped their own lands and forests. Then, a forest guard mapped the state forest and the private, deforested area (his area of control). The third session was conducted in the *Rudari* settlement. They mapped the land they claim for building houses, the forest they would like to have, and the deforested area (where they work mostly in the forest). For theoretical and technical details see Müller et al. (2003).

18 There is no fixed bribe but this was the amount of money most often whispered by *Rudari* and also by villagers.
19 Every family receiving social help has to be socially and economically re-evaluated every year. This evaluation is supposed to be done by social workers from Pitesti. During the four months fieldwork I met them only once. There were two young girls working at the County council. They never saw those families who are supposed to be evaluated. They just signed the papers and after half an hour they went back to the city. The 'social investigation' (*ancheta socială*) is carried out by people from the mayor's office and it is just signed by the specialists. Thus, formally mayor's office employees have an important leverage over *Rudari*. As many authors pointed out (F and K von Benda-Beckmann 2000 [1994] and the literature quoted by them) social security has not only an economic function but also expresses a strong political control especially in the patronage relations where social security programmes may be used as leverage to gain political or electoral support.
20 This is very similar to the situation in the inter-war period when fines were revoked for the same reason.
21 SFD also has a service of forest exploitation. An auction takes place and a private firm gains the right to cut a certain amount of state wood. The lower-quality wood is then sold to whoever needs to buy fire-wood. It is understandable that the production costs which had to cover trees, state expenses and private firm's expenses are far bigger than those of *Rudari*.
22 There are several categories of citizens which are not allowed to be affiliated with a political party: professional solders, policemen, members of the Intelligence Services and public functionaries.
23 *Rudari* generally have only two requirements. The first one is the historical demand Chelcea noticed in his 1944 book: they want some forest of their own so that they will no longer be forced to steal. The second wish is to be allocated 0.4 ha from the communal land on which to build their houses. In most cases there are about six to eight people in a one- or two-roomed house.
24 I thank an anonymous reviewer for drawing my attention to the difference between the 'illegal' and 'legal' commodity chains.
25 I thank M Rusu from the Institute of Agricultural Economics of Romanian Academy for this information.

Chapter 4

The lie of the land
Identity politics and the Canadian land claims process in Labrador

Evie Plaice

4.1 Abstract

Rapid militarization in 1941 and later mining and hydro developments brought about profound change throughout Labrador society, most notably in land use. Local response came during the 1970s, when three native organizations emerged to contest overlapping claims to ownership and control of the land and its resources. Each organization has employed markedly different moral and political strategies to press their respective claim to both land and an enduring local, land-based identity. The choices made, and the processes set in motion by the claims, have divided the protagonists as much as challenged the political status quo. Here I take the case of the Metis, whose disenfranchized position in the process offers the clearest picture of the dynamics involved, to examine the interplay between the politics of identity and claims to land.

Introduction

In their introduction to this book James and Fay outline three stages in their processual model: dispossession, interim and restitution. Like most of the cases explored here, my example fits nicely into the third of these – restitution. Yet restitution processes are predicated upon the nature of the preceding stages: in fact, the process of restitution often comes to redefine both the nature of the dispossession and the interim phase that effectively marginalizes those who were dispossessed. Again, my case is typical in this regard. What makes it unusual is that Labrador has three distinct groups involved in the Canadian land claim process. My focus on the Metis enables me to shed light on perhaps the most pertinent aspect of the whole process: the transformative dynamic through which the claimants themselves are shaped. The Metis case poses the difficult questions of who can make claims to land, how they do so, and why these particular claims are accepted. Of course, this is where assessing a claim also becomes an assessment of the process of marginalization and its point of departure. Once based on the 'level of civilization' demonstrated by those being colonized, the Canadian claim process now requires proof that the claimant group 'is and was an organised society' (Indian and Northern Affairs Canada 2003: 12). Whereas once it was only through treaties that claimants had any legal basis for a claim, now it is a matter of 'aboriginality.' But aboriginality itself is not easily defined.[1] The Labrador Metis claim to land is inextricably linked to their claim to a less than bona fide aboriginal identity because they are the product of several centuries of miscegenation. In their case, degree of aboriginality versus degree of miscegenation is calculated as much by historical and geographical circumstance as by 'bloodlines.' In Fay and James's processual frame, miscegenation situates the Metis firmly in the interim stage. Yet the interim stage also includes massive hydroelectric, mining and military developments that have further dispossessed the claimants, and the inevitable social pathologies arising from such sustained marginalization. The claims of all three Labrador groups reveal the flawed nature of a process that often perpetuates the anguish and misery of dispossession. But none does this more clearly than the Metis, whose claim confronts notions of ethnic exclusivity and the relationship between identity, 'way of life' and land.

Interim

Labrador forms the largest portion of the province of Newfoundland and Labrador, on the north-east coast of Canada. Archaeological work in the 1960s confirmed Icelandic sagas indicating that the Norse had visited the coast towards the end of the tenth century, and Basque, Breton, Dutch and Portuguese whaling and fishing fleets began visiting the coast once the port of St John's was established by British explorers in 1497. Colonization of Canada began at this point, culminating with confederation in 1867, though Newfoundland and Labrador did not join Canada until 1949. Control of the developing Labrador fishery was disputed between the French, British and Americans throughout the eighteenth and nineteenth centuries. It remained a British dominion with Newfoundland until the close of the Second World War, after which the original European interests in fish, fur and forestry grew to include hydroelectric development, mining and the military.

Indigenous populations had of course been thriving in Labrador throughout this period, arriving as soon as the land was free of ice. Over the past 10,000 years the Innu and their predecessors have established a complex nomadic existence around the migrating caribou herds of the Labrador interior, while two distinct Eskimoic populations have occupied the coast for the past 4,000 years. Archaeologically defined as Dorset, palaeo-Eskimos were the likely inhabitants of the coastal region when the Vikings arrived in 896, and were at least partially responsible for the brevity of Norse settlement here. The neo-Eskimo Thule, the direct ancestors of the Inuit, moved into Labrador about 1,000 years ago, probably just after the Norse had left. While Dorset economy had focused on sealing, the Inuit were whalers who had followed the smaller whale species along the arctic coastline into both the Greenland and Labrador sides of the

Davis Strait. Inuit were established along the Labrador coast when British fishermen began to settle in the region around the middle of the eighteenth century, and the present Metis – locally called Settlers – are the result of miscegenation and cultural blending between these two groups. The Metis merged almost indistinguishably with Inuit in way of life and littoral economy, and spread inland where they became primarily trappers.

Labrador Settlers have only recently turned to the term 'Metis' as a more apt description of their mixed heritage. As with any ethnic identification, however, its usage is far from straightforward. Roughly translated to mean 'mixed,' and originally used to describe the French–Indian Prairie fur traders who rose to prominence under Louis Riel, Metis has come to mean a particular population with a distinctive culture and definite political aims. Adopting the term for themselves links Labrador Settlers to a political platform which not all were ready to accept. Nevertheless, the term has grown in popularity over the last few years, with Labrador Metis becoming increasingly involved in politics at local, regional and national levels. One of the ethno-political claims made by the Metis is that their hybrid culture grew out of a combination of adaptations which are intrinsically *of* Labrador, thus testing the potential distinction between 'indigenous' and 'aboriginal'. While aboriginality suggests prior occupancy, indigeneity suggests something that has grown *in situ*. The contrast draws attention to a certain Pan-Canadianness about being either 'Indian' or 'Inuit', which gives an aboriginal person cultural connections across a much wider area. Labrador Metis, however, belong only in Labrador with their particular mix of Labrador native cultures in a specifically Labrador landscape. Since it is land that is at issue in the ethno-political contest currently being waged between Labradorians – indigenous, aboriginal or otherwise – the Metis claim is perceptively salient for, yet largely ineffective in, furthering their cause within the Canadian land claims process.

The restitution process in Canada typically involves a challenge to sovereignty couched in terms of a cultural distinctiveness which demands some form of autonomous land base. The conflicting interests in the land of Labrador are considerably complicated by the need for each group to maintain distinct but overlapping and competing ethnic and local identities which, in turn, give substance to those claims. In this context, claimants need to make claims to both land and identity, and they make each claim with reference to the other. Although this is true for all three cases in Labrador, the Metis claim is hampered by their particular form of adaptation: their *aboriginality* is brought into question such that they are disqualified from claiming land based on either 'way of life' or through the occupation of lands from 'time immemorial' – both of which are given credence through the Canadian land claim process. For the Metis, their disqualification from the claims process is exacerbated by the proximity of two native groups whose case for aboriginality is much clearer. Innu, Inuit and Metis have had to compete for resources on a political as well as an ecological level: the claims process has forced a separation which often contradicts the experience of history. The process itself, then, fundamentally shapes ethnic identity.

The Canadian land claims process in its current form has evolved over the last four decades and has its roots in the treaties of the late nineteenth century. The process is still evolving as a mechanism to address aboriginal demands for control of lands and resources, such that each new case tends to challenge the status quo – often through a court of law. The process is invariably – and usually also drastically – spurred by major development, when the keen economic interest of the developers gives petitioning groups a window of opportunity in which to press their claim. A considerable amount of development had already taken place in Labrador before local groups had become sufficiently organized to contest the inevitable loss of lands that such developments cause. Nevertheless, it also provoked local political organization. Labrador's first taste of development came through the military during the Second World War. Goose Bay Airbase was built with extraordinary speed at the end of 1941, as a direct consequence of American military involvement in the Second World War. The Cold War and the North Atlantic Treaty Organization subsequently became the *raison d'etre* of the base and growing town, and there has been a constant military presence in the region ever since. Iron ore mining and hydro development followed. All these developments posed demands on the land that transformed land use activities throughout the region, none more persistently and pervasively than the military: most recently involving large areas of air space with a severe impact on land use.

Contemporary political awareness began in Labrador during the late 1960s, reflecting the growing regional and ethnic awareness in the rest of the country. The influx of Newfoundlanders and mainland Canadians prompted by the development of Goose Bay Airbase made Labradorians increasingly aware of their provincial and national marginality. They also became acutely aware that Newfoundlanders tended to view Labrador as a large, fortuitous and eminently exploitable source of wealth. Ironically spearheaded by transplanted Newfoundlanders, the rise in Labradorian ethno-political awareness coincided with several significant changes in the broader political landscape: the American black and civil rights movements of the previous decade, the arrival of Trudeau's forward-looking and extremely successful federal government, and the demise of Joey Smallwood's long-standing and by then rather corrupt provincial government.

The extent of the province's underdevelopment had become apparent when Newfoundland joined Canada in 1949. Smallwood's extensive plans for modernization included developing Labrador's resources. However, both northern development and native concerns are managed by the same branch of the federal government.[2] Under the federal Indian Act, those whose forebears had signed treaties, surrendering their lands in return for smaller designated reserves[3] and the provision of basic medical, social and educational services, were registered with the federal government and acquired certain rights and privileges.

Since Newfoundland and Labrador had no such treaties, Smallwood was able to argue that all Newfoundlanders should be covered equally under his provincial administration. Contrary to the rest of Canada, then, federal jurisdiction was never extended to the indigenous inhabitants of Newfoundland and Labrador. They were instead administered provincially with federal moneys through a series of Newfoundland–Canada Native People's Agreements. Native groups were identified by community rather than by the more usual means of registering those with Indian status.[4] It was not necessary to be a native person in order to qualify for native services: any inhabitant of a designated native community was eligible. In part because of this, more recent efforts to identify native groups by ethnic rather than community affiliation have run into problems. But this did become a basis upon which explicitly non-native groups, such as the Metis, were able to lodge claims to restitution.

The value placed on the Indian Act by Canadian native organizations was clearly displayed when the new Trudeau government proposed to repeal the Indian Act in 1969, making provinces responsible for native populations and forcing them to address land restitution. Although cumbersome and discriminatory, the Act still safeguarded some of the fundamental rights aboriginal peoples had gained with confederation and its threatened loss was a major concern for them. Trudeau had all but ignored his promise of 'consultative democracy' (Weaver 1981: 3). Indigenous input through the government-commissioned Hawthorn Report (1966–7) had suggested revising the Act to strengthen the position of native groups through honouring treaties and land claims. Concerted aboriginal rebuke of Trudeau's proposals forced the government to abandon its White Paper on Indian Affairs and to rethink its strategies towards the native population. It has taken several more decades and a Royal Commission on Aboriginal Peoples to bring about any significant change, but land rights, recognition of aboriginal title, the resolution of dishonoured treaties and clear options for political autonomy remain paramount for all native groups.

It was, in fact, bitter outrage against development that spurred Labrador's initial political response. Outside federal jurisdiction, Labradorians lacked federal arbitration when Smallwood proposed hydroelectric development for Labrador. No lands had ever been set aside for exclusive native use in the province: development went ahead without any consultation of the native inhabitants, who then received neither compensation for loss nor benefits accruing from such activity. The Churchill Falls hydroelectric project took massive tracts of valuable hunting and trapping territory to provide power for the burgeoning mining industry of western Labrador. And indeed, most of the power left the province entirely.[5]

The backlash against the Churchill Falls development was a regional response aimed primarily at Newfoundland. Subsequent organization has been greatly enhanced by outside political influence, including government management of indigenous affairs which has encouraged Labradorians to compete among themselves for local and regional ethnic symbolism in support of claims to land. Inuit, Innu and Metis have increasingly formed their own agendas to meet their own specific needs. The Inuit dominate in the northern coastal tundra, the Innu dominate the forested interior, and Metis straddle both domains as well as being more ready to incorporate Western-inspired changes. The eligibility of Metis to join Labrador native organizations became a perennial problem because, despite the membership numbers they represent and the western-oriented skills and contacts they bring, their ethnic identity is seen as marginal to those of aboriginals. These factors have had to be juggled with the need to construct and maintain an acceptable aboriginal image, and all have had some influence on the careers of each of the native organizations subsequently formed in Labrador. The Native Association of Newfoundland and Labrador (NANL) was first, in 1973. Instigated by Newfoundland Mi'kmaq, NANL soon found that it could not accommodate the increasing intensity of Labrador ethno-politics. After successfully lobbying to exclude the Metis, the Innu left NANL to form the Naskapi-Montagnais Innu Association (NMIA) in 1975 and have remained closed to Metis. The Inuit had already left to form the Labrador Inuit Association (LIA), which took a much more interesting position on Metis membership.

Based in Labrador's northernmost community of Nain, the LIA formed as a local branch of the Inuit Tapirisat of Canada (ITC) and as such had to abide by ITC's guidelines for membership. But the complex social and ethnic histories of most northern communities were not so easily accommodated. Specifically, the issue of Metis membership had to be addressed. The distinction between Metis and Inuit is in no way clear:[6] kinship ties linking Metis and Inuit extend throughout Labrador and across into Ungava and Quebec; the way of life is shared almost indistinguishably in all the northern communities; and some knowledge and use of both Inuktitut and English is standard for Inuit and Metis alike (Kennedy 1982). Identification with either group in any of the northern communities is the concern of the individual. The ITC requirement of fluency in Inuktitut excluded many Metis, including some of the LIA's principal ethno-politicians. In 1974, the LIA had resolved to include Metis and to retain the bilingual requirement only for its executive members – something they have retained with the new Nunatsiavut government formed in 2005. The LIA facilitated this in two remarkable ways: by defining ethnic identity in terms of 'way of life' rather than the usual recourse to bloodlines and genealogies; and by adopting the geographical guidelines previously used by the Newfoundland–Canada Agreements. Membership was extended to anyone living in the five designated northern communities whose forebear had been born there prior to 1941, a proviso that acknowledged the role of Goose Bay Airbase in exacerbating the destruction of the 'Labrador way of life' (Brice-Bennett 1977).

The LIA definition, however, does not cover Metis from outside the Association's geographical mandate,[7] namely those in central Labrador. The geographical dimension was part of the substitution of 'way of life' for bloodlines.

Predictably this has caused problems in other areas of membership assessment where personal histories *do* come into play. Internal migration fomented by the base actually complemented as well as exacerbated the regular seasonal movement of fishing, hunting and trapping families such that defining a separate northern population from a central one has become extremely difficult. There are at least three layers of potential LIA members in central Labrador, then: those born in northern Labrador who moved to central Labrador when the base was built; those central Labradorians whose transhumant activities periodically took them out to the coast, or who were born east of the LIA claim line, and those who although born in central Labrador before the base was built and who share a way of life with other coastal Labradorians, are excluded because their links with the land lie to the west of the area mandated by the LIA. The first category has no difficulty in becoming LIA members. The second two are encouraged or discouraged from seeking membership according to the immediate requirements of the LIA, who have other elements to juggle through manipulating their potential membership. The growing numbers of potential central Labrador members threaten to outnumber their northern and coastal membership, thus challenging the ethnically more credible northern stronghold. Yet LIA interests in central Labrador can only be secured by a central Labrador membership, since northern members are the guests of central Labrador land users. The LIA was able to hedge its membership bets until 1983, when the Labrador Metis Association (LMA) emerged to challenge their monopoly over Metis membership.

Squeezed between development and aboriginal claims to land, and excluded from existing organized native associations, central Labrador Metis needed a political voice. But the problems common to any nascent native organization – gaining credibility, public support, and dealing with internal divisions – have been exacerbated for the Metis by the existence of already established competing organizations and by the problems inherent in being of 'mixed' ancestry. The existence of the established organizations made acceptance of an independent Metis organization difficult. As a rule, Metis groups gain most of their ethnopolitical strength by becoming the allies of aboriginal groups, as had been the case with the Metis in the Mackenzie Valley in western Canada. In other circumstances, Metis might gain considerable recognition in areas where there was no other aboriginal competition for land and allied resources, as is the case of the Conne River M'kmaq in Newfoundland. Neither was the case in central Labrador, and the established groups were not interested in a liaison with the LMA because it brought them little that they did not already have. Ethnopolitically speaking, then, central and southern Labrador Metis were in a weak position. But the fact that the LIA already had Settler members left the Metis with at least some exploitable ambiguity in creating an acceptable ethnic identity for themselves outside the established groups. However, the inherent heterogeneity of the Labrador Metis rendered the nascent Metis Association much more vulnerable to the destructive polemics of internal conflicts than would have been the case had they been able to unite behind a strong public image. In this light, it is easy to see the mischief that could be made by the competitive membership tactics of the LIA. One of the deep ironies of native politics in Labrador, and one which was in part responsible for the exclusion of the central Labradorians, was that nativeness was not based upon bloodlines so much as place of residence, and *place* was central to Labrador Metis identity. Moreover, the relative absence of the more usual French–Indian heritage meant that Labrador Metisness had to be accepted differently – both by the Labrador Metis themselves and by the allies whose support they wished to enlist. The LMA was very much aware of the need to promote the right kind of image to a wider public, and this concern forms a constant thread in the internal discussions of the Association. Like many nascent native organizations on the east coast, most of whom had suffered from European colonial influences over a sustained period, the LMA began its ethno-political career by borrowing institutions from its more confident and established compatriots. Difficulties over membership criteria were essentially a legacy the Metis Association inherited from the LIA when they followed the LIA's lead in using 'way of life' as their defining criteria. But the LIA had already claimed the moral ground for an authentic ethnic identity, ironically one that also included Metis. The LMA has had a long and largely fruitless battle to try and reclaim some of that ground from the LIA. In the meantime both other native organizations were preparing to claim rights and land through the new Canadian land claims process.

Restitution

The land debate that was to affect Labrador during the 1980s had already been building in the rest of Canada for over a decade. Changes in the legal position of native peoples within Canada had been set in motion by the demise of the 1969 White Paper on Indian Affairs, and by major development projects occurring in the north. Major northern developments had always posed a threat to native ways of life because they invariably competed with renewable resource harvesting. During the late sixties the need for new sources of energy prompted large, invasive developments in areas where the majority of the population was native. They helped to bring to a head the issue of aboriginal title and native rights in Canada. In fact, Trudeau's drive to dismantle the Indian bureaucracy and assimilate the native population could be seen cynically as an attempt to remove the question of land rights before it became a problem for northern development. Far from removing the problem, however, the White Paper became a conduit for the reassessment of native land rights. While Canadian native peoples tested their rights in Canadian law, then, development projects were moving into the traditionally native lands of the north.

The extent to which the rights of native peoples were recognized in Canadian law was explored through a series of court cases held during the 1970s, and the federal land claims process was born in the wake of three seminal cases: the James Bay Cree; the Dene of the Mackenzie Valley; and the Nisga'a of British Columbia. Between them the three cases provided the templates for other land claims, including those in Labrador, and introduced the fields of human rights, international law and environmental impact assessment to the claims process. They had, however, markedly different points of departure. Two were spurred by the growing energy needs of the 1960s, and two resulted in the recognition of aboriginal title.

Bourassa's hydroelectric plans for the 133,000 square miles of the James Bay hinterland put enormous pressure on the Cree, who had no recourse to treaties. Construction began in the summer of 1972. By October, the Cree had been granted an injunction by the Quebec Superior Court. Despite the later overturning of this injunction the legal implication was that, even without a treaty, the Cree had sufficient grounds for a land claim. At roughly the same time, in the famous Calder case concerning the Nishga'a Indians of British Columbia, three Supreme Court judges had found that such a thing as aboriginal right existed in Canadian law regardless of prior recognition by treaty. Legal recognition of the existence of *aboriginal* (that is, untreatied) title to land forced the federal government to accept land claims based on aboriginal title, which it did in November 1973.

The amended land claims process had a number of components.[8] Claims without treaties were known as comprehensive claims and, according to the British law through which such aboriginal claims were acknowledged, these had to be supported with evidence of occupation since 'time immemorial'.[9] Native groups petitioned the federal government for money drawn against any future settlement to compile, submit, and later use as a basis for negotiations a detailed survey documenting their land use and occupancy of a specified region. Negotiations were entered into on the understanding that once aboriginal rights had been established, they would automatically be abrogated to Canada. In effect, the process made modern-day treaties with native groups so that the federal government could acquire title to their lands and clearly establish Canadian sovereignty over them. This treaty-making policy is made explicit by the fact that reserves subsequently set aside for native use are owned by the resident native band collectively and not individually, and cannot be disposed of except to the Canadian government (see Chapter 5, Nadasdy, in this book).

The recognition of aboriginal title opened the way for a large number of hitherto unassessed land claims from across Canada, resulting in a backlog of work for the federal land claims office that severely impeded progress.[10] However, most claims in the last 20 years have been negotiated under pressure from large-scale development projects. Although such development enables native groups to jump the queue, they leave the native organizations with little room for manoeuvre. Negotiating organizations use what political space they have to extract as substantial a settlement as they can from the situation. But this means that the value of the claim is linked to the expected costs and revenues of the development rather than to the value of a way of life and the resources it needs to remain viable. Native groups invariably end up with far less land than they had anticipated. Moreover many settlements made in the last two decades have yet to be fully honoured from the government side – the James Bay Agreement being a prime example.[11]

The case of the Dene and the Mackenzie Valley Pipeline project differed in a number of ways. First, the project area was covered by Treaties 8 and 11. Secondly, the Dene had the experience of the Cree and the Nisga'a cases behind them for their case. Thirdly, the Dene were able to link their cause to the very emotive one of safeguarding Canada's fragile Arctic wilderness.[12] This led to the establishment of the Federal Environmental Impact Review Process as part of any land claim where development is anticipated, and gave the Dene a magnificent political platform. Even more critically, the Dene used international human rights law to support their case. This body of law allowed for a much broader interpretation of the notion of aboriginal inheritance by suggesting that it included the rights to self-determination and the maintenance of a traditional way of life. The Dene wanted the Canadian government to acknowledge them as a nation, with attendant rights to self-determination within their own homeland, and refused to abrogate their aboriginal title to the federal government. They wanted to join Canada as a distinct new Dene province. Although the Dene have yet to be successful in this regard, Nunavut was created in 1999 with provincehood as the eventual goal.

Native organizations in Labrador were able to capitalize on the experiences of the Cree, Nisga'a and Dene when they petitioned for recognition of their claims. By the mid-1980s, Labrador was facing massive militarization. This raised the stakes on all sides considerably, although the impact was to be felt most in central Labrador. The choice before the Innu and Inuit as they contemplated the land claims process was between accepting the modern-day treaty agreement of the claims process as it stood, or following the Dene initiative in their attempt to push the federal government into acknowledging a much wider appreciation of aboriginal right. Tanner (1983) describes these distinct strategies as 'accommodationist' and 'exclusivist.' His broad generalization characterizes the Inuit as more accommodationist and the Innu as more exclusivist.

The associations

The Labrador Inuit Association

Originally intended to form part of the ITC's comprehensive survey of much of the eastern Arctic, the LIA began researching its land use and occupancy study in the summer of 1975. *Our Footprints are Everywhere* was submitted to the federal government for review in 1977 but the LIA had to wait until 1989 to begin negotiations. Nunavut, the autonomous Inuit homeland of the ITC, was created to the exclusion of Labrador in April 1999. The LIA got its homeland of

Nunatsiavut in December 2005. The trajectory of its eventual formation, however, was somewhat more convoluted than the outcome might suggest. The LIA accepted Canadian sovereignty in return for a degree of autonomy in its local area. In other words, in true 'accommodationist' form, it had chosen the path of the modern-day treaty: negotiations were a matter of pressing for the maximum settlement by whatever means, and not a matter of debating the extinguishment of title. In accepting the invitation to negotiate in 1989, the LIA had tacitly accepted the clause on abrogation, believing that extinguishment could still be resisted from *within* the process. In fact, the LIA has benefited from the campaigns of others in this matter.

The NMIA has never accepted the federal government's terms and stipulations. Although it had received federal money at much the same time as the LIA had done, it did not submit a land use and occupancy study until expanding militarization forced them to do so in 1989. The Innu have always felt that the onus was on the Canadian government to petition them for rights to Labrador because the Innu had never surrendered any of their territory. Such an ideological position was never likely to be accepted by the federal government, of course, but it underlined the NMIA's refusal to accept the extinguishment clause in the land claims process. Like the Dene, the Innu were asking for autonomy and the right to self-determination. They became the Innu Nation, in their homeland of *Nitassinan*, from the mid-1980s and have remained 'exclusive' in their rejection of the federal land claims process in its entirety.

The 'accommodationist' and 'exclusivist' ethno-political philosophies of the two organizations underpinned differences which go much further than their contrasting approaches to the land claims process itself. Well before it was invited to negotiate, for instance, the LIA had pursued three clear objectives which were related to the Association's anticipated settlement. First, it made northern Labrador the centre of its organization. Second, it pushed for tangible interim improvements for its people. And third, it continued to research and consolidate its claim to land. The LIA also maintained close ties with its political allies, the ITC, which boosted its ethnic credibility as much as its northern focus has. Jobs arising from the LIA's growing organizational structure and business schemes directly benefited northerners as well. Living conditions improved as a result, and the LIA has secured a core support base from which to expand. Nain has succeeded in attracting some of the political limelight away from central Labrador; the LIA attracts federal money to the province, and so Newfoundland had to acknowledge its responsibilities in Nain including giving the LIA some local political power. Taking its cue from the old Native Agreements and the provisions of the Indian Act, the LIA began negotiating for free education, dental and medical care for its members. The affiliated Labrador Inuit Development Corporation (LIDC) manages a number of successful Inuit business interests including a variety of traditional craft ventures, a commercial caribou hunt employing experienced local hunters, and a joint experimental shrimp fishery with Greenland. The Association had also continued to research its land use and occupancy in Labrador. By the late 1980s it had interests extending to the north and south of its original 1977 claim, and it was able to use these in bargaining for a better overall settlement. The LIA has been extremely successful in appreciating the extent of its bargaining power with the government. It has achieved an impressive local political structure which has secured a better standard of living for a majority of its people throughout Labrador. In 'accommodationist' mode, the LIA had been able to secure a healthy position within the land claims process.

The Innu nation

The NMIA on the other hand remains reluctant to participate in the federal land claims process and has few of the tangible achievements the LIA could show. Besides, the Innu case is more difficult than that of the LIA. To begin with the Innu Nation heartland is in central Labrador. Not only has this been the seat of white business and administration for well over a century, inevitably making a claim here contentious, but it is also on the doorstep of the recent military expansion. It has not been easy, therefore, for Innu politicians to establish a clear stronghold in central Labrador. Doing so would set their organization in direct competition with already well-established administrative structures, and having not done so leaves the Innu much more vulnerable to the present military encroachment. Furthermore, the pan-Canadian Indian movement was much more diverse and less focused than the ITC and was not in as good a position to provide the Innu with political guidance. Despite these difficulties the Innu had a moral claim to central Labrador that the federal government could not overlook, particularly as military interest in Goose Bay increased.

These reasons undoubtedly influenced the political strategies the NMIA chose to follow. Innu politicians still appeared to be wedded to the idealistic stances that had initially won them public moral support, and which have been summarized by Tanner (1983) as 'winning by losing'. That is, they retained public sympathy and support if they continued to be seen as unfairly treated by government and military. Bringing a claim to the negotiating stage would cost them their ideals and this particular support base. What federal funding they did secure – some at least for researching their claim – was seen as their due for lands already subjected to developments from which they had not benefited. Such funds were, however, a tacit acknowledgement of the legitimacy of their claim.

Nevertheless, the window of manipulation available to native organizations confronting massive development is finite and ephemeral, and military interest in Goose Bay was burgeoning in the pre-Glasnost era of the 1980s. Since Goose Bay Airbase was in the heart of Innu territory, and low-level flight zones spanned much of their hunting grounds, increased military activity would affect the Innu far more than the LIA. In addition, the federal government preferred to negotiate with all potential claimants in a given area simultaneously. The LIA had submitted its land use study and was ready for negotiations. By the mid-1980s, then, the Innu had to come to some sort of understanding with the Canadian government or risk being swept aside by military expansion and sidelined by the LIA negotiations. But the Innu carried their exclusivist resistance into the fray. First, the failure of their previous idealistic position and the mounting pressure of militarization caused a sea-change in Innu internal politics. Innu ethno-politics was briefly and effectively commandeered by several strong women who were driven by their personal experiences of the dissolution of Innu society to demand better services and more humane attention from the media and the authorities. Their patently reasonable demands were not predicated upon unrealistic ideals. Women often bear the brunt of social collapse, and the Innu women who forced their way into public view with their concerns did so out of sheer frustration. Since Innu society is not confrontational, they often acted at considerable personal cost (Wadden 1991).

Second, the Innu began a highly visible campaign of protests to draw attention to what they felt was the military's questionable right to be in Labrador. Innu protesters began by hiking into restricted military areas in the interior to expose military bombing activities, producing evidence to suggest that the military were exceeding their agreed-upon weapons use. Innu families then began a series of sit-ins on the base runways. Many protesters were arrested, some were detained and a few were gaoled in St John's. On behalf of the military, the Crown intended to prosecute the protesters for trespassing on military property. The Innu's response was that, until such time as their claim to the land was resolved, it was the military who were the trespassers. With typical wit and irony several Innu set up a camp at the end of the runway while the court case was in progress, with placards to inform people that they were now on Innu land and entering the camp would require passes issued by the 'Innu Minister of Foreign Affairs'. Both forms of protest and the court case dovetailed to create a period of intense media and public attention for the Innu, and the Innu were invited to negotiate their claim in 1989. They still refused to accept the clause on abrogation.

The Labrador Metis Association

Beleaguered on all sides, the LMA was still mired in internal conflicts and problems of authenticity, and it held the weakest position vis-à-vis the land claims process and militarization. The Association had not set out with the intention of submitting a land claim; it openly acknowledged the priority of claims lodged by the established native organizations, and had sought instead to safeguard its members' hunting, trapping and fishing activities in central and south-eastern Labrador and secure input on the region's future and development. In light of this, the issue of development had become one of the Association's most divisive problems. Without federal support such as the LIA and NMIA commanded, the LMA knew its members and other Metis who fell outside the aegis of the established native organizations were dependent on militarization for jobs. However, the LMA was also well aware that the position of most native groups was anti-development; it could not really expect to achieve recognition as a native group if it took a strongly pro-military stance. It was a classic 'catch-22' position: it could neither attract federal recognition without members, nor gain members without the offer of federally funded benefits. Well aware of the vulnerability this created for the Metis, the LIA challenged every upswing in the fortunes of the LMA by mounting its own vigorous membership campaign in central Labrador.

Prevarication over the issue of development also lost the LMA ground in the business world. The local town council and chamber of commerce are dominated by a number of townspeople who run very prosperous businesses servicing the needs of the military. They formed their own highly vocal group in support of military expansion in Labrador, the Mokami Project Group (MPG), which was not concerned with the land per se, but it had substantial funding from the conservative-led Newfoundland government of the time. Newfoundland still suffers from the notion that Labrador represents its 'big lucky break' in terms of economic opportunity. The last thing it wanted to see was the military frightened away by native land claims campaigns. Financing the one obviously and excessively pro-military Labrador lobby group was one way for influential business people to prevent this. Thus afforded high visibility and vocality, the Project Group was able to fulfil the function of a more general pro-development voice in the region. Metis who feared the loss of their income if the military were forced to leave the region could rely on the MPG to voice these concerns for them. However, few were ever openly supportive of the MPG which did not in any case need a strong local support base. The MPG elicited very mixed feelings from the central Labrador Metis community, and in the end was viewed with extreme suspicion because it represented the demands and desires of the business elite rather than the Metis. More significantly, it showed little concern for the land or its peoples. It may have been used as a foil in many heated debates about the development of the land, but it was definitely not *of* Labrador. Along with the pro-military stance of the town council and chamber of commerce, the MPG's powerful voice tended to negate the local Metis population's opposition to development. Their tacit support from the local Metis community was assured, however, because of two things: Metis valued their jobs, and they shied away from confrontation and overt political activity. The maintenance of the status quo was guaranteed as long as the Metis remained politically silent. And on the issue of development, the LMA was unable to provide decisive leadership; with both pro- and anti-development positions taken, the LMA was left to negotiate a narrow band of moderation between the two.

By 1989, then, the LMA had not gained any strength as a political player in the debate over land. The problems encountered by the Association mirror the peculiarities of the Metis themselves: they have tended to be independent, individualistic and adaptable. Their ability to adapt to new environments and make use of a range of traits and qualities has made them a hybrid group. They may not be able to argue for aboriginal or ethnic purity (a dubious claim in any case); they *can* argue for regional uniqueness. While this argument might be seen as not, so far, having achieved much, the groups laying claim to such purity have not fared any better.

Conclusion

At the close of the century, the three Labrador ethnic organizations were still on very different trajectories. Of all the native organizations in the province, the Inuit Association had fared best in terms of securing funding and federal support. The organization had made significant inroads into the problems facing its remote northern communities, and improved direct funding had given impetus to economic initiatives that linked Labrador Inuit to southern markets – albeit small and regional – for its caribou products, and Greenlandic fisheries. With the declaration of the new Nunatsiavut government in December 2005, the LIA achieved its aims. Land remains of paramount concern for this new third level of government within Canada, but the legal recognition of inherent aboriginal right now reinforces rights to land for aboriginal groups rather than extinguishing them. The Inuit are winners in more ways than one: their accommodationist stance brought them benefits and improvements from the outset, but they have also benefited from the more ardently idealistic positions of their exclusivist compatriots, the Innu.

The Innu themselves, however, have gained little. They are still struggling through claims negotiations, frequently stalling on issues of control and inherent right. The Innu have paid dearly for their political integrity. While the Inuit were receiving federal funding for many economic and social initiatives, Innu communities fell into ever deepening social malaise.[13] In the mid-1990s, reports of gas-sniffing and some of the highest youth suicide rates in the world galvanized media attention and embarrassed the Canadian government into action. Young Innu were flown to special native drug abuse and rehabilitation centres across Canada, but not before severe problems with foetal alcohol syndrome had been uncovered in both Labrador Innu communities. Davis Inlet was eventually relocated to a new community, with new housing and new hope. But Natuashish is as much mired in problems of poverty and despair as Davis Inlet ever was.

The established tactics of the Innu Nation and the LIA exemplify the opposition between exclusivist and accommodationist styles within ethno-politics. The LIA has always sought to work alongside the political structures within the Canadian state. It has maximized the benefits accruing to those organizations working within the system, thus securing a strong support base and, relatively speaking, a good bargaining position with the government. The Innu are much more exclusivist, however. In calling themselves the Innu Nation, and their homeland *Nitassinan*, they lay claim to a distinctiveness through language to support their demands for autonomy. The Innu retained their radical position outside of the land claims process for as long as possible in an attempt to force concessions from Canada; somewhat like the separatists in Quebec, their ideal would be self-determination outside the Canadian state. But both Labrador Innu communities are in a state of despair from which it will be excruciatingly difficult to recover.

The Metis, on the other hand, are just beginning. In September 2003, the Powley case recognized Metis as aboriginals with rights. In response, the Labrador Metis set out a series of objectives. These include achieving renewable resource harvesting rights which, while aiming for conservation, allow for both aboriginal subsistence and commercial exploitation. Like the Inuit, the Metis aim to achieve these as full citizens of Canada. But, unlike the Inuit, the Metis make their focus the insistence that their rights as Canadian citizens will remain unaffected and uncompromized by their claims to land and an associated ethnic identity. It represents yet another shift in the accommodationist versus exclusivist debate: the objective here is that rights as full citizens of Canada are enhanced by rather than set in opposition to rights as a distinct cultural group within the country.

Quite apart from recent successes for Metis generally, the journey taken by the members of the LMA to reach this point illustrates the internal and external struggles for unity, authenticity and recognition common to most emergent ethnic organizations. The example of the Metis raises questions about the way in which an ethnic identity is subject to acceptability in terms of perceived authenticity. Labrador Metis and Inuit share a way of life, and both acknowledge mixed ancestry. But whereas the LMA stipulates mixed ancestry as a prerequisite for membership, the Inuit Association demarcates its membership boundaries geographically. The situation of central Labrador Metis draws attention to the fact that ethno-politics has more to do with the management and presentation of an identity than its component parts. And authenticity becomes a matter of packaging, since any number of traits – including birthplace and an anti-development stance – can be seen as contributing to its veracity. The process of creolization is abundantly apparent in both groups and organizations (and it is also occurring more subtly with the Innu as well). But whereas both groups acknowledge it, the management of creolization is handled very differently in each case. The difference is exacerbated by government handling. Despite Powley, neither mixed ancestry nor way of life appear to be sufficient bases for claims to authenticity or to land. Maybe *because* of Powley, the balance thus far established between way of life and aboriginality is in the process of shifting once again, and Metis from across Canada will be the next wave of claimants at the negotiating tables of the future. If so, will the tenets established in inherent aboriginal right, and questions of aboriginal authenticity, give way to consideration of adaptability and miscegenation in ethnic characterizations?

Returning to the processual framework in the introduction, it is the 'interim' that informs the process of restitution. Governmental policy inevitably shapes this by acknowledging some changes and not others: a 'creolizing' population, an expectation of ethnic permanence, homogeneity, recognition, difference and competition. At all stages, and as in many other examples in this book, the influence of the state is paramount, and most native organizations end up dancing to their tune. In this instance, I have explored the inevitable processes of change in ethnic identities, especially those pertaining to accommodation versus exclusivity. The Labrador Metis are the product of centuries of intermarrying, adaptation and change, qualities that have rendered them less authentic because they are perceived as being less aboriginal. In order to have any form of restitution, claimants have to be identified and their histories of disenfranchizement made evident. Protest, resistance and legal challenges then force changes. The process is costly, time consuming, enervating and divisive. But these are the foundations upon which claims to land are made in Canada.

References

Asch, M (1997) *Aboriginal and Treaty Rights in Canada: Essays on law, equality, and respect for difference*, Vancouver: University of British Columbia Press.
Barnard, A (2006) 'Kalahari Revisionism, Vienna and the "Indigenous Peoples" Debate', *Social Anthropology* 14(1): 1–16.
Berger, T (1977) *Northern Frontier, Northern Homeland: Report of the Mackenzie Valley pipeline inquiry*, Ottawa: Government of Canada.
Brice-Bennett, C (ed.) (1977) *Our Footprints are Everywhere*, Nain: Labrador Printers.
Guenter, Mathias (2006) 'The Concept of Indigeneity', *Social Anthropology* 14(1): 17–32.
Hawthorn, H (1966–7) *A Survey of the Contemporary Indians of Canada: Economic, political, educational needs and policies*, 2 vols, Ottawa: Government of Canada.
Heinen, Dieter (2004) 'Discussion: on the Return of the Native', *Current Anthropology* 45(2): 262.
Indian and Northern Affairs Canada (2003) *Resolving Aboriginal Claims: A practical guide to Canadian experiences*, Ottawa: Government of Canada.
Kennedy, John Charles (1982) *Holding the Line: ethnic boundaries in a northern Labrador community*, St John's: Institute of Social and Economic Research (ISER).
Kenrick, Justin and Jerome Lewis (2004a) 'Discussion: on the Return of the Native', *Current Anthropology* 45(2): 263.
—— (2004b) 'Indigenous Peoples' Rights and the Politics of the Term "Indigenous" ', *Anthropology Today* 20(2): 4–9.
Kuper, A (2003) 'The Return of the Native', *Current Anthropology* 44(3): 389–402.
—— (2004) 'On the Return of the Native', *Current Anthropology* 45(2): 265–7.
Morse, B (1991) *Aboriginal Peoples and the Law: Indian, Metis and Inuit rights in Canada*, Ottawa: Carleton University Press.
Persky, S (1998) *Delgamuukw. The Supreme Court of Canada Decision on Aboriginal Title*, Vancouver: Douglas and McIntyre.
Plaice, E (1990) *The Native Game: Settler perceptions of Indian/Settler relations in central Labrador*, St John's: Institute of Social and Economic Research.

Tanner, A (1983) *The Politics of Indianness: Case studies of Native ethnopolitics in Canada*, St John's: Institute of Social and Economic Research.

Wadden, M (1991) *Nitassinan: The Innu struggle to reclaim their homeland*, Vancouver: Douglas and McIntyre.

Weaver, S (1981) *The Making of Canadian Indian Policy: The hidden agenda 1968–1970*, University of Toronto Press.

Notes

1 See, for example, the debates in *Current Anthropology*, June 2003, and *Social Anthropology*, Spring 2006 (Kuper 2003; 2004; Heinen 2004; Kenrick and Lewis 2004a, 2004b; Barnard 2006; Guenter 2006).

2 Now Indian and Northern Affairs (INAC), the name has changed over time: Department of Indian and Northern Affairs (DIAND); Department of Indian and Northern Affairs (DINA). Inuit were brought under the legal aegis of the Act in 1924.

3 In the nineteenth and early twentieth centuries, when most treaties were signed, this would have also offered a source of protection from the rapidly expanding, largely European, settler population.

4 The communities thus recognized tended to change over time: Nain, Hopedale, Makkovik, Postville and Rigolet (Inuit); Sheshatshit and Davis Inlet/Natuashish (Innu); occasionally also North West River, Mud Lake and Black Tickle (Metis).

5 The contract allowed Hydro-Quebec to resell Newfoundland power to New York at seven times its original price for forty years, with a renewal option to resell for a further 25 years at 10 times its buying price. By that time (2025), the losses to Labrador would be enormous.

6 Brice-Bennett (1977) and Plaice (1990), for example.

7 The LIA boundary follows the Atlantic watershed, cuts across to Lake Melville just before Mulligan and encompasses a portion of Sandwich Bay.

8 The Indian and Northern Affairs Canada website lists them as: (1) submission of claim; (2) acceptance of claim; (3) framework agreement; (4) agreement in principal; (5) final agreement and ratification; (6) implementation. See www.ainc-inac.gc.ca/pr/pub/rul/rul_e.pdf, accessed 26 March 2008.

9 For a full argument of the legal implications of the recognition of aboriginal title, see Lester (in Brice-Bennett 1977), Morse (1991) and Asch (1997) among others.

10 Initial estimates suggested a backlog of 150 years to complete already acknowledged claims under the original claims process, which allowed for six negotiation tables at any one time. And there were still outstanding claims at that point. However, changes to the process, including removal of the six-table limit in 1990, have since speeded up negotiations considerably.

11 The Cree recently used the commencement of Phase II of the James Bay Project to draw attention to this fact.

12 This would entail protection against such events as the 1989 Exxon Valdez disaster.

13 The Innu did receive funding, but the general infrastructure was not in place – nor was the political will to effectively make use of it.

Chapter 5

The antithesis of restitution?
A note on the dynamics of land negotiations in the Yukon, Canada

Paul Nadasdy

Abstract

Although the negotiation of aboriginal land claim agreements in northern Canada appears to have much in common with land restitution processes elsewhere in the world, these Canadian agreements are not in fact supposed to be about land restitution at all. Rather, they deal with the cession of land held under aboriginal title to the federal government. In this article, I focus on the negotiation of Kluane First Nation's (KFN's) land claim agreement in Canada's Yukon Territory. I examine talk that took place at the negotiating table and some of the legal and administrative mechanisms negotiators used to negotiate landownership. I show that political inequalities among the parties transformed what was in theory a process of land cession, in which KFN granted lands to the federal government, into one of restitution, in which the government gave lands to the First Nation. Reframing the process in this way gave the federal government a degree of control over the land claim process that was unjustified by the legal theory that gave rise to the negotiations in the first place.

Most of the chapters in this book deal with the *restitution* of land, that is, the return of land – or payment of compensation in lieu of the land itself – to those who claim to be its rightful owners. On the face of it, the negotiation of aboriginal land claim agreements in northern Canada have much in common with processes of land restitution elsewhere in the world. Legally speaking, however, land claims agreements in the Canadian North are not about the restitution of land at all. In contrast to what took place in most of the rest of the continent, the history of native–white relations in the North is, for the most part, *not* one of wholesale dispossession. Because the Arctic and Subarctic are not suitable for agriculture, there was little demand for northern lands by encroaching Euro-American settlers. Although Euro-American newcomers did appropriate some land – especially in and around urban/industrial centres – northern native peoples have for the most part been able to retain access to and use of the lands on which they have hunted, fished, and trapped for generations. Because there was no great demand for land in the Arctic and Subarctic, neither the US nor Canadian governments bothered to negotiate land cession treaties with northern aboriginal people.

Starting in the 1960s, however, new communication and transportation technologies made it possible for Euro-Americans to exploit some of the mineral and energy wealth that had been locked away in the North and largely inaccessible to southern markets. The last quarter of the twentieth century saw the development of numerous multi-billion dollar mega-projects across the North (pipelines, mines, hydroelectric projects). While these projects often caused an influx of large numbers of Euro-Canadians from the south, much of this immigration was temporary, lasting only so long as construction work remained. Most of those southerners who did remain tended to settle in the urban industrial centres. Indeed, the vast majority of non-aboriginal people living in the North today reside in urban centres like Anchorage, Whitehorse and Yellowknife and work either for government or industry. The oil fields and mines themselves – massive though some of them are – are local phenomena, industrial enclaves within a vast northern landscape, most of which remains free of agricultural or industrial development. Northern aboriginal people continue to hunt and fish on these lands; and indeed, most remain dependent to some degree on hunting and fishing for their subsistence (Nadasdy 2003; Receveur *et al.* 1998; Wenzel 1991).

While, generally speaking, industrial development in the North did not directly force aboriginal people from their lands, it did force both Canada and the US to deal with outstanding aboriginal claims to land. No corporation or consortium is going to invest the billions of dollars necessary to build a pipeline, mine, or hydroelectric project in the North if there is any uncertainty at all about who owns title to the land on which it builds. Without certainty of title, there is always the danger that a corporation might lose its investment as the result of a lawsuit brought against it by aboriginal people. The US Congress unilaterally created certainty when it passed the Alaska Native Claims Settlement Act in 1971. In Canada, however, the need for certainty led the federal government to begin negotiating modern land claim agreements across the Canadian North.[1]

In its 1973 decision in *Calder v Attorney General of British Columbia*,[2] the Canadian Supreme Court ruled that First Nation people in Canada retained their aboriginal title to land except where it had been *explicitly* extinguished by treaty (see Isaac 1995: 20–34). This had profound consequences in the North, where no treaties had ever been signed. It meant that in some sense First Nation people still 'owned' the land, and that therefore the federal government had an obligation to settle aboriginal land claims before development could proceed. Thus, in theory at least, land claim negotiations are the very antithesis of land restitution. Rather than returning land to its original owners, land claim agreements are supposed to create certainty of ownership, and they do this by explicitly extinguishing aboriginal rights and title to those lands *not* retained by First Nations under the agreements.[3] According to Canadian law, then, aboriginal land claim negotiations are not about restoring land rights to First Nation people; rather they are about First Nations ceding land rights to the federal government. Thus, First Nation and government negotiators wrangle not over which lands the government will give (or give back) to First Nations, but over which lands First Nations will cede to the federal government and which they will retain.

That, at least, is the theory. In practice, however, negotiations do not resemble this theory very closely. There is a huge power disparity among the parties to these negotiations. Regardless of the opinions of the Supreme Court, the Canadian government has long had de facto control over the land, administering and managing it as a sovereign power. The Canadian government also has vastly greater resources (of time, money, and personnel) at its disposal than does any First Nation. First Nations are dependent upon the federal government to fund the basic costs of local governance, to provide and administer a whole array of programmes and services, and even to cover the costs of First Nation participation in the negotiation process. As I have noted elsewhere (Nadasdy 2003), the preponderance of state power enables the state to dictate the conceptual assumptions underlying the land claims process and the rules by which negotiations will proceed – even as state officials engage in the negotiations as supposedly equal players (see also Verdery 2003). As a result, First Nation people have been forced to speak the Euro-American language of property law, adopt Euro-Canadian-style political institutions and develop bureaucratic infrastructures that mirror those of the Canadian government – all as prerequisites for even sitting down at the negotiating table.

These unequal power relations do not change once the parties actually begin negotiating, so it should hardly be surprising that land claim negotiations have usually proceeded *as if* it were the federal government giving land to the First Nations, rather than the other way around. This is a difference that makes a difference. It has shaped the very process of negotiations as well as the resulting agreements. In the remainder of this chapter, I will focus on one particular set of land claim negotiations: those among the governments of Canada, the Yukon Territory, and the KFN, whose citizens are the aboriginal inhabitants of the south-west Yukon. I observed these negotiations for two and a half years, the last year of which I served as a negotiator on behalf of the First Nation. In addition, KFN tape-recorded eight years of negotiations, all of which have now been transcribed. Most of those who sat at KFN's negotiating table were well aware of the formal theory underlying land claims that I have just described: that it was the First Nation giving land to the government and not the other way around. As we shall see, however, the day-to-day process of negotiations over land was not consistent with this theory. Although some KFN negotiators at times actively sought to enforce the formal view of land claims, both in the way people talked at the table and in the formal procedures of the negotiations, they were ultimately unsuccessful. Although for the most part everyone at the table avoided overt talk about government 'giving' land to

KFN, such a dynamic remained implicit in the process by which land was negotiated.

Giving land

Negotiations over land took place as follows. KFN had previously agreed to retain a certain 'quantum' of land (350 sq miles) within their Traditional Territory (approximately 15,000 sq miles).[4] In consultation with First Nation members, KFN's Lands Committee chose and mapped a series of 'land selections', the combined area of which equalled their total land quantum.[5] KFN negotiators then presented these land selections to the federal and territorial governments at the negotiating table. While government negotiators quickly agreed to some of these selections, others they rejected outright. Most of the selections, however, were accepted provisionally, subject to more or less intense negotiations over their precise boundaries.

The language of 'land selections' was neutral with regard to who owned the land; one could view it as a matter of KFN selecting the land it would retain (this was the official account of the process) or, alternatively, as the selection of lands they would receive from the government. Most of the time, government negotiators were careful to avoid any explicit statements to the effect that the federal government was 'giving' land to the First Nation. And on those rare occasions when one of them did, they stumbled over one another to correct the mistake, as in the following exchange from January 31, 1997:

> *Yukon negotiator*: And I think that's why the agreement is as thick as it is – the UFA [Umbrella Final Agreement], because it doesn't just deal with . . . [inaudible] money. It's giving the First – well, I shouldn't say 'giving;' I mean – (('establishing'))
> *Federal negotiator*: (('creating'))
> *Yukon negotiator*: or 'creating' . . .
> *Federal negotiator*: . . . possibilities for a First ((Nation and other))
> *Yukon negotiator*: ((And sharing of)) of . . . of how we address the . . .[6]

Despite the lengths government negotiators went to avoid talking in terms of 'giving' land to KFN, it is clear that that at least some of them did see the land claim process in this way. This is evident in their frequent assertions throughout the negotiations that all land in the Yukon not held under fee simple title[7] was 'crown land', as in the following:

> *Federal negotiator*: because gravel permits might, or gravel might, be a YTG [Yukon Territorial Government] interest, but it's a process like I've said. You know, *roads* might be a YTG interest, but they were *ours* until a few years ago, and the land is still primarily crown land, but it's gonna be devolved, so –[8]

Implicit in such statements is the assumption that the federal government *already* possessed underlying title to all land in the Yukon. If this had been unambiguously the case, however, there would have been no need for land claim negotiations at all. That such statements were not just occasional slips of the tongue is evident in the frequency with which government negotiators referred to unoccupied lands as 'crown land', despite the fact that KFN negotiators sometimes explicitly challenged them on their use of the term, as in the following discussion over the status of a gravel pit:

> *Federal negotiator*: Yeah, it's a borrow pit for NPA [Northern Pipeline Act], and [name of Yukon negotiator] said it's a gravel pit for YTG [the Yukon Government].
> *KFN negotiator*: And it's a land selection for KFN.
> *Federal negotiator*: And it's federal crown land at the moment (laughs).
> *KFN negotiator*: Oh no. [inaudible]. You have to keep in mind that this is *our* land. We were here before the federal government.
> *Federal negotiator*: You're right.
> *KFN negotiator*: We lived here anyways. I mean, for ever and ever.[9]

Significantly, however, it was several KFN negotiators – mostly elders – rather than government negotiators, who were most likely to speak in terms of the federal government 'giving' land to KFN:

> *KFN negotiator (elder)*: We are the smallest band in the Yukon, right? We got gypped out of the money part. We got gypped out of the *land* part. What I wanna ask the government, are you guys willing to give us more than we got now [that is, increase KFN's land quantum]? Would you be willing to do that, to show your good grace, that you're negotiating in good faith with us? I mean, say, 'hey you guys; we know we gypped you' but give another hundred kilometers . . . more miles of land (inaudible) to have for my people? [If] it could be done, would you . . . will you consider it?[10]

Younger KFN negotiators, however, who were generally more familiar with the legal theories underlying land claim negotiations – and who were often openly hostile to any hint of paternalism – regularly reminded government negotiators that it was the First Nation and not Canada that owned the land. Even so, there were times when everyone at the table – First Nation and government negotiators alike – tacitly acknowledged the inequalities of power that confined such distinctions to the realm of theory. In a lighthearted exchange on 26 September 1997, for example, negotiators likened the federal government to Santa Claus and KFN to an expectant child on Christmas morning:

> *KFN negotiator*: . . . And I don't think we are *far* apart on Schedule B

[Schedule B of chapter 10 in the agreement deals with the Kluane Game Sanctuary. This statement was tongue in cheek, because the parties in fact disagreed considerably on how to deal with the Sanctuary: KFN wanted it to become a First Nation Park, while the federal and territorial governments insisted that it become a territorial park]. It strikes me, what we tabled *I think* you probably could live with in the context of the territorial park concept, that's entrenched as part of our agreement (laughter). *I am* only dreaming now.
Federal negotiator: Make a wish.
KFN negotiator: OK? It's almost Christmas. (laughter) You know it's almost Christmas when the Sears wish book is out. So.
Yukon negotiator: Just remember Santa usually delivers *some* of the things you wanted. (much laughter)
KFN negotiator: He's a very selective Santa. OK, on *that note* . . . of the *stingy* Santa . . .[11]

This theme became a running joke for the rest of the day. Later, for instance, government negotiators invoked it again and in doing so successfully rebuffed a serious complaint from a KFN negotiator regarding the contentious issue of the inherent right to self-government:

KFN negotiator A: I think these inherent rights. . . . *Our* agreement could've been different because of those rights. Seeing that it's not on the table today, *our* agreement becomes weaker [inaudible] because of that. So why don't you give us the inherent right *today*, so we can beef up our *agreements*, and we'll have it [negotiations] wrapped up by Christmas . . .
Federal negotiator: It's on the list, right? (laughter)
KFN negotiator A: I'm asking yes or no.
Yukon negotiator: It's a little stocking stuffer. (laughter)
KFN negotiator B: Oh my gosh. Mom and Dad, look! I got the inherent right.
(overlapping talk and laughter)
Federal negotiator: My fear is that I remember one or two Christmases where *nothing* on my list arrived under the tree.
KFN negotiator B: So you know how that feels . . . (laughter)
Federal negotiator: . . . And I wouldn't wanna do it at this table.
KFN negotiator A: If you would give us that, just think how you'd be marked in the history books in a hundred years. You'd be greeted right across the country from coast to coast [by First Nation people and] [inaudible] given a lot of fish eggs and what else? Rabbit tails (much laughter).

Interestingly, during this interchange, the KFN negotiator initially refused to go along with the joke, insisting instead that the government negotiators answer his question. It was not until a second KFN negotiator joined in the joking that the first gave up and joined in himself. Even, then, however, he refused to play along with the Christmas morning metaphor. Rather than acceding to the idealized one-way gift implied by the figure of Santa Claus, he invoked an image of true reciprocity: if the government negotiators would only recognize First Nation needs, he said, First Nations across the country would repay their generosity by honouring them with gifts of native food (though his reference to 'rabbit tails' was clearly a joke, fish eggs are an important food and marker of Indianness), thus drawing them into First Nation society.

In likening the federal government to Santa Claus and KFN to an expectant child on Christmas morning, the joke brought into sharp relief the power differential between the two. Legal theories about aboriginal title aside, it was the federal government – not KFN – that controlled the land. The federal Santa Claus might grant KFN land and other rights, but only if they were good. And, they should remember, no child ever gets everything they want for Christmas; rather, the choice of gifts is ultimately left up to the parents masquerading as a benevolent man in a red suit. Because it was 'only a joke', government and First Nation negotiators could give voice to their understanding of how things 'really' worked, despite the façade they normally had to maintain at the negotiation table.

In their study of joking among scientists, Mulkay and Gilbert (1982: 592)[12] note that humour arises from the incongruity that results from a juxtaposition of distinct interpretive frameworks 'which are both appropriate to a common range of topics but which are normally kept separate'. They describe a whole class of jokes told by scientists the humour of which derives from the 'gap between the formal literature and informal talk about science' (Mulkay and Gilbert 1982: 595). Analysis of this sort of humour, they argue, is important because it reveals the interpretive work people do in their efforts to create social meaning (Mulkay and Gilbert 1982: 606). I suggest that the Christmas morning joke was funny for many of the same reasons described by Mulkay and Gilbert; it played on the disconnect between the formal interpretive framework of land cession and everyone's informal understanding of how things 'really' worked.

How things really worked was also clearly evident in the structure of the land negotiation process. Once KFN negotiators had tabled their land selections, government negotiators compared those selections to government maps and consulted with officials from other departments within their respective governments. If they identified any existing government or third-party rights or interests to that land, they either returned the selection to KFN for modification or rejected it outright. Many years before, Yukon First Nations had agreed not to claim any land already held under fee simple title. Without such an *a priori* agreement, it is unlikely that negotiations could have proceeded. Yukon private property owners had initially feared that land claims would undermine their property rights. Without assurances to the contrary, sentiments against land claims among non-First Nation citizens in the territory would likely have been overwhelming. KFN negotiators, however, were dismayed to find that it was not only fee simple title that trumped their claims (see Council for Yukon Indians 1993: section 9.4.0). Rather, government negotiators gave precedence to *any* pre-existing right or interest at all – regardless of how temporary or contingent it might be. Such rights included, for example (to name just a few), the right-of-way for a pipeline that might never be built, bureaucratic 'notations' identifying possible future use by government departments, and grazing leases.

In one particular example of this, government negotiators refused to allow KFN to include in one of their land selections land that the government had recently leased out to a third party for grazing horses.[13] This infuriated KFN negotiators who maintained that since the land was theirs, the government should never have leased it out in the first place. This particular grazing lease was especially contentious because the area in question, around the Little Arm of Kluane Lake, is extremely important to Kluane people. Not only do they hunt and fish there regularly, but the area figures prominently in the social and spiritual life of the village (for example, the popular song *Little Arm Tatay*, referring to narrows on the Little Arm of Kluane Lake, known and sung by Athapaskan people throughout the Yukon and interior Alaska, is owned by the Kluane people). What is more, KFN negotiators argued, the grazing lease had infringed on a KFN citizen's prior legal rights and interests in the area. The KFN citizen in question had long had a cabin and trapping concession on the Little Arm, and the presence of horses in the area had made it impossible for her to set traps for wolves. Why, KFN negotiators asked, would the government grant third parties rights in land that infringed upon long-standing KFN interests like this, yet refuse to approve all KFN land selection that conflicted with any third party interest – even one as contingent and temporary as a grazing lease? KFN negotiators complained that when it came to negotiations over land, their interests were 'at the bottom of the barrel'.[14] It was clear from the dynamics of this process that – despite the rhetoric – it was the federal government that was granting land rights to KFN and not the other way around. And, in the granting of those rights, the government accorded First Nation interests the *lowest* priority; the existence of *any* other interests whatsoever in a land selection was enough to prevent the government from approving it.

That in reality it was the federal government that was 'giving' land to KFN was also evident in the way land negotiations proceeded even in the absence of third-party interests. Government negotiators insisted that KFN provide them with an exhaustive and detailed description of all the interests they had in any particular land they selected. That is, they wanted to know all the ways KFN members had used that land or planned to use it in the future. Government negotiators used this information to evaluate the selection and prepare a response to it that was consistent with government policy. KFN negotiators objected to this process, because they felt that government negotiators were requiring them to justify their land selections. They repeatedly stated that since

KFN owned all the land, it was the federal and territorial negotiators, rather than KFN, who should be identifying their interests and justifying their choice of lands.

Competing conceptions of 'balance' in land selection

Although government negotiators did reveal government and third party interests *after* KFN had tabled their land selections, they refused to do so beforehand. There were sound practical reasons for this; since KFN was retaining only about 2 per cent of their traditional territory, it made more sense to research the interests in KFN's selections than the other 98 per cent of the territory. Often enough, however, even when there were no specific government or third-party interests in KFN land selections, government negotiators objected to the selections (or parts thereof) on the grounds that they conflicted with some government policy. As a result, land negotiations frequently pitted specific KFN interests against government policy. Although government policy did not *always* prevail in such situations, it was only due to the assumption that the land *already belonged to the government* – and not the First Nation – that policy could play the key role it did in the negotiations. To see what I mean, consider the following example.

One important policy guiding government negotiations over land had to do with the notion of 'balance'. In laying out the guidelines for land selection, the Yukon Umbrella Final Agreement states that:

> To establish a balanced allocation of land resource values, the land selected as Settlement Land shall be representative of the nature of the land, the geography and the resource potential within each Yukon First Nation's Traditional Territory, and the balance may vary among Yukon First Nations' selections in order to address their particular needs.
> (Council for Yukon Indians 1993: section 9.5.1)

The federal and territorial approach to land negotiations was based on an interpretation of this clause as meaning that First Nations should not select an 'excessive' amount of high value lands, such as those with lake or highway frontage, and that they should instead select equal proportions of mountain top and muskeg. As a result, government officials scrutinized KFN's land selections along Kluane Lake and the Alaska highway particularly closely, and they regularly insisted that KFN needed to reconfigure those selections to make them 'shorter and deeper' (that is, to include less lake/highway frontage and more of the muskeg and mountains deeper in the bush). KFN negotiators, on the other hand, understood the concept of 'balance' somewhat differently. As one KFN negotiator put it: 'Yeah, I mean you gotta *understand*. *We're* giving up *everything* else, *everything else*. So when you're looking at our 350 square miles, we're balancing this with *everything* else, which is a *huge* amount of land. So, I mean, that's the way I look at it. I mean, the balance is – the other way around'.[15]

KFN negotiators argued that the government negotiators' concept of balance was incorrect, because it was based on an assumption that KFN was *gaining* something as a result of land claims (and that therefore the land they gained had to be balanced). They argued that government negotiators were confusing figure and ground when they looked at maps of KFN's land selections: 'When we're looking at a lake package, we're looking at what we've had to leave out. I mean, in a sense we're gaining, but at the same time we're losing'.[16] If one kept in mind what was supposedly *really* going on, that is, that KFN was *giving up* the vast majority of land, then all that 'extra' land they were giving up had to be factored into any assessment of how balanced their selections were. As another KFN negotiator put it:

> No, I just want to take a look on the map at what [name of different Kluane negotiator] is talking about, like the use down in here. There's lots of available land left over. This section here and all over, you know. There's all that other land left over, too, right? So, I mean, that's why we're having a hard time [accepting] your point that there's too much lake frontage. And then another thing too: for our whole traditional territory, the whole

Figure 5.1 Retained KFN settlement land.

territory are like sacred *grounds* for our whole First Nation. *The whole thing* is very important to us . . .[17]

Despite repeated protests of this sort by KFN negotiators, however, the government negotiators prevailed, and KFN had to reconfigure their lakefront and highway selections to make them 'shorter and deeper'. Government negotiators prevailed by simply refusing to give in. In theory, KFN could have played the same waiting game, but practically speaking this was not an option. In addition to financial constraints that limited KFN's flexibility in this regard, there was the added pressure of possible land alienations. Because it was the federal government that really controlled the land (they could, after all, continue granting property rights to third parties, thus diminishing the lands KFN could potentially select[18]), KFN was under increasing pressure to conclude an agreement as soon as possible. Thus, political inequalities between KFN and government transformed what was in theory a process of land cession, in which KFN granted lands to the federal and territorial governments, into one of restitution, in which government gave lands to the First Nation. Reframing the process in this way gave the federal and territorial governments a degree of control over the land claim process that was unwarranted by the theory that gave rise to the negotiations in the first place.

References

Asch, Michael and Norman Zlotkin (1997) 'Affirming Aboriginal Title: A New Basis for Comprehensive Claims Negotiations', in Michael Asch (ed.) *Aboriginal and Treaty Rights in Canada*, Vancouver: University of British Columbia Press, pp 208–29.

Blackburn, Carole (2005) 'Searching for Guarantees in the Midst of Uncertainty: Negotiating Aboriginal Rights and Title in British Columbia', *American Anthropologist* 107(4): 586–96.

Council for Yukon Indians (1993) *Umbrella Final Agreement Between the Government of Canada, the Council for Yukon Indians, and the Government of the Yukon*, Ottawa: Minister of Indian Affairs and Northern Development.

Isaac, Thomas (1995) *Aboriginal Law: Cases, Material, and Commentary*, Saskatoon: Purich.

McCormick, Floyd (1997) 'Inherent Aboriginal Rights in Theory and Practice: The Council for Yukon Indians Umbrella Final Agreement', PhD dissertation, Edmonton: Department of Political Science, University of Alberta.

Mulkay, Michael and Nigel Gilbert (1982) 'Joking Apart: Some Recommendations Concerning the Analysis of Scientific Culture', *Social Studies of Science* 12(4): 585–613.

Nadasdy, Paul (2003) *Hunters and Bureaucrats: Power, Knowledge, and Aboriginal-State Relations in the Southwest Yukon*, Vancouver: University of British Columbia Press.

Receveur, O, N Kassi, HM Chan, PR Berti and HV Kuhnlein (1998) *Yukon First Nations Assessment of Dietary Benefit/Risk*, Report prepared for the Centre for Indigenous Peoples' Nutrition and Environment (CINE).

Verdery, Katherine (2003) *The Vanishing Hectare: Property and Value in Post-Socialist Romania*, Ithaca, NY: Cornell University Press.

Wenzel, George (1991) *Animal Rights, Human Rights: Ecology, Economy, and Ideology in the Canadian Arctic*, Toronto: University of Toronto Press.

Woolford, Andrew (2005) *Between Justice and Certainty: Treaty Making in British Columbia*, Vancouver: University of British Columbia Press.

Notes

1 On the issue of certainty, see Blackburn (2005) and Woolford (2005). Both of these scholars point out that while 'certainty' is what motivates federal and provincial/territorial governments to engage in land claim negotiations, First Nations have other motivations.

2 [1973] SCR 313.

3 'Extinguishment' has been a sticking point in all modern Canadian land claim negotiations. Initially, Canada insisted on the total extinguishment of aboriginal rights and title, so that these under-defined terms would not undermine the certainty the agreements were meant to achieve. Yukon First Nation people, however, were understandably reluctant to sign away their as-yet-undefined rights. Eventually, Canada began to soften its position, enabling the parties in the Yukon to sign an agreement that does not entirely extinguish aboriginal title on those lands retained by a First Nation (see Council for Yukon Indians 1993: sections 2.5.0, 5.2.1, 5.2.2; McCormick 1997: 67–8). See Asch and Zlotkin (1997) and Blackburn (2005: 592–3) for discussions of the relationship between certainty and extinguishment.

4 Each First Nation's land quantum is laid out in the Yukon Umbrella Final Agreement (UFA), signed in 1993. This framework agreement was negotiated by the Council of Yukon Indians, which represented most First Nation people in the territory. The UFA was never ratified, because it is not an agreement in itself, but rather forms the framework for the negotiation of individual First Nation Final Agreements. The process of negotiating each First Nation's land quantum under the UFA was too long and complex to deal with adequately here, but it is worth noting that some First Nations were permitted to retain considerably more land than others.

5 In fact, KFN selected an area equal to 110 per cent of their total land quantum, and these lands were temporarily withdrawn from disposal by a federal Order-in-Council on 31 December 1993. The idea was that these lands were to be protected from development while the parties finalized KFN's land selections, at which time only 100 per cent of the land quantum would be permanently transferred to KFN. The interim protection order was revised and renewed on 5 December 1996 and again in 1999 and 2000.

6 31 January 1997. Yukon Archives accession number SR234–61B, transcript p 19. Copies of negotiation tapes and transcripts are all located in the Yukon Archives in Whitehorse, YT. Note on transcription: I use [square brackets] to indicate my own comments and ((double parentheses)) to indicate overlapping speech.

7 Fee simple is the legal term for private property in which the owner has the unqualified right to control, use, and transfer property at will (as opposed to fee tail, an archaic form of property in which inheritance was limited to some particular class of heirs, as in feudal estates). In the Yukon agreements, 'fee simple title' is used in contrast not only to other forms of Euro-American property rights, but also to 'aboriginal title', which, though not precisely defined, is viewed as a form of collective property right. On those lands retained by KFN under its agreement (where aboriginal title is not entirely extinguished), KFN is deemed to possess 'the rights, obligations and liabilities equivalent to fee simple' as well as the right to

govern on and manage those lands (Council for Yukon Indians 1993: section 5.4.1).
8   2 May 1997. Yukon Archives, SR234–69B, p 18.
9   24 March 1997. Yukon Archives SR234–64B, p 7.
10   1 May 1997. Yukon Archives SR234–68A, p 7.
11   26 September 1997. Yukon Archives SR234–26, p 2.
12   I thank Derick Fay for drawing my attention to this article.
13   31 January 1997. Yukon Archives SR 234–61B, pp 21–8.
14   Nadasdy negotiation fieldnotes 1997, p 141.
15   31 January 1997. Yukon Archives SR234–61B, p 19.
16   28 February 1997. Yukon Archives SR234–62A, p 16.
17   28 February 1997. Yukon Archives SR234–62A, p 16.
18   Although there was a general moratorium on the outright sale of 'crown land' in the Yukon pending the settlement of First Nation land claims, the federal government could and did continue to grant other forms of property rights in KFN's traditional territory, including, for example, grazing leases and mining claims. Even interim protected lands (see above n 5) could be adversely affected. According to the interim protection order, the federal government could extract gravel from lands under such protection. In 1996, the federal government authorized the extraction of gravel from what was then an interim protected land selection along Edith Creek for use in the reconstruction of a stretch of the Alaska Highway. KFN negotiators complained bitterly about this development. Federal negotiators responded that the new gravel pit did not affect their land selection; KFN was still free to select the land in question. KFN negotiators wondered aloud why anyone would want to select a big hole in the ground, and they redrew their land selections in the area. This event drove home to KFN citizens the fact that even interim protected lands would not be safe until after their agreement had been signed.

Chapter 6

Enacting sovereignty in a colonized space

The Yolngu of Blue Mud Bay meet the native title process

Frances Morphy

Abstract

The Yolngu people of Arnhem Land consider that they live in 'two worlds', encapsulated but not colonized by the Australian settler state. This study of courtroom interactions in the Blue Mud Bay native title case reveals, first, how the Australian legal system enacts the sovereignty of the state over those to whom some form of restitution is being offered under native title law. It then discusses how Yolngu witnesses inserted a discourse about sovereignty into the proceedings through an insistence on the incommensurability of rom (their 'laws and customs') and native title law, and through carefully positioned enactments of rom.

> This land was never given up
> This land was never bought and sold
> The planting of the Union Jack
> Never changed our law at all
> Treaty (1991)
> Mandawuy Yunupingu with
> Paul Kelly and Peter Garrett

Introduction

The colonial encounter between the settler society and Australia's indigenous peoples has been uneven in its consequences in time and space. In the east and south-west of the continent, the dispossession and forced relocation of Aboriginal people began almost from the time of the arrival of the First Fleet in 1788. In the tropical north of the Northern Territory, on the other hand, the colonial frontier did not reach the outer fringes of country fit for cattle until the late nineteenth and early twentieth centuries, and there the violently disruptive effects of settler occupation were stalled for a crucial moment in time. As a result, the Aboriginal peoples of Arnhem Land were never forced off their lands. Dispossession (through the declaration of sovereignty at a distance) and the first partial act of restitution (through the declaration of the Arnhem Land Aboriginal Reserve, comprising 960,000 square kilometres, in 1931) both occurred with few perceptible effects at the local level, and largely outside the ken of the local population. Consequently, this chapter is in some ways a study of a paradox. It concerns an encounter between the restitutive legal machinery of the settler state and a people who, although conscious of the encapsulating power of the state, had hitherto not felt themselves to be dispossessed. The 'temporalities of restitution' outlined by Fay and James in the introductory chapter are here disturbed in ways that starkly reveal the disjunctures between the 'imagined communities' of the state and its colonized subjects.

Numbering today between 5,000 and 6,000, the Yolngu-speaking people of north-east Arnhem Land are one of the most intensively studied Aboriginal groups in Australia.[1] Between 1931 and 1976 the entire Yolngu landed estate fell within the Arnhem Land Aboriginal Reserve. The 1920s had seen the start of missionary activity in the Yolngu area, with the establishment of Methodist missions at Milingimbi, Yirrkala (in 1934) and Elcho Island (Galiwin'ku). This activity was prompted by the state's desire to 'pacify' the Yolngu (classified as 'wild blacks' in the settler Australian parlance of the day), who had, a few years earlier in two separate incidents, disposed of two Euro-Australian 'adventurers' and the crew of a Japanese pearling vessel, all of whom according to Yolngu accounts had violated Yolngu law, and then killed a member of a police party sent in to apprehend the killers of the Japanese (see Williams 1986 for a fuller account of these events).

Australia has a plethora of legislation addressing the restitution of land and waters, or of certain rights in land and waters, to its Aboriginal and Torres Strait Islander peoples. The Blue Mud Bay claim over parts of the land and sea estates of a group of Yolngu clans is unusual in that it was heard simultaneously under two very different legal frameworks – the Aboriginal Land Rights (Northern Territory) Act 1976 (ALRA) and the Native Title Act 1993 (NTA). These are both Commonwealth statutes (the states also have the power to legislate on matters to do with land in their own jurisdictions), but they are very different in their scope and intent.

The Aboriginal Land Rights (Northern Territory) Act 1976 (Cwlth)

The Yolngu of the Yirrkala area were key agents in the events leading to the declaration of the ALRA in 1976. In the mid-1950s the Commonwealth government granted mining exploration licenses over the large bauxite reserves on the Gove Peninsula, where Yirrkala stands. The local Yolngu landowners were neither informed nor consulted. In 1963, when mining activities started to become evident on the land of the Gumatj clan, Yolngu leaders sent a petition on bark to the Commonwealth Parliament, on which a text in the Gumatj dialect of Yolngu-matha (Yolngu-language), with English translation, asked for a Parliamentary Inquiry into recognition of their rights to their traditional lands. The text was framed by paintings referring to the creation myths of the lands in question, which Yolngu equated to 'title deeds' to the land. When the petition failed the Yolngu went to the Supreme Court in the Northern Territory. Here they were brought face to face with the institutions of the colonial power, in what became known popularly as the Gove case.[2] The case failed, with Mr Justice Woodward finding in 1971 that although the Yolngu had proven that they had lived for thousands of years on their clan lands, Australian law could not recognize their intricate system of law in relation to land as property relations.

The announcement of this judgment coincided with a period of radicalism in the wider Australian polity that led to the election of the Whitlam Labor government in 1972. Whitlam pledged support for land rights in his election campaign, and in 1973 instituted a Commission of Inquiry under Mr Justice Woodward, who handed down his final report in 1974. Woodward recommended that the existing Aboriginal reserves in the Northern Territory should be granted to their traditional owners as inalienable freehold title in fee simple – the strongest available form of freehold title – and that a Land Commissioner be appointed to hear claims by traditional owners to unalienated Crown lands, Aboriginal-owned pastoral leases, and smaller areas on other pastoral leases and in town areas on the basis of need. Woodward envisaged that this land rights regime would also extend to waters abutting Aboriginal land for a distance of 2 km out to sea. While the ALRA legislation was being prepared the Whitlam government was dismissed from office by Australia's Governor General, and the Frazer (Liberal-Country Party) Coalition came to power. The ALRA as it was finally passed contained some significant amendments, of which one was the restriction of the extent of Aboriginal 'land' to the low water mark. As it was to transpire later, the status of the column of water over the intertidal zone remained unclear. The reason for running the Blue Mud Bay case under the ALRA alongside its running under the NTA was to clarify the status under the ALRA of this column of water.

In many ways, the passing of the ALRA was a significant moment for Aboriginal people in the Northern Territory. For the majority of those on the Arnhem Land Reserve, including most Yolngu people, it was an act of restitution that had taken place almost before effective dispossession had occurred. As originally conceived it was not primarily concerned with protecting its beneficiaries from the 'ravages of the market', but rather as an act of pure restitutive social justice.[3]

The Native Title Act 1993 (Cwlth)

The NTA is a very different piece of legislation. It had its origins in the *Mabo* decision of 1992, when the High Court of Australia recognized that the Meriam people of Torres Strait held native title over part of their traditional lands. This decision had the effect, among other things, of overturning Woodward's decision in the Gove case, and made necessary the drafting of legislation that was Australia-wide in its scope to reconcile potential native title claims with Australian common law relating to property rights. The acknowledgment of the existence of native title was originally seen as a significant victory for indigenous land rights, but it has proved to be an ambiguous one at best.[4] As it has evolved through amendments to the Act and through the precedents set by particular cases, native title as enshrined in the NTA has become increasingly restrictive in its application. It has come to be viewed as a 'bundle of rights' which may be individually extinguished by the past acts allowed or instituted by government. There are provisions for 'future acts' of extinguishment. Cases may be settled by arbitration through the National Native Title Tribunal, but if litigation is involved it takes place before a judge of the Federal Court, and that court's rules of evidence and adversarial system apply (in contrast to ALRA cases which are heard before a Land Commissioner under relaxed rules of evidence).

Perhaps most significant is the interpretation over time of the clauses relating to the proof of applicants' 'connection' to the area under claim. Applicants have to prove that their 'rights and interests are possessed under the traditional laws currently acknowledged and the traditional customs currently observed' and that they have 'a "connection" with the area in question by those traditional laws and customs'. Several cases have turned on the interpretation of the word 'traditional', to the detriment particularly of Aboriginal people in 'settled' Australia where the historical effects of colonization and dispossession are most marked.

The native title process, then, is an arena in which, among other things, the sovereignty of a colonizing society over its colonized subjects is enacted. As Julie Lahn (2007: 135) points out, native title is based on a 'radical assumption of sovereignty' and the legislation and the growing body of native title case law 'can be said to continue to exercise the power that defines sovereignty ... [a]nd in this sense, it is certainly possible to contend that native title is as implicated in ongoing processes of colonization, as providing a remedy to aspects of it'.

Colonization and encapsulation: the Yolngu view

The Yolngu response to the native title process in the Blue Mud Bay case was in continuity with a long-term tradition of political interaction with the colonizing society and its institutions.[5] It is a response that declares, in essence, 'we know we are encapsulated, but we are not colonized'. Yolngu have never fully acceded to the proposition that their sovereignty has been eclipsed by the process of colonization. When sovereignty was asserted over their region by the colonial power – in abstract and at a distance – their ancestors knew nothing of it. The colonial frontier encroached upon the fringes of their region many years later in the early years of the twentieth century, and there was no significant permanent Euro-Australian presence in the Yolngu heartlands until the establishment of the first missions in the 1920s and 1930s. At the time Yolngu did not perceive the coming of the missionaries as an act of colonization nor did they view their own response as a ceding of sovereignty. Nancy Williams writes that: 'From a Yolngu perspective it was Mawalan, as head of the land-owning Rirratjingu clan, who granted permission to Chaseling, as agent of the "mission" to establish the station at Yirrkala' (Williams 1987: 20).

For 30 years the Yolngu have held their land – but not their waters – under the ALRA. Their view of the Gove case and its aftermath is that although they lost that particular battle they won a longer war: the existence of the ALRA was perceived as a direct result of, and as a reparation for, that earlier loss. At the time of the Blue Mud Bay case, the ALRA seemed a permanent and inviolable part of the landscape. But for the Yolngu traditional owners of the Gove mine site and its associated mining town of Nhulunbuy the passing of the ALRA had represented something of a pyrrhic victory. The leases over the two sites were a fait accompli, and the traditional owners had little say over what happened in those places. Senior leaders lobbied unsuccessfully for a ban on alcohol in the mining town, fully conscious of the potential effects of its free availability. As those anticipated effects began to take hold, those Yolngu whose clan lands lay outside the immediate area, who had been drawn into Yirrkala by the Methodist mission, began to vote with their feet and return to establish permanent small settlements on their own clan estates. The outstation movement, as it became known, saw the establishment of settlements in the Blue Mud Bay area, well to the south of Yirrkala, in the early 1970s.

The Blue Mud Bay case was the first Yolngu encounter with the native title regime. From its inception, the native title 'recognition space' has been highly politicized. But the politicization of the space can come from more than one direction. Today's Yolngu are not naïve, nor are they in a state of false consciousness about the nature of the political situation in which they find themselves. They see and understand the power relations that allow the Australian state to assert its sovereignty over them. But they also consider that this sovereignty was imposed without their consent, and that there never was an act of conquest. They see the ALRA as an acknowledgement of that fact by the state, and to that extent they question the legitimacy of the state's assertion of sovereignty over their estates. In their view the native title process, too, was as much about the issue of sovereignty – at least in the sense of the recognition of the jurisdiction of Yolngu 'law' – as about 'rights', and their participation in the court process must partly be understood as a political act.

This much was clear in discussions with their representing barrister during preparations for the case. The view they put to him rhetorically was, in paraphrase: 'We know that we own our sea country under our law. Why is it not sufficient for us simply to state this to the court? Why do we have to prove our law under *ngapaki* [white] law?'.[6] The barrister's response was, in effect, that as citizens of Australia they were subject to what they were calling *ngapaki* law, that *ngapaki* law was not just for *ngapaki* but for all Australians. He acknowledged that this situation had come about through a prior act of colonization, but, to paraphrase again, 'that's just the way it is, and that's what we have to work with'.

For the late Mr Justice Selway, who heard the Blue Mud Bay native title case, sovereignty was naturally not at issue. The very existence of the Federal Court and of the NTA presupposes the sovereignty of the state, and, moreover, '[f]ollowing *Mabo (No 2)* the High Court rejected attempts to use native title as a vehicle to claim indigenous legal and political sovereignty' (Mantziaris and Martin 2000: 28). But the judge did recognize explicitly that the applicants considered this case as: 'merely the latest aspect of a more protracted campaign. For my part it is difficult to imagine what more the Yolngu people, including the claim groups, could or should have done lawfully to enforce their rights' (Selway 2005: 213).

From the anthropologist's point of view then, the Blue Mud Bay hearing can be seen as Yolngu discourse about the sovereignty of *rom* (Yolngu 'laws and customs') embedded in a native title discourse about rights under European law. In analysing this 'discourse within a discourse', this chapter looks first at the constraints created by the form and structure of the court, and then at the strategies Yolngu applied to insert their assertions of sovereignty. Their political agenda was rarely explicitly stated, but rather manifested in the strategies that they adopted in their responses to questioning and in their deliberate placement, at two carefully selected points in the proceedings, of performances of *rom*.

Performance and enactment: the ritual space of the court

A native title court is an arena for the enactment of law – European law. *Rom* is present, and it may under certain circumstances be performed, but it is not enacted in the sense of having any legal force in this arena. This distinction between performance and enactment is central to the analysis presented here, for sovereignty is asserted through enactment. In the court, European law is sovereign in that it is simultaneously performed and enacted – or is enacted through its performance, whereas *rom* is the object of discourse; it is explicated through the mediating discourse of examination and cross-examination. If performances of *rom* are inserted into the proceedings, these do not count – from the court's point of view – as enactments of *rom*. They do not even count as evidence about *rom*, unless they are also explicated in oral or written evidence.[7]

But from the Yolngu point of view (for reasons that will be elaborated later), any performance of *rom*, in whatever context, simultaneously constitutes an enactment of *rom*. Its performance in the context of the court is therefore, among other things, a demonstration of its sovereignty.

The arena

The forms and rituals of the court come as second nature to those who are expert practitioners, but they are as exotic and potentially impenetrable to Yolngu claimants in a native title case as Yolngu ritual forms are to non-Yolngu.

The performance space – the courtroom – is a constructed ritual space. This much was obvious to Yolngu because the court was held in a building at Yirrkala to which everyone normally has access – the adult education centre. The space was transformed symbolically by the placing of the symbol of the court – the Australian coat of arms bearing the figure of the kangaroo and the emu – at the front of the room, and then this symbolic space was divided into clear zones.[8] In front of the kangaroo and emu stood a table – the 'bench' – at which sat the judge and his associate. The court recorders sat to one side and the witness and the interpreter sat opposite them, to the other side of the judge.

The space between these two flanking tables was empty. Facing the judge across this space were two lines of tables and chairs. The first row was occupied by the teams for the applicants and the most active respondents (the Northern Territory and Commonwealth governments), including the expert witnesses, and the second by the less active respondents and me (an expert witness with a non-speaking part). This completed the arena in which action took place. In the back half of the room, again separated by an empty space from the actors in the proceedings, was the space for the 'public' to sit.

Adjoining the public court there was a restricted space to which only the judge and the court officials had access.[9] The entry of the judge from the restricted space into the public space took place through a door at the front of the court. Everyone else entered through the door at the rear of the court.[10]

Who gets to speak, and how

The Australian court system has an elaborate set of rules for proper discourse, in which different actors have different roles according to their status and function. Certain categories of persons can speak publicly; others – solicitors and expert witnesses who are not on the stand – can give written advice to their colleagues with speaking parts, but may not themselves speak. The discourse rules are well understood and are manipulated (with varying degrees of subtlety) by the actors in the court who have legal training, but they are not transparent to, nor are they explicitly laid out for, the 'lay' actors – the witnesses – who must attempt to learn the rules as they go along. The system is also hierarchical, and that hierarchy is made manifest in the degree of constraint to which different actors must submit themselves. At the top of the hierarchy is the judge, who is the least constrained. It would appear that he or she can speak at any time, freely interrupting the speech of others.

The hierarchy of constraints is ostensibly designed to control the flow of information into the official record of the court, in such a way as to maximize the production of objective 'facts' that are relevant in law to the particular case, according to a particular set of 'rules of evidence'. It is a highly positivist enterprise. In native title cases it has a paradoxical effect, when viewed from the perspective of the applicants – the purported 'native title holders'. They, who are the most knowledgeable about their own system of 'laws and customs', have the most severely curtailed rights to speak in the body of the court. They may only speak when spoken to. Their barrister, who has spent time with them preparing the case and is likely to have more knowledge of their 'laws and customs' than any of the other counsel present, is bound by the rules of evidence to act 'as if' he knew nothing, because he may not ask leading questions – that is, he may not ask questions that contain knowledge that he and the applicants know that they all hold in common.[11]

Prior to the court hearing, a set of detailed witness statements had been prepared. The witnesses had understood that these were to form the basis of questioning that they would be facing in the court hearing. There had been some discussion at the directions hearings preceding the court hearing about how these statements were to be used. The respondents had wanted full statements in writing, and to have the portions to which they raised no objections accepted as the witnesses' evidence in chief. In the case of objections, the relevant paragraphs were to be lead orally from the witnesses. Counsel for the applicants had objected to this process. He favoured providing summaries of the evidence and otherwise leading evidence orally. The judge noted his objection to the process advocated by the respondents.

The judge was concerned to make the proceedings as short as possible. Accordingly, at the beginning of the court proceedings large portions of the witness statements were indeed accepted into evidence, with no objection from the respondents. But there remained certain paragraphs or sentences that the respondents did not allow into evidence, and insisted should be the subject of oral examination in the court. Although the counsel for the applicants was not explicitly confined to leading only the evidence in these excised portions of the witness statements, in practice the timetable set by the judge made it impracticable to do anything else.[12] As a result, the witnesses found themselves being asked a very narrow range of questions.[13] Towards the end, the last witness (X) obliquely voiced his frustration with this state of affairs:

> *Counsel for the applicants (CA):* Now, I'll move on to [paragraph] 66 [of X's witness statement]. Just – this deals with, X, this deals with the idea of catching a turtle or a big animal on a person's country. Can you tell us what happens when if you catch a turtle or a big animal on somebody else's country?
>
> X: Yes, I think we are all aware about that. We had three – six people sitting down here telling the same stories. Now I'm going to do the same thing and tell the same stories. When we get turtle from – from another country . . .[14]

The counsel acting for the respondents are free to ask leading questions if they so wish, and are not confined to leading evidence from the witness statements. They may even, as a tactic, pose questions that are deliberately founded on ignorance or wilful misunderstanding of the facts. The latter were sometimes deliberately deployed to attempt to confuse the witness, or to lead them towards a conclusion that they would not freely subscribe to.

From the point of view of the uninitiated – Yolngu or non-Yolngu – the structure of the discourse imposed by the court seemed designed, whether intentionally or not, to emphasize the power of the European law by systematically constraining the ability of the knowledgeable practitioners of *rom* to express *rom* clearly in its own terms and in its fullness.

This was a paradoxical effect, because the judge's intention had been quite different. He was proceeding from the premise that he only needed to know from the witnesses that which was relevant to native title law and the ALRA – it was not his role, as he said, to become an anthropologist or an expert in Yolngu law. He was also clearly concerned to minimize the adversarial aspects of the judiciary process on the witnesses: he enjoined the respondents not to attack their credit, and he clearly wished to set limits on the number of witnesses, and on the length of their appearances on the stand, not simply to expedite the hearing and confine proceedings to what he saw as the relevant facts, but also to minimize the potential for adverse impacts on the Yolngu claimant group.

To some extent, then, the judge and the claimants were at cross-purposes. While the judge was concerned to minimize the impact of the proceedings on the claimants, the claimants were concerned to produce as much of an impact on the court as they could. They saw the court as a platform for demonstrating the power of *rom* and the depth of their knowledge about it – as a site for persuasion.[15] This is in continuity with earlier Yolngu views of the court in the Gove case, as described by Nancy Williams:

> The Yolngu leaders perceived the court less in adversary terms than as a setting where their role was to assist the court to learn about their ownership of land. They saw an opportunity 'to explain', and *explanation in their terms involved 'to demonstrate'* . . . *For the Yolngu the situation was marked by explanation that would result in understanding*. They found it difficult to accommodate defence counsel's mode of questioning, and of attempting to elicit from them inconsistent or contradictory responses . . . the Yolngu leaders were unprepared for a situation in which Europeans explain only enough to 'win'.
> (Williams 1986: 159; emphasis added)

During the proofing stage of the Gove land rights case WEH Stanner and the claimants' solicitor Frank Purcell were taken to a place where they were shown sacred objects. Stanner recalled: 'One of the men said to me: "Now you understand". He meant that I had seen the holy *rangga* which in a sense is the clan's title deeds to its land, and heard what they stood for: so I could not but "understand" ' (Stanner 1979: 278).

In the Blue Mud Bay case, the claimants were more conversant with the conventions of court hearings than their forebears had been, having had more direct or indirect experience of the adversarial system in the intervening years. However, the connections between explanation, demonstration and understanding, as detailed by Williams and Stanner, hold equally strongly for Yolngu today.

The witness statement – neither fish nor fowl?

From a sociolinguistic point of view, the 'witness statement' is an interesting and problematic document. The judge in this case considered it to be a valuable tool. In his judgment (Selway 2005) he said in part:

> 182 . . . in many cases it is convenient to have evidence in chief given wholly or largely by means of a prepared statement. This not only reduces the time involved in the hearing – it also assists in ensuring that the applicant's case is prepared well in advance of trial and that the respondent(s) is not taken by surprise . . .
>
> 183 I accept that this may need to be qualified in relation to some witnesses who may be disadvantaged by this course, which may include some Aboriginal witnesses . . . However, I do not think that those disadvantages arose in this case. The Yolngu witnesses were all obviously intelligent. Most of them seemed relatively sophisticated as to the ways of European society . . . All the witnesses were senior law men in relation to a legal system of considerable complexity. These are not simple and naïve people. *Subject to potential issues arising from translation between Yolngu language and English* I do not think that the Yolngu witnesses were disadvantaged by the procedure adopted.
>
> (emphasis added)

I would not quarrel with His Honour's concluding sentence, in this particular case. However, I want to pick up on the phrase that has been italicized. For the process involved in the construction of a witness statement is much more complex than this, and it is not, strictly speaking, translation.

If it were possible to translate word for word between Yolngu-matha and English, and if we were only dealing with 'layman's' English, then maybe the process would be straightforward. Once the lawyers had written up the statements in English, it would simply be a matter of reading the statement back to the witness (or translating it word for word into Yolngu-matha and reading it back), or getting the witness to read the statement over for themselves. The Yolngu witness might find the formal style of the statement unfamiliar, but that would not be a barrier to comprehension. However, neither of these 'ifs' hold.

First, there are very few words that can be translated literally from one language to the other. There is, for example, no English equivalent of the word *gurru*t*u*, and no Yolngu-matha equivalent of the English word 'permission' (see Figure 6.1). For an English speaker to understand what *gurru*t*u* means, it is necessary for them to be familiar with the operation of the Yolngu kinship system, and for a Yolngu person to understand what 'permission' means (in the context of native title) it is necessary for them to be familiar with Anglo-Australian notions of property.

Second, and this is something the Yolngu witnesses are not privy to, many of the words that appear in witness statements – words like 'permission', 'speak for', 'resource', 'sing for' and 'connection' – have come to have particular meanings for lawyers who work in native title. Some are defined in the NTA itself, which gives them status as legalese; others are quasi-legalese – terms that have commonly been used by lawyers in native title cases, and which are in the process of definition as legal terms, with very particular meanings. The trouble is that they sound like ordinary English words. So a phrase like 'without first having to ask permission' could conceivably mean something very different to the Yolngu witness to whom it is read from what it means to the lawyer who reads it to him – even if that witness has reflected at length on what 'permission' might be equivalent to in the Yolngu system (as at least one witness had done). To a Yolngu who has not reflected on the meaning of the word, the phrase is, quite possibly, meaningless.[16]

With a moment's reflection, it is possible to see that the 'translation' of a witness statement 'back' into Yolngu-matha so that it can be verified as his own by a Yolngu witness with poor English, is a near impossible task, and one that

Yolngu-matha concept, e.g. *gurru*t*u*, with no direct translation equivalent in English.	A statement by a Yolngu witness, in English, about 'permission': For example, my mother's mother came from X... yeah, I still have permit, or permission which is, that's *balanda dhäruk* [English word], our *dhäruk* is *gurru*t*u*. I always know in my mind that I always call that country is my *märi* [mother's mother]...
Statement is read to the witness by the NLC lawyer, with an interpreter present to assist, amended if necessary, and then **sworn** by the witness.	A statement about permission as written up by the NLC lawyers as part of a witness's affidavit: I can go hunting, camping or travelling across W, X, Y or Z countries, without first having to ask **permission** of the owning clan. This is because I have **close relationships** with these clans and because I know the countries.

Figure 6.1 Problems of translation.

would be extremely time consuming. For such a document is a hybrid.[17] It purports to be the statement by the witness about 'laws and customs' (*rom*), but it is to some degree actually a lawyer's statement about native title. It belongs fully to neither of its authors, and its meaning is inherently indeterminate.

The witness statement is a particular instance of what Mantziaris and Martin have in mind when they write that:

> native title involves a process of translation from indigenous 'relations' defined by traditional law and custom to native title rights and interests enforceable within the Australian legal system. This process of translation becomes difficult, or impossible, when the terms of the translation are incommensurable.
> (Mantziaris and Martin 2000: 29)

I do not take the strong position that incommensurability is inevitable and always uncircumventable. However, I do take the witness statement to be an instance of 'enforced commensurability' in the context of an unequal power relation.

The Yolngu response

I now turn to a consideration of how the Yolngu witnesses viewed this arena, how they chose to act in it, and to what end. Although the witness is the most constrained of any of the actors in the court, there is still scope for alternative ways of acting in that role. It is fair to say that the Yolngu witnesses had a very precise appreciation of the ritual nature of the court and of the power relations that obtained within it. The second point on which most witnesses were pretty clear was the nature of the hierarchical relationship between customary law and native title, within the context of the court. But it is one thing to acknowledge differential power, and quite another to acquiesce to the legitimacy of the relationships so constituted, or to view them as just.

I will discuss two kinds of action that the Yolngu took within the constraints placed upon them, and their reasons for those actions. The first is the insertion of performances of *rom*. The second is the Yolngu commentary on difference, and insistence on difference, and on the need for *rom* to be seen in its own terms – the insistence on incommensurability. Through both these kinds of actions Yolngu were making statements about sovereignty, not simply about 'rights'.

The insertion of performance: sacred power made manifest

The Yolngu announced to the court that they wished to perform a short ceremony before the court started in order to 'welcome' the judge and the court. This wish was granted. A group of men, followed by women, all wearing white paint on their foreheads, processed into the court chanting loudly and calling out ceremonial names of the country to the accompaniment of clapsticks. They bore with them two very large public ceremonial objects representing the walking sticks of Yirritja moiety ancestral beings associated with a place within the claim area called Gänganbuy, richly adorned with feather-string. The choice to evoke this place was very deliberate. For the Yolngu clans of the Blue Mud Bay area it is the place from which the *rom* of the Yirritja moiety originates.

In order to accommodate the performance inside the courtroom it was necessary to disrupt the spatial ordering of the native title court by moving aside the tables and chairs facing the judge's 'bench', where the judge sat. The performance in the confined space of the court was visually and aurally extremely powerful – the lawyers and other court officials were displaced to the periphery of the arena. The judge, significantly, was not; he sat at his 'bench' throughout the performance, which ended with the ceremonial objects being laid against the bench, and the Yolngu leaving the court. The court space was reconstituted, the ceremonial objects were moved out of the courtroom, and the court then got down to its business. But for a moment, it must have seemed to the non-Yolngu present, as it certainly did to the Yolngu, that *rom* had momentarily displaced Australian law in its own space.

The second insertion of a performance of *rom* took place on the first site visit to the homeland settlement of Yilpara on Blue Mud Bay itself. The Yolngu had chosen this time very carefully, situating it near the beginning of the proceedings, and had been preparing for it for months. The male members of the court were taken to the men's ceremonial ground. Female members of the court, by consent, and including the female counsel for one of the respondent groups, were led to the edge of the ceremonial space, but then were led back (by me under instruction from the ceremonial leaders) to sit with the women in the main settlement while the men went to the restricted ground. As the men returned the women (including the non-Yolngu women) sat with their backs to them, only turning under instruction when the men were close. This was not just a performance of *rom* in its own ritual space, but an enactment that incorporated the members of the Federal Court as actors, under the terms and the strictly defined gender differentiations of *rom*.

The advantages of giving 'non-evidence'[18]

These two ritual performances could have been admitted as evidence, had the ground to do so been prepared. But before the welcoming performance, no one had suggested to counsel for the applicants that it should be regarded as having evidential content. In the case of the performance on the ceremonial ground, there was an issue about procedural fairness, because the other parties had had no opportunity to ask questions, at the time of the performance, about what was happening. The judge was concerned about what an appeal court would make of the event in the absence of a transcript or other recording of it. His decision in the end was to treat it as a 'view', 'to be understood by me as a background or context to understand later evidence'.[19] He considered it to have been a 'wonderful experience',[20] and went further when counsel for the applicants tried to persuade him that at least the explanatory statements made by one of the witnesses in the 'restricted session' could be regarded as evidence:

> CA: ... I appreciate – I accept fully that my learned friends haven't any or any adequate opportunity to cross-examine, but that ...
> HH: But they didn't have any capacity to object. It was – *the Federal Court of Australia was not in session*. I can't see how anyone could think we were in session. It wasn't –
> CA: Well, I'm in your Honour's hands.
> HH: *It would have been completely inappropriate, completely rude, completely out of the question for that to be the Federal Court of Australia having a session.*
> CA: I hear what your Honour says.
> HH: It simply was not that. That's not what it was.[21]

Although the judge did not then elaborate as to 'what it was', the implication was clear. The men's ceremonial ground – or perhaps the nature of the performance that took place there – was not within the jurisdiction of the Federal Court. Had the Yolngu submitted these performances as evidence, this arguably would have lessened their force, because once situated within the frame of the court as 'evidence', they would have been deemed by the court to be performances but not enactments.

These Yolngu performances were deployed in a politics of persuasion, as part of their embedded discourse about sovereignty. Although not evidence, the power of these performances, in their enactment, inevitably became part of the wider context in which their evidence in court was then heard.

The Yolngu were not necessarily fully aware of the court's distinction between performance as 'evidence' and performance as 'view', nor of its legal implications. Nor was it relevant to them, in that, to borrow Nancy Williams' terminology, demonstration is in and of itself explanation in the Yolngu view. Indeed, the informal space of the 'view' is arguably the most effective space for an embedded discourse about sovereignty precisely because it is not subject to the adversarial discourse of cross-examination. Thus the Yolngu had achieved exactly what they had set out to do in their two ritual performances. They had estimated, correctly, that the person whose opinion really mattered was the judge's, and they had asserted that *rom* had its own jurisdiction, by enacting it through performance.[22]

What happens to the discourse about sovereignty when it becomes overt in the context of the court is demonstrated by the following passage from the court transcript – an exchange between the counsel for one of the respondent parties and witness W:

CR: ... Now, in that paragraph you say that Yolngu law applies to everyone on Yolngu country whether they are Yolngu or Aboriginals from other parts of Australia or even non-Aboriginal people; is that right? Does Yolngu law apply to non-Aboriginal people just because they're on Yolngu country?
W: Yes.
CR: So you really expect non-Aboriginal people who are on Yolngu country to follow all of Yolngu law?
W: Yes.
CR: Okay. Now, under Yolngu law people are either Dhuwa or Yirritja, is that right?
W: Yes.
CR: But non-Aboriginal people like the ones living at Nhulunbuy, they're living on Yolngu country, aren't they?
W: Yes.
CR: But they're not either Dhuwa or Yirritja, are they?
W: No.[23]

The same question and answer routine was then deployed to extract a 'no' answer about clan membership, initiation ceremonies, and correct behaviour with kin, and the passage ended thus:

CR: So really Yolngu law doesn't apply to non-Yolngu people, does it, just because they're on Yolngu country?
W: Yes, it does.[24]

It is hard to know what counsel for the respondent was trying to achieve here, apart from the undermining of the witness's confidence to soften him up for subsequent questions. It was notable that he did not touch on those aspects of 'Yolngu law' relevant to native title – aspects relating to permission – until after this exchange. W's final response is interesting, since it seems at face value to be merely defiant, and to be unsupported by his answers to the previous questions.[25] It is, however, supported by a deeper logic concerning the nature of sovereignty.

Ancestral forces insert their own performance

On the second site visit it seemed that the sea itself had decided to make manifest its ancestral forces. In the preceding days it had been like a millpond. Indeed, this time of year had been chosen for the hearings because it was usually a time when Mungurru, this named body of deep saltwater, was calm.[26] But when the court arrived at Blue Mud Bay on the day appointed for the view by boat, the weather had worsened. The party set off in two big boats and an aluminium dinghy, but once out in the bay, in big seas, it became clear that the view would have to be aborted. The dinghy turned back first. The judge, fortunately, was in the biggest and best-protected boat, and he and the witnesses and barristers who were with him suffered only a bit of a buffeting. Those of us in the second boat returned somewhat battered, shivering and soaked to the skin.

In the boat, at the height of the battering, one of the interpreters had said to me, *sotto voce*, 'they won't forget the name of Mungurru now'. Later on the same day I heard Yolngu saying to one another that Mungurru had been offended by the presence of so many strangers. At least some of the non-Yolngu who experienced the power of Mungurru on that day were prepared to give some credence to this idea, or at least to acknowledge the strength of the Yolngu belief. In court the next day, the following exchange took place between one of the respondents' barristers and the witness who was then in the box:

> CR: ... Mr X, a last question from me: yesterday when we went out to sea, it was very rough; do you have a belief or an explanation as to why it was rough yesterday?
> X: I felt it myself too. Yes, I felt it; maybe the country didn't want us, or the sea didn't want us.
> CR: Was that the Mungurru you think?
> X: That's the Mungurru I'm talking about.
> CR: So was that the reaction you think he may have had?
> X: Yes.
> CR: Thanks very much, Mr X.
> X: Thank you.[27]

The Mungurru episode and its interpretation holds the key to understanding W's final assertion – that Yolngu law does apply to non-Yolngu people – in the passage quoted above, and to the Yolngu insistence on incommensurability discussed below. For the basis of *rom*, in the Yolngu view, is not something that they as human agents have the power to determine. It is determined – always was and always will be – by the ancestral creator beings of the Yolngu world, and such forces are not something over which humans – any humans – have sovereignty. In that sense then, Euro-Australian law can never have sovereignty over *rom*, no matter what mundane power relations hold, in a political sense, between the two communities.

The insistence on difference

Technically speaking, Yolngu are Australian citizens and Australian law is 'their' law as much as it is any other Australian's. But their way of modelling the relationship between the two laws shows clearly that they view the matter rather differently. As one witness put it:

> We're living in the two worlds today, for example. Your world is change

every day or every month or every year. My law and my story, it can't change.[28]

It is not simply that Yolngu value their difference and assert their 'right' to be different. From their point of view it is not a matter of choice. They feel themselves to be fundamentally and intrinsically different from 'white' people because of their relationship to their country and its ancestral forces. As the same witness put it, succinctly, 'You stand for power, white people, but we stand for our land and the sea'.[29]

In the context of the court hearing, Yolngu constantly asserted difference. They pointed out the non-equivalence of concepts, and the problems of translation between the two systems, and in particular they asserted the permanence of *rom* (as opposed to 'law'). Here is just one example of several, in which a witness's evidence is being led by the counsel for the applicants. There are many things going on in this dialogue. One is an assertion of the difference between Yolngu *rom* and Euro-Australian 'law', but there is also, in effect, a debate about the nature of the translation process, in which Yolngu are compelled to use English terms such as 'law' when talking about their own institutions:

> CA: ... you mentioned your law, or 'our law' I think you said. Well, what do you mean by that? What do you mean by your 'law'?
> X: My law.
> CA: Yes.
> X: Well, what's that 'law' mean?
> CA: That's right.
> X: What in your ...
> CA: That's the question I'm asking you.
> X: I'm asking too: what is 'the law' means?
> CA: Well, you ...
> X: In *balanda* [English/white person's] way, what youse call it?
> CA: You – you said, 'Under our law, we line the turtle shells up', as I understood you.
> X: Okay, exactly ...
> CA: That's part of your law. What did you ...
> X: Well, exactly what I'm talking now. When I'm using *balanda* English, well, you should know better than me, you know, because I'm – I'm talking in Yolngu way too you know? My – my tongues are turning around, like, Yolngu way I'm talking, and if I'm using your English now, you should understand this is new to me ... my really language is Yolngu language ... And I cannot – you know, when you talk to me, you know – what is Yolngu story, what this 'law' means, you know, well, I just pick up the English, 'law'. My *ngarraku rom*, my *ngarraku rom* is different. I call it *rom*.[30]
> CA: And what does that word mean?

> X: Well, I'm telling you it – the law been there forever. It was given from our ancestors to our grandfathers to our father to me. This is what I call *rom* and law. I'm just putting that English into my – in my way of using of – using or thinking, you know, law. You call it law; I call it *rom*.[31]

This insistence on incommensurability might not necessarily have been to the applicants' advantage in the context of a native title hearing. And it is notable that X introduced it in a dialogue *with his own counsel*. He was, in effect, restating the Yolngu position as summarized earlier. Yolngu *rom* has been encapsulated by *ngapaki* (*balanda*) law, but it has not been colonized by it. It cannot be – it remains distinct, it is everlasting, and it is incommensurable with *ngapaki* law. In this witness's view, stated in another context, so long as Yolngu hold fast to their own *rom* they will be Yolngu. If they abandon *rom*, the *rom* will remain in the country, but Yolngu will no longer be Yolngu – they will just be 'Aborigines'. Yolngu identity is thus deeply bound to the fundamental underlying principles of governance generated by *rom*. It is, as they say, the 'foundation' of their existence and identity.

Native title as a process seeks to impose commensurability between *rom* and law in order to make the former legible to the latter, and so potentially 'recognisable'. In the face of this, Yolngu find themselves in a complex double bind. To submit *rom* to commensurability is in itself impossible in the Yolngu view, whatever the pretensions of the *ngapaki* native title law. To submit their own conceptualization of *rom* to a process of enforced commensurability risks alienation from *rom*, and from their identity as Yolngu. Yet in resisting commensurability they potentially deny themselves advantages that might accrue from recognition of 'their' native title. Their response to this double bind – seeking to maintain a discourse about sovereignty within the dominant discourse of native title – was equally complex.

Conclusion

At the time of writing, the Blue Mud Bay case is still in the court system. The initial determination found that Yolngu have exclusive native title to their land country and non-exclusive native title to their sea country, and while Mr Justice Selway felt himself bound by the *Yarmirr* decision in the High Court to say that exclusive native title rights and land rights under the ALRA do not extend to the waters over the intertidal zone, this did not, in his opinion, reflect the situation under customary law which is no different to that on the land proper:

> The Northern Territory also submitted that the evidence did not establish a right to exclusive occupation of the sea. In this regard the Northern Territory referred me to the factual findings of Olney J in Yarmirr TJ. In that case his Honour was not satisfied that the relevant Aboriginal tradition

involved a right of exclusive possession. I can only assume that his Honour was faced with different evidence to that which is before me.

(Selway 2005: 214)[32]

This initial finding can be seen as a partial victory – the most that could realistically be expected under the native title regime. It states, in effect, that prior to colonization *rom* was sovereign both on the land and in the sea. But the Yolngu did not see this as a victory, and nor indeed was it, in terms of realpolitik, since it did not give them the present-day control that they were seeking over their sea country. For his part, Mr Justice Selway regarded his conclusions as problematic for reasons to do with the relative status of various kinds of European law, particularly the status of the common law 'right to fish' as against the status of fee simple under the ALRA, thus giving possible grounds for appeal. In the appeal to the Federal Court, three Federal Court judges overturned the part of his determination relating to the operation of the ALRA in the intertidal zone, so that the waters over the intertidal zone now come under the ALRA (at least for the moment), and Yolngu (and all other traditional owners with coastal estates on ALRA land) have the right to exclude others from their intertidal waters. The case was due to go to the High Court in Canberra, in early December 2007.

In the 'recognition space' of the native title arena the Yolngu, despite convincing the Judge that under their customary law they had the right to exclude others from their sea country, failed to get that exclusive right recognized in Australian law. Their interim victory on first appeal relies on the ALRA rather than native title, so has no implications for others outside the ALRA lands. From the perspective of the applicants if not from that of adherents of Euro-Australian legal procedure, involvement in the appeals process is shot through with ironies. The only protagonists in this process are judges and other lawyers – practitioners of Australian law. If Yolngu attend it is only as 'the public', although it is the fate of their sea country and of their relationship to it that is in the balance.

The Yolngu experience of the native title process has thus far been relatively benign, certainly by comparison with the experiences of some other claimant groups (see, for example, Redmond 2007). They started from a position of strength. They already held their land country under ALRA. Like claimants in several of the other case studies in the present book (see Chapters 5, Nadasdy; 4, Plaice, in this book), they had never been alienated from or forced off their land estates so that many of the issues about identity faced by actively dispossessed people did not arise. As a collectivity they were able to show a united front, and to put forward a coherent, consistent and convincing account of their system of 'laws and customs'. There were no competing claims. They brought to the arena a strong view of themselves as uncolonized subjects. The fact that part of the case related to ALRA rather than to native title was also an advantage, since under ALRA there was the prospect of gaining delimited exclusive rights, whereas under native title, because of *Yarmirr*, there was really no prospect of gaining exclusive rights to the sea. They also encountered a judge with whom they were able to forge a relationship of mutual respect, even if neither party fully understood the other's agenda. The combination of Mr Justice Selway's clear insistence on the limits of his interests in the case, legally speaking, and his evident respect for their system of 'laws and customs', provided a space for Yolngu to reaffirm their sense of sovereignty – at least to themselves, and for the time being. Through resisting commensurability in the court, they have been able also to hold firmly to their 'two worlds' model, in which the state's particular objectification of 'their' native title is seen by them as essentially irrelevant to *rom* and the social field that is founded in it.

This view of relative strength, however, must be counterposed against the limitations placed upon its eventual realization. In the court's terms the dialogue could be perceived at most as being about jurisdiction, and 'rights'. In the longer term the Yolngu view of themselves as encapsulated but not colonized – as 'living in two worlds' – will come under increasing pressure. They have been able to sustain that view until now because ALRA, unlike most European law, appeared immutable. In reality, however, it can be changed like any other piece of Euro-Australian law, and its effects can be substantially undermined by a government with the will and the power to do so. The current neo-liberal Commonwealth government views the ALRA not as it was originally conceived but as an impediment to the 'development' of the Northern Territory's remote Aboriginal populations, in a manner similar to that described by Nadasdy (see Chapter 5, in this book). The state wants to let the market loose on the ALRA lands, and because it currently has control of the Senate as well as the House of Representatives in Australia's bicameral system, it has the power to alter the ALRA. It has already begun the process, and if it wins the upcoming election, the Northern Territory will likely see the entrenchment of an 'end to restitution' that closely parallels processes described by Tiedje (see Chapter 11, in this book) for Mexico. Whether the Yolngu sense of their sovereignty as people will survive such a process, only time will tell. It would only collapse, in their view, if they were to abandon *rom* for a more generic state of colonized Aboriginality.

References

Barnes, J (1967) 'Inquest on the Murngin', *Royal Anthropological Institute Occasional Paper No. 26*, London: Royal Anthropological Institute.
Berndt, RM (1951) *Gunapipi*, Melbourne: Cheshire.
—— (1952) *Djanggawul*, London: Routledge and Keegan Paul.
—— (1962) *An Adjustment Movement in Arnhem Land*, Paris: Mouton.
Berndt, R and C Berndt (1984) 'Collection of Essays on Aboriginal Land Rights for the Guidance of the Government of Western Australia Aboriginal Land Inquiry 1983–1984', Special Issue, *Anthropological Forum*, 5(3).
Claudie, D (2007) ' "We're Tired from Talking": The native title process from the perspective of Kaanju People living on homelands, Wenlock and Pascoe Rivers, Cape York

Peninsula', in B Smith and F Morphy (eds) *The Social Effects of Native Title: Recognition, Translation, Coexistence*, CAEPR Research Monograph No. 27, Canberra: ANU E Press. PDF. Available at http://epress.anu.edu.au (accessed 31 October 2007).

Evans, N (2002) 'Country and the Word: linguistic evidence in the Croker sea claim', in J Henderson and D Nash (eds) *Language in Native Title*, Native Title Research Series, Canberra: Aboriginal Studies Press.

Gawirrin Gumana & Ors v Northern Territory of Australia & Ors (2004) Federal Court Transcript.

Hiatt, L (1984) *Aboriginal Landowners: Contemporary Issues in the Determination of Traditional Aboriginal Land Ownership*, Oceania Monograph No. 27, Sydney: University of Sydney.

Keen, I (1994) *Knowledge and Secrecy in an Aboriginal Religion: Yolngu of North-East Arnhem Land*, Oxford: Clarendon Press.

—— (2003) *Aboriginal Economy and Society on the Threshold of Colonisation*, Melbourne: Oxford University Press.

Lahn, J (2007) 'Native Title and the Torres Strait: encompassment and recognition in the Central Islands', in B Smith and F Morphy (eds) *The Social Effects of Native Title: Recognition, Translation, Coexistence*, CAEPR Research Monograph No. 27, Canberra: ANU E Press. PDF. Available at http://epress.anu.edu.au (accessed 31 October 2007).

Maddock, K (1970) 'Rethinking the Murngin Problem: a review article', *Oceania* 41: 77–87.

Mantziaris, C and D Martin (2000) *Native Title Corporations: A Legal and Anthropological Analysis*, Sydney: The Federation Press.

Merlan, F (1998) *Caging The Rainbow: Places, Politics, and Aborigines in a North Australian Town*, Honolulu, HI: University of Hawai'i Press.

Morphy, H (1983) ' "Now you understand": an analysis of the way Yolngu have used sacred knowledge to retain their autonomy', in N Peterson and M Langton (eds) *Aborigines, Land and Land Rights*, Canberra: Australian Institute of Aboriginal Studies Press.

—— (1984) *Journey to the Crocodile's Nest*, Canberra: Australian Institute of Aboriginal Studies.

—— (1991) Ancestral *Connections: Art and an Aboriginal System of Knowledge*, Chicago, IL: University of Chicago Press.

Morphy, H and F Morphy (2001) 'The Spirit of the Plains Kangaroo', in T Bonyhady and T Griffiths (eds) *Words for Country: Landscape and Language in Australia*, Sydney: University of New South Wales Press.

—— (2006) 'Tasting the Waters: discriminating identities in the waters of Blue Mud Bay', *Journal of Material Culture* 11(1/2): 67–85.

Peterson, N (in collaboration with J Long) (1986) *Aboriginal Territorial Organization: a Band Perspective*, Oceania Monograph No. 30, Sydney: University of Sydney.

Povinelli, E (2002) *The Cunning of Recognition: Indigenous Alterity and the Making of Australian Multiculturalism*, Durham, NC: Duke University Press.

Redmond, A (2007) 'Some Initial Effects of Pursuing and Achieving Native Title Recognition in the Northern Kimberley', in B Smith and F Morphy (eds) *The Social Effects of Native Title: Recognition, Translation, Coexistence*, CAEPR Research Monograph No. 27, Canberra: ANU E Press. PDF. Available at http://epress.anu.edu.au (accessed 31 October 2007).

Reid, J (1983) *Sorcerers and Healing Spirits: Continuity and Change in an Aboriginal Medical System*, Canberra: Australian National University Press.

Rumsey, A (1989) 'Language Groups in Australian Aboriginal Land Claims', *Anthropological Forum* 6(1): 69–79.

Selway, J (2005) 'The "Blue Mud Decision" *Gumana v Northern Territory of Australia*' [2005] FCA 50.

Shapiro, W (1981) *Miwuyt Marriage: the Cultural Anthropology of Affinity in Northeast Arnhem Land*, Philadelphia, PA: ISHI.

Smith, B (2003) ' "All been washed away now": tradition, change and indigenous knowledge in a Queensland Aboriginal land claim', in J Pottier, A Bicker and P Sillitoe (eds) *Negotiating Local Knowledge: Power and Identity in Development*, London: Pluto Press.

Smith, B and F Morphy (eds) (2007) *The Social Effects of Native Title: Recognition, Translation, Coexistence*, CAEPR Research Monograph No. 27, Canberra: ANU E Press. PDF. Available at http://epress.anu.edu.au (accessed 31 October 2007).

Stanner, WEH (1979) 'The Yirrkala Case: dress-rehearsal', in WEH Stanner, *White Man Got No Dreaming: Essays by WEH Stanner*, Canberra: Australian National University Press.

Sutton, P (2003) *Native Title in Australia: An Ethnographic Perspective*, Cambridge: Cambridge University Press.

Thomson, DF (1949) *Economic Structure and the Ceremonial Exchange Cycle in Arnhem Land*, Melbourne: Macmillan.

Toussaint, S (2004) *Crossing Boundaries: Cultural, Legal, Historical and Practice Issues in Native Title*, Melbourne: Melbourne University Press.

Warner, WL (1958) *A Black Civilization*, Chicago, IL: Harper and Row.

Williams, N (1986) *The Yolngu and Their Land: A System of Land Tenure and the Fight for Its Recognition*, Canberra: Australian Institute of Aboriginal Studies.

—— (1987) *Two Laws: Managing Disputes in a Contemporary Aboriginal Community*, Canberra, Australian Institute of Aboriginal Studies.

Notes

I thank Sturt Glacken for his thoughtful and perspicacious comments on the first draft of this chapter, and for saving me from solecisms that were the product of my unfamiliarity with matters of the law. I would like to have addressed all his comments, but that would have turned this into a different – and longer – chapter. The second draft benefited greatly from Tom Keely's detailed comments, and I hope that I have gone some way towards taking them properly into account. I also thank Daniel Lavery, David Martin, Howard Morphy and Rebecca Morphy for their comments on the second draft. Needless to say, all remaining solecisms and errors of fact or interpretation are my responsibility alone.

1 The Yolngu have been the subject of several significant anthropological monographs; roughly in chronological order according to when the authors undertook their fieldwork, these include Warner (1958), Thomson (1949), Berndt (1951, 1952, 1962), Shapiro (1981), Peterson (1986), Williams (1986, 1987), Reid (1983), Morphy (1984, 1991) and Keen (1994, 2003). The complex, asymmetrical Yolngu kinship system was the subject of the 'Murngin controversy' that occupied much space in anthropological journals in the 1960s (see, for example, Barnes 1967; Maddock 1970).

2 For a detailed account of this case (*Milirrpum v Nabalco and the Commonwealth of Australia*) and the Yolngu response see Williams (1986).
3 There is developed anthropological literature – which includes a significant critical dimension that I do not have the space to explore here – on Australia's various State and Territory Aboriginal Land Rights Acts. See for example Berndt and Berndt (1984); Hiatt (1984); Merlan (1998); Morphy and Morphy (2001); Rumsey (1989); Smith (2003).
4 See the contributions to Smith and Morphy (2007) for a detailed examination of the social effects of native title cases in a variety of contexts. Although they maintain a focus on native title practice, Sutton (2003) and Toussaint (2004) also both make valuable contributions to the anthropological theorization of native title, whilst Povinelli (2002) contains a significant critique of the effects of native title.
5 The initial determination of the Blue Mud Bay case can be found at *Gawirrin Gumana v Northern Territory of Australia (No. 2)* [2005] FCA 1425. The determination of the Full Federal Court hearing may be found at *Gumana v Northern Territory of Australia* [2007] FCAFC 23. Links to the two determinations may be found on the website of the National Native Title tribunal at www.nntt.gov.au/ntdetermination/1136779170_3832.html (accessed 4 September 2007).
6 David Claudie, a Kaanju political leader and elder from Cape York Peninsula in Far North Queensland (2007: 89, 101 and n 15), takes a similar view.
7 Sturt Glacken (personal communication, 9 November 2005) notes that there is legal provision for evidence by performance. 'If it is used', Glacken notes, 'there would then need to follow conventional evidence explaining its symbols'. In this case, bark paintings made by the claimants that depicted their land and sea country were used as evidence in precisely this way.
8 Ironically, the emu is one of the main ancestral beings for one of the Yirritja moiety clans involved in the case, and the wallaby has the same status for one of the Dhuwa moiety clans involved.
9 Yolngu witnesses saw a parallelism between the public and restricted spaces of the court and the public and restricted grounds of Yolngu ceremonial performance. That only the judge (and his court officials) had access to the restricted space was seen (correctly) as an indication of his pre-eminent status in the proceedings.
10 An exception was made for the witnesses and interpreters when it was realized that entry through the back door was impossible once all the barristers and others were seated.
11 This was not true in the original version of the NTA, which was similar to the ALRA in terms of its attitude to evidence. The Act was amended in 1998, so that 'normal' rules of evidence now apply.
12 I am grateful to Tom Keely (personal communication, 3 April 2007) for explaining the finer points of the leading of the evidence to me. Any remaining errors of fact and interpretation are mine.
13 In the week immediately prior to the hearing, the young adult daughter of one of the main appellant witnesses died suddenly and unexpectedly. During the period of the hearing, her body was in Darwin for the coroner's inquest into the cause of death. One of the issues that the respondents' barristers wished evidence to be led on was the question of the closure of areas of the sea and shore following a death. So a side-effect of the strategy adopted by the court was that the witnesses (apart from the father), several of whom were also closely related to the young woman, were subjected to lengthy questioning on the topic of death and its consequences. While people found this emotionally difficult, they nevertheless saw that it strengthened their evidence to be able to show how they were acting in relation to this death.
14 Court transcript (henceforth T) 815.26–35.

15 On Yolngu and the concept of persuasion, see also Morphy (1983).
16 The noun 'permit' is certainly in the everyday lexicon of most Yolngu people because of the permit system that applies on ALRA land in the Northern Territory. However, its meaning has been extended in Yolngu contexts in a way that makes the Yolngu lexical item 'permit' different from the Standard Australian English lexical item. For example it is possible for a Yolngu to say 'he is my permit for this country', referring to the *gurrutu* relationship with another person that gives the individual 'standing permission' to access the resources of their relative's country.
17 By this I mean hybrid in the third sense listed by the *Macquarie Dictionary*: 'anything derived from heterogeneous sources, or composed of elements of different or incongruous kind'.
18 This section of the chapter has benefited greatly from comments by Tom Keely (personal communication, 3 April 2007).
19 T221.46–7.
20 T221.38.
21 T222.28–43; emphasis added.
22 It may be that the Yolngu actually wanted to achieve more through the enactment of *rom* – namely to force the recognition of its sovereignty in relation to Yolngu land and sea. However, although the judge was explicit in his recognition that this was a separate system of law with its own jurisdiction, he was not thereby making a statement about sovereignty. As noted before, like all the other non-Yolngu involved in the case he was working from the premise that the Australian legal system and the Australian law is, unequivocally, an expression of the sovereignty of the Australian state over all its citizens. I am grateful to Sturt Glacken (personal communication, 9 November 2005) for comments that helped me to clarify my thinking on this point.
23 T643.04–28.
24 T644.26–29.
25 It should be noted, however, that in cases where Yolngu forge friendships with non-Yolngu people those people are, invariably, incorporated into the Yolngu kinship system, and thus into a moiety and a clan. In many cases they are also given a Yolngu name.
26 For a detailed discussion of the sea country of the Yolngu and their relationship to it see Morphy and Morphy (2006).
27 T904.33–905.03.
28 T284.02–04; the witness did not mean by this that *rom* cannot accommodate new circumstances, but that its basic and underlying principles are eternal and immutable.
29 T295.47–296.01.
30 T126.41–127.39
31 T127.45–128.05.
32 Nicholas Evans, in a paper on the linguistic evidence in the Croker (*Yarmirr*) case, points out that 'much of the evidence that led Mr Justice Olney to this conclusion [that the permission system applied only to Aboriginal people] turns on modal verbs [for example, 'can', 'must', 'should] in the witness' evidence' (2002: 87). He goes on to show that Mr Justice Olney misinterpreted a key witness's non-standard use of modal verbs, deriving a meaning from the witness's statement that was precisely the opposite of what the witness had intended by his evidence. There is a strong case for saying, then, that Mr Justice Olney did not in fact hear evidence that was substantially different from that heard in the Blue Mud Bay case, but rather that the judgement in the *Yarmirr* case was based on flawed analysis of the evidence, with potential repercussions down the line for the Blue Mud Bay case and, indeed, all subsequent native title cases that concern the sea.

Chapter 7

Ethnoracial land restitution
Finding Indians and fugitive slave descendants in the Brazilian Northeast

Jan Hoffman French

Abstract

This chapter considers how a desire for land and development can lead to a refashioning of ethnoracial identities and identifications. Debates in development studies have centered on culture as an impediment to development. I turn that debate on its head and argue that new assertions of cultural particularity have in certain settings advanced the equity goals of development. The chapter explores the contrasting responses of two neighbouring communities of related African descended, mixed race rural workers who over a 25-year period (1975–2000), under new laws, were recognized and given land by the Brazilian government. One was identified as an indigenous tribe, the other – the primary focus of this chapter – as a community of descendants of fugitive slaves. Struggles for recognition and land have provoked a hardening of family feuds and ethnicization of disputes, but have also reformulated the way in which 'community' and 'race' are expressed.

> [When I learned I was an Indian] the emotional impact was very powerful, because I was born and raised on that land. Being a day labourer without education working the land, when suddenly I came to know that I was a person belonging to a community that had a past and that now we have a history . . . History that I never knew. I had no idea.[1]

This remark, made to me on my first research trip to the north-eastern state of Sergipe, the smallest state in Brazil, by Apolônio, the 40-year-old former leader of the Xocó Indians, introduces some key themes relating to land restitution in the Brazilian Northeast. It shows how the claiming of land both awakens, and is nurtured by, new assertions of cultural particularity. It demonstrates how such assertions give rise to a sense of an identity valorized by history: one which is experienced as vastly superior to the devalued, and culturally non-specific, definition of poor labourer. At the same time as land restitution in this context generates new ideas about identity, a concurrent sense of community, and promises of economic development which might accompany these, it also generates fierce contestations within such new communal formations.

The deep-seated conviction about a rediscovered cultural identity expressed in this statement belies the contingent and fluid character of such an identity. From within the same broad grouping of African-descended, mixed-race rural workers, some were recognized by the Brazilian national Indian agency as Xocó Indians[2] while others claimed an identity as *quilombolas* or slave descendants. It is with the latter group that this chapter is primarily concerned.

During that same visit to Sergipe, I met Maripaulo, a 37-year-old agricultural labourer and cousin of Apolônio from the neighbouring village of Mocambo. As a leader of his community, this son of a Xocó man and a self-identified black woman had been instrumental in the struggle to win legal recognition of the residents of Mocambo as descended from a *quilombo* – a rural black community that is recognized as dating to the time before the abolition of slavery in 1888. The 1988 Constitution, in a one-sentence provision, guarantees land to the residents of *quilombos*.[3] This constitutional provision, enacted as part of a negotiation with national leaders of the black consciousness movement, is often referred to as the 'Quilombo Clause'.[4] Its effects for villagers like Maripaulo were striking. As he told me when I met him for the first time, 'People from Mocambo are afraid of talking to whites, to people from the outside. It's a legacy of slavery', said Maripaulo. 'Before the struggle, I used to be [silent] like that too. Now I can talk to anyone – even the Pope'.

Apolônio, Maripaulo, and their families live in neighbouring settlements in the semi-arid backlands of the Northeast, Brazil's poorest region. With one of the world's 10 largest economies, Brazil has a population that exceeds 180 million. The north-eastern region has 30 per cent of the population of Brazil, but has 20 per cent of all poor people and about 30 per cent of the rural poor. A place of cattle ranches, cowboys, bandits, fervent folk Catholic practices and millenarian movements, it is best known for its cyclical droughts, intense poverty and bleak environment requiring a hardscrabble existence. In this part of the backlands, discourses about collective identities as Indians and descendants of African slaves have taken on new meaning since the late 1970s when the military regime, which came to power in 1964, began to open up political life under pressure from massive protests. With the consolidation of political democracy, which was reinstituted in 1985, peasants and rural workers who had been making a living by sharecropping rice on the fields of nearby landowners began to struggle for their own land through newly available legal means. In the process they began to reconfigure village life on new terms. Their struggles were influenced by, and pursued under, new laws interpreted and applied by local Catholic church activists, non-governmental organizations (NGOs) and government agencies.

In this chapter, I thus consider a situation in which land restitution claims have led to a refashioning of ethnoracial identities. The form of land restitution under consideration here involves the 'return' of land to people claiming that their ancestors lived on the land prior to the current landowners. These owners, it is said, obtained legal title as the result of violent seizure of the land and expulsion of its residents. Once this was accomplished, those same residents are said to have been re-incorporated as landless rural workers and sharecroppers on the land where their ancestors had lived. Opportunities for a better life were then presented in connection with legal provisions granting land to those people, but this time based on ethnoracial identities assumed to predate the law itself. In this chapter I explore how such opportunities, once taken up by rural people living in the Northeast backlands, operate to transform their ethnoracial identification, reconfigure their local cultural practices, exacerbate pre-existing tensions when new identities draw on historically negative categories, and help us think about the possibility of alternative modernities.[5]

Land restitution claims as spurred by the disappointment of development projects

The context for these two struggles and the accompanying identity transformations is that of the Brazilian Northeast: an area which has been the concern of international development agencies and Brazilian government internal development projects since the Second World War, and which was an important focus of the Alliance for Progress in the 1960s. Attention to the area increased at this point, in the wake of the 1959 Cuban Revolution, particularly because there was a growing peasant movement and increased demands for agrarian reform and rural worker unionization, principally in the north-eastern state of Pernambuco, the original home of the Peasant Leagues (Julião 1962).

Drought cycles in the Northeast and the poverty and hunger they bring have been a concern of the Brazilian government since the early twentieth century, by which time the human role in droughts was already understood: Euclides da Cunha (1944 [1902]) wrote of desertification, the impact of cattle raising and introduction of cash crops. The first Brazilian anti-drought agency (Superintendency of Studies and Works against the Effects of Droughts) was established in 1906 inspired by Theodore Roosevelt's Reclamation Service. Over the course of the twentieth century, this spawned an 'industry of drought' in Brazil which gained speed in the 1960s and 1970s. It led to capital-intensive projects (often referred to as pharaohonic) and political positioning that benefited government contractors and their supporters rather than resulting in sustained improvement in the lives of the rural poor.[6] Both large-scale dam projects and irrigation projects have featured in development efforts in the drought-ridden Northeast. Both have affected the people who have come to self-identify as either Indians or *quilombolas* in the backlands of Sergipe.

Crucial to understanding the unusual route taken by those engaged in land struggles along the São Francisco River is the catalyzing role played by the Catholic diocese where the Xocó and Mocambo communities are located. The bishop for almost three decades, Dom José Brandão de Castro, arrived in

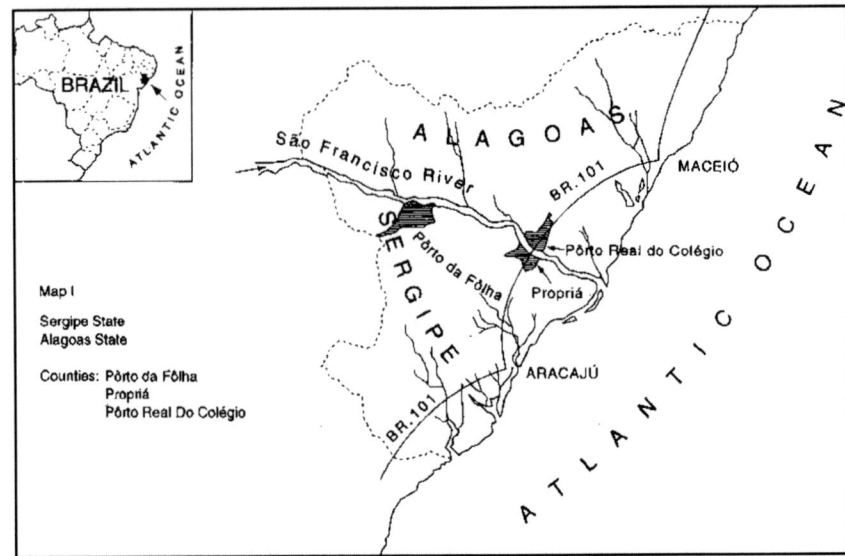

Figure 7.1 Map of Sergipe with São Francisco River.
Source: Mota (1997)

Sergipe in 1960. He came to be known as a 'red bishop', in recognition of his efforts to minister to rich and poor alike and to iron out inequalities. Initially, like the Brazilian Catholic Church more generally, a supporter of large-scale development projects as a means to achieve this end, he soon changed tack. His earlier support for a large irrigation project downriver from the island claimed by the Xocó Indians, for example, arose from his conviction that it would improve agricultural development and provide employment to his parishioners. He thought it would amply compensate those who might be displaced. However, when he visited the project and learned of the pain his poor constituency was suffering as the result of the project, he changed his mind. He could see that those being displaced were left with even less than they had before and were not being compensated. At this point, he took action, based on the education he said he was receiving from his parishioners – that such forms of development needed to be questioned. From the 1970s onwards he became one of the leading liberation theology figures of the Northeast, and an instigator of identity-oriented social movements.[7]

Dom José Brandão almost immediately helped initiate a movement of poor people affected by these developments. Alongside his antipathy to the irrigation project, he mobilized the populace in opposition to a massive hydroelectric dam that was being built upriver at Paulo Afonso, one of many being constructed in the Northeast at that time.[8] In Sergipe, as in many cases of dam-building, the effects of its construction were multiple and unexpected. In addition to the outright displacement of people living in the path of the dam, as well as inadequate compensation and failed resettlement plans, there were also collateral effects. The lowering of the river's level visited drastic impacts on peoples' livelihoods and cultural practices. Particularly relevant to the communities along the São Francisco River was the tragic disappearance of the rice lagoons. People who lived along the river, including both those in the area of São Pedro Island and in the village of Mocambo, had formerly sharecropped the rice on plots of land belonging to a wealthy landowner. This agricultural activity had been accompanied by the performance of dances (such as the *samba de coco*) associated with the stages of the harvest (see French 2002). The disappearance of the rice lagoons, caused by the construction of the dam, is often cited as the beginning of Mocambo's conflicts with this landowner. Indirectly, it then led to their eventual restitution claim and their assertion of an identity as *quilombolas*.

'Discovery' of indigenous and black identities

Beginning in the early 1970s, around the same time that Dom José Brandão was learning of the pitfalls of development in his diocese, the Native American movement was gaining momentum in North America and Amazonian Indians were becoming central to indigenous politics in the western hemisphere. During the darkest days of the Brazilian military regime, African-descended rural workers in Brazil's Northeast began to win government recognition as Indians. The Xocó recognition in 1979 marked the first emergence of over 30 such 'rediscovered' tribes in the Northeast, where it was assumed for more than a century that descendants of the indigenous inhabitants in the Northeast had been assimilated into the local peasantry when their land was taken for cattle raising by wealth-seeking families moving into the hinterlands from the coast. These 'new Indians' in non-Amazonian regions of Brazil are composed primarily of mixed-race individuals with few of the 'traditional cultural diacritics'. Almost all of them speak only Portuguese, and their Indianness is 'not always evident from their physical appearance' (Ramos 2003: 370). Their recent re-recognition is described by Brazilian anthropologist João Pacheco de Oliveira (1993) as 'ethnogenesis'.

In the case of the Xocó, it was a dispute with their employer, a local oligarchical landowning family, the Brittos, that started this claim for indigenous identity. Spurred on by this conflict, Apolônio, their leader at the time, accompanied by his mother, grandfather, and 22 other families, illegally occupied the Island of São Pedro in the São Francisco River, claiming it as their ancestral home. Spurred on by the arrival of a liberationist priest who had been brought to the diocese by Dom José Brandão, and assisted by the expansion of the definition of 'Indian' in the Indian Statute of 1973, it was also reinforced by anthropologists' reports and historical research, and by connections forged with other land struggles sponsored by the Catholic Church. Xocó success in being recognized and receiving permanent access to land (French 2004) soon looked set to become a reality.⁹

When they first illegally occupied São Pedro Island to claim it as their ancestral home, the rural workers who would soon definitively become the Xocó Indians planted a Brazilian flag on the sandy beach. Although this action seemed to signify a collective aspiration to full citizenship by people who had been the objects of patron–client relations and hence marginalized from power for generations, it had ironic implications. By becoming Indians in the 1970s, these rural workers were forfeiting full citizenship rights because Indians were (and continue to be in many respects) wards of the Brazilian state, considered and treated as children, relatively incapable of conducting their own affairs (Ramos 1998).

It was only 20 years later that the inhabitants of the neighbouring village of Mocambo began the long march to self-recognition. As in the Xocó case, what started the process for Mocambo villagers was a land dispute, but in this case the landlord – and their primary employer – was a former community insider who had become a landowner. She was the daughter of a Mocambo resident who had made good and purchased the land on which all of her father's neighbours worked as sharecroppers. Again, it was partly at the instigation of a liberation theologian that villagers took action. Mocambo residents, advised by a nun-lawyer, made moves to take advantage of the Brazilian Constitution's

Figure 7.2 Xocó Indian with Bishop.

Quilombo Clause, which allowed them the collective ownership of the lands putatively occupied since colonial times. The lawyer had heard of a claim in the neighbouring state of Bahia at a Church meeting in 1993 and introduced the possibility of such a claim to Mocambo. In 1997, the Palmares Cultural Foundation, an agency of the Ministry of Culture, recognized Mocambo as a *remanescente de quilombo* (descendant of fugitive slave community) under the Quilombo Clause and other articles of the 1988 Constitution that govern cultural patrimony preservation. It was through these sets of materially similar circumstances, yet contingent and idiosyncratic contacts and networks, that the two communities ended up being classified along such distinct lines. But in both cases, the result was some form of land restitution.

With recognition – of the Xocó as an indigenous group and of the neighbouring Mocambo's residents as a *quilombo* – came land access. In the case of the Xocó, the full swath of land they claimed finally became an indigenous reserve in 1991, while Mocambo received title to its land in 2000.[10] A land grant, however, was just the first step in meeting the basic needs of people who only received electricity in 1997, still have no running water, and are competing for the primitive concrete outhouses which serve as 'bathrooms'.

Multiple meanings of land and their impact on the value of restitution

The value and meaning of land when granted as restitution for ancestral dispossession can be more symbolic than concerned with economic viability. This was

Figure 7.3 Quilombo supporter.

Figure 7.4 Quilombo women of Mocambo dancing.

especially true for the Xocó and Mocambo, both of whom received possession of land that was not particularly arable. Most of it had for many years been used for cattle raising. Rainfall in this region is at best unpredictable, and irrigation, technical assistance and the machinery necessary to make the land truly productive have not generally accompanied government land grants based on indigenous or *quilombo* identity claims. Nonetheless, land has multiple meanings for members of these groups, involving a depth of feeling that in many respects goes beyond practical considerations. The struggle to obtain land both enhanced that 'structure of feeling' (Williams 1977) that gave its protagonists an enhanced sense of their own identity and history, and simultaneously undermined this by leading to or entrenching family feuds. Indeed, it created new fault lines among community members who agreed on needs but not on the means to achieve them.

In Mocambo, as with many other cases discussed in this book, present-day land struggles were premised upon conditions experienced as a result of those experienced in the past, with the state as a forceful interventionist presence (see Chapters 2, Fay; 11, Tiedje; 10, Nuijten and Lorenzo, in this book). In the area of Mocambo, back in the 1940s, in connection with a state land reform attempt, some of the older workers had been given individual title to small parcels of land, the size of which was based upon the number of children in the family. Each family was given a receipt that served as the equivalent of a deed. About 20 years later, most of the recipients of these parcels took advantage of their legal ownership, sold the land and moved to the village of Mocambo, itself built on land purchased by the state from a local landowner during the same land reform period in the 1940s. As the use of the land in the area changed from crop production to cattle by absentee landowners who had pieced together large holdings, those who had worked on the land moved their families to Mocambo, which grew to the 90 houses it now has. Landless families newly concentrated in the village began to work as sharecroppers, or collected state retirement pensions. Since each of the three rows of houses share walls to ease the burden of building entirely new dwellings, the demographic configuration of the area was radically changed from scattered dwellings and families living far apart to a concentrated settlement. This change in land use and the resulting change in settlement pattern was instrumental in the later ability of community and church activists to organize the *quilombo* movement.

What clearly distinguished this later episode – clearly conceptualized as restitution – was the element of struggle and the sense of a need to self-identify culturally. The receipt of individual titles in 1946 had been a welcome windfall, viewed as an entitlement like a pension.[11] By contrast, the land now held under collective title in the name of the *quilombo* association was directly linked to the struggle for recognition of history and culture, even though some of the land involved was the same as that which had earlier been individually owned (and sold) by members of the community. Unlike the individual, alienable land grants of the 1940s, the collective, inalienable title of the year 2000 carried with it meanings grounded in cultural and ethnoracial identification that had developed as the result of collective struggle.

A more recent example reinforces this conclusion. An important member of the Mocambo community is a man who owns a large house about a mile up the road from the nucleus of Mocambo. He runs a bar out of his house where people in the area stop to chat and socialize on their way back from working in the fields or visiting the county seat. This man, whose son, a metalworker in São Paulo, has paid for improvements to the house over the years (see Figure 7.3), decided early on that he was willing to forfeit his individual, alienable title in exchange for an untried, collective title that would leave him without the right to sell his property. By doing so, he is also risking the inheritance of his son and other children, since the question of whether children automatically succeed to the membership of their parents in the *quilombo* association upon death is entirely unresolved. In other words, this man has exchanged a known property right for a right, the legal status of which is unknown and untested. Land, in and of itself, is thus not enough to provoke action or commitment. Rather, it is the process and form of obtaining it and the concomitant sensibilities that are produced through that process that provide the meanings of both land and struggle.

In addition to the way various forms of struggle influenced the changing meanings of land, the requirement of communal ownership also affected the way the new owners worked on the land. Because the government stipulated that the land be held collectively on the grounds that the key index of *quilombo* identity was the communal use of land, during the planting and harvest of 2000 an effort was made to intensify the collective nature of land use. By insisting on communal land title, the government's ostensible purpose was to distribute land in a way that would not disrupt pre-existing land-use patterns. This insistence embodied an inaccurate assumption about the nature of community amongst *quilombo* descendants. In the case of Mocambo, areas on the riverbank had been occupied by individual families on individual plots, and the only communal work was that which they had done as sharecroppers. It was only once they received their large parcel of land collectively as a *quilombo*-descended community that the villagers for the first time began to work it communally on their own account. Therefore, the government's interpretation of the Quilombo Clause requiring land to be owned collectively by an association was instrumental in consolidating, if not provoking, a shift in land use that paralleled, and coincided with, the shifts in the meaning of land.

Behind the state directive lay romantic assumptions about the collective nature of African-descended communities. As I watched their early attempts at collective production, both with co-operative milk sales (from the cows that were individually owned) and with bean planting, harvest, distribution and sale, it became obvious that there was much to be learned before they became successful collective farmers. It did not come naturally, particularly for people who for generations had worked on other people's land and lived their lives in an individualistic society.[12]

Although Dom José Brandão, the bishop who was crucial to the commencement of land struggles in this part of the Northeast, was no longer alive by the time Mocambo received land through its claim as a *quilombo*, it is instructive to consider how his particular critique of development projects might be affected by the Mocambo story. For those in Mocambo with a staunch belief that the government would come through for them, the land had long been seen as a harbinger of development. For them, development did not mean large irrigation projects, the building of dams or the re-routing of rivers. As academics and activists involved with issues of ethical development might posit, it did signify the possibility that their basic needs would be fulfilled: healthy food on a regular basis, consistent medical care, clean water, sewers, paved roads, means of travel to the county seat to collect mail and pension cheques, visit doctors, means of communication like telephones, refrigeration, means of cultivating their land, seeds and agricultural technical assistance, a tractor, irrigation equipment, and sufficient cash to have dental work done and to purchase clothes and shoes.[13] Whether all residents of Mocambo shared the view that government recognition as a *quilombo* was the best path toward development in this sense is the subject of the next section.

Factions and ruptures in the Mocambo 'community'

The tenacity with which people viewed the new, collective title granted to Quilombo Mocambo by the government was, in part, attributable to the opposition they faced from within their own families in the village. The strategy for achieving improved conditions through 'good change' (Edwards 1999) is not always agreed upon by the members of a community. Almost from the beginning of the *quilombo* movement there were families in Mocambo who were opposed to pursuing recognition. In hindsight, now that more than 5,000 acres of land have been declared the property of Quilombo Mocambo and now that the political shift to the left at state and national levels has begun to bring attention to the plight of the rural poor in Brazil, it seems difficult to imagine why people living under the impoverished circumstances of the early 1990s in Mocambo would have opposed a move that would eventually provide such rewards. However, when an untried law is invoked there are risks as well as rewards to consider. In this case, both factions – residents in favour of self-identifying as a *quilombo* and those opposed to it (known as *contras*) – thought their route was the better way to achieve an improved life with the amenities mentioned above. The problem, from the point of view of the *contras*, was that to get such modern improvements they were being asked to identify themselves with a pre-modern sensibility, a slave category and a racial category that had been reviled since the moment their ancestors arrived in Brazil, whether as slaves or colonizers. To buy into the possibility of an 'alternative modernity' (Gaonkar 2001) would require a leap of faith that the *contras* were not quite ready to take.

By the year 2004, approximately two-thirds of the 90 families living in Mocambo were participants in the *quilombo* movement, while the other third belonged to the *contra* faction. This faction included people who could have qualified as *quilombolas* (members of the *quilombo* based on their heritage and long-term residency), as well as relative newcomers to Mocambo who were less eligible for this status – families who had been forced to move when the land they lived on was expropriated for the Xocó reserve. The *contras* and their allies had determined, from the early days of the struggle, that it was to their benefit to remain loyal to local politicians who for years had been the only source of promised services. Such politicians provided favours in exchange for political support at election time, leaving many people, particularly those who preferred the losing candidates, with practically no access to resources such as agricultural technical assistance, irrigation equipment, seeds for planting and legal help with claiming pensions and resolving disputes. Despite these disadvantages for the losers, the federal untried promise of *quilombo* collective landownership and use initially seemed less reliable than local clientelist political configurations that were at least predictable, if often unfair or unjust.

There was also a strong element of competition between the leader of the

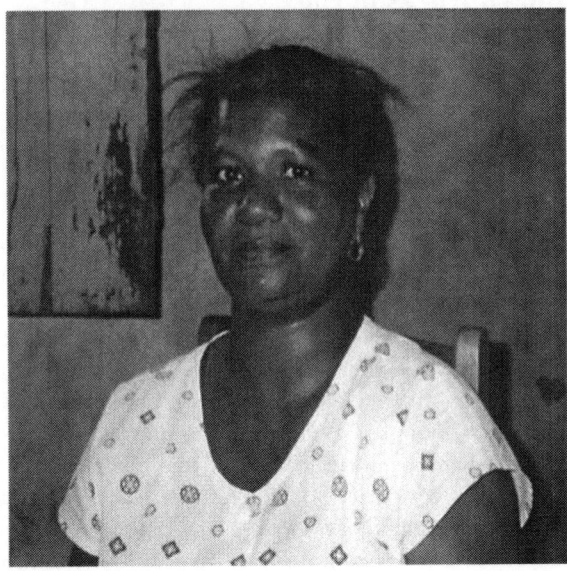

Figure 7.5 Supporter of *contra* opposition to Quilombo movement.

contras and some of the leaders of the *quilombo* movement who were also his first cousins. Within the first three years of the struggle for recognition, this had developed into a full-scale family feud, with some tragic results. For example, the matriarch of one of the leading *quilombo* families, Dona Maria, did not speak to her sister, Dona Rosa, the mother of the leader of the *contras* who lived three doors down the street, even though Rosa was dying of cancer. On Dona Rosa's part, shortly before she died, their 80-year-old brother walked the 100 yards from Dona Maria's house to visit Rosa who berated him so severely for being a *quilombola* that it reduced him to tears: a shameful situation in the eyes of the rest of the family.

The moment most identified with a hardening of positions was the disagreement in late 1995 over whether the already constituted community association, whose president was to become the official leader of the *contras* (Dona Rosa's son), would be a viable entity which could hold title to the *quilombo* land. This was a crucial issue because Brazilian land law has no provision for collective ownership. The Palmares Cultural Foundation, the body charged with facilitating *quilombo* land access, required that title be held in the name of an association formed expressly for that purpose. In the face of opposition from the *contras*, a new community association was formed to hold title to the land. Only residents who had supported the struggle for recognition were entitled to membership and hence to indirect landownership when the land was finally titled in the name of the new community association in July 2000. There is evidence to suggest that a pre-existing power struggle was being acted out through the *quilombo* movement and was, perhaps inadvertently, being exacerbated by the nun-lawyer who was responsible for drafting the new association's by-laws.

Talk of 'community' works 'to reduce and deny social differences and power relations' within a particular group (see Chapter 8, Beyers, in this book). Moreover, it is often used to paper over the fractures, feuds and cleavages that are always present, constituting and reconstituting, that make a community a dynamic, processual space and place. Additionally, in Brazil the word '*comunidade*' is associated with Catholic liberationist-based ecclesial communities (CEBs) so that there is always a religious connotation lurking behind the everyday use of the term. CEBs are locally based groups in which 'poor people, inspired by their interpretations of biblical images of justice, solidarity and liberation, seek to transform the world' (Vásquez 1998: 2). As a result of this liberation theology practice, the word 'community' has come to signify a site of both struggle and solidarity. In the case of Mocambo, once the *quilombo* movement began in earnest, the invocation of 'community' became a point of intense dispute. Could it still mean the entire village, or had it become something to which membership needed to be actively asserted or denied? Initially used as a definitional term tied up with religious belief, it acquired new meanings once the land was granted to the *quilombo* community association. At that point, it also became an invocation of exclusion.

The premise of perfect social solidarity and unity has long been called into question by ethnographers, who have shown that 'within the nearest kinship group rivalries, dissensions, the keenest egotism flourish[ed]' (Malinowski 1926 [1972]: 48), and have questioned whether 'a focus on regularity and consistency should not be replaced by a focus on change, on process over time, and on paradox, conflict, inconsistency, contradiction, multiplicity, and manipulability in social life' (Moore 1975: 217).

The case of Mocambo illustrates the proposition that 'incompletion' is the principle of community, 'an uninterrupted passage through singular ruptures' (Nancy 1991). At the same time, the relations among the factions in Mocambo revealed themselves to be moments of articulation, times when the two factions took shape in relation to one another, in the 'play of the juncture' (Nancy 1991: 76).

As these sliding articulations manifested themselves in Mocambo, the atmosphere there remained tense throughout the entire decade of *quilombo* mobilization. The question of community membership even extended to disputes over entitlement to the government-provided cement outhouse 'bathrooms'. When government workers arrived with materials, a drama unfolded over who was or was not a *quilombola* qualified to receive these facilities. What complicated matters further was that the exclusivist definition enforced by the *quilombo* association contradicted the more inclusive approach of the federal attorney who insisted that all the 'black' residents of Mocambo were entitled to the land.

Being black or Indian when land is at stake

Once the land was titled in the name of the *quilombo* association, the *contras*, even though they were black, were excluded from working on the land. This has also led to a refashioning of what it means to be 'black' in this part of the Northeast backlands. Whether community members would assume a black identity had been a subject of concern since the *quilombo* recognition movement began in 1994. Choosing to 'be' black or to 'assume' a black identity was a new phenomenon in Mocambo. Recognizing the fundamental importance of each such personal decision advances an understanding of how the transition from a typical backland community to a legally recognized *quilombo* has affected racial self-identification. Stuart Hall describes his own experience of 'becoming black' in Britain after migrating from Jamaica where initially the label 'black' was simply not available, even though almost everyone there was African-descended. In Britain, however, 'black was created as a political category in a certain historical moment'. It included South Asians as well as immigrants from the Caribbean and East Africa and was 'created as a consequence of certain symbolic and ideological struggles . . . [plucked] out of its negative articulation and articulate[d] in a new way'. This led to a 'change of self-recognition, a new process of identification, the emergence of a new subject' (Hall 1991: 55, 54).

In Mocambo, 'becoming black' as a political process is tied up with the repeated exhortation to 'assume' one's identity as black. The assumption of a black identity, however, is more than 'a narrative tie that connects micro-political conflicts to macro-political ideological clashes' whilst not altering very much the micro-political terms (Arruti 2002: 393). Racial identification, here, is more than a formal nominalism since it has definite material effects. With new categories tied to land and promises of a better life has come a self-recognition that can open up 'a new world of new possibilities and impossibilities [that are] born when acts of objectifying racial classification move [people] to understand themselves, to formulate aspirations, and to plan future courses of their lives under descriptions of themselves as black . . .' thus 'actively contribut[ing] to the construction of their identities as black persons' (Gooding-Williams 2001: 243). *Quilombolas* in Mocambo are discovering that some of the 'most politically salient modes of being a black person involve the assignment of a *collective* significance to being black' (Gooding-Williams 2001: 243).

In Mocambo, the majority of residents are taking seriously this new 'collective significance to being black' – celebrating Black Consciousness Day, and dancing their *samba de coco* dressed in a way that creates a tie to Afro-Brazilian religious practices, even though they are Catholic. A similar process has taken place with the Xocó, in the context of their history and struggle (French 2004). They, too, have adopted dances and rituals that have come over the past 25 years to be required for indigenous recognition in the Northeast.

Conclusion

In both cases discussed here, new identities are being experienced in the crucible of struggle for land and a better life, as the people in the northeastern backlands perceive it. We can see through these examples that as new legal categories interact with ethnoracial transformations, universalist goals promised as a result of land restitution, such as better living conditions and improved access to crucial services and resources, are called upon to incorporate cultural and ethnoracial difference and the value of diversity. Notions of community, while playing a key role in precipitating self-identification by some as Indian and by others as the descendants of black slaves, are also keenly contested. Restitution, while shaping groups, also serves to exclude many from them.

References

Amit, V (2002) *Realizing Community: Concepts, Social Relationships and Sentiments*, London: Routledge.

Arruti, JMA (2002) ' "Étnias Federais": O processo de identificação de "remanescentes" indígenas e quilombolas no Baixo São Francisco', unpublished thesis, *Museu Nacional*, Rio de Janeiro, UFRJ.

Berger, PL (1976) *Pyramids of Sacrifice: Political Ethics and Social Change*, Garden City, NY: Anchor Press/Doubleday.

Creed, GW (2004) 'Constituted through Conflict: Images of Community (and Nation) in Bulgarian Rural Ritual', *American Anthropologist* 106: 56–70.

Cunha, ED (1944 [1902]) *Rebellion in the Backlands (Os Sertões)*, Chicago, IL: University of Chicago Press.

Edwards, M (1999) *Future Positive: International Co-operation in the 21st Century*, London: Earthscan.

Escobar, A (1994) *Encountering Development: The Making and Unmaking of the Third World*, Princeton, NJ: Princeton University Press.

Ferguson, J (1990) *The Anti-Politics Machine: Development, Depoliticization, and Bureaucratic Power In Lesotho*, Cambridge, New York: Cambridge University Press.

Foster, GM (1965) 'Peasant Society and the Image of Limited Good', *American Anthropologist* 67: 293–315.

French, JH (2002) 'Dancing for Land: Law Making and Cultural Performance in Northeastern Brazil', *Political and Legal Anthropology Review* (PoLAR) 25: 19–36.

—— (2004) 'Mestizaje and Law Making in Indigenous Identity Formation in Northeastern Brazil: "After the Conflict Came the History" ', *American Anthropologist* 106: 663–74.

—— (2006) 'Buried Alive: Imagining Africa in the Brazilian Northeast', *American Ethnologist* 33: 340–60.

Gaonkar, DP (2001) *Alternative Modernities*, Durham, NC: Duke University Press.

Gaspar, D (2004) *The Ethics of Development*, Edinburgh: Edinburgh University Press.

Gooding-Williams, R (2001) 'Race, Multiculturalism and Democracy', in R Bernasconi (ed.) *Race*, Malden, MA: Blackwell Publishers.

Gordon, ET, GC Gurdián and CR Hale (2003) 'Rights, Resources, and the Social

Memory of Struggle: Reflections on a Study of Indigenous and Black Community Land Rights on Nicaragua's Atlantic Coast', *Human Organization* 62: 369–81.

Goulet, Denis (1971) *The Cruel Choice: a new concept in the theory of development*, New York: Atheneum.

Hall, S (1991) 'Old and New Identities, Old and New Ethnicities', in AD King (ed.) *Culture, Globalization and the World System: Contemporary Conditions for the Representation of Identity*, New York: Macmillan.

Harrison, LE and SP Huntington (eds) (2000) *Culture Matters: how values shape human progress*, New York: Basic Books.

Healy, K and Helen Kellogg Institute for International Studies (2001) *Llamas, Weavings, and Organic Chocolate: multicultural grassroots development in the Andes and Amazon of Bolivia*, Notre Dame, IN: University of Notre Dame Press.

Joseph, M (2002) *Against the Romance of Community*, Minneapolis, MN: University of Minnesota Press.

Julião, F (1962) *Que São as Ligas Camponesas*, Rio de Janeiro: Editora Civilização Brasileira.

Lebret, L-J (1967) *Développement – Révolution Solidaire*, Paris: Les Editions Ouvrières.

Malinowski, B (1926 [1972]) *Crime and Custom in Savage Society*, Totowa, NJ: Littlefield, Adams & Co.

Moore, SF (1975) 'Epilogue: Uncertainties in Situations, Indeterminacies in Culture', in SF Moore, SF and BG Myerhoff (eds) *Symbol and Politics in Communal Ideology: cases and questions*, Ithaca, NY: Cornell University Press.

Mota, Clarice Novaes da (1997) *Jurema's Children in the Forest of Spirits: Healing and Ritual among Two Brazilian Indigenous Groups*, London: Intermediate Technology Publications.

Nancy, J-L (1991) *The Inoperative Community*, Minneapolis, MN: University of Minnesota Press.

Pacheco de Oliveira Filho, J (1993) 'Povos Indígenas no Nordeste: Fronteiras Étnicas e Identidades Emergentes', *Tempo e Presença* 15: 31–4.

Ramos, AR (1998) *Indigenism: Ethnic Politics in Brazil*, Madison, WI: University of Wisconsin Press.

—— (2003) 'Pulp Fictions of Indigenism', in DS Moore, J Kosek and A Pandian (eds) *Race, Nature, and the Politics of Difference*, Durham, NC: Duke University Press.

Sen, AK (2001) *Development as Freedom*, Oxford, New York: Oxford University Press.

Taylor, C (2002) 'Modern Social Imaginaries', *Public Culture* 14: 91–124.

Vásquez, MA (1998) *The Brazilian Popular Church and The Crisis of Modernity*, Cambridge, New York: Cambridge University Press.

Walley, CJ (2003) 'Our Ancestors Used to Bury their "Development" in the Ground: Modernity and the Meanings of Development within a Tanzanian Marine Park', *Anthropological Quarterly* 76: 33–54.

Williams, R (1977) *Marxism and Literature*, Oxford: Oxford University Press.

Notes

Funding for this research was provided by the International Dissertation Field Research Fellowship program of the Social Science Research Council, a Fulbright Dissertation Grant, a National Science Foundation Dissertation Improvement Grant, and travel grants from the Duke University Latin American and Caribbean Studies Center. Thanks go to Derick Fay for his useful comments and to Fay and Deborah James for organizing the panel at the American Anthropological Association meeting in Washington, DC in December 2005 where this chapter was presented.

1 I conducted preliminary research in 1998 and 1999, and then moved to Sergipe for the entire year 2000 to conduct ethnographic field research in Mocambo and on São Pedro Island, and in the state and national capitals. I returned to Sergipe in the summers of 2002 and 2004 to conduct follow-up research. I conducted participant observation and interviews with residents of the two villages and surrounding areas, former landowners, lawyers, anthropologists, activists, priests, nuns, politicians, and government officials. I also conducted documentary research in court, government, Catholic Church, newspaper and personal archives.
2 'In Brazil [the term] Indian has gone through phases of denigration and of regeneration. The indigenous movement of the 1970s and 1980s reappropriated the term and infused it with a substantial dose of political agency' (Alcida Ramos 1998: 5). Janet Chernela (personal communication 5 May 2004) explains that the term 'Indian' is imposed by the state and when it is accepted and used by indigenous people, it is a means of articulation with the state.
3 The 1988 Constitution was the first democratic constitution promulgated since the military coup in 1964, after a year-long Constituent Assembly involving people and interests from around the entire country.
4 The word 'Mocambo' is synonymous with *quilombo*. Both are African-derived words meaning, among other things, a settlement of runaway slaves.
5 Traditional cultures adapt and change under stresses of modernization and push to enter into modernity (Gaonkar 2001; Taylor 2002). 'Modernity' is the reified label for complex, contradictory and contested processes and beliefs with multiple temporalities and jagged edges (Walley 2003:34).
6 A similar dynamic has been playing itself out upriver from my field sites, where there is a proposal to divert water from the São Francisco River for use in the more northern states in the Northeast. The *transposição*, as it is known, has been debated for many years and its potential success doubted. The World Bank denied funding at one point in the process because studies showed that it would be a waste of resources and money. Moreover, its effects on the communities and cities along the lower São Francisco (Sergipe and Alagoas) were taken into account. In 2005, Catholic Bishop, Dom Luiz Flávio Cappio, went on a hunger strike to oppose its construction, which was scheduled to begin in 2006, with some revisions meant to appease opponents (one source indicates that the volume to be taken from the river has been reduced from 6.2 per cent to 1.4 per cent). The movement to save the river has many adherents in the area.
7 Dom José Brandão's critique of development in his diocese foreshadows the kind of critiques put forth by anthropologists in the 1990s (Escobar 1994; Ferguson 1990), while his analysis of the pain caused by development and the balance between economic and human development is in keeping with analysts who were creating the subfield of development ethics beginning in the late 1960s and early 1970s (Berger 1976; Goulet 1971; Lebret 1967).
8 The struggle of people deleteriously affected by dam projects became known as the movement of *atingidos* (literally, those reached by the water) and is still active throughout Brazil wherever dams displace communities.
9 For an account of Xocó recognition and the Indian Statute of 1973, see French (2004). For an account of the use of the Quilombo Clause by Mocambo, see French (2002, 2006).
10 Indian land in Brazil is not transferred to the indigenous group or to individual Indians. Rather it is held by the government for the use of the tribe in perpetuity.

However, the possession of the land does not include the subsoil: in many parts of the Amazonian region, for example, mining by private enterprises is permitted.

11 See Chapter 10, Nuijten and Lorenzo, in this book, for a similar point about Mexican land reform.

12 George Foster's (1965) 'Image of Limited Good' is an instructive way to think about the issues raised by an imposed collectivity among peasants under a capitalist system. Foster proposed that peasants view their environment as one in which all desired things in life (land, wealth, health, friendship, love, manliness, honor, respect, status, power, influence, security) exist in finite quantity and are always in short supply. There is no way directly within the peasant's power to increase the available quantities. 'Good' is to be divided but not to be augmented (Foster 1965: 296). An apparent relative improvement in someone's position with respect to any 'good' is viewed as a threat to the entire community. Since there is often uncertainty as to who is losing, any significant improvement is perceived, not as a threat to an individual or family alone but as a threat to all individuals and families (Foster 1965: 297), hence the reaction is one of extreme individualism (Foster 1965: 301). When benefits are provided from outside the system, it is seen as luck and each person looks for ways to maximize that luck (Foster 1965: 308). Such a view of the social and economic universe might present problems when land is given to these individuals who must exercise power locally, rather than as agents of outside forces.

13 Edwards' normative definition of development comes closest to the desires that motivated both the Xocó and the *quilombolas* in Mocambo to use the law to help them redefine their ethnoracial self-identifications. Edwards defines development as an increased opportunity for valuable being: 'the reduction of material want and the enhancement of people's ability to live a life they consider good across the broadest range possible in a population' (Edwards 1999: 4). For him, development is 'good change' and is subjectivist in that the specification of valuable being is left to each group, but having said that, he also believes that people agree on a lot and those things, it is fair to say, are the elements of the meaning of development for the people who live on the banks of the São Francisco River in Sergipe. For Edwards, 'good change increases the fulfillment of these aspirations' (Gasper 2004: 44). He identifies the following universal aspirations: to be free from poverty and violence and the servitude these bring in their wake; to be loved and enjoy a sense of belonging; to feel more in control and less vulnerable to the vagaries of unaccountable power; and to be subjects of their own destiny rather than the objects of the intentions of others (Edwards 1999).

Chapter 8

The will-to-community
Between loss and reclamation in Cape Town

Christiaan Beyers

Abstract

This chapter examines popular constructions of 'community' in the land restitution process in District Six. 'Community' is theorized as a structure of aspiration born of a particular socio-legal context. As the restitution process moves from an initial phase of mobilizing claims to a subsequent phase of settling claims, a fundamental tension arises between desire and expectation. The aspiration to 'community' variously (and imperfectly) reconciles claimants' idealized desires for redress – based on memories of a sense of solidarity and order in the former neighbourhood – with their feelings regarding what might realistically be expected of restitution. The chapter examines how this tension is resolved in the shifting ways in which 'community' is 'imagined,' and analyzes attendant forms of class and race-based social exclusion in the context of group formation.

Introduction

Group claims for the restitution of land are framed in many of the cases in this book as being undertaken by a 'community', underscoring that land is a crucial source of collective belonging, and a fundamental anchor for associational identification. Talk of 'community' works to reduce and deny the social differences and power relations within the social groups thus represented, and to elide the social and political processes through which these groups are constituted and mobilized. The central contention of this chapter is that a fundamental tension arises in the course of the formal legal processes of land restitution between an initial phase, in which 'community' – largely ideational in character – is mobilized in order to claim rights, and a subsequent phase, in which these rights are to be settled. During this latter phase, where group resettlement is involved, the practical challenge is to actualize 'community' as a functioning social unit in the world. But how then is this tension discursively resolved, and moreover, what happens to 'community' in the process?

A current case of land restitution that epitomizes these processes is District

Six, Cape Town, where there has been much discursive traffic around the idea of 'community'. Based on over 90 interviews carried out between 2001 and 2005, this chapter examines the construction and mobilization of 'community' as an object of political practice. It first discusses 'community' as signifying loss, and the restitution process as a movement from loss to reclamation. It argues that while the community-construct works towards an equalization of the experience of those considered part of it, insistent differences are underscored by legal-political and social historical dynamics, the influence of which can be observed in the differing orientations towards the restitution process by various sub-groupings. The chapter describes the tension between ideational projections of identity based on memories of associational life in the former District Six, and more strategic calculations based on individual projections of material gain and social prejudice. Over time, it is argued, the balance between these two kinds of orientations shifts from the former to the latter, as the restitution process moves from the stage of mobilizing and processing claims to the stage of settling those claims. This leads to a preliminary examination of some of the lines of differentiation and exclusion *within and on the margins of* the symbolic typography of 'community' attendant to differing value orientations towards 'return' and levels of attachment to 'community' amongst claimants.

Background

District Six is a prime area of real estate lying on the slopes of Devil's Peak – part of the famous Table Mountain – adjacent to the Central Business District of Cape Town. It was a neighbourhood which consisted of a largely low-income population. It was racially diverse, but the majority of its residents were classified 'Coloureds' – a residual racial category designating a very diverse group of people considered neither 'White' nor 'African' but somewhere in between.[1] Amongst the so-called coloured people of District Six, the largest group was Muslim, who were and continue to be the most organized and vocal sector[2] (Ridd 1981). District Six was proclaimed a 'whites-only' area in 1966, after which the majority of its estimated 30,000 to 70,000 residents were forcibly removed to the barren and windswept area known as the Cape Flats, but many District Sixers classified as 'African' had been removed beforehand: in successive stages dating back to the turn of the twentieth century. Today, a large portion of District Six remains undeveloped, lying empty as what is often referred to as a scar in the centre of the city. The apartheid government was largely unsuccessful in its bid to turn District Six into a white residential neighbourhood due to concerted opposition first from the popular sectors – who made the case known internationally – and later from developers and corporations – who did not want the mark of District Six on their name (Soudien 1990).

The apartheid government agency responsible for carrying out the original forced removals, the cynically entitled Department of Community Development, rationalized that District Six was a dilapidated slum, and that moving people to state housing projects on reclaimed flood plains on the Cape Flats contributed to their 'social upliftment'. In fact, the overarching rationale for the removals was not just to expel blacks from the city centre, but to excise the heterogeneity and hybridity of which District Six was emblematic (see Soudien 2001). 'Africans' were duly moved into their own encampments on the furthest outskirts of the city, or banished from the region altogether and forcibly moved to the Transkei or Ciskei – two so-called tribal homelands in the Eastern Cape. 'Coloureds' and 'Indians' were afforded intermediary levels of citizenship, and were each moved to their own respective residential areas. There was further differentiation within each of these racial categories: former low income tenants and sub-tenants were relocated in 'sub-economic' areas further away from the city centre, while former owners – who received some monetary compensation at the time of removals – and more prosperous tenants were able to afford to relocate to 'economic' or comparatively more affluent areas. This history is memorialized by the well-known District Six Museum (D6M), which has played a very important role in conscientizing and mobilizing claimants (see Jeppie and Soudien 1990; Rasool and Prosalendis 2001).

One reason why the redevelopment of District Six is a prize case for the land restitution programme is that it presents the possibility of moving a large population of low-income people who formerly were racially excluded back into the *centre* of the city. The restitution of District Six involves the restoration of some 40 ha of remaining vacant land (Le Grange 2003: 6), on which it is hoped that somewhere between 10,000 and 15,000 District Sixers will be resettled. This entails a huge development effort which is at the same time a *re-development*, since its ultimate aim is ostensibly to rebuild 'community'. The nature of this re-development is in the process of being determined in a complex legal and political process between key stakeholders: the District Six Beneficiary and Redevelopment Trust (D6BRT), representing the 'community' of claimants, the City of Cape Town, and the national government's Land Claims Commission. Crucial to the planning of the new neighbourhood are questions of what life was really like in District Six, and what kind of diasporic 'community' currently exists among District Sixers. While the official planning and policymaking processes are beyond the scope of this paper (see Beyers 2007), it should be noted that there has been considerable frustration and anxiety among claimants about the slow pace of these processes. Some 10 years after the inauguration of the programme, the project has thus far only seen the completion of a pilot phase of 24 houses.

The value of any particular claim depends upon whether it is made by a former owner/trader (businessperson), or a former tenant. For those in both categories who wish to resettle, the value of their claim is almost equal (except for former owners/traders with claims to properties in excess of 600 m^2 who are entitled to additional monetary compensation on a sliding scale).[3] The value of claims differs more sharply for those claimants opting for monetary compensation. The monetary settlement package for former tenants consisted of a once-off payment of R17,500, an amount which has recently increased to R22,550 and then to R25,580.[4] In most cases, this payment is divided among a number of family members represented under a single claim. The claims of former owners and traders opting for monetary compensation, on the other hand, are still being processed. They are entitled to a base amount of R40,000 for property claims of up to 600 m^2, and additional compensation on a sliding scale for larger claims (see n 3, below). The total number of claimants – approximately 2,600 – represents only a small proportion of the original population of the district, even when one considers that each claim usually consists of several family members. There is a sizeable and growing group of ex-residents who did not submit a claim by the official nationwide December 1998 deadline (since extended), but who are mobilizing to be included in the process. In the interest of augmenting the existing pool of claimants who intend to resettle, the D6BRT – which is ultimately in a position to make the final decision on what is to be done with the vacant District Six land – has indicated that these would-be-claimants will through a broader selection process have first rights to any undeveloped plots that are not used to resettle legally recognized claimants.

For many claimants, restitution offers a panacea of 'return' to the good days of old (Fortune 1996; Ebrahim 1999). This entails not only resettlement in District Six, but a symbolic reinstatement of a lost 'community' (cf. James 2007; Robins 2001; Walker 2004). Others, however, are sceptical that there will be a place for them in the new District Six: 'District Six will never, *never* be the same!' is a common lament. They fear having to pay high rents, or that the gangsterism and crime of the Cape Flats will find its way into District Six. Alternatively, they express class- or race-prejudice against their potential future neighbours. The question, then, is how we can make sense of this bewildering complexity in the context of citizenship struggle, in a way that goes beyond the current affirmation within social science of 'community' as a product of social construction, and without merely leaving our answer as a description of a formless plurality of voices.

The question of community

It has been widely recognized that the relationship between locality and forms of association such as 'community' and citizenship has become increasingly elusive and at the same time intensified in the context of increasing displacement and de-territorialization in late modern society (Gupta and Ferguson 1997; Amit 2002). Identities are re-territorialized in displacement (Malkki 1997), and these processes are greatly intensified – and, as is largely the case in District Six, sometimes dramatically sparked (cf. Robins 2001) – by land restitution. In South Africa as elsewhere, land restitution greatly complicates existing social relations between beneficiaries by providing new opportunities for social mobility and social differentiation. Indeed, as one observer notes, 'Land claims . . . have become a catalyst for processes of ethnogenesis that reproduce apartheid-like ethnic categories and essentialist discourses' (Robins 2001: 844). These processes and discourses often centre on the concept of 'community'. In District Six, the principal cultural and political agents acting on behalf of the claimants – the D6M and the D6BRT – have for the most part worked hard to promote an alternative, less rigid form of associational identification based on the district's former hybridity and heterogeneity. This would appear to echo the approach of the Canadian Labrador Metis Association (see Chapter 4, Plaice, in this book), except that the aforementioned agents in District Six explicitly disavow – or at least downplay – any invocation of ethnicity or race as throwbacks to apartheid ideology (see Soudien 1990; Beyers 2008, forthcoming). However, as I will demonstrate below, popular discourses of 'community' amongst District Sixers at large have their own dynamics. They prove to be less flexible, more essentializing.

Much recent thinking in anthropology on the subject of 'community' is informed by Fredrik Barth's (1970) situational boundary method and especially Benedict Anderson's (1991) 'imagined communities'. Apart from their articulation of broadly defined 'conditions of possibility', however, there is little in these approaches to connect symbolic and discursive constructions of 'community' with the forms of desire and aspiration through which these constructions are mobilized. Veret Amit criticizes the increasingly widespread use of 'imagined communities' to represent de-territorialized social relations (for example, Appadurai 1996) for assuming 'that if people imagine themselves, even when they do not know each other, to share a distinctive collective identity, then they can mobilize themselves as a community', and thus for presuming 'that to imagine community is already to constitute a community' (Amit 2002: 24). While her call for greater attention to 'the difficulties of structure, logistics, persuasion, ideology and opportunity involved in constructing actual as opposed to imagined communities' (Amit 2002) is entirely persuasive, one should not throw the baby out with the bathwater. The concept of 'imagined communities' may be useful for thinking about social and political mobilization, or lack thereof, provided that it is adequately grounded. What is lacking is any kind of relation to volition – a sense of how the diverse *aspirations* and *desires* of people who imagine themselves as part of community are mobilized in *a particular direction*, with apparent *collective intent*. Indeed, even if their aspirations and desires for 'community' are only apparently in concert, what is it about this appearance that merits such deep commitment? Addressing these issues requires interpreting the social and phenomenological reality of the construct (Jackson 1996: 4): obtaining some kind of understanding of what is at stake (Bourdieu 1991 [1984]: 240) in 'community' for a range of people who often strongly believe in 'its' existence, and feel an intense sense of attachment to 'it'. 'Community' is always already in the process of formation, and given that this is particularly true in the dynamic context of land restitution, which usually involves great flux in both the key temporal and spatial referents of identity, it is a highly productive field for observing such formation and, indeed, formativeness.

How, then, do District Sixers at large see 'community'? As might be expected, an analysis of the interviews reveals 'community' as a highly contested idea which, in giving an account of a rich social history, also articulates diverse sets of interests and aspirations. The old District Six is widely commemorated as a diverse, devil-may-care, cosmopolitan 'community', where so-called coloured, Muslim, Indian, African and white people coexisted in a spirit of tolerance and mutual support. The interviewees repeatedly speak of Muslims and Christians living together harmoniously, and recall District Six as being a kind of retreat from the racialism of the apartheid world surrounding it. According to the leadership of the D6BRT representing District Six claimants, the aim of re-development is to reinstate these conditions of social diversity under the banner of an officially sanctioned 'multiculturalism'. The D6BRT and the Land Claims Commission have been actively promoting resettlement over monetary compensation, given the former's greater potential to contribute to a significant social transformation.

In District Six, there is a very strong sense of community despite the size and diverse socio-cultural and racial composition of the group. Given that so much is at stake, and that much still needs to be settled about the nature and character of 'community', it tends in practice to be posited as an existential social question about the nature and extent of a social group, rather than as a predetermined secure basis from which legal and state processes can proceed. 'Community' is manifested, in the concrete form of a social group, fundamentally as difference, not sameness – as agents' positions of distinction in relation to one another in social space (cf. Bourdieu 1991 [1994], 1997). And yet, despite this constitutive condition of difference, 'community' discursively works towards commonality. It is thus necessary to delve into the question of what might be called the 'will-to-community': the collectivizing drive to revive, recover, regenerate the sense of community, in a way that articulates diverse desires and aspirations. In District Six, this process of mobilizing commonality occurs in the nexus between loss and the possibility of restoration, and is manifested at both spatial and temporal levels (cf. Verdery 1994) – in a 'feeling of togetherness', in the words of more than one interviewee, that is both about setting sights on the centre of Cape Town, and about recalling a bygone era when life was somehow better.

In that the 'community'-building project in District Six was prompted and enabled by the state-initiated land claims process (cf. Greenhouse et al. 1994, see also the Introduction to this book) one could say that the will-to-community answers, or addresses itself, to the state and its laws. In its political form this will-to-community is answerable to the land claims process, as the concrete instantiation of the 1994 transition to democracy. While the will-to-community takes the social group as an object of identity and belonging, at another level it also constitutes a 'buy-in' to the formal and legal processes of justice administration. In articulating the level of associational practice with a particular political-institutional domain, it constitutes a public sphere and thus significantly contributes to the emergence of a substantive field of social citizenship struggle (Somers 1993; Rocco 2000; Isin and Wood 1999), a topic which can only be broadly invoked in this chapter. The will-to-community is differentiated and differentiating, to be sure, but coheres around an object of volition which is widely perceived to be held in common. This object has unity only in an ideational sense – a matter to be considered shortly, after first underscoring some of the main social differentiations in question.

To begin, the formal division between tenancy claims and ownership/trader claims is reflected in their respective decision rationales regarding how to settle their claims. This is in part because this division constitutes a rough indication – although admittedly imperfect – of the influence of class differences on aspirations and strategic practical orientation (cf. James 2007; Walker 2004). In spite of significant upward or downward social mobility in the case of certain families, the general trend has been that former tenants have continued to be less affluent than former owners/traders, due to not having been able to afford to relocate to comparatively more affluent suburbs at the time of the removals. Former tenants – particularly those still living in 'sub-economic' areas – tended to be much more likely to view restitution as enabling the reestablishment of the former ethos or 'spirit' of District Six. They thus tended to argue for an egalitarian new District Six, in which there are not major differences in standard of living amongst inhabitants. In contrast to most tenancy claimants' communitarian invocations, ownership claimants – and some of the more affluent tenancy claimants – often took a more individualistic and pragmatic approach, and tended more readily to use the language of property rights to articulate their claims. Indeed, former owners often resented the fact that if they were to opt for resettlement, they were formally entitled only to a base-package with a value equivalent to that offered to former tenants.

Two further forms of social differentiation that are highly significant for the District Six case are racial and religious ascription. Only the former will be addressed in this paper. The next section interprets claimant decisions regarding the settlement of their claims in light of the history of racially differentiated citizenship in Cape Town. This will lay the foundation for elaborating the concept of the will-to-community in the rest of the chapter.

Racially differentiated citizenship

The political significance of District Six, both historically and at present, has to be cast in light of the politics of the region. Under the apartheid regime, particularly during the 1980s, the state not only furnished people then classified as 'coloureds' with more rights than 'Africans' in the Western Cape, but also became a direct employer of significant sectors of the 'coloured' population. The Group Areas Acts of 1950 and 1966 formed the foundation for segregated education, health and social services, as well as the territorial basis for establishing putatively representative coloured institutions of government, in the form of elected municipal councils and eventually a tricameral parliament

(Unterhalter 1987). The Coloured Labour Preference Policy, in tandem with policies controlling the influx of Africans into the Western Cape, was designed to protect coloured people from African competition in the labour market and politically to appease coloured people in light of their disenfranchisement. In the longer term, the implicit objective was to secure white dominance in the Western Cape by securing the compliance of the coloured majority (Goldin 1987).

The field of District Six politics and discourses about the area have been dominated by coloured voices, in part because the majority of the population of District Six was coloured – and increasingly so after the earlier removals of African people. In large part this can also be attributed to the relatively privileged citizenship status of coloured people vis-à-vis African people, and the much higher level of domination experienced by African people – their virtual expulsion from the region, and especially from the city centre, where their presence had been precarious and controlled. Before being declared 'white', District Six was thus first defined as 'coloured' in ethno-nationalist terms by the ruling hegemony (Western 1981). When District Six was destroyed to make way for a proclaimed 'white area', the removals were paternalistically rationalized according to what would be in the presumed best and rational interest of 'the Coloured population'. The liberal press lamented the loss of this 'Coloured homeland'. The *Cape Times* averred that 'If there ever was an area in which Coloured people were entitled to live by tradition, by occupation, and by human right it is District Six', thus deploying a minority rights discourse to lament the 'Coloureds' bereavement of 'their' territory, their most solid foothold in an otherwise ostensibly sparse cultural tradition (*Cape Times*, 14 February 1966). Local conceptualizations endorsed, while differing in detail from, these insistences on the coloured character of the area. The construction of District Six as a 'coloured space' (Soudien 2001) was thus not just a matter of an externally imposed ascription. According to Bickford-Smith et al., the demolition of District Six 'meant the destruction of a kind of mother city within the Mother City for many coloured Capetonians' (Bickford-Smith et al. 1999: 183, 186).

This historical context directly affected the decision rationales of claimants regarding the settlement of their claim. One of the most striking findings from the interview data is the evident importance of 'returning' to District Six and thus recovering a sense of belonging and identity for coloured and Muslim claimants, set against the near absence of such a motive amongst African claimants. This is reflected by the disproportionately small number of African claimants in general, and specifically of African claimants who have opted to resettle. It is not merely the case that coloured or Muslim ex-residents are most likely to have submitted a claim, and – particularly for those from a working class and lower income background – to opt for resettlement. In addition, those opting instead for monetary compensation tended to see the latter as a consolation prize when resettlement was not considered viable or desirable. Prominently factored into their decision rationales was the question of whether or not symbolic 'return' was possible in any practical sense. For coloured and Muslim claimants opting for compensation, a common reason was that 'District Six won't be like it used to be'. The question of 'community' is thus resolved on the grounds of the possibility of restorative justice as a means to reclaiming an identity.

Remarkably, however, neither these rationales nor the general motive of 'return', figured significantly for claimants now living in African townships (including two women who self-identified as coloured). They do not, then, appear to frame their relationship to the area in terms of a similarly strong sense of belonging or identification. This suggests that there was no build-up or 'hype' regarding the claims process in African townships comparable to that which existed in non-African residential areas. Once again this reflects the history of spatial segregation, and the long-standing dominant perception that District Six was and still is a 'coloured area'. African claimants tended to have a more practical attitude about resolving their claims, considering their options not in terms of 'return' or reinstating 'community', but in terms of using monetary compensation for improving their living conditions in their current areas of residence or, for the more severely impoverished, simply surviving. They were much less likely to be nostalgic about life in the former District Six due to the much harsher realities most of them then faced in terms of legal status, access to employment and sources of livelihood, access to public institutions, physical mobility, and racial prejudice in everyday interactions. This included iniquities suffered at the hands of other District Sixers.

In sum, there has clearly been a formation of a dominant perspective among restitution claimants, in keeping with the socio-historical construction of District Six as a 'coloured space'. While this perspective does not neatly correspond with any particular social sub-grouping, it is possible to identify broad differences in orientation between claimants who continue to be categorized in terms of race and class, and continue to live in separate residential areas.

The broken self

For those most emotionally invested in the project of reclaiming 'community', 'return' offers a profound possibility of self-recovery amidst the ongoing reality of trauma and alienation. For many claimants, the restitution meetings, and the interviews themselves, were the occasion for rehashing painful memories of removals. Their testimonies make strikingly clear that removals were not merely a hardship endured in the past, but are an ongoing process of struggle and mourning, one which informs a strong desire to return. An important reason for opting for resettlement, often coupled with the motive of 'return', is to leave or escape the areas in which claimants currently live. The place to which they were removed is seen as lifeless, dull and empty – in direct contrast to the 'liveliness' and 'vibrancy' of District Six (Ngcelwane 1999; Adams and Suttner 1988; Rive 1986). The loss represented by removals is taken to be intimately tied up with illness, disorder and death. Not surprisingly, these concerns were expressed with particular urgency by claimants that currently resided in poorer areas with heightened levels of criminal activity and violence, such as Hanover Park, Guguletu, and Lavender Hill.

For most claimants, therefore, the traumatic rupture of removals was not a one-time occurrence, now left behind; it is an inseparable part of the ongoing ordeal of displacement, insecurity and disempowerment that continue to characterize their lives on the Cape Flats. The plunge from the familiar into the unknown is the background for the emergence of the currently prevailing narratives and practices of 'community'. 'Community' emerged from the ruins of forced removals as the pre-eminent collectivizing signification of experiences of loss. It originates in an indignant sense of injustice, and as an object of ideation, 'community' manifests a countervailing sense of justice. One can already see the beginnings of this early on; for example, a 1974 memorandum[5] protesting the removals vividly demonstrates the birth of District Six as itself an idea of justice:

> District Six was for so long the essence of throbbing vital life. Could new hope not there be bred into the hearts of all men? ... Might not the Mother City cradle a new life? Could the Phoenix of a new South Africa not arise from the ashes and the dust of District Six?
>
> (Section 3.2)

The longing to 'return' to a better place and time is in most cases inseparable from a desire to leave the place where claimants currently reside. As Tahir, a Muslim man given to allegory, states:

> Let's face it, the community, if you see it, has never been broken. If they had been broken they would not cry to come back. Only a broken man come back to home, because a forest is not a place for a broken man. And where we were put was a forest.

This apparently paradoxical statement exemplifies the ambivalent character of narratives of return. Return here is as much about 'the forest' as it is about 'home'. The broken man can reconstitute himself in 'community', where the bond of those in relation to which he had first constituted himself as whole, has in some sense 'never been broken'. Restitution offers an opportunity to transcend the post-removals context of a loss of self by enabling one to regain a sense of wholeness, or at least of the possibility of becoming whole.

District Sixers were rendered voiceless, powerless, and in their own terms, 'less-than-human' by removals. This is first of all a brutally sensual and 'material' fact, so evocatively stated in interviewees' memories of their first experiences as residents on the sandy wastes of the Cape Flats – the 'stables' of Guguletu, the '*hokkies*' [cages] of Manenberg and Hanover Park, the long early morning hikes through darkness to catch the trains, the strange neighbours. The most pressing imperative for District Sixers, as in other cases of forced removals, is to reinstate their humanity as a victim of forced removals. To recognize and restore a right in land, particularly through the resettlement option, begins to answer this imperative.

It needs to be remembered that the majority of claimants are over 60 years of age. Most elders who have opted for resettlement are looking for a peaceful *denouement* to often difficult lives – and this includes a retreat from politics. Thus Ina, who has lost her husband to illness and has had to deal with the intense level of gangster activity for which Valhalla Park has become notorious, is looking for a kind of refuge:

> That it will look like it did before, that you can walk in the streets. You don't need to be afraid. You could be outside late at night in District Six. Your children could be outside late [in the evening]. You don't have to be afraid. It shall all just be nice like it originally [*eers*] was there. So we hope to live like that again, and that neighbours will again be together.

These aspirations are shared by many of the claimants now living in impoverished areas who have opted for resettlement. Many, however, are in search not merely of a personal refuge, but also of an alternative life for their children. They hope that those that follow them will give rise to a new kind of society, one that derives its impetus from the character of 'community' in the old District Six as they remember it. In this respect, opting to resettle in the new District Six is sometimes taken as evidence of commitment to a revival of the old 'community' that is nonetheless oriented to the future generations.

Although nostalgic commemorations of the past and concomitant ideas of justice are most common amongst older claimants who could remember living in District Six, it is not just the elderly who have a strong sense of attachment to that area. According to Martin, an upwardly mobile 28-year-old man with a young family, who was moved from District Six at the age of five:

> I live in Rosebank which is fairly white, and students and old people live there. And I was looking to buy a house, and I don't feel at home anywhere else. And I know that I'll feel at home in District Six, because this is where I lived. This is where I grew up. This is where my brothers grew up, I was beaten (laughs), we used to do naughty things . . . my childhood. And you know, I wish that I lived here a little bit longer so that I could have had more memories.

Martin's rationale for opting for the resettlement package combines a general feeling of belonging to District Six, a strategic assessment of the property market and the nostalgia of childhood – the memory of which is filtered through the stories recounted by his parents, who now live in the low income area of Lentegeur.

It is important, therefore, that the claims process is not simply about pragmatic considerations of material gain and social mobility. Many claimants, especially elderly coloured and Muslim people, express a strong desire to 'recapture' in some way or form what life was like. While many approach the process pragmatically, having resigned themselves to the fact that the restitution process can not itself enable this to happen, many others harbour hopes of 'return' in the larger sense of the word, or express disillusionment and sorrow that such 'return' is not possible. Underlying these rationales is a longing – which to varying degrees was reignited or intensified by the restitution process – for a time, an ethos, a social universe where one's humanity had not yet been removed, when the fragile thread of belonging was not yet severed.

Reconciling the old and the new

Interviews with coloured and Muslim claimants are populated with statements such as: 'We want to change life, to go back', 'What one wants to come back to is what District Six used to be', and 'Home is home, you cannot find another place that is home'. At the same time, the prevailing wisdom is that 'It will never, *never* be the same!', and that 'We are separated, in other words, we are broken apart from one another [*gebreek van mekaar*]'. There is tension between these two kinds of narrative orientation. Indeed, a respondent often contradicted her or himself throughout the interview, by stating for example that District Six can never be the same (with emphatic emphasis on the 'never'), but affirming moments later her or his intent to resettle in order to experience District Six again as it used to be. What can one make of this?

Interviewees who recognized the tension or contradiction between the desire for 'return' and its impossibility usually resolved it as follows: 'Everybody says it's not going to be same, but I hope it's going to be like that!'. This sense of hope is often an outcome of interactions with others at restitution meetings and reunions. According to Abieda, a 48-year-old Muslim woman from an 'economic area' in Mitchell's Plain:

> I am happy, I wanted to come back. I loved District Six. I wanted to come back. I want to show my children how I lived. I hope it is going to be the same, I hope the people are going to be the same as the others – the old people that [lived] there. I met a lot of them here, the other day when we come together and met, and all their children are all so big. And they can't believe we're turning out the same as we were when we were young. Ja! I was young and I didn't let anybody tell me something (. . .) But I changed over the years, I changed a lot over the years.

It is interesting to note the shifts in Abieda's response: first she notes the tremendous sense of reaffirmation in discovering that people hadn't changed since living in District Six. This is no doubt in part a result of the nostalgia of the reunions, where one has the opportunity to re-enact one's sense of the past by experiencing one's interactions with others according to one's memory of oneself and of them. Abieda then says that she has changed a lot over the years, probably also a result of the recognition that comes from remembering how one was when one was younger – perhaps less fearful and more carefree. Finally, a moment later she states: 'It must be like the old District Six, if it doesn't . . . I know it's not going to be like the old District Six, but I hope so'. This willed imperative is echoed by other claimants who say that District Six *must* be the same – and indeed be even better than it was before, since there should be no gangsterism and they should be more affluent. In the end, as if responding to sceptics, Abieda weakens this imperative to a counter-intuitive hope.

The evident discord between desired and expected outcome – between optimistic and sceptical voices – tends to be resolved in the first instance not by an objectivist explanation of how the ideal may be brought about externally in the world, but by an imperative in the form of a subjectivist affirmation of internal hope and faith. As Ina avers: 'It will again be like it was before – not actually [*eintlik*], but we know, we shall make it that it will be like . . . it was before, in District Six'. This kind of assertion of personal volition is usually both active and passive. Thus Wareda, a 45-year-old woman, states:

> The community as such, the people of District Six, they are no longer, they are gone. And it's their children, their grandchildren. (. . .) we'll have to wait and see. Maybe we can – the children of the people that used to stay in District Six – maybe we can build a community, and our children and grandchildren can carry on the legacy of District Six, you know? I just hope so, for myself and for District Six, I hope that is what can happen. That we can be a wonderful community like we used to be. I know . . . I'm sure it's not going to be the same as it was 30 years ago, but we can try. We can try to make it work.

Wareda's approach ultimately reflects the kind of circular and constitutive relation between an individual's personal hope and desire that the 'community' be reinstituted and the aggregate or collective volition that would be required to reinstate it. The implicit narrative logic is: 'Through *my* act of volition, *I* am part of a community-willing-a-community-to-come'. The key feature of the willed 'community' is that it is conceived of both in a primordialist sense – as a set of essential communal traits shared by members and carried over time – and in a constructivist sense – as a 'communicative community'.

When asked whether it would be possible to recreate a sense of 'community' in the new District Six, Henry's response was: 'Well, it all depends on the communication, how the people will communicate towards each other'. Indeed, the question of 'return' rests on finding 'once again' the 'communicative ethos' of District Six – and in doing so, finding the way that one was unto others. The regeneration of this ethos requires a combination of memory-work and political mobilization; hence the potentially pivotal role of the D6M, which is dedicated to precisely this kind of task. But it would also require communicative work at the level of interpersonal relations. As Ismail puts it:

> The community shall build [*sal bou*]. (...) Look, if you are a child, you can't simply walk, you must first crawl, you understand? Now the community can be the same: people must become acquainted, you understand? ... Now if we know each other well [*lekker vir mekaar ken*] and the children, then the community will emerge [*opkom*].

It is crucial that the type of 'community' that is envisioned bears the essence of what ex-residents remember of the character of life in District Six: a dense network of intersubjective relations among people who are roughly equally poor, an ethic of mutual care and support, and the prevalence of an informal dialogized mode of communication (see McCormick 2002).

There is, then, if not a broad agreement, a 'structure of aspiration' regarding 'community' in the new District Six shared by a certain critical mass of claimants. It is shared, in particular, by coloured and Muslim claimants that have opted for resettlement. Claimants in this central contingent call forth 'community' as a potentially unifying project of salvaging the past. Furthermore, the aspirations for 'community' in a new District Six are to some extent grounded by a roughly shared set of memories of what the old District Six was like. There is, for instance, considerable consensus among claimants – particularly of the older generation – that the new District Six should conform to general standards of respectability – that, as one younger woman put it, '[we] keep away from the hooligans (laughs)!'. There is also agreement that a new District Six should have something of the egalitarian ethos of mutual care and support, on the one hand, and respect for cultural and religious difference, on the other, of the old District Six. Such a project is sharply contrasted to the violence, deprivation, and alienation characterizing life in many townships and suburbs of the Cape Flats. Volition is thus mobilized around the urgent need for social solidarity: one might say that its object is a community-imperative.

For a minority of interviewees the gap between expected and desired outcome cannot be bridged. They insist that 'community' cannot be 'brought back', not only because 'the past is past', but because this change is perceived to include many District Sixers who it is thought are no longer sufficiently generous of spirit, and who will thus not have the collective resolve, willpower, and stamina required for a 'community'-building project of this nature. Thus Sandra doubts that the 'community' would ever be the same as it was – in spite of the fact that 'lots seem to think it'. She claims that 'my friends were old people and they've all died'. She occasionally crosses paths with other District Sixers living in the area, 'but each one of them was now living for themselves'.

Practical aspirations for a new District Six

Having seen how the tension is resolved at an abstract level between the desire to 'return' and the recognition that return is practically impossible, I now turn to its practical resolution. The problem, as one claimant put it, is how 'the old and the new are supposed to integrate'.

Most claimants bring an egalitarian sentiment to their aspirations for a new district, and are apprehensive about the potential consequences of much increased socio-economic differentiation among District Sixers since their removals decades earlier. According to Abdulatief, ' *"die hoog" van hulle moet nie daar wees nie, nè* ["the high (attitude)" of them musn't be there, *nè*] ... – how can I say it in English, like uh, you're better than me, like that attitude, you see'. Ewald, who lives in Belhar Extension 13, articulates the concern as follows:

> Let's say they build fancy houses, streamlined houses and so forth, the space-aged kind of thing, you know? Ok, then that is now going to be the elite and so forth, it's going to cost more and so forth. And now on the opposite side of the road, now there you have something plainer, that is now more the 'sub-economic', you know? Then you see ... then it's not going to be like the old District Six where, you know, where I look over the road and ... I'm just like you, you know? (...) Then you see that can change the spirit of the people ...

While there is widespread agreement, at least in principle, that a general socio-economic standard of life ought to be ensured for District Six's new inhabitants, it is less certain what standard precisely is called for. Thus Sedick, a former tenant who lives in Rocklands, a more affluent area than those in which Ewald or Abulatief live, concurs that 'once this place is redeveloped we should be very equal to one another', but thinks that the type of housing needed in a new District Six are 'decent two or three bedroom house[s] – you must be proud of it, you must know that for sure that you can stand up and say "Well, I'm back in District Six and this is my house" '. In fact, many claimants appear to imagine the planning of the new district in terms that are roughly consonant with suburban design. Rayda and Allie echo this general sensibility, and are hoping for 'roomy town houses' that are similar in character, with a garage downstairs, and the option of extending the home if one wants to – as long as it conforms to existing standards of uniformity. Other indications of a generally suburban vision include mention of guarding privacy, having a front garden, lots of trees and grass, and ample playgrounds and public facilities for the young.

This perhaps suggests an imminent shift in the conception of the nature of the social order from a (remembered) 'loving community' based on very intimate family-like relations, towards something more in line with Weber's version of rationalized society, where relationships between individuals tend to be mediated by contracts, and are thus more narrow and purposive (Weber 1968: 668ff). In this respect, claimants' views on what the new District Six should be like, and how the redevelopment will change the city, tends to be cast more in terms of social mobility, in contrast to their discussions about the reasons for claiming and the rationales for claims settlement decisions which usually evoke an egalitarian collective identity. In general, claimants hope that the new homes will have a considerably higher standard than in the old District Six, and than the homes into which they were subsequently forced to move. Moreover, these aspirations are supplemented by an implicit subtext of 'social upliftment'. Gadija from Bonteheuwel hopes that with redevelopment, the children of elderly claimants will:

> ... now maybe come right [*regkom*], *nè* ... mix between decent people and so ... but as the time goes on then we shall again learn to know one another [*mekaar leer ken*] again, and rise [*opbou*] again, the community [*gemeente*] will rise again like it was before ... that love for one another.

For her, a revitalized 'community' ethos will be the means of assimilating and civilizing the other within. The concern with upliftment dovetails with broader security concerns, particularly of older people. Thus Kevin, a 70-year-old Christian man currently living in middle-class Strandfontein, hopes for 'peace and comfort', and says that his 'prayer' is that a redeveloped District Six will be a 'clean place': that it 'should be drug-free, gangsterism-free, shebeen-free. Because we had those things in the past.... and I don't know, it should not mushroom like it did before'. Others envisioned the need for state or police protection, or community-based forms of vigilantism.

Despite the emphasis on social mobility, it should be stated that the latter is not necessarily opposed to concerns of social redress and social justice. Tahir polemically casts social mobility as a need, and frames redevelopment in terms of an appeal to humanity:

> Mankind is not a doll to stay in something two by two rooms! You'd rather put a pigeon and say this is your prison camp! Give us something that we can live in! You've got to integrate the old and the new together, that it must combine, because we want the world to come and see us again, to visit us, to live with us, enjoy us, and come to know us better – how we are!

Moreover, aspirations of social mobility should not be seen as simply contradicting the cultural project of reviving 'community'. It was thus frequently stated that among other social benefits of redevelopment, the city's churches and mosques would be bolstered. However, cultural revival is not seen as requiring that the design of the old District Six be replicated. Although many would like to see elements of the built environment carried forward from the old District

Six, they imply that the most essential thing is that the conditions be in place for the creation of a similar 'culture', ethos, and social atmosphere. Robert sums up the general sentiment, when he responds to my question of whether the new District Six would be similar to the old:

> Not similar, but the culture will be there, you see. Now the people are more advanced. They're building their houses, making their houses nice. That time it was clay houses, now its bricks. . . . It won't be a slum area, it will be an upgraded area.

Whatever the balance between redress and mobility in the various particular narratives of entitlement, it is possible to discern a general shift in consciousness between an initial phase of the struggle for restitution, where former residents are mobilized to claim rights, and a subsequent phase, presently moving into gear, in which these claims are to be practically settled. In the former, the general target is 'land', as the spatio-temporal location of that which was lost and is now reclaimed, while in the latter it is 'property', as a means of social mobility and personal security, and something with clear boundaries that is possessed and defined against others (cf. Verdery 1994). While the use of property rights discourse is not yet dominant, it is most evident amongst current property owners and upwardly mobile claimants. The figure of 'community' is important throughout, but its emphasis moves from signifying a context of memory, healing and sometimes transformative vision, to signifying a space where property relations are respected and where new relations between neighbours may be inspired by the district's former ethos, to be sure, but can nevertheless be negotiated according to individual preference.

Apprehensions for a new District Six

Ex-residents intending on resettling in District Six are also apprehensive about the nature of their aspired-to community. One of their principal sources of apprehensiveness is that they will not be able to select who their neighbours are, and more broadly, who will live in the neighbourhood. Indeed, the presumed district-wide solidarity – which I have suggested should primarily be seen as a result of the symbolic work of community-formation in the wake of removals – will first be put to the test in the formation of neighbourly relationships in the new District Six. But more than unfamiliarity, the apprehension is about the effect of time: whether District Sixers that had been living in very different social conditions in the intervening decades since removals continue to share the same virtues and values as before. Do they, as a whole, continue to be 'God-fearing', without pretension, respectful of parents and elders, hardworking, and sociable and amiable?

While interviewees thus believe that the 'spirit' of the old District Six can be rekindled, they think that time and work will be required. Those moving back will bring with them the respective localisms associated with the places in which they have been living. One might say that whereas integration in the old District Six was greatly facilitated by the existence of a common ethos and code of conduct, the new District Six will have to contend with the existence of distinct cultural and behavioural codes thought to prevail in places as distinct as Guguletu, Langa, Hanover Park, Belhar extension 13, Greenhaven, Rhylands and Woodstock. Older people are especially concerned about the younger people that will move in, who may have little or no experience of the 'old times'. When I asked Jeanette, an African woman who intends to resettle, about the potential difficulties with redevelopment, she responded simply and pointedly: 'You can see for yourself, things are not like they were before. You youngsters are twisting things, you are not like we were before'.

Moving back to District Six, although it reverses the original situation of removals in which interviewees suddenly had to adapt to strangers from diverse locales, is often seen as analogous to it. This is particularly the case among older interviewees, and figures either as a rationale for the decision not to resettle, or as an apprehension for those who do intend to resettle. There is an anxiety amongst claimants about other District Sixers who now live in neighbourhoods and townships which are feared or looked down upon. Class-based prejudice is most commonly expressed in terms of the 'respectability' of District Sixers versus its relative absence in the case of their fellow denizens on the Cape Flats, particularly in the 'sub-economic' areas. In many cases, District Sixers have personally witnessed the effect of bad surroundings on good people in their areas of current residence, and see people as having become 'raw' – as one evidently devout Anglican woman put it.

There is also considerable apprehension about the extent to which different racial groups will be able to coexist. While a handful of the coloured interviewees expressed the wish that a redeveloped District Six would incorporate a significant number of Africans, and that the neighbourhood would be even more diverse than previously was the case, most expressed a considerable amount of ambivalence in this regard. Although Sofia had told me before that there was no 'colour-bar' amongst District Sixers, she suddenly blurted indignantly that Africans had lived in 'caves' in District Six: 'how can *they* presume to tell a tourist about District Six?'. Ewald, on the other hand, is concerned about the immigrants from other African countries who he believes will probably also come to settle in District Six. 'I think that now you'll probably have more of a cultures clash than before'. African claimants are, of course, not exempt from racial fear or prejudice; they sometimes saw Muslims and coloureds as actively working to exclude them. The latter were portrayed as 'not belonging in Africa' or as 'having no culture'. Although some interviews displayed genuine 'non-racial' sentiments, the widespread ambivalence around race, and the increasingly explicit expressions of anxiety in this regard when interviewees switched from discussing the past of District Six to its anticipated future, is perhaps a cause for concern.[6]

There is clearly a tension, then, between evocations of what one D6BRT member called 'unity in diversity' and the apprehensions about that diversity defined in racial and class terms. This recalls the tension noted earlier between the present aspirations to social mobility and the commemoration of past egalitarianism and relations of mutual support. This is in part a manifestation of the use of the language of individual rights to manifest a sense of entitlement, on the one hand, and the fact that the ideational and normative dimensions of entitlement are based in a desire to recover the fractured self – a self which is remembered as formerly existing through communitarian relations of mutual support and defence – on the other. It is not accurate to say that the impulse for 'community' sides with the latter, in a kind of romantic defence of the past against the ravages of late modernity. Rather, 'community' is precisely about the projection of certain reified interpretations of the past into the context of present aspirations, and has the effect of masking power differentials and otherwise divisive forms of social distinction (cf. Greenhouse et al. 1994). Now, these tensions have not posed a decisive practical problem in the restitution process yet, partly because communitarian invocations occur at a level that is sufficiently general and nostalgic to trump social mobility and/or anxieties about 'undesirable others', and partly because in the current phase of heightened discursive production, compatibilities are emphasized over incompatibilities. By thus interpreting social mobility and apprehensions as a counter to the disorder, alienation, and social privation of the post-removals world, the compatibility between rights claims and communitarian rememberings is asserted. However, with housing reconstruction under way and the first claimants resettled, there is a need to 'imagine community' in a much more practical sense. This will need to take stock of the range of materially embedded interests and to acknowledge the prevalence of 'essentialist discourses' on race, ethnicity and class.

Conclusion

Based on the narratives of loss and entitlement by restitution claimants, this paper has conceptualized 'community' as an ideational object born of a sociolegal relation, which manifests a set of roughly compatible normative orientations towards restorative justice. It has traced the shifting and dynamic formation of a dominant perspective on 'community' in District Six. While the majority of claimants rationalize their claims in terms of 'return', they nevertheless generally believe that 'return' in any substantial sense is impossible. And while for many claimants this impossibility does not pose a decisive dilemma in the stage where claims are mobilized and the claimant group consolidated, the problem remains to be solved at the moment when claims are settled. How to reconcile the desire to 'return' with its practical impossibility is resolved by what I have called the 'will-to-community': that is, by self-consciously internalizing 'community' as an object of volition and ideation.

The will-to-community mobilizes 'community' within a collectivizing structure of aspiration, imagination and desire – one that is political in the final instance, since it owes its form to the bid for citizenship. As the dominant trend among claimants, this mobilization of 'community' also needs to be seen as constituting a symbolic strategy within and in relation to a particular social group, consisting mainly of working-class and lower-income coloured and Muslim claimants engaged in a particular field of citizenship struggle. This mobilization of 'community' comes with dynamics of social exclusion, most clearly exemplified by the marginality of African claimants. This chapter, in beginning to address such questions, points to a broader field for future investigation. The shifting inclusionary and exclusionary dynamics of this will-to-community, expressed through a variety of different projections based on different memories of a past 'community' as refracted through the various spaces of displacement and relocation, is a fertile arena for exploration in studies of restitution.

References

Adams, H and H Suttner (1988) *William Street: District Six*, Cape Town: Chameleon Press.

Amit, V (2002) 'An Anthropology without Community?', in V Amit and N Rapport (eds) *The Trouble with Community: Anthropological Reflections on Movement, Identity and Collectivity*, London: Pluto Press.

Anderson, B (1991) *Imagined Communities: Reflections on the Origin and Spread of Nationalism*, revised edn, London: Verso.

Appadurai, A (1996) *Modernity at Large: Cultural Dimensions of Globalization*, Minneapolis, MN: University of Minnesota Press.

Barth, F (1970) *Ethnic Groups and Boundaries: The Social Organization of Cultural Difference*, London: Allen and Unwin.

Beyers, C (2007) 'Land Restitution's Rights Communities: The District Six Case', *Journal of Southern African Studies* 33(2): 267–85.

—— (2008, forthcoming) 'The Cultural Politics of "Community" and Citizenship in the District Six Museum, Cape Town', in C Neveu (ed.) *Anthropologica*, Special Issue: 'Citizenship, politics and locality: Anthropological Perspectives'.

Bourdieu, P (1991 [1984]) 'Social Space and the Genesis of "Classes" ', in *Language and Symbolic Power*, Cambridge, MA: Harvard University Press.

—— (1997) 'What Makes a Social Class? On the Theoretical and Practical Existence of Groups', *Berkeley Journal of Sociology* 32: 1–18.

Bickford-Smith, V, et al. (1999) *Cape Town in the Twentieth Century*, Cape Town: David Phillip Publishers.

Dubow, S (1995) *Scientific Racism in Modern South Africa*, Cambridge: Cambridge University Press.

Ebrahim, N (1999) *Noor's Story: My Life in District Six*, Cape Town: District Six Museum.

Fortune, L (1996) *The House in Tyne Street – Childhood Memories of District Six*, Roggebaai: Kwela Books.

Greenhouse, CJ et al. (1994) *Law and Community in Three American Towns*, New York: Cornell University Press.

Goldin, I (1987) *Making Race: The Politics and Economics of Coloured Identity in South Africa*, London: Longman.

Gupta, A and J Ferguson (1997), 'Beyond "Culture": Space, Identity, and the Politics of Difference', in Gupta and Ferguson (eds) *Culture, Power, Place: Explorations in Critical Anthropology*, Durham, NC: Duke University Press.

Humphries, R (1992) 'Administrative Politics and the Coloured Labour Preference Policy', in WG James and M Simmons (eds) *Class, Caste and Colour: A Social and Economic History of the South African Western Cape*, New Brunswick: Transaction Publishers.

Isin, E and PK Wood (1999) *Citizenship and Identity*, London: Sage Publications.

Jackson, M (1996) 'Introduction: Phenomenology, Radical Empiricism, and Anthropological Critique', in M Jackson (ed.) *Things as They are: New Directions in Phenomenological Anthropology*, Bloomington, IN: University of Indiana Press.

James, D (2007) *Gaining Ground? 'Rights' and 'Property' in South African Land Reform*, London: Routledge.

Jeppie, S (2001) 'Reclassifications: Coloured, Malay, Muslim', in Zimitri Erasmus (ed.) *Coloured by History, Shaped by Place: New Perspectives on Coloured Identities in Cape Town*, Cape Town: Kwela Books.

Jeppie, S and C Soudien (eds) (1990) *The Struggle for District Six: Past and Present*, Cape Town: Buchu Books.

Le Grange, L (2003) *District Six: Heritage Impact Assessment*, Lucien Le Grange Architects and Urban Planners.

Malkki, L (1997) 'National Geographic: The Rooting of Peoples and the Territorialization of National Identity among Scholars and Refugees', in Gupta and Ferguson (eds) *Culture, Power, Place: Explorations in Critical Anthropology*, Durham, NC: Duke University Press.

McCormick, K (2002) *Language in Cape Town's District Six*, New York: Oxford University Press.

Ngcelwane, N (1999) *Sala Kahle District Six: an African Woman's Perspective*, Roggebaai: Kwela Books.

Rasool, C and S Prosalendis (eds) (2001) *Recalling Community in Cape Town: Creating and Curating the Museum*, Cape Town: District Six Museum.

Ridd, RE (1981) 'Position and Identity in a Divided Community: Colour and Religion in the District Six, Walmer Estate, Woodstock Area of Cape Town', unpublished thesis, Oxford University.

Rive, R (1986) *Buckingham Palace*, Cape Town: David Philip.

Robins, S (2001) 'NGOs, "Bushmen" and Double Vision: The ≠khomani San Land Claim and the Cultural Politics of "Community" and "Development" in the Kalahari', *Journal of Southern African Studies* 27(4): 833–54.

Rocco, R (2000), 'Associational Rights-Claims, Civil Society and Place', in E Isin (ed.) *Democracy, Citizenship and the Global City*, London: Routledge.

Somers, MR (1993) 'Citizenship and the Place of the Public Sphere: Law, Community, and Political Culture in the Transition to Democracy', *American Sociological Review* 58: 587–620.

Soudien, C (1990) 'District Six: From Protest to Protest', in S Jeppie and C Soudien (eds) *The Struggle for District Six: Past and Present*, Cape Town: Buchu Books.

—— (2001) 'District Six and its Uses in the Discussion about Non-racialism', in Z Erasmus (ed.) *Coloured by History, Shaped by Place: New Perspectives on Coloured Identities in Cape Town*, Cape Town: Kwela Books.

Unterhalter, E (1987) *Forced Removal: The Division, Segregation and Control of the People of South Africa*, London: IDAF Publications.

Verdery, K (1994) 'The Elasticity of Land: Problems of Property Restitution in Transylvania', *Slavic Review* 53(4): 1071–109.

Walker, C (2004) ' "We are Consoled" – Reconstructing Cremin', *South African Historical Journal* 51: 199–223.

Weber, M (1968) *Economy and Society: An Outline of Interpretive Sociology* (R. Guenther and C Wittich, eds), trans. E Fischoff et al., New York: Bedminster Press.

Western, J (1981) *Outcast Cape Town*, London: George Allen and Unwin.

Notes

I wish to thank Deborah James, Derick Fay, Richard Wilson, Jane Cowan, and Kerry Bebee for invaluable comments and corrections of earlier versions of this chapter. The research for this article was supported by a Canadian Social Sciences and Humanities Research Council Doctoral Fellowship, and by the Centre for African Studies at the University of Cape Town, which provided institutional support.

1. In apartheid discourse, the term was commonly capitalized in order to indicate its status as a proper name corresponding to an ostensibly 'scientific' ethnoracial category – along with the other official categories (see Dubow 1995). Anti-apartheid and unofficial discourses in turn often disavowed this usage, and instead used the uncapitalized form. The issue of capitalization continues to be contentious today. Rather than attempt to distinguish between various usages, this chapter reverts to the uncapitalized form hereafter, for the sake of simplicity.
2. The official apartheid usage of the term 'coloured' included a subcategory of 'Muslims', or 'Cape Malays'. In current popular usage, this all-encompassing designation continues to be frequently employed, but 'coloured' and 'Muslim' are also often referred to as two separate categories – where 'coloured' typically has a more Christian or secular connotation (see Jeppie 2001). This chapter uses 'coloured' to denote the former sense of the term, except where it is useful to distinguish the two subcategories, in which case explicit reference is made to 'Muslim' in addition to 'coloured'.
3. Properties exceeding 600 m^2 are to be settled at R40 for every m^2 up to 1800 m^2, at R20 for every m^2 up to 3,000 m^2, and then at R10 for every m^2 up to 20,000 m^2 (Project Officer of Finance for District Six, personal interview, 15 July 2005). If ownership claimants are unhappy with this settlement offer, they have the option of pursuing an independent property valuation process.
4. These increases reflect increases in the housing subsidy, which are implemented to account for inflation.
5. Memorandum of September 1974, signed by Rev. JF Forbes of Zonnebloem College, and 'four other people/groups'.
6. There is particular cause for concern in light of increasingly public expressions of racial fear following the announcement in 2003 by the City to fund a massive housing project targeting informal settlements along the N2 highway, and culminating with District Six. Proposed plans involve, among other things, building 500 new houses in District Six in which beneficiaries currently living in informal settlements, who are alleged to be recent African immigrants from out of province with no personal history with District Six, would be resettled.

Chapter 9

Through the prism
Local reworking of land restitution settlements in South Africa

Yves Van Leynseele and Paul Hebinck

Abstract

Displaced communities living under conditions of land scarcity and poverty in South Africa have used land restitution policies as a means of historical redress. In mediating resettlement of their ancestral land, community representatives deploy discursive strategies that refer to cultural discontinuity suffered at the hands of apartheid's architects. The consequent reconstitution of claimant groups along traditionalist lines however becomes problematic when development agencies enter local arenas using an agenda of rural development that aims to create a new class of African farming entrepreneurs. This 'shifting articulation' of land as development object provokes a set of responses that unfold as multiple modernities. Through interaction between agencies and beneficiary communities, development parcels may be subject to disintegration and selective appropriation. Fragmentation occurs: intended broad-based reforms are essentially aggregate outcomes of hundreds of micro-level interfaces between programme beneficiaries and agencies of reform.

Introduction

This article explores contemporary processes of land restitution in post-apartheid South Africa and highlights the problematic marriage of historical redress with present-oriented production. Analysing the land restitution process, two distinct moments can be perceived: the resolution of historical land rights is followed by the so-called 'post-settlement' stage when a developmentalist language of production (a predominant feature of the parallel land redistribution programme) predominates. Although development agencies often separate the symbolic and political act of reconciliation from the 'post-settlement' stages of restitution, to local people land embodies a complex composite of multiple meanings and multiplex social relations that cannot easily be dissembled. In line with current modernity approaches in anthropology (Arce and Long 2000), we rather contend that the material and symbolic manifestations of land restitution are inseparable. These different elements become part of people's body of knowledge, experiences and physical environment, which in turn are the building blocks of future narratives in the ongoing renegotiation of development objects. They unfold as temporary constellations or multiple modernities.

Two case studies describe distinct manifestations of land restitution. The Mandlazini case gives an account of the fragmentation of exogenous land-use planning and the Makhoba case highlights the endorsement and materialization of a language of African rights and tradition. From the two cases together it becomes evident that intervention parties promote a number of uncertainties when land rights are formally resolved, and promote a consequent re-articulation of land as productive asset when claimant groups are confronted with modernization trajectories. By focusing mainly on localized appropriations of the bifurcated 'language of development' we describe restitution processes as a theatre where values are contested, internalized and reinterpreted by virtue of reflexivity and human agency.

In focusing on land restitution we show how it has created new fora of contestation and negotiation. We problematize the multiple objectives of the programme, which seeks to marry value-based issues (for example, participation, democratization and social equity) with concerns over viable production and sustainable land use. A persistent characteristic of rural transformation processes comes to the fore: the interfaces between the development agencies and communities resettled on their claimed land are points of only partial connection. Policies unfold in often unexpected ways which generate considerable ambivalence. As members of these rural populations interact with state- and non-state development agencies, they strategically produce traditionalist resettlement narratives, thus affirming their relative autonomy in the local setting.

Competing discourses of land restitution

Land restitution in South Africa was designed as a means to redraw the apartheid map of racially and unequally distributed land after the first democratic elections of 1994. But the miscellaneous legislation that supports restitution encodes divergent goals (see MacAuslan 1998; Cousins 2000). On the one hand, the objective of 'just and equitable redress' refers to the undoing of a painful past when racially motivated acts of dispossession confined black landholding to 13 per cent of the land. It involves the compensation by government of a group defined as 'historically disadvantaged' for past grievances and the loss of land rights. On the other hand, concerns are expressed by the state and the international donor community over sustainability, productivity and farm efficiency. The prospects of environmental degradation and the collapse of the capitalized and commoditized commercial farming sector have proved potent counter-arguments to a populist wide-scale land redistribution programme.

Reflecting its legalistic nature, restitution was 'designed as a stand-alone, legally driven programme without linkages to other planning or development processes' (Turner and Ibsen 2000: 12). The limited scope of restitution policies led the Commission on Restitution of Land Rights (CRLR), more commonly known as the Land Claims Commission, to view land restitution primarily as a legal process with the core responsibility of fulfilling the constitutional requirements of 'just and equitable redress'. Its remit has thus been restricted to the formal resolution of land rights. The lack of strategic advance planning has meant that much of the subsequent activity has been outsourced, with contract consultants, financing institutions, local farmers' associations and local municipalities assuming a prominent role in post-settlement stages of land restitution.[1] Accompanying the role of these actors and development agencies, there is a shifting articulation, from land seen as a means of reconciliation towards land as an economic asset to be commoditized or safeguarded from exhaustive usage.

At the 'post-settlement' stage when the land rights have been formally settled, extracts from a developmentalist language of production (a predominant feature of the parallel land redistribution programme) are inserted into the process. Co-ordinated land-use planning is then introduced by a conglomerate of state- and non-state interests that draft business plans with claimant representatives and restitution officials. Negotiations over land and land use then take place in different arenas where 'expert knowledge' assumes a critical position in mediating the transfer from an undesired state of subsistence farming to a more efficient production style which meets standards of efficiency and sustainability. Landownership is, in many cases, nominally transferred to restitution claimants (through the land rights stages) without any effective change in current land use and production patterns. This has been termed the 'same car, different driver' principle (van den Brink 2003: 20); it bears a striking similarity to the process in which haciendas in Peru were allegedly 'endowed' to peasants but with minimal changes in personnel, production structures and farming styles (see Chapter 10, Nuitjen and Lorenzo, in this book).

The setting up of new production regimes involves a switch from the preoccupations of the earlier phase of restitution. Intervention, at this stage, no longer involves an attempt to arrange structures of governance or to manage land relations. Instead, it is directed towards encouraging commercial farming and commoditization. Although it offers restitution beneficiaries the prospect of sustainable livelihoods and may thus be seen as a welcome alternative to earlier cases in which restitution beneficiaries were simply dumped on their ancestral land with few means of survival (Lahiff 2003), what is less welcome is that it involves mentorship by external parties in farm management and land resettlement. In the process of this change, significant alterations occur in the role of the landholding 'entities' – CPAs or Trusts – which were established through state legislation as part of the restitution process. During the initial stages, through which land rights were being claimed, groups grappled with issues pertaining to political representation and the nature of effective ownership. Subsequently, in the post-settlement phase, they find themselves thrust into land-use planning sessions with other 'interested parties' that are identified as stakeholders in the delivery of post-settlement assistance. Matters of effective governance and property-holding become marginal (see James 2006).

Land restitution as a bifurcated intervention strategy problematically blends a state-led compensatory mechanism for victims of historical land dispossession with a productionist agenda aimed at promoting commercial farming. The re-articulation of the meaning of land through the consecutive stages of restitution, with a corresponding thrust by state officials to denude it of its symbolic and political value, entails a significant shift of which the contingent outcomes are explored in the two case studies.

Case study 1 – Cattle and the struggle for the city: Mandlazini[2]

On a Sunday morning in mid-February 1996, one of us attended a general meeting between staff members and students from the then Department of Agriculture of the University of Zululand and the Mthiyane community at Mposa Hill on the outskirts of Richards Bay, an Indian Ocean coastal town in the north-eastern corner of KwaZulu Natal. Dressed in the white robes of the followers of the Shembe church, the crowd sat on the ground and listened to the chairman of the Mandlazini Development Committee announcing the arrival of the foreign visitors. Being introduced as agriculturalists with a university connection, our group was heralded as future partners that would provide support services such as advice and vegetable seedlings. It was agreed that we would collect data on the various aspects of the past and present of the people and their landscape. At the time of the meeting about 50 families had already settled on their recently reclaimed ancestral land where they had built simple houses. Some vegetable gardens had been established, cattle were grazing freely, and the primary school held classes under the trees. The construction of a community hall was almost finished. The preparation of roads, land surveying and pegging of plots was still going on.

The Mandlazini case is considered one of the first land restitution cases in South Africa. The claim, like many of its kind, dates back to the period before the first democratic elections of 1994. The Mthiyane community was in 1976 forcefully removed from their ancestral land to what was then referred to as Reserve 6, designated as Trust land. The removal was effected to allow for the construction of a deep sea harbour and the expansion of the industrial and residential areas of Richards Bay.[3] The Mthiyane were resettled to Manbuka and Ntambanana (AFRA News 1993), areas remote from the coast and from the urban area where it was more difficult to make a living. Ntambanana was less suitable than their ancestral land for livestock and crop production because of lower and unreliable rainfall. It had limited infrastructure and hardly any formal employment opportunities. Land scarcity and limited development options had made subsistence in their new home virtually impossible. Compensation given to them by the then Department of Bantu Administration, comprising land and some basic services, had been insufficient.

With the advent of the first free elections and the drive for reconciliation, people began manoeuvring to regain control over their land with the thought of improving their livelihoods as well. In 1993, a year before the passing of the Restitution Act through parliament, the Mthiyane residing in Ntambanana location formed the Mandlazini Interim Committee, later renamed the Mandlazini Development Committee (MDC), in an effort to negotiate a claim for the return of their ancestral land. They held negotiations with the then newly-formed municipal structure, the Richards Bay Transitional Local Council (RBTLC) which represented the municipal authorities of Richards Bay. Richards Bay had in the meantime evolved into a thriving seaport town, with the biggest deep-sea harbour and the biggest aluminium smelter in the world. Given the comprehensive developments on much of the claimed land, the MDC realized that restoration (that is, physical restitution) of their ancestral land was not realistic. Consequently, the MDC, on behalf of its constituents and with historical reference to a holy tree and ancestral graves, claimed the area between the airfield and Lake Mzingazi. The claim proposed a resettlement of the claimant population in combination with subsistence and commercial agriculture.

Religion, land and politics

The driving force behind the restitution claim was not the chief (*inkosi*) but a religious leader. An unintended outcome of the forced removal was that the Mthiyane had been cut off from their traditional leader *Inkosi* Mthiyane and his *Induna* (headman) who for undisclosed reasons decided to settle in eSikhawini (a township near to Richards Bay). The Mthiyane thus fell under the authority of a different chief, the *Inkosi* of Ntambanana, which had the effect of making them feel like a minority group. In addition their relocation subjected them to the violence of the fighting between the ANC and its ethnically nationalist rival Inkatha which was raging during the 1980s. Not only did they face the physical difficulties of the landscape but they were also subjected to the whims of the Inkatha-led provincial government. Among the Mthiyane many stories circulated about attacks on ANC supporters among their ranks and about informal justice meted out by Inkatha cadres for minor crimes. The resulting grievances and fears proved to be a fertile seedbed for the emergence of religious leadership. Skulu, a local priest of the Shembe church, an African Independent Church with many local adherents, occupied the political space and emerged as the driving force of the struggle for independence from the *Inkosi* of Ntambanana. In a vision, he saw that 'his people were living in peace near Mposa Hill', a piece of holy land near Lake Mzingazi. By publicly narrating his dreams that some day the community would return to this place, he strategically linked the political struggle over control of people with a claim regaining control over ancestral land.

The group of people Skulu rallied around him, together making up the MDC, began negotiating to return to their ancestral land. The MDC gained much respect and support among the Mthiyane people and played a critical role in forming a new community identity by emphasizing Shembe religious and cultural values, addressing the need for peace, and enhancing development. It also employed strategically placed discursive means during the negotiations with the local municipal authorities. The brother of the priest and a key member of the MDC, dressed in traditional Zulu clothes, delivered a compelling speech to the municipal council to emphasize that the land belonged to the Zulu people. Evoking grand memories of traditional values intrinsically linked to the landscape, the speech, according to a participant in the meeting, made a big impact and the deal was speedily approved. The MDC in this way manoeuvred itself into a privileged position. Not only did it present itself as the local authority in Mandlazini, it also created an institutional structure in which the MDC was the exclusive negotiator with outside agencies. In the end it was Skulu and not the urbanized *inkosi* Mthiyane who initiated negotiations with the municipal authorities. The *inkosi* formally endorsed the claim but played a minor role in mobilising popular support. Hence, the Shembe religion and the priest became the critical factors in the success of the ancestral land claim. This resulted in, but was also nurtured by, a shift of political power from hereditary to religious leaders.

Agri-village and settlement

The claim was approved at a time, pre-1994, when restitution legislation was only provisional (the Provision of Certain Land for Settlement Act). This Act, like the restitution policies that followed, dictated that the number of households to be resettled should be in line with the carrying capacity of the land, thereby implying that productivity and environmental sustainability criteria should guide prospective resettlement. The Conditions of Designations, art 1.3. specified that 'Returning to Richards Bay, the Mandlazini Community Trust (MCT) acknowledges the necessity of the Mandlazini people to be integrated into the life and fabric of the town, to support existing by-laws and the town planning development controls, which are necessary for orderly settlement' (RBTLC and MCT 1993).

The Mthiyane claimants in their turn demanded a further division of the land according to their own wishes and perceptions. The negotiations resulted in a statement that 'settlement in respect of the agri-village concept shall attempt to create a self-sustaining community, by cultivating cash crops through productive small-scale farming methods in order to supplement the involvement of the people within the broader economy of Richards Bay' (RBTLC and MCT 1993). The agri-village idea implied that only 12 per cent of the total 5,000 families residing in Ntambanana – that is, 570 beneficiary households – could actually be resettled. Fearing the overgrazing that by experts is typically associated with communal tenure husbandry systems, it was agreed that 'the MCT shall ensure that, in view of the limited carrying capacity of the land and in view of the number of families (570 families) to be accommodated on the site, no livestock be permanently kept within the agri-village' (RBTLC and MCT 1993). To effect this, each family head signed a document. It was also agreed that plots of 4,000 m^2 would be pegged, with the option that these could be subdivided in the future. A subsidy to build houses was finally approved in 1995 and as per agreement settlement would take place in five phases. The means to purchase the land from Richards Bay municipality (about R6.3 million in 1993) and for the delivery of infrastructure and services such as water, electricity and roads came from the government's settlement land acquisition grant (SLAG).

The question of how many people could be resettled was not just a 'numbers game' but rather one concerning competing bodies of knowledge and contesting interpretations between MDC and experts. The contest was over how to understand the concept of 'agri-village' and the land's resources. Hired by the MDC, Cedara, a research institute of the Kwazulu-Natal Provincial Department of Agriculture, conducted a study to calculate the carrying capacity of the land as decided in the Conditions of Designation. Cedara subdivided the area according to physical characteristics and limitations. The soil is classified as sandy and hardly capable of retaining water and low fertility. Cedara's experts were therefore highly sceptical of Mandlazini's agricultural potential: '... due to irrigation requirements and other quality management inputs this could not be considered for a rural agricultural scenario' (Cedara 1993: 2). One other key limitation was that Lake Mzingazi is a nature conservation area restricting the use of fertilizer. But 'with good agricultural practices, making use of cuttings that are nematode tolerant, sweet potato yields of 20–30 mt/ha could be easily achieved. Realistically, however, 8–15 mt/ha would probably be closer to the mark. This could be marketed at approximately R800 per metre realizing a gross income of approximately R600–R12,000 per hectare. Costs, if any, would be discounted from the above to result in a gross margin' (Cedara 1993).

Notwithstanding this gloomy scenario, two resettlement options were proposed to be negotiated with the claimant representatives. The first one consisted of a wetland plot of 1,500 m^2 in combination with a 1 ha plot higher up for each family. An alternative scenario proposed a plot of 4,000 m^2 upon which housing and cultivation could be combined (Metroplan 1994). The community preferred the latter scenario because it allowed more people to be settled. Both Cedara and the consultancy firm Metroplan hired for the physical town planning aspects considered this as the most appropriate scenario as it would enable settlement of 178 to 228 families. However, against the backdrop of mounting pressure on the MDC by the larger claimant group and against the economic rationality of the planners, it was decided to resettle the 570 families mentioned in the original 'agri-village' proposal. But even this involved excluding some. Eventually, in response to further pressure, about 3,000 families were listed as potential beneficiaries: those considered by the MDC to be among the poorest. It was realized that the restitution process had just begun and that more claimants might later materialize. However, in stretching the perceived carrying capacity to its outer limits and in erroneously interpreting the scale of the map, the planners of Metroplan had made a crucial mistake: they had grossly overestimated the sizes of individual plots.

Reworking and fragmentation

Integrated Planning Services (IPS) was given the task of supervising the further but orderly implementation of the resettlement project. In 1994, the preparations for resettlement started with the pegging of the settlement plots. The first 50 families arrived in the course of 1995. The first erected houses were simple shacks. Vegetable gardens were demarcated and shortly afterwards the first crops were planted (mainly vegetables and staple crops like maize). In contravention of the restrictions, livestock was also reintroduced. By 1996/7 two large herds were to be found grazing freely in the Mandlazini settlement area. During later visits, it appeared that more and more cattle had moved in. Since communal grazing land was neither readily available nor had been accounted for in the planning, and no feed and fodder crops were purchased or grown, cattle increasingly ventured into the predominantly white suburbs of Richards Bay, Birdswood and Meerensee. A number of complaints by the dismayed townsfolk soon featured in the local newspaper, the *Zululand Observer*.[4]

Ira Stone, the frontline IPS employee for the Mandlazini project, commented in 1997 defensively on how grazing needs had not been foreseen, 'It was not planned, I realize, but it could not be prevented. People do as they like and don't want us to intervene'. She also complained about the Richards Bay municipal authority not showing much interest in what was going on, saying that they clearly did not have the political means to enforce the by-laws that were part of the conditions for settlement.

Follow-up visits showed that the settlement scenario unfolded in a way that was not foreseen in the initial agreement. This showed that the proposal for an agri-village was reworked and redesigned according to the people's own perspectives. Besides the 'cattle question', the five-staged settlement process was clearly not being implemented. Families came and settled as they saw fit. The vegetable gardens, one of the core elements of the agri-village construct intended to cater for subsistence needs, were withering and untended. Moreover, most plots had been subdivided into three to four smaller plots as an alternative strategy for deriving income from the urban settlement. Houses were built on these smaller plots and rented out to tenants many of whom were probably not listed beneficiaries (in restitution terms the 'original occupants or descendants thereof'). In a testimony to the rising economic vibrancy of this urban periphery, the shacks from the first phase of settlements were almost all replaced by new brick houses and some of them were upgraded to bungalows.

Some plot owners have moved to the nearby settlement of eSikhawini whilst subletting their houses to newcomers.

Mandlazini today shows how land restitution has provided a vehicle for a community to create and recreate a landscape. The landscape appears fragmented; divided between urban-style concerns and rural ones. Certain elements of the landscape reflect how the area has been integrated into the urban economy and lifestyle. The subdivision of plots and the subletting of houses has produced the imaginary of a township. The withered state of the vegetable gardens indicates that wages have been substituted for the production of food. In their turn supermarkets have been assigned a major role in the supply of food. The garden committee, once the driver of at least this part of the agri-village idea and headed by women, is now defunct. This urban landscape converges with the lifestyles of the youth, who have no interest in living like 'traditionalist subjects' whose livelihood and dignity depend upon the ability to maintain a healthy stock of cattle and goats. For them restitution has been a forward-looking affair rather than one evoking the past.

Other elements of the landscape, however, indicate that the elderly generation sees a possibility to continue their traditional rural lifestyle. The most visible indicator of this is the key role that cattle play in Mandlazini. More than half of the settlement's families own and keep cattle, and the elected cattle committee, headed by a member of the Shembe-dominated MDC and originally set up to restrict the extent of cattle ownership and grazing, is still operational and run by elderly men. To the group of elderly men, the Mandlazini claim does not imply a break with the past (in contrast to the younger generation); it rather reflects an element of cultural continuity. When the shortage of feed and fodder was pointed out, some committee members responded by saying 'there is enough grass and water behind Alusaf' (the grounds of the aluminium plant). This statement resonates with a proposal first suggested in 1998: that new ancestral claims on land nearby (such as a eucalyptus plantation) would resolve the issue of limited grazing. Although the prospects for new pastures may be limited given that that land is poisoned[5] and unsuitable for grazing in the short term, and that there are difficulties in finding suitable herd boys to exploit distant soils, elders continue to dream about the great Zulu tradition of cattle and pastures. This is supported by the fact that these elders enjoy much prestige and have the discursive means to connect their dreams of a 'traditionalist lifestyle' to contemporary restitution options.

Contrary to this impression of divergent urban- and rurally-oriented concerns, however, Mandlazini in fact represents a locally specific blend of urban and rural, of modern and traditional lifestyles. These identities are wrought into a coherent unfragmented whole providing meaning to residents' livelihood. Internally the role of cattle is not disputed – they continue to play a key role in Shembe rituals and as a provider of social status. Cattle in town constitute a key element of contemporary indigenous modernity. The land restitution process has thus catered for those who seek proximity to the city and also for those looking for ways to combine a 'traditional' lifestyle with a modern urban setting.

The Mandlazini case shows that a developmentalist discourse of restitution has been significantly redesigned by members of the various social categories in the community to suit their interests. The constitutive elements of contemporary modernities, rationalism and romanticism that together formed the Mandlazini landscape, indicate the relative autonomy of social actors such as restitution beneficiaries. Religion, and the way cultural symbols and tradition are used in the negotiations, appear as a useful set of discursive means. Moreover, evidence indicates that expert knowledge was contested; the role of the IPS in particular is noteworthy in that its regulatory role was pre-empted. After the claim was negotiated and formally settled, the various actors went their own way, leaving the state on the sidelines.

Case study 2 – Seeking common ground, finding hidden claims: the Makhoba Community Project[6]

On 12 April 2002, the presidential helicopter touched down on the dusty Sonderwater farm. As President Mr Thabo Mbeki alighted, an exultant mob greeted him with singing and dancing. He was led into the party tent erected on behalf of the Commission on Restitution of Land Rights, to take part in a symbolic transaction. Intended to mark yet another step in the long march towards reconciliation of the divided people of the 'Rainbow Nation', this was the transfer of a 11,000 ha farm to a large group of land restitution beneficiaries. Ambrose Makhoba, Chief of the Makhoba people and chairman of the newly formed Community Trust, proudly accepted the hastily drawn-up draft agreement while a group of white farmers in their characteristic khaki outfits sat to one side, somewhat withdrawn and intimidated by the proceedings. They explicitly featured in the final act of this spectacle when Chief Makhoba solemnly addressed his new neighbours and expressed his hope that these farmers would assist the resettlement community in the appropriation of modern farming methods.

This politicized event was typical of what is known in restitution terms as the 'settlement celebration', a definitive moment in the resolution of land rights issues during which claimants are handed a copy of the settlement agreement. It symbolizes the finalization of the compensation of historical land rights by the Land Claims Commission and is intended to lead the way for resettlement of the ancestral land by the claimant group. It also marks the beginning of a new stage in land restitution when resettled claimants are faced with the question how to develop their ancestral land.

The resettlement narrative

As early as 1927 the white farmers adjacent to the 4,000 hectare Makhoba's Location had called for their removal, claiming that they resided in an 'otherwise

European area' (Eastern Cape Regional Land Claims Commission 1999). This 'black spot' removal, finally effected in 1946 with the characteristic display of violence, would be recalled through re-enactment some 50 years later when the land restitution option presented itself. When they lodged their land restitution claim in 1995, a group of people descended from the original residents who had resisted the forced relocation revisited their dispossession history. In reconstructing the event in the company of land restitution officials, they emphasized the suffering they had endured at the hands of apartheid's architects and stated an explicit wish to be united again under strong traditional leadership on their ancestral land where they could pick up their lives as pastoralists and agriculturalists.

What formed the core of their original resettlement experience, and what became a key theme of its later re-enactment, was the keen sense of the temporal and social discontinuity they had suffered as a result of the act of dispossession. In the official account by the Eastern Cape Regional Land Claims Commission we find some of the components of a traditionalist resettlement paradigm: its reference to a 'past state of things' and the injustice felt at being newly placed in an area where the presence of various ethnicities poses a real threat to sustainable livelihoods. One instructive passage in the research document indicates the imperative for resettlement and the cry for a restoration of a traditional leader on the claimed land:

> the claimant community is adamant that they want to go back to their ancestral land for they cannot keep on staying on the New Makhoba Location. The reasons brought forward are the stock theft and the cross border raids that ensue. The community is feeling insecure for the danger of tribal strife is always there ... The claimants would like to start their lives where their forefathers are resting. There is a feeling that, as the area is used for farming, most graves have been desecrated and for Africans their lives cannot be stable. They would like to continue with farming operations as they used to do in the past. The Makhoba Community would like to get their respect back and resume the life of enjoying their culture under their leader'.
> (Eastern Cape Regional Land Claims Commission 1999: 12)

The desire for restoration of their ancestral land reflected the worsening conditions at 'New Makhoba', the resettlement area in the former Transkei homeland to which the Makhobas had been moved. According to accounts from present-day claimants, uncontrollable cattle theft is the main factor undermining the Xhosa way of life, affecting in its wake customary institutions such as *lobola* (bridewealth). Blame is laid on the weak state that is no longer able to curtail raiding parties by members of the neighbouring Basotho nation, as well as on the erosion of the chieftaincy institution through historical compromises with cunning white officials. Moreover, the relegation of the once-proud

Makhoba people to reliance on state pensions and welfare grants has been attributed to the poor leadership of the sitting headman, who is commonly referred to as a drunk and an incompetent. The dispossession narrative carries the weight of historical injustices, asserts the right to be compensated and stresses the reconstruction of a tribal community, returning it to an implied 'original state' before the moment of disintegration. Restoration, to the claimant group, hinged on a dual mechanism: the installing of a Chief on the claimed land and the physical resettlement of the entire claimant group.

Driving the vast distance to the East London Restitution Commissioner's office to lodge the community claim was Ambrose Dlamini, cousin to the sitting headman. The chairman of the first claimant committee had approached him to give the claim what it needed – a community leader who could deal with the state to negotiate the best settlement for the claimants. Various respondents have pointed out that even though he was 'young', implying a limited experience in the function as community leader, he had the vital characteristic of being 'educated', a description referring to his familiarity with external notions of progress and development. These qualities related to his high-level education and his involvement in urban life while working on the mines prior to becoming a secondary school teacher. At the same time, his proximity to the ruling family in kinship terms made him of 'royal blood'.

When the claim had been validated and a new Makhoba Community Trust was formed to hold and manage the land on behalf of the claimant community, the young man claimed his place as hereditary leader on the restituted land. His position remains much disputed, given that it was an earlier dispute over the traditional leadership at Makhoba that had led to the sitting headman being validated as the rightful hereditary leader by the overarching Bisho traditional authorities of the former Ciskei homeland. In discussing his formal installation with members of the Eastern Cape Land Claims Commission, it proved difficult to trace the former civil servants who had accepted his appointment as leader of the claimant group in 1995 – a testimony to the social mobility of state employees in post-apartheid South Africa.

The endorsement of the new traditional leader, however, seems to reflect the South African government's objective to build alliances with 'progressive chiefs' (Department of Land Affairs 1997) whilst seeking to reform or replace chieftaincy institutions that do not have the capacity to adjust to modern conditions and emergent development options. It also points to the way political representation is reconstructed through the interfaces that are formed between democratic institutions and 'modern actors' who find ways of vocalizing and linking their day to day struggles over resources and power to discourses on land reform. In the implied 'reinvention of tradition' in evidence here, rural people mobilized in order to latch onto new policies and to connect their personal projects to the values encoded in the grand narrative of reconciliation and land restitution. Chief Makhoba, in assuming the role as chairman of the Community Trust, materialized the alignment between the Land Claims Commission and the group of land restitution claimants. The new legal landholding and political entity over which he presides stands at the crossroads between local conceptualizations of power, as expressed through existing chieftaincy structures, on the one hand, and modern imposed conceptualizations of democratic representation negotiating the restitution process with external development agencies, on the other.

Traditionalist narratives accompanying land restitution claims are thus often fabricated by sections of the beneficiary community in their bid to gain access not only to land and development assistance but also to power and authority derived through partnerships with the authorities dispensing land reform and rural development. They serve as the means for entering the realm of state politics in terms which have been deemed as acceptable. In South Africa, traditionalist representations of society are becoming increasingly popular, and the ANC has endorsed the existence of the chiefship in no uncertain terms. Accommodating ancestral land claims, and promoting the reinvention of traditional institutions by acknowledging their stake in community development, is a sign of this turn in state politics. In the process, however, there has been a reconstruction of 'false' representations of communities by powerful claimant groups who attempt to gloss over intra-local heterogeneity and underlying conflicts through the use of traditionalist motifs of communal identity. The fallacy of these constructs is evident when land claims are actually resolved. Reconstituted communities are heterogeneous groups made up of disparate parts, which then become further divided through the very process – state-induced land restitution – that was intended to unite them (Du Toit 2000; James 2000).

The fragmented New Makhoba population similarly faces renewed stratification through the claim. The so-called original descendants are divided in two: one group following the aspirant chief to the ancestral land and another remaining loyal to the sitting headman. There is also a division between the group of newcomers (resettled on location after the Makhobas) and earlier occupants excluded from the legislative process.

Enter development values

When the land claim was validated on the basis of archival research and informal interviews with key informants of the large claimant group, the Eastern Cape Regional Land Claims Commission (RLCC) was faced with the prospect of delivering a land resettlement scheme to this group. Its numbers had more than quadrupled in the interim, jumping from 330 to 1,440 households in the one-year period prior to the signing of the settlement agreement in 2002. This increase was underpinned by pragmatic motives – but of rather different kinds. From the commission's point of view, the greater number of beneficiaries boosted the 2002 achievement statistics considerably, thereby proving government's commitment to the restitution of land to former homeland communities. From claimants' point of view, there was much promise in being part of this resettlement project, which at the time was being launched as one of the most prominent cases involving a former homeland community and as a test case for the recent 'developmental approach' in land restitution.

In order to harmonize the seemingly divergent political objectives of large-scale resettlement and continued productivity, the commission, together with the national Department of Agriculture, incorporated the land resettlement into the Integrated Rural Development Programme. This brought with it a government promise of sustained commitment: the Makhoba case was designated as a pilot case intended to operationalize the uneasy marriage between the 'Africanization' of landholding and the new promotion of farmer productivity.

To the Makhoba claimants these goals represented an imposed, and not necessarily welcome, redesign of their original objectives. Although the new plan held the attraction of prospective jobs, it also represented an expenditure of finances in a manner which was planned by state officers rather than by themselves. The restitution award (the standard monetary compensation offered to each beneficiary household for settlement and development planning) would now be used to develop the land into a 'viable farm unit' capable of providing 'sustainable livelihoods'. In the process, new partnerships were forged with a range of development agencies acquiring a stake in the project, involving further expenditure. In order to ratify the commercial farming orientation towards sustainable livelihoods, the Land Claims Commission set up a new stakeholder network, the Project Steering Committee, which could deliver the knowledge and additional financial means needed to turn Makhoba beneficiaries from 'subsistence' to commercial farmers. In the months following the April 2002 settlement celebrations at Sonderwater farm, a diverse group of development 'experts' (including their future white neighbours) visited the Makhoba location to sensitize the prospective inhabitants to their new future.

The dedication of the Land Claims Commission to commercial farming first involved a 'situational analysis' of the resettlement area and the beneficiary population. The Commission together with contracted researchers of the Agricultural Research Council (ARC) conducted livelihood assessments of the Makhoba community (Agricultural Research Council 2002). Simultaneously, evaluations were made of the grazing capacity and output potential of the restituted land. The findings culminated in a planning document that divided the land into separate areas for grazing, arable farming and residential purposes and laid out the necessary inputs to achieve short-term production goals and the management guidelines.

The resulting document described Makhoba livelihoods as being subsistence-oriented and based on so-called 'traditional farming systems'. In the light of the proposed transformation to commercial production, it termed the community's existing skills 'problematic': an account typical of much 'expert rhetoric'. The envisioned transformation process – implicitly part of the 'same car, different driver' intervention strategy discussed earlier – was not merely a matter of transferring technical and managerial skills but rather one of changing the attitudes of restitution beneficiaries towards their antiquated notions of agricultural production.

Two central aspects of the business plan were the concentrated settlement or 'agri-village' concept and the new labour regime. The Makhoba Community Project, as the resettlement scheme was renamed, proposed that three of the 16 members of the Makhoba Trust join the so-called Operating Company, which makes the day-to-day farm decisions. It also prescribed that 20 to 40 beneficiaries be employed on a full-time basis to work as farm labourers. The remainder of the beneficiary community would be allowed to settle on the land but their contribution to agricultural production would be restricted to farming their small garden plots, since no arable fields would be allocated to individual households. The notion of 'agri-village', proposing to optimize productive land use by resettling families on 35 × 35 m plots of land designated for residential purposes, appeared as a means of justifying that resettlement.

Both aspects – but particularly the proposed concentration of residential settlement – were met with considerable antagonism by the beneficiary population. As Chief Ambrose Makhoba explained, the claimants had envisioned plot sizes that mirrored the ones they had originally received from the apartheid government's South African Native Trust upon resettlement in the former Transkei homeland – 70 × 70 m residential plots and 3 morgen (2.4 ha) of 'black soil' for each household. Their fierce commitment to this historical plot size countered whatever new economic policies were being proposed. The Community Trust and the commission eventually settled for a compromise: 50 × 50 m for each residential allotment without further specifications regarding arable fields. Despite reaching a formal agreement, many claimants felt that they had been robbed by national government and their representatives. When asked about moving to the restituted land it emerged that many respondents had lost interest, stating that they could not live under 'location' conditions – a reference to the dreaded life in the townships where livestock rearing and land allocation is subject to rules and regulations prescribed by external authorities and where municipal services and rent must be paid.

At the time of writing, the resettlement scheme had been shelved and the claimants remained divided over the future prospects at 'Old Makhoba'. The type of houses offered (the standardized Reconstruction and Development Programme (RDP) one-bedroom variant, widely known as 'RDP houses'), the uncertainty over allocation of arable fields and the connotations of becoming wage labourers under the contracted interim farm manager, were reasons for people's reluctance to participate in the model 'community project'. After a period of leasing the land to the neighbouring white farmers – a strategy that provoked a heated debate about landownership and accusations that the young chief had sold the restituted land – the farm is now being developed by the Operating Company, using the money from the restitution award of the listed beneficiaries. The majority of the target group proposed as future farm labourers expressed fervent doubts about the project. The role they would have to play in the project simply did not match their approach to 'sustainable livelihoods'. To be absorbed into a collective that was governed by the rules of an external development agency run by a cosmopolitan elite and a new class of African entrepreneurs, seemed little different to being subject to the rules and regulations of the apartheid era, with its earlier vision of agricultural development.

Epitomizing the cleavage between the two stages of land restitution is the bifurcated position of the newly empowered Chief Makhoba. Whilst still embodying traditionalist images of the chiefship on the one hand, on the other – having effectively become the broker of the new development language – he appears in community meetings to present the latest developments regarding the housing scheme and the progress in setting up the commercial farm. At the time of our research, this role was putting considerable pressure on his function as community leader. The popular support originally afforded him by the successful land claim was now becoming increasingly dependent on what the project could deliver.

Resolving this dilemma of dual appeasement, he subsequently decided to start a Committee on Traditional Affairs to ensure that principles of tradition and customary law be upheld at Old Makhoba. The idea is that the elected committee (an expression of new democratization values) nonetheless safeguards custom and restores the chieftaincy institution to its former glory. When asked which aspects of behaviour would be affected, he gave his interpretation: no wearing of trousers for women, abstinence before marriage and organization of ritualistic tribal gatherings. Regarding the critical questions of communal tenure, communal grazing and the allocation of arable fields to community members, traditionally associated with the function of chief, he explained that these functions had not yet been defined. It appeared, then, that he was taking refuge in ritual and behavioural aspects of traditionalism but leaving the new landownership propositions unmodified.

9.6 Emergent properties of land restitution

Land restitution policies in South Africa have given rise to claims based on ancestral land rights. The land rights orientation of the programme has led to the endorsement of historical claims based on oral histories and affidavit statements of claimant groups. These statements invoke a sense of collective suffering, political and cultural ruptures in the face of dispossession, and related problems of being concentrated in native reserves where various ethnicities were collected together. When claimants strategically refer to a coherent tribal society, dismembered and robbed of its collective identity upon dispossession, an idealized community construct emerges through interfaces with what is now a benevolent state. A multiracial ideology reaffirming 'tradition' is couched in a reconciliatory dialogue between restitution beneficiaries and land restitution agencies. The emergent properties of this shared imaginary entail the reconstruction of representations of communities by powerful claimant groups who attempt to gloss over intra-local heterogeneity and underlying conflicts. The fallacy of these constructs becomes evident when land claims are resolved and when resettlement of the ancestral land involves social fragmentation. Restituted communities appear as highly heterogeneous groups through processes of land reform (see MacAllister 1999; James 2000).

Now, just as during apartheid, a co-ordinated effort by powerful local actors and a legitimating state ironically endorses and ensures the continuing importance of the chieftaincy institution in rural society. Through 'interlocking actor projects' (Long 2007), disputed 'hereditary leaders' assume prominent roles. As part of this process we found well-situated 'modern' actors articulating exclusionary scripts that asserted their rights to leadership functions and privileged the land rights of the beneficiary group over that of 'newcomers' (see also Magadlela and Hebinck 1995). The co-production of this narrative by state and non-state actors is reflected in its materialization: the Communal Property Association (CPA) or Community Trust as a hybrid legal form is organized around the harmonization of 'modern' notions of democracy with those of customary rule (see James 2006).

These social and material constructs, however, exist by virtue of the partial and heterogenous connections out of which networks of actors and their practices are constituted (Arce and Long 2000). From the hybridized and sometimes historically perverse nature of these emergent realities, we can see how the resolution of land rights provokes the emergence of 'indigenous modernities' (Robins 2003) as complex composites that connect social and political struggles over land to the modern state. Uncertainties in the land-rights-based aspect of land restitution reflects the way national policies are reinterpreted and translated.

Traditionalist identities reverberate in a wider policy environment, where they interface with alternative meanings and newer approaches to land as 'development object'. The symbol systems that emerge at the point where land rights are negotiated may coexist uncomfortably with other macro discourses of 'change' and 'progress'.

We have argued that land restitution practices unfold in roughly two stages: that oriented to the restoring of land rights and that of post-settlement. Resettlement comes with a re-articulation of land as development object, with its problematic reduction of 'rights to purely economic terms', implying calculated effects in terms of transaction costs, added value and farm productivity (Skapska 2003: 23). This re-articulation, in effect, involves a second and completely separate settlement negotiation by claimants. Where in the land restitution phase communities grappled with notions of communal tenure and traditional leadership, they are now thrust into planning sessions involving the reform of farming practice to meet contemporary standards of efficient management and commoditization.

The problematic situation of new subjectivities such as 'tribe' and 'historically disadvantaged' can then be seen in terms of the colonizing concepts of a neo-liberal master narrative. This narrative posits such abstract qualities as 'efficiency', 'productivity' and 'sustainability' and such equally abstract spatial entities as 'agri-village' and 'viable farm unit'. Paradoxically, what was first a legitimate discourse on tradition and custom, sanctified by the Department of Land Affairs in the process of compensating restitution claimants, in later stages becomes associated with antiquated livelihood approaches held to be inefficient, exhaustive to the land and the root cause of rural poverty. In implementing new land use and farm management models, community participation is then defined as problematic. The lack of farming skills and management capacity to run a commercial farming enterprise becomes the motivation for a range of educational, technocratic and administrative interventions geared at changing local perceptions on livelihoods and meeting the 'critical success factors' stated in planning documents.

When implementation of policies implies stringent principles and prescriptions that are explicit about the behaviour they intend to promote, the traditionalist approach to land and livelihoods loses its bargaining power and beneficiary communities are expected to trade 'backward attitudes' for 'progressive practices'. The case of the proposed labour regime and concentrated resettlement entailed in the commercial farming model demonstrate this. The interpretation and enactment of new messages takes place in an altered network of social relations. The entry of management consultants and local government as playing important roles within the newly redefined 'commercial farming project' leads to the reformulation of 'progress'. As mentioned earlier, and as discussed in several chapters in this book (see Chapters 2, Fay; 10, Nuitjen and Lorenzo; in this book), those expecting restitution of their lands now find themselves ensnared in externally imposed policy frameworks, in which earlier relationships of power and wealth are continued. Although there are 'different drivers', they are in the 'same car'.

Conclusions

Land restitution processes at Makhoba and Mandlazini took place in two separate yet interrelated negotiated developments: the resolution of land rights and the consequent developmentalist intervention. The endorsement of ancestral land claims and the instalment of new landholding entities by the land restitution bodies are achieved at the interface between local actors and national policy communities. Through the endorsement of claims, land restitution has become a vehicle for the construction of traditionalist identities around the shared imaginary of reconciliation. The manifestations of these social constructs can be treated in terms of human agency: claimant representatives reinterpret and project historical events into a socio-political constellation where they derive meaning through association with the grand narrative of restitution and reconciliation. This implies interaction, with external messages meeting subjective and local experiences and practices. The result is a co-production of meaning across various scales and social institutions.

At first this interaction, centred on the political function of land and claims to existentialist identities, looked set to produce a mutually agreeable outcome. But fissures appeared with the shift to post-settlement planning. Commitment to land restitution began to waver, as the case studies demonstrate. In Mandlazini there was outright rejection of the development imperatives and land-use planning was reconfigured to match contemporary local approaches to livelihood in which urban and rural were unevenly combined and in which 'expert discourses' on commercial farming had no place. Negotiations led to a materialization of social relations of production parallel to contemporary 'struggles over the city', with agriculture occupying no more than a marginal place. In Makhoba, expert knowledge and external intervention, attempting to reshape farming practices, looked set to prevail, but community opposition rendered new plans inoperative. The chief, unable or unwilling to challenge this project and its accompanying new forms of landownership upon which his power was partly invested, retreated to exert his authority in the restricted realms of ritual and dress code.

In conclusion, the social phenomena and emergent properties that are born out of the encounter between the post-apartheid state and restitution claimants are typical of the concept of 'modernity' (Arce and Long 2000). This refers to the way such restitution processes are located in multiple, semi-autonomous institutional environments, where the interfaces between social actors lead to the production of various modernities that bring together fragmented notions of 'custom', 'tradition' and 'progress'.

References

AFRA News (1993) 'The people shall share – but not our properties', Newsletter of the Association for Rural Advancement, no. 20.
Agricultural Research Council (2002) 'Makhoba Community Project', ARC Consultancy Report.
Arce, A and N Long (2000) 'Reconfiguring Modernity and Development from an Anthropological Perspective', in A Arce and N Long (eds) *Anthropology, Development and Modernities. Exploring Discourses, Counter-tendencies and Violence*, London: Routledge.
Brink, van den R (2002) 'Land Policy and Land Reform in Sub-Saharan Africa: consensus, confusion and controversy', paper presented at Symposium Land Redistribution in Southern Africa, Pretoria.
—— (2003) 'Land Policy and Land Reform in Sub-Saharan Africa: Consensus, Confusion and Controversy', World Bank Discussion Paper, 2 April 2003.
Cedara (1993) *Settlement of the Mthiyane tribe*, Pietermaritzburg: Cedara.
Cousins, B (2000) 'Introduction: Does land and agrarian reform have a future and, if so, who will benefit?', in B Cousins (ed) *At the Crossroads: Land and Agrarian Reform in South Africa into the 21st Century*, Cape Town/Johannesburg: Programme for Land and Agrarian Studies, University of the Western Cape/National Land Committee.

Department of Land Affairs (1997) 'White Paper on South African Land Policy', Government Press: Pretoria, available at http://land.pwv.gov.za/legislation_policies/white_papers.htm.

Du Toit, A (2000) 'The End of Restitution: Getting real about land claims', in B Cousins (ed.) *At the Crossroads: Land and Agrarian Reform in South Africa into the 21st Century*, Cape Town and Johannesburg: Programme for Land and Agrarian Studies, University of the Western Cape and National Land Committee.

Eastern Cape Regional Land Claims Commission (1999) *Makhoba Land Claim Report*, unpublished report.

James, D (2000) 'After Years in the Wilderness: the discourse of land claims in the new South Africa', *Journal of Peasant Studies* 27(3): 142–61.

—— (2006) 'The Tragedy of the Private: owners, communities and the state in South Africa', in F and K von Benda-Beckmann and M Wiber (eds) *Changing Properties of Property*, Oxford: Berghahn.

Lahiff, E (2003) 'Land Reform and Sustainable Livelihoods in South Africa's Eastern Cape Province', Sussex: Institute for Development Studies, IDS Research Paper, No. 9.

Langeveld, P (1997) 'Cattle and Interfaces in the Resettlement Project of Mandlazini', unpublished thesis, Wageningen University.

Leynseele, Y van (2004) 'The Land You Bought, the Land We Never Sold: The Makhoba land restitution case', unpublished thesis, Wageningen University.

Long, N (2007) 'Resistance, Agency and Counterwork: A theoretical positioning', in W Wright and G Middendorf (eds) *The Fight over Food: Producers, Consumers and Activists Challenge the Global Food System*, University Park, PA: Penn State University Press.

MacAllister, PA (1999) 'Anthropology, Identity Politics, Consumption and Development in Post-Apartheid South Africa', in R Farden, W van Binsbergen and R van Dijk (eds) *Modernity on a Shoestring. Dimensions of Globalisation, Consumption and Development in Africa and Beyond*, Leiden and London: EIDOS.

MacAuslan, P (1998) 'Making Law Work: Restructuring Land Relations in Africa', *Development and Change* 29: 525–52.

Magadlela, D and P Hebinck (1995) 'Dry Fields and Spirits in Trees – A social analysis of development intervention in Nyamaropa Communal Area Zimbabwe', *Zambezia* 22(1): 44–63.

METROPLAN (1994) *Mzingazi Village Development Project: Draft development concepts*, Richards Bay: Metroplan.

RBTLC and MCT (1993) 'Conditions of Designation in Terms of Act 126 of 1993', Provision for land for settlement act, Richards Bay.

Robins, S (2003) 'Whose Modernity? Indigenous modernities and land claims after apartheid', *Development and Change* 34(2): 265–85.

Skapska, G (2003) 'Restitution of Property in East Central Europe: On the importance of symbolic aspects of property rights', paper presented at conference Changing Properties of Property, Halle, July.

Turner, S and H Ibsen (2000) *Land and Agrarian Reform in South Africa*, Research Report No. 6, Programme for Land and Agrarian Studies, Cape Town: University of the Western Cape.

Notes

1 Integrated planning has now officially become one of the tasks of the provincial Regional Land Claims Commissions with the introduction of specialized Settlement Support and Development Planning Units (van Leynseele 2004; Lahiff 2003: 15–19). However, the understaffed departments rely heavily on outsourcing skills transfer and development planning, thereby restricting their roles to making rudimentary livelihood assessments and managing information flows on behalf of restitution claimants.
2 This section is partly based on Langeveld (1997) and frequent visits by Hebinck between 1995 and 2000.
3 'Trust' land was that purchased by the state under the 1936 Native Trust and Land Act, to be added to the extent of the homelands in order to accommodate both their existing population and its natural increase and to provide space for the settlement of people relocated into them with the infamous 'population removals' of the 1950s and 1960s. Richards Bay's expansion took place on the alienated Trust land as well as on state land.
4 A (white) inhabitant complained about 'cows wandering the streets of Birdswood and Meerensee, rabbits, ducks, etc. demolishing ratepayers' property and absolutely nothing is being done. If I wanted to live on a farm, I would have stayed in the Northern Transvaal. For goodness' sake – you'd say we are living in the Wild West!'. She continues by stating that 'the next cow that sets foot on my property, I will confiscate'. She refers to benefits such as biltong as a nice product, and that cow meat fetches a good price. The authority that should address the matter here is the municipality. A letter with a similar content was sent to the *Zululand Observer*, on 29 March 1999.
5 Eucalyptus trees leave a poisonous substance in the soil. It takes about seven years before soils in uprooted plantations can be safely used for growing and grazing.
6 The data collection for this case study was done from November 2002 to March 2003 following a six-week period with the Eastern Cape Regional Land Claims Commission (see van Leynseele 2004).

Chapter 10

¡Dueños de todo y de nada! (Owners of all and nothing)

Restitution of Indian territories in the Central Andes of Peru

Monique Nuijten and David Lorenzo

Abstract

For centuries the Indian communities in the highlands of Peru have fought for restitution of territories which were taken away from them under the colonial regime and throughout independence. The Peruvian land reform of the 1970s was a reaction to increasingly fierce invasions and demands by Indian communities for restitution of stolen lands. But the land reform of the 1970s involved 'endowment' rather than restitution; instead of reclaiming land that had belonged to their ancestors, Indian villagers received it as an endowment for which they had to pay. The official change from 'indigenous community' into 'peasant community' during the land reform of the 1970s and the removal of all notions of Indianness in relation to the highland communities underscores this change from a restitutive to a distributive approach. In addition, the land was not handed over to the communities but to an associative enterprise, the so-called Agrarian Association of Social Interest (SAIS) which held it on their behalf but was managed by state officials. This put Indian communities directly under state tutelage: it meant a disregard of their ancestral rights. In response, the communist movement Shining Path, active in the highlands of Peru in the 1980s, prioritized the return of SAIS land to Indian communities. Drawing on ethnographic and historical material in one member community, Usibamba, we explore the 1970s land reform, showing how its relationship to the Túpac Amaru SAIS changed as a result of the insurrection by Shining Path, even though it did not result in the restitution of community lands.

Endowment versus restitution

In order to avoid some of the complexities of land restitution programmes, many Latin American states have opted for land reform framed in terms of endowment rather than restitution. In endowment procedures the appeal is not to a legal title but to a general principle of justice. Such procedures, equivalent to those termed 'redistribution' elsewhere, are based on the principle of ironing out extreme inequalities of land distribution. Since they do not require evidence of previous occupation or links with ancestors who were robbed of their land in the past, no complicated investigations to establish the original ownership of land or the reasons for present land inequality are necessary. In land endowment programmes the criteria for eligibility are practical and forward-looking, rather than focused upon the past. A village that is mostly dependent on agriculture, has a certain number of inhabitants, is demonstrably lacking in farmland, and/or is situated next to large landholdings that are apt for expropriation is – in the case under discussion – considered an ideal candidate for such redistribution.

For a peasant community, the obvious advantage of endowment over restitution is that it is generally easier to fulfill the requirements. This became clear during the Mexican land reform (1917–92) in which communities could choose between restitution and endowment. Indigenous communities were privileged in being entitled to claim restitution where their peasant counterparts had no such entitlement. But even they, being unable to deliver the requested proof of ownership through ancient property titles (Nuijten 1997), were generally compelled to switch this into a request for endowment. Although this seems to be no more than a difference in terminology, as the practical effects in terms of the amount of land redistributed were often the same, this distinction has political and ideological implications. The change from restitution into endowment entails an ideological disadvantage. Whereas restitution is expressed in terms of 'giving back what was rightfully theirs', endowment is presented in terms of 'a grant from the state'. Many indigenous communities that fight for official recognition of their ancestral land rights – and redress for the injustices committed in the past – want this to be expressed as a legitimate 'restitution' rather than as a 'gift' for which they have to be grateful. As we will show, these questions about the meaning of transactions played a role in the Peruvian land reform of the 1970s.

Indian highland communities: between haciendas and valley towns

Under the colonial regime (1530–1821), the Indian population in the Peruvian Andes lost much of its land to colonial administrators and *hacendados* who extended their landholdings by invading communal lands. Especially in the early colonial period, land rights were granted to Spanish settlers as a reward for their loyalty to the Spanish Crown (Faron 1985: 30). These invasions forced the Indian peoples to move towards the highest and poorest regions in the mountains (del Castillo 1992: 39). At the same time, however, Indians were 'permitted to use the Spanish legalism of long-standing practice ("from time immemorial") to press claims to land in colonial courts' (Guillet 2005: 95, 96). 'Indians actively contested the usurpation of their communal lands and water rights in the courts. Even though legal struggles were long and costly, persistence often paid off' (Guillet 2005: 96).

After Peru's independence from Spain, in 1821, the Peruvian state put territorial reorganization at the top of its agenda. In the central Andes the highland communities (*anexos de altura*) came under the political jurisdiction of provincial valley towns (*comunidades madres*). Thus, after independence the Indian highland villages remained under the command of the valley centres for which they had to perform a variety of services, among which were the herding of cattle and the construction of bridges and roads (Roberts and Samaniego 1978; Smith 1989). Indian territories remained under threat of invasion by regional power-holders who now were supported by the independent Peruvian state.

This vertical domination of valley over highlands had racial and colonial dimensions as the lowland people were mostly *mestizo* populations descended from the Spanish colonists, whereas the uplands were populated with indigenous Quechua or Huanca-speaking communities (Alberti y Sánchez 1974). In other words, Peruvian society had become racialized according to a vertical axis (de la Cadena 2000).

In addition to having to perform onerous tasks for those who inhabited the lowland centres, the Indian population also maintained tense relationships with the neighbouring haciendas. Community territories bordered on the hacienda landholdings and many indigenous communities functioned in close relation to the hacienda system for which they formed the main labour force. *Hacendados* – mostly *mestizos* – wielded considerable power over the Indians and interfered in many dimensions of their lives.

In the central highlands an important driver in this land alienation process was the Cerro de Pasco Corporation, a US mining and railway company. By 1917 this North American company decided to construct a smelter at the town of Oroya. The smoke of the Oroya smelter caused extensive damage and destroyed productive resources in the region. Its operation significantly altered the agrarian economy and the system of land tenure in the central highlands by the late 1920s. Because of the decline in productivity, the majority of the good high pastureland near the Mantaro Valley passed to the Cerro de Pasco Corporation for a rock bottom price. The corporation became the owner of several haciendas in the region (Mallon 1983: 226–336).

The law and 'the problem of the Indian'

As Guillet recounts, 'Indians were not completely powerless in their relations with *hacendados* . . . Indigenous communities continued to pursue legal solutions [and] Indian *alcaldes* quickly learned to address their petitions to the republican authorities of the new urban administrative hierarchy' (Guillet 2005: 99). As a result of these petitions 'an 1828 law declared Indians to be the owners of the land they occupied, including communal land held through periodic distributions' (Guillet 2005). Other legal mechanisms supported indigenous communities against encroachment from haciendas. Despite the passing of these national laws which recognized ancestral claims to land and protected indigenous communities, land distribution in the Andes remained extremely unequal.

Rural rebellions at the beginning of the twentieth century brought the 'Indian problem' more openly into the public field. Finally, the Peruvian constitution of 1919 provided for the registration of all Indian community lands. The constitution recognized special responsibilities of the central government towards indigenous groups which had held land without interruption since pre-hispanic times (Dobyns 1970: 11). The state endowed lands to landless communities by expropriating private property for which it then compensated the owners. Special offices were established with the task of processing and approving the petitions for the recognition and official inscription of 'indigenous communities'.[1]

However, laws and government programmes do not necessarily lead to the outcomes they promise. As Handelman argues, describing the first decades of the twentieth century in the Peruvian highlands:

> legislation governing the *comunidades indígenas*, failed to put an end to serious land disputes between *latifundistas* and *comuneros*. Hundreds of villages throughout the *sierra* spent much time and money over a number of years vainly trying to recover their lands. In the eyes of their leaders, there was little hope of legally regaining community lands ... Many of them shared a deep-seated resentment against the large landowners and felt exploited by the political and economic system that gave the *hacendados* support.
>
> (Handelman 1975: 34)

The new legislation, thus failing to respond to the grievances of communities, was unable to prevent the increasing peasant unrest and political mobilization. Conflicts between communities and haciendas continued, as well as land seizures and invasions.

In the decades that followed the new constitution of 1919, the highland peasantry became increasingly vigorous in their demand for a serious land reform and the abolition of the haciendas. Intense conflicts between large landowners and *comuneros* emerged and social movements were growing.

Usibamba: gaining ground and fighting for independence

Usibamba is a community of approximately 2,500 inhabitants[2] at an altitude between 3,600 and 4,100 m, in the San José de Quero district, department of Junín. At the end of the nineteenth century, the villagers of Usibamba started their struggle for recognition as an autonomous community.[3]

Until then, Usibamba had been an *anexo* of Mito (*comunidad madre*), one of the biggest communities in the Mantaro valley. This meant that the Usibambinos had to carry out *faenas* (working parties), undertaking the construction of churches and bridges and the cleaning of roads for the landowners of Mito. At the same time, the Usibambinos worked on the Cónsac hacienda that bordered their village. In return for being allowed to graze their cattle on the hacienda or to take stones and cow dung (used for cooking and heating), they were required to carry out a variety of services for the hacienda, from agricultural activities to construction work.

In 1896 the Usibambinos won a lawsuit against the Lozano family of Mito and were given property rights to the disputed land. They then, in 1907, bought an additional tract of land from the Lozano family, while simultaneously maintaining an interest in acquiring the lands of the neighbouring Cónsac hacienda with whose owners they had long had close working relationships. When the hacienda was sold to a new owner, Usibamba became involved in many border disputes with the new landlord.

At the beginning of the twentieth century Usibamba applied for official recognition as an Indigenous Community. In the application for recognition, the community defined their territory, declaring that these lands formed a vital part of the community and had been in their peaceful possession from the time of their forefathers onwards, since time immemorial, without problems ever having arisen with their neighbours. The ministry decided that the documents and reports provided by Usibamba indeed proved the historic existence of the indigenous community and the possession of communal land, and conferred upon them the official status of Indigenous Community in 1939. At that time the population consisted of 492 persons.[4]

By far the largest part of the 3,640 ha of land that the *comunidad* of Usibamba possesses today is divided into private plots and worked on an individual basis. This does not, however, amount to private ownership, since community members (*comuneros*) are allowed to use and work their plot only during their lifetime and provided that they follow community rules. After their death, or if they infringe local community regulations, their plot is allocated to other *comuneros*. To become a member of the *comunidad* and acquire access to a private plot of land one has to fulfill a series of requirements. Young married men from the age of 18 can become *comuneros* upon payment of an entrance fee. Once they have joined they are required to perform many duties: take part in committees, attend meetings and generally behave as responsible and respectable persons. Among other things, this means taking care of the education of their children, not being drunk at meetings and not committing adultery. Through their participation in *faenas*, and fulfilling of *cargos* (public functions), the *comunero* builds up a personal record. This record is taken into account when land comes free and is reallocated among *comuneros*. Every year in August the re-allocation of plots takes place.

Usibamba fits the image of a typical Andean *comunidad* as a strictly organized and disciplined institution, where rigorous local forms of order and justice are followed (Paerregaard 1987). The highland indigenous communities are known for their strong local institutions, such as well-established forms of reciprocity, elaborate festive ceremonies and *faenas*. As the state has been largely absent in these areas, local forms of communal governance have developed with strict rules and punishments (Yambert 1980). At the same time, community life in Usibamba has been characterized by multiple struggles, divisions, fights and quarrels.

Like many other highland communities, Usibamba continued its fight for the recovery of more land. To that end, in 1964 they collected money and bought part of the Cónsac hacienda, still owned at that time by the Cerro de Pasco Corporation. Although expensive, the land was of very low quality.

Given the context of the early 1960s, which was witness to a serious land-seizure movement throughout the Peruvian highlands, this land purchase by Usibamba was hailed by conservative political groups as exemplifying the value of following legal procedures rather than seizing land through violent and illegal invasions. A newspaper article published on 20 July 1964 argued that by buying hacienda land the *comunidad* of Usibamba had demonstrated that agricultural lands could be acquired without invasions.[5] Rather than being represented as violent acts committed in protest by a civil population against abusive authorities, uprisings were glossed as barbarian savagery to which Indians were typically prone (Orlove 1994: 83). Here 'the categories of Indian, Communist and rebel overlapped considerably' (Orlove 1994: 84). In the newspaper article the executive committee of Usibamba was reported as having framed their actions in similar terms. 'The red agents', they are quoted as saying, 'constitute a danger as they generally try to provoke riots and to break the order imposed by the Constitution and the laws . . . The peasants expressed their willingness not to listen to the red violence'. In their efforts to downplay the political background of land invasions the newspaper thus presented Usibamba as a community that, by following the law, distanced itself from barbarian Indian practices.

The Peruvian land reform: the SAIS as creature of the state

The military regime of Velasco (1968–75) became aware of the urgent need to intervene in land distribution, and carried out an extensive agrarian reform in which large-scale cattle haciendas were expropriated and handed over to highland communities. The principles that informed this process were, however, distinct and novel ones. In the decades before the agrarian reform, indigenous identity had been decisive for land entitlement. But the new land reform of the 1970s represented the state's attempt to avoid the legal and political intricacies of 'land restitution' by moving towards 'land endowment'. This was presented not as a way of restoring lost land, but as a means to change the highly unequal land distribution in the countryside and create productive associative enterprises. Communities were considered by the state to be ancient institutions that should be replaced by modern co-operatives (Nuñez 1995: 36). *Comuneros*, however, saw this new endowment process as an opportunity to claim and attempt to recover communal land: a restitutive approach which clearly clashed with the state's modernizing interests (Nuñez 1995).

During this new land reform of the 1970s, then, property was 'given' rather than 'returned' to communities, and the original owners were compensated by the state for the expropriation. What is more, expropriated hacienda lands were not directly handed over to communities but to the SAIS of which communities became members. Thus, beneficiary communities were amalgamated into large associative enterprises. In the department of Junín six SAIS were established: Cahuide, Mariscal Castilla, Heroínas Toledo, Túpac Amaru, Pachacutec and Rámon Castilla. Many SAIS were named after national Indian heroes, such as Túpac Amaru, the last leader of the Inca people executed by the Spanish in 1571. Notably, however, no SAIS was named after Indians who had rebelled against Peruvian large landowners (Martínez-Alier 1973: 39). The victory of Indian communities over *mestizo* haciendas was symbolized and discursively expressed by the Peruvian state in terms of 'national heroes fighting against foreign invaders'. In this way they denied the specific Indian demands for recognition and protection within the borders of the Peruvian nation state.

Figure 10.1 The symbol of the Túpac Amaru SAIS.

Owing the state: 'gifts' and the Agrarian debt

The alleged 'gift' of this land was a misnomer. In reality, communities were given 20 years to pay for the land, animals and equipment which the state had bought from its previous owners, the *hacendados*, and handed over to the SAIS. Communities considered this payment unfair and contrary to the spirit of restitution. They were opposed to compensating former owners of the haciendas, maintaining that these lands had belonged to the Indian peoples and had in the past unlawfully been taken away. Agreeing with this stance, critics of this state project went so far as to suggest that this requirement for Indian communities to pay for the land amounted to the theft of their territories from them (Zaldívar 1971 in Martínez-Alier 1973: 49). Along the same lines, Renique argued that 'in privileging the associative enterprises as a substitute for the traditional hacienda, Velasco's agrarian reform failed to resolve these historic demands for the lands stolen by *hacendados*' (Renique 1994: 226).

Communities were expected to collect the money for this repayment through the proceeds of the SAIS. This meant that each SAIS started with a huge debt. In addition, many *hacendados* had de-capitalized their productive enterprises before they were expropriated. For that reason the SAIS had a difficult start. Officially, it was only when the community members of the SAIS had fully paid their debts that they could become absolute owners of the lands, cattle and installations. Until that time, their control over SAIS operations was limited by the extraordinary powers of intervention retained by the government (Roberts and Samaniego 1978: 244).

Beneficiaries felt utterly betrayed by the fact that instead of receiving the restitution of what rightfully belonged to them, they were forced to become members of a landholding association run by external officials. This seemed a far cry from the recovery of land illegitimately taken from their forefathers. Indeed, there was very little change in the appearance of hacienda life or its productive structure, given that the majority of technical and administrative personnel of the former haciendas kept their posts alongside the workers and labourers in different sections. Although the owners had been removed, everything else remained the same (Sánchez 1989: 87, 88). In fact, 'the associative enterprises reproduced the oppressive traits of the traditional haciendas' (Renique 1994: 241). Although officially the member communities were the 'owner of all' they felt, as the title to this paper indicates, that they were left with 'nothing' (*dueños de todo y de nada*).

This inadequate and unfair restructuring of landownership during the land reform laid the grounds for further episodes of struggle over land in which the highland communities fought for the dismantling of the SAIS and the transfer of its resources to its member communities.

From restitution to endowment: from Indian to peasant

The military government of Velasco, however, was very proud of the SAIS. They considered it a Peruvian invention effective in pacifying Andean Indian communities (Martínez-Alier 1973: 41). The state tried to modernize the Peruvian agrarian production system by converting backward Indians (superstitious and lazy, almost by definition) into modern peasants (effective and dynamic entrepreneurs, commercially-oriented farmers). But there were other less noble objectives as well: 'by taking the "associative" option, the government sought to preserve the administration and assets of the expropriated estates while at the same time defusing and controlling peasant demands for land' (Renique 1994: 227).

The move from a restitutive towards an endowment approach by the Peruvian state was underscored by the systematic removal of the notion of 'indigenous' or 'Indian' from all legal and administrative references to Andean highland communities. From 1969 onwards the official term *'comunidad campesina'* (peasant community) replaced *'comunidad indígena'* (indigenous community). There were other changes as well. 'Known in the past as "The Day of the Indian", 24 June was henceforth declared to be "The Day of the Peasant" to emphasize the dissolution of Indian identity and the inception of national identity among Peru's indigenous population' (Seligman 1995: 59).

This change from Indian into peasant was supported by academic trends at that time. In the first half of the twentieth century Peruvian anthropology, sponsored by the Peruvian state, had focused on 'indigenous cultures' and 'Andean beliefs' as its object of study. However, from the 1960s onwards, accompanying a decline in the Peruvian state's support for anthropology, the earlier Indigenista culture-history nationalist rhetoric was replaced by an economist discourse (de la Cadena 2005: 18). According to the famous Peruvian Marxist author Mariátegui, the *Indianista* ideology had a racist connotation and diverted attention from the economic problems that formed the core of indigenous people's oppression, particularly the unfair system of land tenure. Both advocates of modernization and leftist academics thus preferred to talk in terms of peasants instead of Indians.

With the removal of the 'Indian' or 'indigenous' from the formal agrarian system, restitution-style land claims based on ancestral rights lost their importance. The change from Indian to peasant thus accompanied that from land restitution to land endowment.

Usibamba and the Túpac Amaru SAIS

During the Peruvian land reform of the 1970s Usibamba became one of the 16 member communities (*comunidades socias*) of the Túpac Amaru SAIS. Túpac Amaru was established in 1970 through the expropriation of 19 properties, haciendas of the Cerro de Pasco Corporation. In total it received 216,499 ha of land and all the equipment and effects of the former haciendas. The value of all the land, the construction and installations, and the animals was precisely calculated. On the basis of this calculation the total debt of Túpac Amaru SAIS to the state was established in January 1970. This huge debt had to be repaid in 20 equal yearly payments, starting from 1976.[6]

Of the 30 communities that applied for membership, 14 were disqualified and 16 selected on the basis of the following criteria.[7] It was required that agriculture play a central role in the local economy: communities with a primarily non-agricultural base were disqualified, and calculations were made about the importance of income from agricultural activities in relation to other sources of income. The relationship between the number of residents and the productive potential of the community was also taken into account. More important, the community had to possess fields adjacent to the pastures of the SAIS. The existence of lawsuits between the community and the former owner of the land, the Cerro de Pasco Corporation, was a positive indicator, since it was argued that existing legal problems about borders and land invasions could be resolved more easily if the community were to become a co-owner of the new associative enterprise, the SAIS. Finally, the harm done to the community through the pollution caused by the Oroya smelter was a positive factor for inclusion in the SAIS.[8]

These claims were considered in the selection process not because they pointed towards the restoration of past injustices of dispossession, but because of logistical convenience. Of the communities which eventually formed the Túpac Amaru SAIS no less than 13 had claims against the enterprise by virtue of 'immemorial possession' or colonial land titles (Hobsbawm 1974: 148). The fact that lawsuits and damage claims against the former owners were considered as selection criteria did, however, give the endowment process more than a taste of restorative justice. While from the state's point of view this was a pragmatic approach through which incorporation and co-optation would solve disputes, there was nonetheless something upon which communities could seize as a sign that past wrongs were being redressed through what appeared as the return of land.

Social interactions over land displayed several continuities with earlier property regimes. Between Usibamba and Cónsac, one of the haciendas expropriated for the establishment of Túpac Amaru SAIS, there was a long history of work-based relations and later border problems. These have continued virtually unchanged. Officially Cónsac now became one of the centres of production of Túpac Amaru (Unidad de Producción Cónsac). Yet, *comuneros* of Usibamba still speak about the Cónsac hacienda as they maintain the same feudal relationships with it. In their eyes, the hacienda continues to exist and to exploit them.

The member communities were understandably dissatisfied with the creation of the SAIS, and in particular with their resulting indebtedness to the state.[9] Feeling strongly that they should not pay for what was theirs by rights, they believed themselves entitled, in particular, to the lands of the Cónsac hacienda where *tapadas* (secret treasures) of the Cónsac hacienda are alleged to be buried.

The state justified transferring land to the SAIS rather than to communities on the grounds that economies of scale would allow for the more efficient organization of production. In attempting to maintain these economies of scale it was set on avoiding a relapse into typical indigenous subsistence economies. This justified allowing the organizations of the former owner, the Cerro de Pasco Corporation, to continue working in the same way as before even though the land had changed ownership. A bigger enterprise would also result in higher salaries for the many labourers. The member communities would share in the yearly proceeds of the SAIS according to specific percentages. The SAIS was sited in the premises of one of the expropriated haciendas, Pachacayo, and all employees of the Cerro de Pasco Corporation, from directors and administrators to labourers, were hired by the new SAIS enterprise. To tend the large herds of sheep and cattle, Túpac Amaru SAIS also hired many shepherds (*huacchis*), who were charged with keeping *comuneros* from invading the lands of the SAIS in return for usufructuary rights over the pastures where they were entitled to keep their own animals – called *huaccho* – next to the extensive herds of the enterprise (Sánchez and Lovón 1991: 64). Their role was much resented.

The SAIS was in essence a paternalistic institution. Considering peasants' lack of management capacity, it was alleged that state institutions would support its administration and organization. All communities who were selected as members had to sign an agreement in 1969 in which they expressed their conformity with the intervention of technical and administrative personnel of the General Direction of Land Reform and Rural settlement and the National Office of Co-operative Development. Usibambinos clearly discern this paternalistic impulse, depicting Túpac Amaru SAIS as 'a mother who rejects her children, who cannot accept that her children have grown up and have become adults'.

In the present day, the *comuneros* of Usibamba feel that they are the rightful owners of the land, but they see few of its benefits. In contrast, the directors and labourers of Túpac Amaru SAIS earn good incomes and have all kinds of additional benefits (such as cheap meat). The larger part of SAIS profits are spent on remuneration for the workers, technicians, and administrators, leaving little for member communities.

Contradictorily, the sector that ought to benefit most, according to the original idea of the SAIS as a company providing income, services and other benefits to its members, is that which receives fewest profits from the SAIS. This drawing, included in a folder for the first training and participation meeting for the directives of the member communities of Túpac Amaru in 1987, illustrates the contradictions, perhaps unintentionally. It appears to reflect the ideal of concerted effort towards a common goal, but in fact depicts the struggle and difficulty community members experience in sustaining the SAIS.

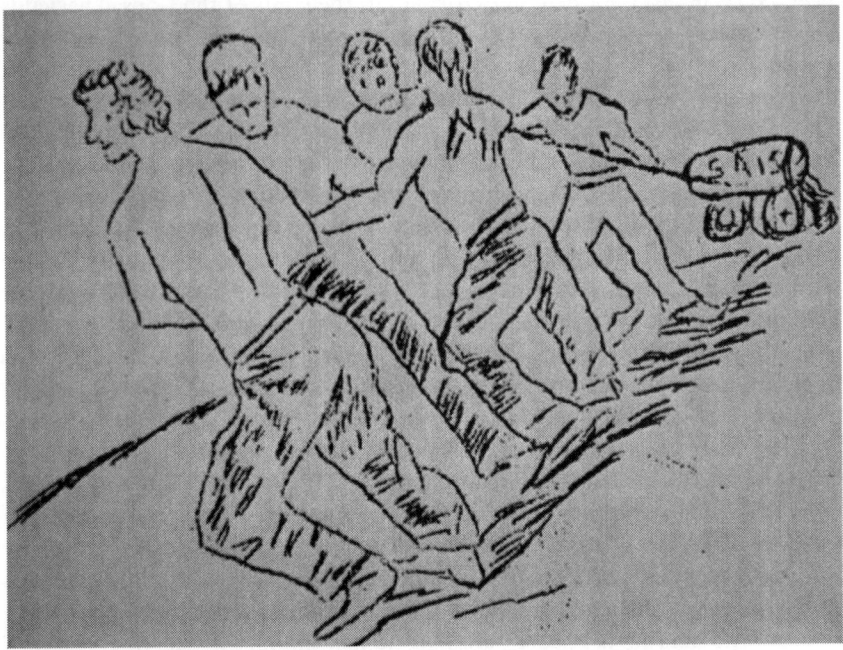

Figure 10.2 Illustration from a training folder for SAIS community delegates.

Túpac Amaru SAIS is managed by a team of directors – engineers and other professionals – that is accountable to the general assembly. The general assembly is the highest authority and elects the directors. The general assembly can vote to remove the directors from office and can alter SAIS policies and budgets. To this body, each member community sends a representative (*delegado*) who holds office for two years. In addition to these community representatives, the general assembly includes one representative of the Túpac Amaru service co-operative. In theory, through this system, member communities thus have considerable power in the general assembly of the SAIS.

In practice, however, several mechanisms conspire to reduce member communities' control. First, directors try to secure the loyalty of the delegates to the SAIS instead of to their constituents, by giving them benefits and material compensations in the form of payment of expenses, cheap products and food. The weekly supply of meat is especially important for the delegates as eating meat is generally only possible for wealthy families. Delegates receive a full salary for two years and can improve their administrative and political skills in this process. They receive additional payment for each meeting they attend. These financial compensations are substantial in comparison with the modest earnings of *comuneros*. The fact that even in times of crisis when the Túpac Amaru SAIS cannot pay their employees the delegates still receive their remuneration, shows their privileged treatment. As a result, they easily accept the 'rules of the game' and work less in the interests of the community they are representing than of the managers, often striking deals with them before meetings. But even if the delegates want to defend the interests of their constituents, there is very little possibility of their participating effectively in decision-making. The directors make use of the existing division among the member communities to play the delegates off against each other. Significant interests are at stake and delegates who do not comply with 'the rules of the game' imposed by the directors even run the risk of being killed.

The remission of the Agrarian debt: the state's betrayal

From the day Túpac Amaru SAIS was established, the member communities fought to dismantle it, and to have the land divided and transferred directly to themselves. At every meeting of the SAIS, petitions are presented by communities for more land to be given to them. Some appeasement has been attempted and some tracts of land handed out. Much community division is generated in the process, but these attempts merely fuel community resentment and suspicion.

Members know the SAIS is capable of violence and murder in pursuing its aims. One means by which members have tried to dismantle the company is by fighting for a change in SAIS statutes. According to the SAIS statutes the association can be dismantled if two-thirds of the delegates request this change. As the member communities are aware of the pressure the directors exert on the delegates to vote against dismantling, they have tried to change the statute with a majority of half plus one instead of two-thirds of the votes. SAIS directives have attempted to annul these initiatives, even – it is alleged – through homicide if necessary. Moises Camacho, a *comunero* from Chalhuas, for example, was killed in 1987 together with his wife. This killing was alleged by *comuneros* to have been ordered by the SAIS because of Moises' vigorous efforts to change the statute during his term as delegate.

In frustration at the difficulties of legal change, several member communities have started to invade and incorporate SAIS property. Countering these invasions as well as the countless lawsuits filed against them by member communities, Túpac Amaru SAIS has levelled many accusations in public. For example, in a newspaper report about the invasion of SAIS land by member communities, the Usibambinos were accused of being communist agitators and ultra-leftists. Accusations continued and in 1979, in the name of their 750 labourers, the SAIS publically denounced the provocation of an ultra-left-wing peasant confederation that supported invasions of its lands.

Comuneros were paradoxically disappointed when in 1980 the Peruvian state remitted the SAIS debt. They had never intended to pay this debt in the first place, since they considered themselves the rightful owners. But they had hoped that the outstanding debt would eventually result in the bankruptcy of the SAIS and hence in the transfer of the land to its members. 'The government condoned the debt, otherwise we would now be the owners of those lands', as a *comunero* put it. Instead, the remission of the debt enabled the official transfer of the ownership titles of the land and other properties from the state to the SAIS.

In 1988, several letters and requests were written by peasant confederations to president Alan García (1985–90) in which they decried the lack of benefits received by member peasant communities from the SAIS. They complained that the aims of the Associative enterprise had not been fulfilled and that the SAIS had turned into a bureaucratic enterprise damaging its members. While SAIS managers worked short hours for good salaries, shepherds, they maintained, worked far longer for minimal returns. The transfer of agricultural and pastoral lands formerly controlled by the *gamonales* and landholders to the SAIS, they alleged, amounted to the continuing exploitation of the rural population. They requested the dissolution of the SAIS to enable the distribution of land, animals and machines among its members, in this way finalizing the process of agrarian reform.

The kind of dismantling being demanded here was, indeed, widely accomplished throughout Peru, since many SAIS were dismantled because of internal conflicts and bad management, and today only a handful of the 53 original associations remain (Paerregaard 2002: 63). What definitively altered the terrain for Túpac Amaru SAIS, however, was a new and external factor: the revolutionary Maoist movement Shining Path which became active in the 1980s. It was the intervention by Shining Path, rather than internal dissent and conflict, that forever altered the relationship between the member communities and Túpac Amaru.

Sendero Luminoso *(Shining Path) and Túpac Amaru SAIS*

Shining Path was initiated by intellectuals in the city of Ayacucho and then spread to other Andean regions and the capital of Lima (Degregori 1996). It propagated a revolutionary agenda directed against 'the enemies of the people'. This included all authorities, but those of the state were particularly suspect. (Degregori 1996; Fumerton 2001). The abolition of the SAIS as a state-run enterprise and the restitution of the land to the highland communities fitted well with *sendero*'s political agenda.

It also proposed a thoroughgoing reform of rural society and the abolition of thieving and adultery. In general the population in the highlands was sympathetic to this agenda of social order. What peasants in Usibamba liked most, however, was *sendero's* agenda of bringing down the SAIS and dividing the property between its member communities.

What caused disenchantment and horrified the community populations, however, were the brutal killings of authorities and the regime of violence that the *senderistas* introduced. Instead of a visionary project aiming towards a more egalitarian future, the revolutionaries turned life into a nightmare of violence, threats and war (Starn 1995: 552). The rebels also angered the villagers with their demands for food and forced recruitment.

The time of *sendero* remains a sensitive topic. Although the directors or executives of many SAIS were violently attacked or even killed, in Usibamba relatively few people were harmed and none of the SAIS community authorities were sacrificed by *sendero*. For that reason other communities accuse Usibamba of having collaborated with the Maoists. This type of accusation is still used in conflicts within and between communities.

During the years of subversion, SAIS member communities were uncomfortably positioned between the revolutionaries and the establishment. Either attracted by *sendero's* propaganda or 'moved by the threat of force, dozens of peasants participated in the massive attacks on the associative enterprises and in the sacking of goods and livestock which took place after the armed attacks' (Renique 1994: 235). One event much recounted in Usibamba was when in 1989 the *senderistas* forced villagers to kill SAIS bulls in the main square and divide the meat amongst themselves. Later that same day the army arrived and accused the *comuneros* of having stolen the bulls from the SAIS. The *comuneros* were extremely frightened by the prospect of being punished by the military. They explained that they had been forced to kill the bulls by *sendero* and immediately returned the meat to the military. The military took the meat but fortunately did not punish them. However, a few days later two *comuneros* who had supposedly been involved in this action were taken away by soldiers driving a SAIS truck and never returned. In Usibamba this event is known as 'the revenge of the association' (*la venganza de la empresa*).

The worst years for Usibamba were 1989 and 1990. Don Rafael was president of the executive committee of the *comunidad* of Usibamba in the years of strong subversion, 1990 and 1991. He narrates the following:

> The *senderistas* ... told us very clearly 'We are going to knock down the SAIS for you'. They went together with other *comunidades* to Cónsac to kill, burn, destroy ... That's no good. Who wants to do this?
>
> We did not go out of our own will. That was not how it went. We were obliged by the subversives 'at gunpoint' (*a punta de cañon*). The entrance was not peaceful, they entered to kill. The company had the support of the government, the army and the police. What can a *comunero* do when faced with the army? ... The ideas of *sendero* were good in theory, but they were not here when the army came. Their ideas were good, they tried to help the *campesino*, but in practice they only pushed us to destroy things.[10]

Because of the attacks by *sendero* the Mariscal Castilla SAIS was dismantled in 1986. Two further associations, Heroínas Toledo and Cahuide, followed two years later and were closed down in 1988. Their lands were distributed to member communities as well as to neighbouring communities that had not formerly been members. Being one of the largest associations, Túpac Amaru received much support from the national military and police. In this way it survived despite suffering many *sendero* attacks in which a total of 11 people were killed: six employees; one military officer; one delegate; two wives of delegates; one community leader.

Usibamba, like other communities, used this time of political unrest and attacks on the SAIS to intensify the pressure on the state authorities to redistribute their land. For example, in a letter written by the authorities in Usibamba to the director of the Ministry of Agriculture in 1987 they argued the following:

> we are overpopulated in the little village where we live with only 3,810 hectares of land to support 2,840 inhabitants . . . this is a continuing problem which we try to resolve through your respected intervention, through . . . an extension of 12,000 hectares, which corresponds to us as member of . . . the SAIS Túpac Amaru

These are the 12,000 ha of the former Cónsac hacienda which, according to them, belong to Usibamba. In 1988 and 1989 – the years of severe violence in the region – Túpac Amaru SAIS responded by transferring first 230 ha and then 570 ha to Usibamba. But it transferred only the use rights in the land, retaining official ownership. Although the *comuneros* perceived this as a strategic move by the SAIS in order to appease them, they were nonetheless pleased to receive the land 'in their own hands'. They were not appeased for long. In 1990 they sent another letter, this time to the delegates, requesting the dismantling of the SAIS given its non-fulfilment of the aims for which it had been created.

Communities involved in land claims were labelled pro-*sendero* by SAIS and therefore seen as potential 'terrorists' or *terrucos*. Although some villagers did, indeed, participate in *sendero*'s activities, most *comuneros*, fearing military retaliation, tried to keep a distance from the violent conflict. Seven *comuneros* of Usibamba disappeared during the worst years of violence, between 1987 and 1989 – among them two men who worked as *huacchis* for the Túpac Amaru SAIS – but it was never known who was responsible.

In 1991 civil defence committees (*rondas campesinas*) were organized to protect the population and a national army base was established in the region. The heads of the *rondas* were trained by the military. Although officially the army came to protect the people against *sendero*, in many instances they turned against those whom they had been sent to defend. As a *comunero* put it: 'the *terruco* betrayed you, the armed forces betrayed you and the police betrayed you'. This period of civil defence lasted some five years: from 1991 when the army began the massive distribution to Andean peasants of more than 10,000 shotguns (Starn 1995: 553), through 1992 when the leader of *sendero*, Abimael Guzmán, was captured by the Peruvian army and life in the Andes became more peaceful, to 1996 when the self-defence committees ceased functioning in this region.

Relations between Túpac Amaru SAIS and its member communities, already uneasy, had now been further disrupted. Struggles over land assumed new forms, but the balance had shifted in the communities' favour. As several *comuneros* from Usibamba said: 'it is only since *sendero* that the SAIS started to respect us'.

Changed relationships: comuneros and the huacchis of the SAIS

The violent invasions of *sendero* had a lasting effect even after the movement had been subdued by the Peruvian army. Communities now felt able to challenge SAIS authority, or at the very least openly to defy it. This applied particularly in respect of grazing rights. 'Since terrorism it has become easier', they say, 'now we can let our animals graze during the day'. Whereas formerly *huacchis* temporarily impounded animals grazing illegally, or fined their owners, this is no longer the case. People now travel openly and in broad daylight to SAIS pastures, making no attempt to hide their activity as they used to do. If the *huacchi* evicts them from the pasture they simply wait until he has left in order to cross the fence and enter the SAIS again. 'Today I even make fun of them [the *huacchis*]', commented an old *comunero* 'But they made us cry as children. One day I promised myself, I won't be a man until they respect us'.

Member communities of Túpac Amaru keep on fighting, however, for what they really want: to get their land back. By way of appeasement, the association has agreed that 2,000 ha will be restored to each of 15 communities: 30,000 ha in total. So far, only 12,000 ha has been transferred. Member communities, dissatisfied with the small proportion of the total they were promised and the even lesser proportion that has been restored, have continued their invasions and lawsuits. In January 2004 one of these communities, San Juan de Ondores, fenced off a large terrain as a means to claim property rights. Inhabitants occupied 14,000 ha of land and claimed a further 8,000 ha. After the executive committee of the SAIS filed an unsuccessful lawsuit, the police arrived to defend the rights of the people of Ondores, much to the outrage of the SAIS directors. Such a thing would have been unthinkable in the days before *sendero*, but the balance of political power had now subtly shifted.

While peasants claim the right to subdivide SAIS lands for redistribution, the executive committee has been attempting quite the opposite: they aim to turn Túpac Amaru into a private joint-stock company. This transformation has already taken place in the case of the Pachacutec SAIS in the department of Junín. As the head of Túpac Amaru SAIS told us during an interview in 2003:

> The SAIS is an associative enterprise that consists of 15 communities and a labourers' co-operative. That is an old-fashioned form of enterprise. It makes efficient decision making impossible, as well as the further development of the enterprise. The SAIS should become a joint-stock company.[11]

However, in order to effect such a change, they need the agreement of two-thirds of the assembly, which they have so far not managed to secure. Efforts will need to be made, they claim, to promote the idea. All indications are, however, that such promotion will not be enough to counteract the opposition of member communities. Since 2001 they have convened several meetings, mobilizing around the memory of Moises Camacho (the *comunero* from Chalhuas who was allegedly killed by the SAIS in 1987), at all of which the *comunidades* resolved not to accept the change of the SAIS into a joint-stock company. So far they have been able to close ranks and forestall this change. Their slogan 'land to the tiller' (*la tierra para el que la trabaja*), resonating with similar slogans worldwide, is an emotive reminder of their determination to oppose the further alienation of their land.

Restitution of land and indigenous rights in a new political climate

The original substitution of 'peasant' for 'indigenous' to designate Andean highland communities, which was introduced by the military regime in the 1960s, was applauded by many as an important step in the fight against racism. As Dobyns argued in 1970 'The fundamental thing in changing the designation of the communities from "indigenous" into "peasant" is to switch a racial connotation for a socio-economic designation that better corresponds to the socio-cultural reality of the population of Peruvian communities' (Dobyns 1970: 13). It is unlikely, however, that the formal abolition of a form of ethnic categorization will lessen discriminatory practices against marginalized populations who, in daily life, continue to be defined in these terms. Despite the disappearance in formal policy talk of the term 'Indian' or 'indigenous' to refer to Andean populations, ethnic categorizations and discrimination against highland people in Peru are very prevalent (cf. de la Cadena 2005). As Faron argues, replacing '*indigenuus*' with 'peasant' with the Agrarian Reform Law of 1964 has left unaltered the conceptualization of a natural hierarchy based on phenotype (Faron 1985: 142), with 'major patterns of land and labour allocation founded on bio-ethnic considerations that began in the colonial era and middle republican period' remaining largely unaltered (Faron 1985: 129). In Peruvian society one of the most enduring distinctions is that between *mestizos* and Indians. Indians are seen as pre-modern populations living under harsh circumstances at high altitudes. Lower-lying areas, in the valleys or at the coast, are inhabited by Spanish-speaking *mestizos*, seen as an index of whiteness and civilization (Stepputat 2004: 246). Thus, the term 'Indian' is used in pejorative ways to depict backward, superstitious, pre-modern, violent highland people. Highlanders, perhaps responding defensively to this stereotype, do not, themselves, self-define as indigenous or Indian. As Paerregaard rightly points out, in contemporary Peru:

the ethnic label of 'Indians' thrust upon the Andean peasantry by the outside world has become highly controversial; indeed most of Peru's rural population do not identify themselves as indigenous. Rather than employing ethnic or cultural categories, they refer to economic position or regional origin when accounting for their identity.

(Paerregaard 2002: 57)

In the past, by contrast, highland people engaged in land conflicts habitually referred to their Indian roots.

Despite the fact that it left intact the fundamental inequalities of Peruvian society, however, some success is evident in the Peruvian state strategy of abolishing ethnic classification. This contrasts with other Andean countries such as Ecuador and Bolivia, and meso-American ones such as Mexico (see Chapter 11, Tiedje; see also Chapter 7, French, in this book), where Indianness is high on the political agenda today and is used as an important weapon in the fight for justice and recognition of land rights. In these countries, emerging organizations and political movements stress the centuries of exploitation of the Indian population and demand on the basis of this that indigenous citizenship be taken seriously. It perhaps seems puzzling that in Peru 'indigenous mobilization has not taken the explosive forms that have attracted so much attention in Eucador, Bolivia, Guatemala, and Mexico' (García 2005: 164). Peasants in the highlands of Peru do not revert to Indian or indigenous repertoires in order to frame their struggle for justice.

Besides the change from 'Indian' to 'peasant' in state discourse in Peru in the 1960s, several other influences can explain this phenomenon. First, the academic debate about indigenous highland communities in Peru has developed in such a direction that many people have begun to find the term 'indigenous' a distasteful one. We mentioned earlier that *Indigenista* studies in Peru have the connotation of a limited focus on Andean cultures and rituals, at the expense of political analysis. Second, leftist political leaders in Peru originated above all from the coast. In their political programmes they framed struggles and problems in terms of peasants and labourers and they concentrated especially on rural social mobilization in the coastal areas. Indigenous people in the highland areas received little attention. Third, the Shining Path, which was particularly active in the Andean highlands, also expressed its political agenda in terms of class struggles rather than using a language of indigeneity or Indianness: in their view class consciousness would automatically transform Indians into peasants of a modern sort. Interestingly, one could conclude that these leftist and class-based politics have had the effect of making it impossible for Indian people to fight their own struggle. Whereas in Bolivia and Ecuador, restitution claims to land are accompanied by the 'return of the Indian' (de la Cadena 2005: 25) or of what Kuper calls 'the native' (Kuper 2003), in Peru this is not (yet) the case.

Conclusion: rights, recognition and restitution

The unequal distribution of land in the Andean highlands of Peru has an ethnic and racist underpinning, which is the result of centuries of exploitation of Indian people in a political climate of discrimination and exclusion. Land restitution programmes generally express the intention of setting right injustices committed in ancient times when land was illegitimately expropriated from subordinate populations. For various technical, political and ideological reasons, however, restitution programmes have in this setting been changed into endowment/ redistribution programmes in which it is not necessary to establish links to the past. Instead of giving back land that was theirs, endowment procedures talk about the need to restructure because of the highly disproportionate distribution of land. The Peruvian land reform of the 1970s was a clear case in which land restitution was replaced by a redistributive endowment approach: albeit one in which highland indigenous communities were made to pay for the land. The fact that payment was levied for what many saw as their entitlement served merely to compound the injustice.

It is no coincidence that the movement away from land 'restitution' in Peruvian land reform was accompanied by the movement from 'indigenous' into 'peasant community'. The notion 'indigenous' has a legal connotation in the context of land restitution claims based on 'ancestral' rights, or possession since 'time immemorial'. Being a peasant does not have this connotation of linkages to a sacred past. While highland communities hoped that their longstanding claims to communal lands would finally be recognized through land reform, the Peruvian state aimed to create a modern, agricultural sector by changing 'traditional, superstitious Indians' into 'dynamic, entrepreneurial peasants'.

For that same reason, the communities received land not 'in their own hands' but in the form of associative enterprises, the SAIS. By naming the SAIS after national heroes who had fought against foreign invaders (the Spanish, the Chileans) the state imposed a nationalist logic of co-operation between peasants and the state. Peasants, however, did not necessarily share this nationalist agenda, since they felt betrayed by not being entrusted with the independent ownership and management of what they felt to be their land. We have shown how, in the case of Túpac Amaru, the formal structure which officially gave communities decision-making power in fact disempowered them in subtle and less subtle ways. This made it impossible for communities to counter the strategies of managers or to abolish the institution despite decades of struggle.

The Maoist *sendero luminoso* tried to break the power of the SAIS and to hand over its properties to the peasantry. Despite these attacks, Túpac Amaru SAIS survived but was rendered weaker in relation to its member communities. Claims by the *comunidades* that the lands of the SAIS should be given to them have become more strident and it is by no means certain that it will be able to resist these pressures for much longer.

Since the 1990s indigenous peoples in Latin America have increasingly fought for their rights on the basis of ethnic entitlement, shaped by the language of international human rights and multiculturalist discourse (Sieder and Witchell 2001). The United Nations has extended the discourse of universal human rights to cover the rights of historically marginalized indigenous peoples and to demand the reparation of historical wrongs (Sieder and Witchell 2001). Land restitution has been put firmly back on the political agenda in Latin America, through the UN Universal Declaration on Human Rights. In contrast to Bolivia and Ecuador, however, highland Andean communities in Peru do not have recourse to ideas of indigenous rights in order to demand protection and recognition of land rights. Since the 1970s the indigenous question in Peru has been banned from political and academic debates. The question is whether the ethnic upheaval in neighbouring countries will inspire the Peruvian highland peoples to re-appropriate an indigenous rights discourse which was widely employed by them before the Peruvian land reform, or whether they will find some other means to pursue their still-unfulfilled goal of restitution.

References

Alberti, G and R Sánchez (1974) *Poder y Conflicto Social en el Valle del Mantaro (1900–1974)*, Lima: Instituto de Estudios Peruanos.

Cadena, M, de la (2000) *Indigenous Mestizos: The politics of race and culture in Cuzco, Peru 1919–1991*, Durham, NC, London: Duke University Press.

—— (2005) 'The Production of Other Knowledges and its Tensions: from Andeanist anthropology to interculturalidad?', *Journal of the World Anthropology* Network 1: 14–37, available at www.ram-wan.org/e-journal.

Castillo, L, del (1992) 'Tienen futuro las comunidades campesinas?', *Debate agrario* 14: 39–53.

Degregori, CI (ed.) (1996) *Las rondas campesinas y la derrota de Sendero Luminoso*, Lima: Instituto de Estudios Peruanos.

Dobyns, HF (1970) *Comunidades Campesinas del Peru*, Lima: Editorial Estudios Andinos.

Faron, LC (1985) *From Conquest to Agrarian Reform: Ethnicity, Ecology, and Economy in the Chancas Valley, Peru: 1533 to 1964*, Pittsburg, PA: University of Pittsburgh Press.

Fumerton, M (2001) '*Rondas campesinas* in the Peruvian civil war: peasant self-defence organisations in Ayacucho,' *Bulletin of Latin American Research* 20(4): 470–97.

García, ME (2005) *Making Indigenous Citizens: Identities, Education, and Multicultural Development in Peru*, Stanford, CA: Stanford University Press.

Guillet, D (2005) 'Customary Law and the Nationalist Project in Spain and Peru', *Hispanic American Historical Review* 85(1): 81–114.

Handelman, H (1975) *Struggle in the Andes: peasant political moblization in Peru*, Austin, TX: University of Texas, Institute of Latin American Studies.

Hobsbawm, EJ (1974) 'Peasant Land Occupations', *Past and Present* 62: 120–52.

Kuper, A (2003) 'The Return of the Native', *Current Anthropology* 44(3): 389–402.

Mallon, FE (1983) *The Defense of Community in Peru's Central Highlands: Peasant

struggle and capitalist transition, 1860–1940, Princeton, NJ: Princeton University Press.
Mariátegui, JC (1971) *Seven Interpretive Essays on Peruvian Reality*, Austin, TX: University of Texas Press.
Martínez-Alier, J (1973) *Los Huacchileros del Perú: Dos Estudios de Formaciones Sociales Agrarias*, Paris: Ruedo Ibérico; Lima: Instituto de estudios Peruanos.
Nuijten, M (1997) 'Agrarian Reform in Mexico: illegality within the framework of the law', *Law and Anthropology* 9: 72–104.
—— (2003) *Power, Community and the State, the Political Anthropology of Organisation in Mexico*, London: Pluto Press.
Nuñez, P (1995) 'Law and Peasant Communities in Peru (1969–1988)', Wageningen: PhD thesis.
Orlove, B (1994) 'The Dead Policemen Speak: power, fear and narrative in the 1931 Molloccahua Killings (Cuzco)', in D Poole (ed.) *Unruly Order: violence, power, and cultural identity in the high provinces of Southern Peru*, Boulder, CO: Westview Press, pp 63–96.
Paerregaard, K (1987) *Nuevas Organizaciones en Comunidades Campesinas: el caso de Usibamba y Chaquicocha*, Lima: Pontífica Universidad Católica del Perú, Fondo Editorial.
—— (2002) 'The Vicissitudes of Politics and the Resilience of the Peasantry: the Contestation and Reconfiguration of Political Space in the Peruvian Andes', in N Webster and L Engberg-Pedersen (eds) *In the Name of the Poor: Contesting Political Space for Poverty Reduction*, London: Zed Press, pp 52–77.
Renique, JL (1994) 'Political Violence, the State, and the Peasant Struggle for Land (Puno)', in D Poole (ed.) *Unruly Order: violence, power, and cultural identity in the high provinces of Southern Peru*, Boulder, CO: Westview Press, pp 223–46.
Roberts, B and C Samaniego (1978) 'The Evolution of Pastoral Villages and the Significance of Agrarian Reform in the Highlands of Central Peru', in N Long and B Roberts (eds) *Peasant Cooperation and Capitalist Expansion in Peru*, Austin, TX: University of Texas Press.
Sánchez, R (1989) 'Las Sais de Junín y la alternativa comunal', *Debate Agrario* 7: 85–101.
Sánchez, R and G Lovón (1991) 'Empresas Asociativas y Democratización del Agro: el Caso de la SAIS Maragañi', *Debate Agrario* 11: 54–88.
Seligmann, LJ (1995) *Between Reform and Revolution: political struggles in the Peruvian Andes (1969–1991)*, Stanford, CA: Stanford University Press.
Sieder, R and J Witchell (2001) 'Advancing Indigenous Claims through the Law: reflections on the Guatemalan peace process', in J Cowan, M Dembour and R Wilson (eds) *Culture and Rights*, Cambridge: Cambridge University Press.
Smith, G (1989) *Livelihood and Resistance: peasants and the politics of land in Peru*, Berkeley, CA: University of California Press.
Starn, O (1995) 'To Revolt against the Revolution: War and Resistance in Peru's Andes', *Cultural Anthropology* 10(4): 547–80.
Stepputat, F (2004) 'Marching for Progress: Rituals of Citizenship, State and Belonging in a High Andes District', *Bulletin of Latin American Research* 23(2): 22–59.
Yambert, K (1980) 'Thought and Reality: dialectics of the Andean community', in B Orlove and G Custred, *Land and Power in Latin America: agrarian economies and social processes in the Andes*, New York, London: Holmes and Meier Publishers, pp 31–54.

Official documents

Proyecto de adjudicación del complejo Cerro de Pasco a favor de la Sociedad Agrícola de Interés Social (SAIS) Túpac Amaru, 1969 (88 pages).
Estatuto de la SAIS 'Túpac Amaru' Ltda. No 1. Registrado la Modificación de Estatutos en el asiento No. 11, del folio 146 No. 1 del tomo 1 No. 1 de Sociedades Civiles de Junín. Huancayo, 28 de Junio de 1985.

Notes

1 In 1962 there were 1,600 such officially recognized communities in Peru (Dobyns 1970: 12). Today there exist approximately 3.312 officially recognized communities in the highlands (Paerregaard 2002: 56).
2 In 1993 Usibamba had 2,197 inhabitants according to the *Resultados Definitivos de los Censos Nacionales: IX de Población y IV de Vivienda* of 11 July 1993. The estimated population for 2003 is 2,345 according to the INEI projections of 30 June 2003.
3 We are much indebted to two officials in charge of the *División de Comunidades Campesinas y Nativas* of the Ministry of Agriculture in the city of Huancayo for helping us to get access to the official archives. We are grateful for their invaluable assistance, sense of humour and willingness to co-operate.
4 *Expediente relativo al Reconocimiento e Inscripción Oficial de la Comunidad de Indígenas de Usibamba, del Distrito de Aco, de la Provincia de Jauja, del Departamento de Junín. Dirección de Asuntos Indígenas. Sección Administrativa. Minsterio de Salud Pública, Trabajo y Previsión Social.*
5 *La Prensa*, Huancayo, 20 July 1964.
6 The total debt of the Túpac Amaru SAIS to the state in 1970 was established at: 130,827,164.37 soles de oro. *Proyecto de adjudicacion del complejo cerro de Pasco a favor de la sociedad agricola de interes social 'Tupac Amaru'*, 1969.
7 *Proyecto de adjudicacion del complejo cerro de Pasco a favor de la sociedad agricola de interes social 'Tupac Amaru'*, 1969.
8 The 16 member communities were: Usibamba, San Antonio de Tanta, Canchayllo, Llocllapampa, Santa Rosa de Sacco, Huari, Suitucancha, Urauchoc, Santiago de Huayhuay, San Juan Bautista de Pachahaca, Huacapo, Purísima Concepción de Paccha, Chalhuas, Huancaya, Chacapalpa, San Juan de Ondores.
9 Officially the Tupac Amara SAIS consisted of 17 members: 16 member communities and the worker co-operative which was established in 1970.
10 All interview fragments and texts from Spanish sources are our own translations.
11 One of the 16 communities that were included in Túpac Amaru from the start had left the association.

Chapter 11

Que sucede con PROCEDE? (What is happening with PROCEDE?)

The end of land restitution in rural Mexico[1]

Kristina Tiedje

Abstract

This article examines the limitations of Mexican agrarian programmes for agricultural transformation and nationalism by exploring indigenous responses to the end of land restitution in the late 1990s. Mexico's land restitution began with the Agrarian Reform aimed at assisting with post-revolutionary nation-building and appeasing rural unrest. Landless labourers were able to claim rights to land for agricultural production on communally held lands, and landless indigenous peoples could request the restitution of their original land or lay claim to land endowments if they had been displaced from their original lands. With Mexico's opening up to a global economy, the 1992 reform signalled the end of restitution. The Programme of Certification of Individual Rights to Farm Plots, Common Land and Urban Lots (PROCEDE) presently promotes individual titling of former communal lands. For the Nahuas, the reform portends neoliberal restructuring: it paves the way for land sale, and for the division of their communities through the reduction or potential elimination of communal landholdings, which they view as ethnic spaces. I analyse a case of indigenous organizing and argue that terminating restitution is counterproductive to nation-building at a time when Mexico has declared multiculturalism the new brand of nationalism.

Introduction

Questions regarding who owns the land, controls resources, provides labour to make the land productive and derives profits from it, have shaped social, ethnic, and spatial relationships in Latin America over the past 500 years. Like nineteenth-century liberalism, 1980s free-market policies intensified efforts to privatize land and portrayed indigenous communal landholdings as obstacles to agricultural productivity. In Mexico, the end of both land restitution and redistributive endowment set the stage for the latest round of land privatization and left landless indigenous men and women with the dilemma of whether to work as peons or migrant workers.

Roughly at the same time as the reforms of the 1990s, ethnic movements have resurfaced with the new wave of democratization in Latin America that fused multiculturalism with a new brand of nationalism. In what Deborah Yashar has termed the 'postliberal challenge' (2005), indigenous peoples have come together in regional and national organizations to make claims to equal rights: to special rights previously denied to them as native peoples, including land rights (Sieder 2002; Van Cott 1994; Warren and Jackson 2002; Yashar 1999). This round of ethnic movements accompanies growing claims for differentiated rights to land, based in part on ethnic origin, primarily subsistence-based economic systems and a particular relationship with the environment (Plant 2002).

Against this backdrop, I examine the end of land restitution and redistribution programmes in the region known as the Huasteca in Mexico. I am particularly interested in local responses to PROCEDE that, from the 1990s, opened communal landholdings for private rental and sale.

With respect to indigenous communal landholdings and indigenous peoples' identification with the land, the term 'restitution' is a useful one through which to conceptualize the period of implementation of Agrarian Reform in Mexico, since that is how it is commonly understood by the indigenous peoples themselves. Both the *ejido* and the *comunidad indígena* are community-based landholdings to which members have usufruct rights for cultivation usually on individual land plots (Stephen 1997a: 160, 2002: xxvi–xxviii). Strictly speaking, the *comunidad indígena* is a result of land restitution (*restitución*) whereas the *ejido* is a result of redistributive land endowment (*dotación*). *Ejidos* are more common and much more numerous, since many indigenous peoples had been displaced from their original lands during the colonial period and subsequently experienced difficulty in juridically proving their pre-colonial settlement on these lands. This, however, proved to be no obstacle to the creation of new ideas of aboriginality and indigeneity. For the indigenous peoples thus displaced, the land they received (as endowments or restitution) in the 1930s and 1940s became, in their view, 'original' land. Although in reality the 1917 Agrarian Reform and subsequent redistribution campaign restored aboriginal lands to only some indigenous people, while others received redistributive endowments as compensation for lands from which they had earlier been displaced, it is nonetheless often claimed that this was the moment when they got 'their land back'. Typically, the land freed for restitution in the 1920s was that located in less fertile areas which large landowners were willing to give up and make accessible for landless peasants.

Given this history, the concept of restitution is an important one in understanding contemporary indigenous organizing against the state's attempts to transform communal land into individual property. It is these changes in agrarian policy which have been a catalyst causing land claims to be framed in ethnic and indigenous terms. Claims are simultaneously framed, however, in terms of citizenship. People's demanding of special rights – rights to land, collective rights, autonomous judicial spheres and the right to maintain ethnic identities distinct from, but formative of a multicultural state – initiate a debate about what citizenship ought to entail in this context.

My discussion is based on ethnographic fieldwork conducted over a period of 10 years with several extended periods of field research, the longest lasting 14 months during 2002 and 2003, and especially on a total of 22 months between 1999 and 2005. I focused on the eight out of 35 *ejidos* that rejected the land-titling programme in Xilitla *municipio* (a district roughly equivalent to a county), situated in the tropical ecozone of the Huasteca where maize subsistence agriculture is combined with coffee as a cash crop. The *ejidatarios* (members) mobilized to keep local autonomy intact by preventing national and municipal interests from gaining control over their land.

Xilitla's *ejidos* were established in the 1930s in areas with a majority of Nahuatl speakers. The Nahuas are the largest indigenous group in Mexico, spread throughout Central Mexico. In the Huasteca, Nahua peoples live as peasants in the fertile Sierra Madre mountains. I conducted structured and

Figure 11.1 Map of the Huasteca.

unstructured interviews with Nahua peoples, communal shareholders, community activists, local and municipal authorities and government officials.

The narratives people used when talking about the land were generally framed in terms of political, economic and cultural needs, collective rights and citizenship. In some cases, in particular, *ejidatarios* skillfully co-opted the vocabulary of democracy, multiculturalism and economic restructuring. Those who were engaged in local church base communities during the 1970s, and who subsequently founded agricultural co-operatives, have learned to articulate multiple cultural values and practices. They have come to act as cultural intermediaries and community activists, through their interactions with progressive priests and secular clerics, NGO facilitators and officers of the government.

Indigenous organizing and the state

The history of land restitution programmes in Latin America is one of shifting relationships between indigenous peoples and the state. In Mexico, Bolivia, Peru and Guatemala, post-independence republics granted indigenous peoples special rights to land. Such rights were largely eradicated by elites within the nation-state who took their lead from the ideologies of nineteenth-century economic liberalism. This eventually led to rural protests and peasant unrest, and, in the case of Mexico, to revolutionary struggle. In the twentieth century, restitution was deemed necessary to appease unrest and create a new basis for post-revolutionary, state-supported nationalism. State projects sought to remap the nation, redefine democratic citizenship and broaden the responsibilities of citizens. In this context, the agrarian reforms privileged certain types of political and economic identity. Those claiming restitution people tended, from the 1940s to the 1960s, to be construed as peasants rather than as indigenous people.

To understand contemporary indigenous organizing against individual land titling in Mexico, I shall examine the centrality of the state, showing the partial and sometimes unintended impact of its policies on the local level, arguing that state projects cannot be studied in an institutional vacuum (Yashar 2005). State constructions of the variety of indigenous peoples as 'peasantry' (*campesinado*), in vogue in Latin American nationalisms (and echoed in anthropological thought) in the 1930s and 1940s, came into question in the 1960s and 1970s (Kearney 1996). In response, the surge of ethnic movements and the multiplicity of voices in indigenous organizing demonstrated that people could and did have several different identities and were able to express those in different contexts (Nagengast and Kearney 1990; Montejo 2002; Stephen 1997b; Tiedje 2002; Warren 1998).

Mexico has the numerically largest indigenous population in Latin America with approximately 11 million people who identify as indigenous, estimated at 10 to 15 per cent of the total Mexican population (Sieder 2002). In the past, efforts to identify indigenous peoples for national statistics were initially based on diverse criteria such as language, dress, and primarily subsistence-oriented production, with a particular emphasis on maize agriculture and its intrinsic relationship to the seasonal ritual cycle (see Figures 11.3 and 11.4). Such attempts at identification embodied a romantic vision of the indigenous economy, implying closed corporate communities practising subsistence-oriented production (see Chambers and Young 1979; Roseberry 1995; Schwartz 1981). They overlooked indigenous communities' long-standing participation in market-oriented production. In Xilitla specifically, coffee co-operatives have operated since the early 1980s and the Nahua communities have always provided staple food for local markets. When analyzing the impact of the state's economic restructuring upon the construction of indigeneity, it is thus important to recognize Nahua economic activity as one which combines cash and subsistence agriculture.

My research with Nahua peoples in the Huasteca shows a close relationship between Mexico's economic restructuring and the rise of indigenous activism with rural populations insisting on their right to self-define in new ways. Objective economic criteria have given way to an emphasis on more subjective criteria. During the wave of resource rights movements of the 1990s, indigenous activists have emphasized their spiritual, cultural and material attachment to the land, in part as a means to support their territorial claims. In this new vision of indigeneity, subsistence agriculture has become a key attribute in the self-definition of the Nahuas as indigenous. In addition, the geographical space where they live is of considerable importance for the expression of their political, economic, cultural and religious identities. The latter play an important role in contesting and shaping state-projected nationalism and in formulating alternative notions of citizenship.

How wide-ranging and effective, I ask, have state land-titling and land-restitution projects been in Mexico, in the context of that country's broader agrarian and state policies? Recent scholarly work suggests that states are less competent, coherent and capable of governing the whole society than is normally accepted (Scott 1998; Yashar 2005). Nor should we assume that a society will respond predictably to institutional change. Instead, I take my lead from Yashar, in trying to assess – and question the extent of – the 'reach of the state,' its 'penetration throughout the country' and 'capacity to govern society' (Yashar 2005: 6). These questions are particularly complicated, in the case of the Nahua and other country-dwellers, by the changing forms of categorization which the state employs and through which Nahua, in turn, self-identify. The shifting policies of the Mexican state, applied to 'peasants' and 'indigenous people' by turns, have had limited reach and many unintended consequences.

Background to restitution

Over the centuries, land has been central to every political, economic and cultural struggle that has divided the population of Xilitla in the Huasteca. Xilitla *municipio* lies in what is known as the Huasteca Potosina in southern San Luis Potosí (see Figure 11.1).[2] In the mountain hamlets of Xilitla, belonging to an indigenous community was an important ethnic marker in the nineteenth century. With indigenous peoples settling in the mountains when the Spaniards invaded their lands in the fertile foothills and coastal plains, claims to indigenous identity were closely connected to place. In the early colonial period, the densely forested areas of the Sierra made access to these highland areas more difficult and provided some protection to the local population and their lifeways. Spanish paternalism also allowed indigenous communities to retain some autonomy with their *cabildo* leadership and some territorial integrity (based on a unit known as the *fundo legal*) in the indigenous republics.

The nineteenth-century reforms changed the protected status of the indigenous republics. Elite discourses of that time blamed the divide between the 'indigenous' and 'non-indigenous race' on the existence of these indigenous republics, and advocated instead the spread of a universal *mestizo* civilization (of mixed Spanish and indigenous descent). With Independence, colonial racial hierarchies were to be overcome in order to create one nation. The proclamation of Morelos in 1810 declared the end of slavery, racial stigmatization, and indigenous inferiority. In 1821, Agustín de Iturbide declared Mexican citizenship on the basis of equality. In theory, this marked the end of colonial exploitative practices of indigenous land and people. In reality, however, it marked the end of state protectionism for indigenous communities and made them subject to more unforgiving market forces. In 1864, Liberal thinker Francisco de Pimentel argued that the social, ethnic, political and economic segregation between indigenous peoples and *mestizos* was a remnant of colonial rule. According to Pimentel this segregation inhibited nation-building. He described the indigenous population as suffering and marginalized. Assimilation into a *mestizo* nation was depicted as the solution to the 'indigenous problem' (Pimentel 1864: 217). Following this same line of argument, the Liberal economic reform ('*La Reforma*') was aimed at erasing a separate status and a separate lifestyle for indigenous peoples. For Liberal thinker José Luis Mora, the reforms sought to form a unified, homogenized nation where all citizens were to be treated equally and none would be considered inferior (Fraser 1972; Marzal 1993).

Overall, however, the reforms did not turn out to hold the promise to a racism-free equality. Instead, they dissolved the protected status of the indigenous republics, thus rendering them more vulnerable to outside interference. In 1856, economic liberalism promoted the privatization of indigenous lands and church estates with the Lerdo Law, intended to concentrate the population into smaller areas in order to free land for foreign investment. The law declared communal lands illegal and promoted their distribution among shareholders (who were often foreign investors). In the Huasteca, the Lerdo Law was implemented in the 1890s, focusing in particular on rural areas considered suitable for investment. The disamortization of communal lands resulted in an increase of large estates (haciendas) and agrarian societies (*condueñazgos*). Land became concentrated in the hands of *latifundistas*.

The acute land shortage experienced by poorer people as a result of these processes represented one of Mexico's major problems around the turn of the nineteenth century. By 1910, 1 per cent of the population owned 97 per cent of the total land (Eckstein 1966, cited in Marzal 1993: 53), while 15 million people, who made up 95 per cent of the rural population, were landless (De Ita 2003).

The situation in the Huasteca mirrored this. Disamortization laws made it possible for indigenous people's lands to be settled by incomers, particularly by the new immigrants from Europe who were attracted to Xilitla. A number of Mexican families already known for their large landholdings, as well as one American citizen and several Europeans, established haciendas in the area. By the end of the nineteenth century, as a result, 90 per cent of the rural population in San Luis Potosí was landless.[3]

Rural grievances prompted by increasing landlessness began to assume violent form. Small upheavals, such as the indigenous rebellion in Tamazunchale in 1877, had already announced the existence of such grievances in the rural sector protesting against the privatization campaigns. A period of intensified agrarian struggles followed between 1910 and 1919, eventually leading to the collapse of the Porfirian regime during the Mexican Revolution.[4] The armed encounters of the revolution were a direct result of agrarian legislation under this regime.

Land restitution and endowments

The Agrarian Law of 1917, in effect, established the basis for Mexico's restitution programme. Aimed at stopping agrarian rebellions but still intent on 'peasantizing' the indigenous poor in order to forge a homogeneous nation, it enabled state expropriation of large estates in order to return land to people in rural hamlets who had lost their original lands. This means that former private land was eligible for land restitution in order to create small private and communal landholdings. The implementation of the land reform accompanied the creation of the National Peasant Confederation (CNC), the principal government organization established to deal with the rural poor and mediate between land claimants and landowners. Land grants given to rural and indigenous peoples were intended as a means to dismantle the great estates, and either to promote the restitution of land or to establish new *ejidos* through land endowments to those who were not living on their original lands and for whom its restoration was unlikely.

In Xilitla, the first wave of land petitions under the 1917 law occurred in 1921 and 1922 when the inhabitants of a number of *rancherías* (hamlets) demanded restitution of land originally inhabited.[5] The land restitution process involved measuring land, expropriating it from current owners and declaring it and its holders either as *comunidad indígena* or *ejido*: the latter could be formed by any group of dispossessed rural men by soliciting land.

Although the first petitions took place in the 1920s, in San Luis Potosí the largest part of the redistribution happened only *after* the end of the era of the revolutionary *caciques* (1929–34). Until then, many hamlets still occupied territories which had formerly been theirs, but which had been appropriated by private landowners during the Porfiriato. Others had lived on federal or state owned land since the implementation of the Lerdo Law.

In the 1930s, President Lázaro Cárdenas (1934–40) began to promote peasant agriculture as a basis for agricultural modernization. During his years in office, he adopted several measures to this end. One was to implement the Agrarian Law from 1917 in the hope of ending rural unrest. Another was to change agrarian legislation so that land could be redistributed both to rural hamlets whose communal land had been taken by haciendas, and to landless peasants who no longer belonged to a rural community.

Legally, the state retained official titles to the land. *Ejido* land was inalienable and could not be sold or rented. *Ejidatarios* possessed inalienable use rights until their death. The use rights were transferred, on the event of death or incapacity, to a nominated successor. If no successor was present the land would revert to the agrarian community for redistribution to a landless claimant. The *ejido* in its ideal form has been described as 'an institution that exercises domain over the land in a corporate fashion, clearly distinct from private appropriation' (Warman 1980: 286). In practice, however, there was much rental and transfer of *ejido* land, often accompanied by corrupt practices. In the Huasteca, the process of *ejido* distribution was very slow and was often derailed by illegal actions of the political elite. Even though the *ejido* land was legally inalienable, large landowners who were legally excluded from membership continued to exert pressure and sometimes acquired land titles for *ejido* plots.

As was the case for the landless in other areas of Mexico, Nahuas were required to draft land requests, stating the number of household heads. At first only males over 18 were accepted. For the *ejido* to become legal, hamlets went through three phases: a formal request to the government (*solicitud*), measurement (*acta de posesión y deslinde*) and the final paperwork (*mapa y plano definitivo*). The Agrarian Law also permitted subsequent additions (*amplificaciones*) with the increase of population density, provided that public land was in the vicinity or that private proprietors held land in excess of the legal maximum.

In sum, despite delays, corrupt transfers and other problems, land restitution did lead to the creation of many *ejidos* and gave the communities a stable geographic space, which allowed them to carve out a degree of local autonomy that was largely impervious to state institutions.[6] However, it was no longer as 'indigenous' that its residents were conceptualized.

Local memories

The redistribution of hacienda and 'vacant' land (*tierras baldías*) as *ejido* land from the mid 1930s was a significant moment as remembered by local people in Xilitla and in the Huasteca. Whereas, between 1929 and 1934, an average of only 18,826 ha was redistributed in the entire state of San Luis Potosí, the rate of redistribution then increased significantly, jumping to an average of 48,845 ha in 1935 (Falcón 1984). But the really noteworthy increase occurred between 1935 and 1937: from 48,845 ha to 85,605 ha. There were similar rates of increase in other states of Mexico. As recalled by Nahuas and rural *mestizos*, their subjugation to local *caciques* and the resulting land struggles ended only when, in 1935, they requested the intervention of President Lázaro Cárdenas. Cárdenas visited the region in 1936 to enforce the Agrarian Law.

The memory of Cárdenas' visit to Xilitla is evoked by Nahuas as a key event in their history. It is seen as having initiated their visibility as a people and as Mexican citizens. Unlike the indigenous peoples in southern Mexico who tend to claim Emiliano Zapata as a symbol of their inclusion into the post-revolutionary nation-state, in the Huasteca it is Cárdenas who represents the 'good side' of the government for the *ejidatarios* (for southern Mexico see Stephen 2002: 240–86). Cárdenas is described as a heroic figure; as the first one who really listened to the needs of the indigenous people. This was described by Nahua *ejidatario* and political activist Juan who spoke to me in 1988 of his parents' struggle to regain control of the land:

> The Revolution went on for a long time around here, even in the 1920s and 1940s. It was only in the 1930s, around 1935, that we were given land and could begin to work as *ejidatarios*. But until then, the *campesinos* (peasants) were in constant struggle. They possessed no land and they were just *peons* who worked under the *caciques*. At the turn of the century, many people came here from many different countries. When they arrived, they took our best land from us to build their *fincas* (ranches). And they still own the best land in the lower altitudes where rain is abundant throughout the year and it does not freeze the crops in the winter. We, the ones who speak Nahuatl, live here in the communities of the Sierra. Our ancestors were always able to continue their lives, even under the *caciques*. It was when Cárdenas became President, that we were able to have land. This is when the indigenous peoples were given land back.

Juan thus viewed the process of land restitution as a key event in the recognition of their status as the original people of Mexico.

Early twentieth-century nation-building

To understand why the Nahuas tie their local histories to post-revolutionary land reform, it is necessary to examine the nationalist ideologies that sought to eradicate cultural and ethnic differences. Contradictorily, they did so by proposing to augment local autonomy. Nationalist discourses combined with agrarian policies of the twentieth century provided the context in which indigenous ethnic claims emerged at the turn of the twenty-first century.

The notion of a '*mestizo* nation' played a crucial part in early twentieth-century nationalism in various Latin American countries, including Peru and Mexico. As opposed to colonial and liberal practices of othering, Mexico's assimilationist campaigns of the 1930s attempted to impose a national homogeneous identity.[7] These new cross-racial ideologies were prevalent until the early 1970s and sought to build a unified model of the nation whereby ethnically different people were to become subsumed as *mestizo*. This model did not, however, eradicate earlier ethno-ecological stereotypes that had identified indigenous peoples primarily with subsistence-based agriculture, rural lifestyle, and the local autonomy previously granted to them during the time of the indigenous republics and renewed through land restitution. Rather, it built upon these. Land restitution and relative local autonomy were viewed as key factors in achieving the successful assimilation and acculturation of indigenous peoples into '*mestizo* peasants'. This ideology of peasantization, constitutive of Mexican nationalism in its agrarian and economic dimensions, thus retained the relative autonomy of local landholders, but reconceptualized them as peasants.[8]

This ideology was developed in Gamio's book *Forjando Patria* (Forging the Fatherland), originally published in 1916 during the revolutionary war. Gamio adopted Vasconcelos' (1958) definition of nationalism praising the '*mestizo*' – arising through racial and cultural miscegenation – as a 'cosmic race'. Similar to earlier discourses about *mestizaje*, Gamio believed that a homogenous nation should be based on miscegenation with a 'gradual phasing out of ethnic and cultural differences' (Gamio 1992 [1916]: 179). Through the fusion of 'races' and their cultural manifestations, Gamio hoped to attain 'a powerful nation and a coherent and defined nationality' (Gamio 1992 [1916]: 183). In order to achieve this goal, he argued that it was necessary first to get to know the social and cultural differences that existed within the nation in order to reach 'the goal to control their social life'. Only then, he concluded, would it be possible to form a general constitution with specific laws that were 'adequate for the social, ethnic and economic characteristics of the groups as well as the geographical conditions of the region in which they live' (Gamio 1992 [1916]: 31).

Gamio's model specifically suggested using the land as a means to underpin the social life of indigenous peoples by giving them a new cultural and economic identity, that of the *mestizo* peasant. He stated that with the devolution of the original territories, it would be necessary to govern communal property rights through internal ('tribal') democracy, probably in order to prevent further agrarian unrest while slowly introducing a process of peasantization through state projects and achieve economic and cultural assimilation. Gamio argued that it would be best to:

> ... govern these groups with constitutions and federal and state laws ... but at the same time ... respect the genuinely democratic ideas and practices that reign in their interior organization; for instance, associations of

tribal character or the municipal government constituted by elders or individuals who were really elected by the collectivity.

(1992 [1916]: 199, my translation)

In this way his work indirectly promoted a return to a modified form of the indigenous republics that had been relatively successful in pre-independence Mexico. Gamio seems to have been suggesting that a relative autonomy, coupled with definitive integration into the economic system, would eventually lead to the creation of a homogeneous nation. By granting indigenous peoples special rights ('tribal democracy'), he hoped to foster a slow but effective assimilation while avoiding further unrest. For Gamio, land reform coupled with indigenist policies that promoted 'acculturation' seemed to provide a solution to achieving both economic and cultural assimilation.

For the Cárdenas government, *ejidos* reintroduced land as 'a good of production, a means of subsistence with restricted possibilities for being converted into a commodity, capital' (Simpson 1937). The question arises as to whether *ejidos* really were 'Mexico's way out' of agrarian problems: problems which were based on the marginalization of and discrimination against the indigenous peoples who were in the majority among the rural poor. If so, did these state projects achieve their goals by incorporating rural and indigenous peoples into a modernized agriculture and a homogeneous nation?

Ejidos *as material resource or site of autonomy?*

As it turned out, the *ejido* system proved less effective in delivering on its economic goals than in providing a means for cultural and political self-determination.

As a site for agricultural production, *ejidos* were far from ideal. In Xilitla, the land areas were often unsuited for intensive agriculture, and the procedure for legalizing their transfer was long and drawn-out. Despite some success during the 1950s, existing *ejidos* entered a phase of stagnation that led to the impoverishment of many of their members. To compensate for insufficient income, a complex system of state subsidies was put into place by government agencies. Eventually, the rising cost of subsidies also contributed to the economic failure of the system (De Janvry *et al.* 1996). Additionally, rapid population growth was placing a strain on scarce resources, contributing to declining per capita income and forcing out-migration.

The present state of play in Xilitla demonstrates the shortcomings of the system, when measured in purely material terms. Presently, Xilitla has 35 *ejidos* and two *comunidades indígenas*, with a total surface of communal landholdings of 59,983 ha for 4,790 *ejidatarios*. This means that, on average, each *ejidatario* has approximately 12 ha. However, some land in *ejido* and *comunidad indígena* holdings is also reserved for communal use, as sites for the location of schools, rural clinics or coffee processing plants. Individual holdings can vary significantly depending on when people staked their claims and depending on population density, topography, and the location of communal landholdings. Descendants of original inhabitants, for example, are likely to have use rights over larger parcels than more recent arrivals. The larger *ejidos* of Xilitla are located in areas that were former federal lands, which include less fertile land at higher elevations. The other, smaller (former) haciendas in Xilitla remain as *fincas* of the rich *mestizos* in the region to this day. The more productive land of these *mestizos* was never redistributed.

Minifundismo (land plots between 1 ha and 5 ha) also remains a grave problem. Very little extra land was allocated after the original restitution and, four to five generations later, the size of such plots is so small that new offspring cannot be accommodated. Clearly, access to communal lands did not guarantee survival for the rural poor. Although state subsidies did provide some assistance, they also created economic dependency and political patronage (see De Janvry et al. 1996; Ibarra Mendívil 1996; Snyder and Torres 1998). In addition to plot size, poor soil conditions and the marginalization of small-scale farming during the capitalist expansion made it difficult to earn a living wage based on farming alone.

Nonetheless, even though communal landholdings did not bring significant economic gains, Nahua *ejidatarios* feel attached to their land. It did, at least early on, bring improved livelihoods for many. More importantly, it brought a substantial gain in local autonomy. This meant that *ejidos* freed the Nahuas from direct dependence on the rural elite. In 2002, *ejidatario* Francisco from Tlaleta recounted:

> When the *ejidos* were formed it was the first time that the government listened to us! It was when Cárdenas came. Our father had no land at the time ... Three brothers started our hamlet ... They came here more or less in 1930. It was at the time when they began to talk about the restitution and since they had lived in Petatillo ... they said that there was not enough space for everyone. They said they all lived on top of each other (*amontonados*), but up here it was empty ... So they left Pahuayo to live over here. Now we have our community. We organize our work independently here in the community ... We would not be able to live without our land! No one can take it away from us now ... It is part of our community life.

Tlaletla has a total of 265 ha for 120 members. On average, this means that each *ejidatario* has about 2 ha, hardly enough to make a living. Nonetheless, land restitution retains a political and symbolic value for many members, as it does for Francisco. Concretely, it meant local independence for decision-making on crops and resource management. After reforms passed in 1992, members were able to revise their internal rules to include indigenous decision-making structures. In a meeting with the authorities of Poxtla Ejido, Victor from the security council explained that the assembly decides the fate of their land:

Here, we decide everything in our *asemblea*. We meet here in our *casa ejidal* (*ejido* meeting house) and discuss how to organize the community work or the implementation of new projects in our *ejido* amongst ourselves. We then make a decision all together.

As stated here, decisions about *ejido* land, collective use, and individual plots are consensus-based decisions made by the assembly. *Ejidos* and *comunidades indígenas* are not directly subordinate to the *municipios*, although they often work with them. Land restitution, by enabling greater autonomy and independence, thus represented an end to the symbolic and actual violence many had suffered as peons.

Indigenous campesinos

During the 1950s and 1960s, the process of peasantization – the incorporation of indigenous peoples into the nation as peasants – encouraged the Nahuas to privilege their economic identities. State policy in this era militated against the national representation of ethnic difference in Mexico, and led to its invisibility. In Xilitla, Nahua men and women recall that they were encouraged and sometimes forced to stop speaking their own language and 'to look the same' by adopting *mestizo* clothing. Calling themselves *campesinos* (peasants), denying their knowledge of their language for fear of being punished by local school teachers and changing their clothing and hence their physical appearance also

Figure 11.2 Ejido general assembly.

made it easier for national census agents to cast people as 'non-indigenous': a practice coined by Mexican anthropologist Guillermo Bonfil Batalla (1987) as 'statistical ethnocide'.

While these strategies might have worked better in other Latin American countries, such as Peru (see Chapter 10, Nuijten and Lorenzo, in this book) or in other regions of Mexico, superficial visible markers, such as Western clothing, or labels such as '*mestizo* peasant', seem to have been less effective in the Huasteca. In this sense, state projects led to an only superficial and partial peasantization: a lesser one than originally hoped for by nation-builders. In fact, current indigenous self-identification emphasizes Nahua beliefs and practices related to the land rather than only the economic needs and poverty they share with other rural men and women. This is also true for the testimonies I collected on land restitution and ethnically-framed land claims. The Nahuas highlight what I call 'ethno-ecological identities', by appropriating and transforming former negative stereotypes that associated them with subsistence agriculture. Challenging their characterization as an unproductive workforce, they underline their identification with the earth and traditional crops (the triumvirate of corn, squash and beans) as a vital element of their community life. In our conversations about the importance of the communal landholdings, they stated that the *ejido* structure allowed them to decide which crops to grow on their land. Many noted that this was crucial: it allowed them to reserve part of their land for subsistence agriculture alongside coffee cultivation, in which many engage.

Figure 11.3 Harvest Thanksgiving procession.

Figure 11.4 Corn dolls on the altar at Harvest Thanksgiving.

As shown elsewhere (Tiedje 2002), the Nahuas and other rural people have come to self-identify as indigenous *campesinos*, Nahuas, indigenous *mestizos*, Indians or a combination of all four, based on their relationships with the land and their rural way of life, phrased in cultural rather than (only) in economic terms. Why is this the case? For them, land was never only a means of production (although it always has economic significance) but remains the symbolic focus of a way of life that was sheltered by the *ejido* structure. Thus, contrary to the idea promoted by Gamio (1992 [1916]) that land restitution would enhance the assimilation of the indigenous peoples as peasants into a homogeneous nation, the Nahua presently claim the *ejido* as a foundation for their cultural identities. Their identity constructions are fluid and changing but many use the term 'indigenous *campesinos*' to refer to their social-ethnic and ethno-ecological identities when it comes to *ejido* matters. In the *ejidos* with a majority indigenous population, land endowment signified the restitution of their original lands, even if these were not located in the same community. What counted for them is recognition by the government that they had a right to claim land as the original peoples of Mexico. In contrast to *mestizo ejidatarios* who tend to view the land as economic spaces, *ejidos* for the Nahuas are ethnic spaces that also helped them gain respect as citizens. For them, the land endowments as *ejidos* came to mean the restitution of the land of their ancestors (even if, legally, many were only able to claim land endowments as 'peasants').

It is therefore not surprising that people have increasingly come to organize themselves as 'indigenous' and to express their claims for the land in ethnic terms. While the grounds for such an identification may have been established when Nahua inhabited their 'original' land, the *ejido* period served to consolidate it. Its fiercest expression, however, has been in response to the renewed targeting of these communal landholdings by the most recent agrarian programmes.

Neo-liberalism and the end of land restitution

Mexico's *ejidatarios* and the Nahuas in Xilitla are now facing the challenges of global commodity markets under the North American Free Trade Agreement (NAFTA) and the World Trade Organization. Under pressure from these forces, in 1992, an amendment to Art 27 of the Mexican constitution ended the post-revolutionary land reform. Given that communal landholdings had started to be seen as an obstacle to progress, such lands, formerly protected against privatization, were now able to be sold and rented (after several steps: mapping, measuring and titling). This 1992 modification to Mexico's agrarian reform was complemented by PROCEDE, launched in 1993 to 'modernize' the countryside by providing *ejidatarios* and communal landholders with legal property titles to their use-right plots. At a national level, PROCEDE was set in motion with the promise to certify land tenure, regularize agrarian rights, resolve conflicts over border areas, and grant individual property titles that enable proof, sale and rental. Initially, PROCEDE was scheduled to conclude the certification of rights in 1994. However, *ejidos*, agrarian communities, and peasant organizations rejected the programme. In March 2005, 85,562 ha out of 103,515 ha of communal landholdings were certified, leaving 17,953 ha yet to be certified. The *Procuraduría Agraria*, the institution that administers PROCEDE, explained the delay as being due to intercommunity conflict over boundaries. The World Bank acknowledged communities' reluctance to implement the programme, but stated that the rejection rate of PROCEDE was equivalent irrespective of whether areas had a predominantly indigenous or non-indigenous population. Empirical evidence suggests, however, that PROCEDE was more resoundingly rejected in rural areas with large indigenous populations, such as the states of Chiapas, Guerrero and Oaxaca (De Ita 2003). The Nahuas view the efforts to promote land privatization as a threat to their autonomy. Faced with the possibility of dividing their *ejido* into individual property land plots, a number of *ejido* assemblies in Xilitla mobilized to oppose the titling campaign.

The myth of the inefficient ejido

The changes in Art 27 and the subsequent launch of PROCEDE renewed a biased view about the inefficiency of *campesino* farming and communal land tenure (Nuijten 2003, 2004). Similar to earlier elite ideologies of progress, communal farming was once again portrayed as a threat to the economic expansionism of the 1990s. The wave of neoliberal reforms brought up the question that had long preoccupied discussions of land reform. During the early years of post-revolutionary reform, one great concern was whether collective farming could be a means to modernize the countryside. The *ejido* was in fact never 'truly communal' since individual cultivation was practised within it. Given 'the conditions under which at present the *ejido* system develops' and the limited 'resources they possess', Stavenhagen viewed this 'myth of the inefficient *ejido*' as a self-fulfilling prophecy (Stavenhagen 1970: 249). One might even argue that *ejidos* do remarkably well to continue operating given the precarious situations under which they exist.

Some advocates of the PROCEDE reform argue that the new legislation finally frees small farmers from state intervention. They also claim that the free market allows small farmers to engage in joint ventures with foreign and domestic agribusiness. In 2003, I spoke to Engineer Torres from the *Procuraduría Agraria*, who explained that the goal of PROCEDE was to prevent further division of land plots. According to local custom, when an *ejidatario* died, he or she would divide up his land plots among his sons. In Xilitla, this custom led to a large proportion of very small land plots ranging from half to five hectares. Torres stated that PROCEDE supplies *ejidatarios* and *comuneros* with titles to their plots in order to control the further division and parcelling of land. With the property title, a plot cannot be subdivided any further and it can only be sold to other registered members, unless the assembly decides as a whole that *ejido* land can be sold to outsiders.

The rationale behind the programme, then, is phrased in terms which eulogize the greater efficiency and rationality of the free market. In Xilitla this does not ring true. Herculano, an *ejidatario* from Tlaletla and a committed member of church base communities and grassroots organizations for over 20 years,[9] told me that he does not believe in these promises. The *asemblea* of Tlaletla rejected PROCEDE in 2002:

> The Free Trade Agreement [NAFTA]? That's for the rich people, the people with money. That's not for us who are the indigenous peoples . . . Because we continue to suffer just the same, you could say that we continue to get 'screwed' [*seguimos igual de jodidos*]. We cannot go across the border and sell our product there. They would stop a poor man [*un pobrecito*] at customs. It is only for the rich company owners . . . With that treaty [NAFTA], they will only marginalize us more.

Herculano's reasoning is largely based on his experience as an *ejidatario*. He has very few resources in comparison to large landowners, and will be unable to compete with them in a global market. For Herculano, Mexico's opening to free trade is interpreted locally as a renewed attack on indigenous communal lands.

According to state officers, the titling process is 'voluntary'. However, testimonies by the *ejidatarios* in the eight *ejidos* that voted against PROCEDE demonstrate that there have been considerable attempts to influence them. Government officials have made strenuous efforts to persuade them of the programme's importance. The process of introducing PROCEDE unfolds as follows: first, the programme is explained by personnel from the *Procuraduría Agraria*; second, there is a formal presentation followed by a vote of acceptance or rejection by the assembly. The fourth and longest phase entails the measurement of individual and social land plots resulting in a final presentation of the land plot sizes. To conclude, a meeting takes place to distribute the land titles. The assembly then votes on whether to accept full ownership (*dominio pleno*).

The acceptance of full ownership can be a ploy to facilitate the swifter sale of real estate – whether through official channels or informally – to outsiders, particularly in urban or peri-urban settings. San Antonio Xalcuayo, for example, is the sole *ejido* in Xilitla that has voted to accept full ownership. It did so in order to circumvent the rule, originally aimed at guaranteeing the size of the *ejido*, specifying that certified land must be sold to fellow *ejido* members. It lies within immediate reach of the urban boundaries and is marked by a high degree of out-migration to the US. Its *ejidatarios* now sell their land for urban development projects and to develop new residential neighborhoods. Increasingly, Xilitlenses attempt to turn former cultivated land into pasture for cattle or to buy former *ejido* land to invest and build big country houses as the town is growing beyond its boundaries. In the remote locations of the *municipio* however, land values are low due to bad roads, which renders access difficult. Here *ejido* members have tended not to adopt full ownership.

As of June 2003, the *Procuraduría Agraria* reported that 16 agrarian centres (*ejidos* and *comunidades indígenas*) in Xilitla were certified with PROCEDE.[10] In three agrarian centres, *Peña Blanca Comunidad*, *Cerro Quebrado Ejido* and *San Pedro Huitzcuilico Ejido*, the certification process was ongoing as of April 2005. In seven other *ejidos*, the certification process was started but stalled.[11] Additionally, eight *ejido* assemblies[12] denied the entry of PROCEDE at phase two.

Because the Nahuas' *ejidos* mean more than just money, they remain sceptical toward PROCEDE, if not openly hostile.

Nahua ejidatarios mobilize against PROCEDE

Almost two decades of organizing in co-operatives gave some *ejidos* a sense of autonomy and collective productive strategies. Memories of discrimination, land expropriation and labour exploitation were present in the discourses advanced to plead for a rejection of PROCEDE. Nahua *ejidatarios* believe, perhaps with good cause, that PROCEDE, aside from representing challenges to their local autonomy, might in the long run increase their dependence on a global market on which they have no influence. Many also fear that individual land titling engenders potential loss of the viability of local political indigenous institutions that had operated in a relatively stable geographic space.

In Poxtla, the redistribution process began in 1922 when 140 household heads requested that their land be declared as an *ejido*. They had previously inhabited this area that belonged to the *Hacienda de la Empresa*. They requested 1050 ha, but only 733 ha were granted as *ejido* while the remaining hectares stayed with the hacienda. When the PROCEDE was first initiated in 2002, the majority of its members rejected the programme. They did so again in 2005. I spoke to Raúl who lives in Poxtla where the population is predominantly Nahua. He explained members' opposition to PROCEDE as resulting from their history of marginalization:

> We rejected PROCEDE to protect our community. Our parents had to struggle for a long time to regain control over this land and PROCEDE wants to destroy our community. We see it as a threat to introduce outsiders into our communities and onto our land. As *ejidatarios*, we all have the same rights, and we all carry obligations to participate in the *faenas* and care for our community. We are originally from here and have lived here for a long time. Our parents have struggled to get this land after being landless, their struggles were done for us. It is now our responsibility to continue this respect for the land and the community. If we lose the territories of this *ejido*, how will we be able to sustain our children? This is why we rejected PROCEDE.
>
> *Why do you think having the title to your land with PROCEDE will make it easy to lose the land?*
>
> It is easy for some people to sell their land when they are drunk and they don't think of their family. And then, when they are sober they realize what they have done. What could they do? They would have to leave the community or work as *peons*. What would happen to their land? Who would come here to take it? We want to know who our *vecinos* (neighbours) are. It is important that we remain strong as a community, and that we teach our children the importance that this land has for us.

Subsistence agriculture coexists, in many places, with market-oriented production and the insertion of indigenous production into the global economic system. Therefore, Raúl's opposition to individual land titling, rather than being a statement of separatism linked to the world-view of a closed-corporate community, is linked to *ejidatarios*' desire for a place within a national society in which they can exist and persist as a 'people'. His 'selling off of land while drunk' refers to the *arrimadismo* (alienation of land to *mestizo* incomers) mentioned earlier. Raúl underlines that *ejidatarios* have communal obligations (*faenas*) to sustain the land, including its water sources and common use areas. Outsiders, he implies, would not be able to understand community customs that require an attitude of respect to land, water and people.

The multicultural challenge

The constitutional reform that removed the legal basis for land redistribution has proven more controversial than was anticipated, because it became so strongly entangled with the issue of indigenous peoples' rights. In other Latin American countries, most national secondary legislation continues to promote collective land titling for indigenous peoples. In Bolivia, Ecuador, Panama and Peru, governments have dealt with indigenous rights by applying specific laws to specific geographical areas of the country or to the areas inhabited by specific ethnic groups, rather than applying laws of national coverage (Plant 2002: 218). In Mexico, indigenous peoples have begun to seek other ways to claim local autonomy since the democratic opening to legal pluralism in the early 1990s. Multiculturalism has become a feature of recent state projects since Mexico's signing of the Convention (No. 169) concerning Indigenous and Tribal Peoples in Independent Countries and the constitutional amendment to Art 4. Theoretically, indigenous communities should presently be able to claim the special status of differentiated citizenship including claims to political representation, local autonomy and collective land rights. In practice, however, PROCEDE ends the legal use-right and hence the special status of such communities' landholdings. *Ejidatarios* opposed to PROCEDE view the programme as an attempt by the government to re-map the nation along economic lines without respecting their *cultural* rights as indigenous peoples who are also Mexican citizens. In the words of Maria, a Nahua woman:

> We are Mexican citizens and we are members in our community and this is what counts for us. We are the real ones here from Mexico, even if the government does not want to take us seriously. Now they tell us on the radio that we have indigenous rights, but we don't see the promises kept. They want to take our land away so that other people can buy it from us for little money and then where do we go? This is our home.

In Mexico, then, no official legislation has been established to promote collective land titling based on cultural claims. Indigenous communities are thus unable to claim a special or differentiated citizenship that recognizes the cultural meanings of the land. They have pursued alternative strategies to achieve these ends. In Chiapas, indigenous communities in resistance have begun to declare autonomous *municipios* to mark their local autonomy and claim sovereignty. In the Huasteca, the indigenous peoples have mobilized to protect sacred sites in natural protected areas. Rather than highlighting the cultural and religious use of these sites, they were forced to use environmental legislation originally intended to protect endangered species. Only after further negotiation did the state create a new category of natural protected areas, the sacred-natural site, to underline the importance of certain lands for local beliefs and practices (see Tiedje 2005).

Claiming alternative modes of citizenship

This study of indigenous responses to recent state policies and projects demonstrates that the Nahuas phrase their belonging to the land in cultural terms. Their self-identification with communal landholdings indicates that none of these policies – state-projected nationalism, the Agrarian Reform or PROCEDE – achieved the goal of transforming them into Mexican peasants. Rather, the *ejido* system provided them with a stable space to continue local practices while declaring their status as peasants. They used this category to construct an ethno-ecological identity: that of the ecologically sensitive indigenous peasant. In spite of economic failure, *ejidatarios* mobilized to protect the special status provided to them by communal landholdings. They did so for several reasons that I have outlined: because it was through 1930s land restitution that indigenous peoples were first recognized as citizens; because the existence of communal landholdings enabled them to retain or regain local autonomy; and because their access to these landholdings enabled them to control crops associated with ritual practices. The indigenous character of the rejection of PROCEDE thus extends beyond the material use of the land as a productive resource. Their land is the symbolic focus of an entire history, cosmology and way of life.

It is not surprising, therefore, that constitutional changes, although accepted by many peasant communities, met with strong resistance in indigenous ones. The reform of Art 27 contradicts the reform of Art 4 that declares Mexico a multicultural nation. State policies, despite the rhetoric of multiculturalism, continue to target indigenous people as unproductive peasants. Whereas recent reforms privilege the individual as the primary subject of political life with rights and responsibilities, the Nahuas claim their right to distinct modes of citizenship by arguing that their ethnic identities are socially constructed and rooted in the land, and hence must – as with indigenous movements in other parts of Mexico and Latin America – be recognized by the state. For the Nahuas, state–society relations must take into account the collective nature of their identities.

Conclusion

Questions of the land are closely linked to the political economy of identity and the crafting of differentiated citizenship. Territory and identity are linked, as is the idea of a (territorialized) nation. Alternative politics of citizenship emerge in the context of land struggles, through which indigenous people engage with nation-state politics while resisting political, economic and cultural domination to fashion their own notions of citizenship.

This chapter demonstrates how state-orchestrated agrarian programmes have been characterized by disputes between individualist approaches and policies on the one hand and communalist ideas on the other. It argues that recent constitutional amendments aimed at ending land redistribution and promoting privatization have sent mixed messages to Mexico's indigenous peoples without keeping the promise of differentiated citizenship proclaimed by the indigenous rights law. In Mexico these changing state policies – and the actual processes of land restitution/redistribution – have provided a political arena that is highly contested. In the process, it is refashioned by indigenous actors, such as the Nahuas in Xilitla. Contrary to claims by earlier policymakers, who viewed the indigenous republics and later communal landholdings as obstacles to nation-building and progress, the Nahuas view these holdings as the basis of their cultural right to retain a separate status and lifestyle.

Mexico's indigenous peoples thus have a voice and a mode of organization as political actors which is less dramatic, more everyday, than that of the Zapatistas in Chiapas. Indigenous grassroots organizing like this involves the claiming of special collective rights and rejects the ideal of the individual as the primary member of the state. In this sense, indigenous activists question, and threaten, the idea of citizenship in Mexico's putatively multicultural nation-state.

References

Aguilar Robledo, M (1995) 'Haciendas y condueñazgos en la Huasteca potosina: notas introductorias', VIII Encuentro de Investigadores de la Huasteca, Mexico City.

—— (2000) 'Los condueñazgos del oriente de San Luis Potosí, México, de finales del siglo XIX a principos del siglo XX: algunas reflexiones teóricas, Vetas', *Revista del Colégio de San Luis* 2(4): 151–89.

Alemán Alemán, E (1966) *Investigación socioeconómica directa de los ejidos de San Luis Potosí*, Mexico City: Instituto Mexicano de Investigaciones Económicas.

Bonfíl Batalla, G (1987) *México profundo. Una civilización negada*, Mexico City: Grijalbo.

Chambers, EJ and PD Young (1979) 'Mesoamerican Community Studies: The Past Decade', *Annual Review of Anthropology* 8: 45–69.

De Ita, A (2003) *Mexico: The Impacts of Demarcation and Titling by PROCEDE on Agrarian Conflicts and Land Concentration*, Centro de Estudios para el Cambio en el Campo Mexicano, Land Research Action Network.

De Janvry, A, E Sadoulet, B Davis and G Gordillo de Anda (1996) 'Ejido Sector Reforms: From Land Reform to Rural Development', in L Randall (ed.) *Reforming Mexico's Agrarian Reform*, London: ME Sharpe Inc., pp 71–106.

Falcón, R (1984) *Revolución y caciquismo. San Luis Potosí, 1910–1938*, Mexico City: El Colégio de México.

Fraser, Donald J (1972) 'La política de desamortización en las comunidades indígenas, 1856–1872', *Historia mexicana* 21: 615–52.

Gamio, M (1992 [1916]) *Forjando Patria*, Mexico City: Porrúa.

Gutierrez, Gustavo (1973) *A Theology of Liberation: History, Politics, and Salvation*, Maryknoll: Orbis Books.

Ibarra Mendívil, JL (1996) 'Recent Changes in the Mexican Constitution and their Impact on the Agrarian Reform', in L Randall (ed) *Reforming Mexico's Agrarian Reform*, London: ME Sharpe Inc., pp 49–60.

Kearney, M (1996) *Reconceptualizing the Peasantry: Anthropology in Global Perspective*, Boulder, CO: Westview Press.

Marzal, M (1993) *Historia de la antropología indigenista: México y Perú*, 3rd edn, Barcelona: Anthropos, UAM.

Montejo, V (2002) 'The Multiplicity of Mayan Voices: Mayan Leadership and the Politics of Self-Representation', in KB Warren and JE Jackson (eds) *Indigenous Movements, Self-Representation, and the State in Latin America*, Austin, TX: University of Texas Press.

Nagengast, C and M Kearney (1990) 'Mixtec Ethnicity: Social Identity, Political Consciousness, and Political Activism', *Latin American Research Review* 25(4): 61–91.

Nuijten, M (2003) 'Family Property and the Limits of Intervention: The Article 27 Reforms and the PROCEDE Programme in Mexico', *Development and Change* 34(4): 475–97.

—— (2004) 'Peasant "Participation", Rural Property and the State in Western Mexico', *The Journal of Peasant Studies* 31(2): 181–209.

Pimentel, F, de (1864) *Memoria sobre las causas que han originado la situación actual de la raza indígena en México y medios para remediarla*, México: Imprenta Andrade y Escalante.

Plant, Roger (2002) 'Latin America's Multiculturalism: Economic and Agrarian Dimensions', in R Sieder (ed.) *Multiculturalism in Latin America: Indigenous Rights, Diversity, and Democracy*, Hampshire: Palgrave Macmillan, pp 208–26.

Roseberry, W (1995) 'Latin American Peasant Studies in a "Postcolonial" Era', *Journal of Latin American Anthropology* 1(1): 150–77.

Schwartz, NB (1981) 'Anthropological Views of Community and Community Development', *Human Organization* 40(4): 313–22.

Scott, J (1998) *Seeing Like a State: How Certain Schemes to Improve the Human Condition Have Failed*, New Haven, CT, London: Harvard University Press.

Sieder, R (2002) 'Recognising Indigenous Law and the Politics of State Formation in Latin America', in R Sieder (ed.) *Multiculturalism in Latin America: Indigenous Rights, Diversity, and Democracy*, Hampshire: Palgrave Macmillan, pp 184–207.

Simpson, EN (1937) *The Ejido. Mexico's Way Out*, Chapel Hill, NC: North Carolina Press.

Snyder, R and G Torres (1998) *The Future Role of the Ejido in Rural Mexico*, La Jolla: Center for US–Mexican Studies; San Diego, CA: University of California Press.

Stavenhagen, R (1970) *Agrarian Problems and Peasant Movements in Latin America*, Garden City, NY: Doubleday.

Stephen, L (1997a) *Women and Social Movements in Latin America. Power From Below*, Austin, TX: University of Texas Press.

—— (1997b) 'Redefined Nationalism in Building a Movement for Indigenous Autonomy in Mexico: Oaxaca and Chiapas', *Journal of Latin American Anthropology* 3(1): 72–101.

—— (2002) *¡Zapata Lives! Histories and Cultural Politics in Southern Mexico*, Berkeley, CA: University of California Press.

Tiedje, K (2002) 'Gender and Ethnic Identity in Rural Grassroots Development: An Outlook from the Huasteca', *Urban Anthropology and Studies of Cultural Systems and World Economic Development* 31(3–4): 261–316.

—— (2005) 'People, Place, and Politics in the Huasteca, Mexico', *Anthropology Today* 21(4): 13–17.

Van Cott, DL (ed.) (1994) *Indigenous Peoples and Democracy in Latin America*, New York: St Martin's Press.
Vasconcelos, J (1958) *Raza cósmica*, México: Libreros Mexicanos Unidos.
Warman, A (1980) *'We Come To Object': The Peasants of Morelos and the National State*, SK Ault, trans, Baltimore, MD: John Hopkins University Press.
Warren, KB (1998) *Indigenous Movements and their Critics: Pan-Maya Activism in Guatemala*, Princeton, NJ: Princeton University Press.
Warren, K and J Jackson (2002) 'Introduction: Studying Indigenous Activism in Latin America', in KB Warren and JE Jackson (eds) *Indigenous Movements, Self-Representation, and the State in Latin America*, Austin, TX: University of Texas Press, pp 1–46.
Yashar, D (1999) 'Democracy, Indigenous Movements, and the Postliberal Challenge in Latin America', *World Politics* 52(I): 76–104.
—— (2005) *Contesting Citizenship in Latin America: The Rise of Indigenous Movements and the Postliberal Challenge*, Cambridge: Cambridge University Press.

Notes

This research would not have been possible without the hospitality of the Nahuas in the Huasteca. I would like to thank Cecilio Torres at the Procuraduría Agraria. I am grateful to Lynn Stephen for her insightful comments on this project. I also would like to thank Bron Taylor, Deborah James and Derick Fay for thoughtful observations on earlier drafts. Funding from the DAAD Doctoral Fellowship, the International Trade and Development Graduate Research Fellowship, and the CIESAS Research Fellowship allowed me to conduct field research in the Huasteca. The Fyssen Postdoctoral Fellowship made writing possible.

1   What is happening with PROCEDE?
2   The wider Huasteca region extends across three states: San Luis Potosí, Veracruz, and Hidalgo from the Sierra Madre Oriental to the north eastern Coastal Plains, near the Gulf of Mexico.
3   According to data from the 1900 Census, '75 per cent of the population lived in communities of less than 2,500 inhabitants and half of the economically active population was agricultural labourers'. Around 1910, *peons* had houses close to the haciendas where they worked. They were mostly landless, lived in modest houses, and were paid between 18 to 25 cents for a 12-hour workday (Alemán Alemán 1966: 11).
4   It was during the Porfiriato (1876–1910) that the disamortization laws had given rise to haciendas and had converted corporate landholdings into small properties through *arrimadismo*. In this practice, *mestizos* first moved into indigenous hamlets as 'neighbours', initially asking the residents to grant them land use rights as shareholders, but eventually taking over their communal lands to turn them into agrarian societies (Aguilar Robledo 1995, 2000).The goal of revolutionary struggles in San Luis Potosí was not to restructure agrarian property, but rather to use military interventions to liberate land as a 'the source of enrichment of a good number of military chiefs and their allies' (Falcón 1984: 93).
5   The hamlets were Apetzco, Miramar, El Bagazo (La Victoria), Potrerillos, Ahuacatlán, Plan de Juarez, Petatillo, Tlaletla, El Sabino, Xalcuayo, Xilitlilla, Tlamaya and San Pedro Huitzcuilico.
6   Over some 80 years, the Agrarian Reform gave out 103 million ha – 52 per cent of the 196 million ha that make up the Mexican territory, or 56 per cent of its agrarian

land, and 70 per cent of its forests – to 3.5 million communal landholders, integrated in 30,322 ejidos and indigenous communities that constituted the social sector (De Ita 2003).
7 Colonial discourses focused on indigenous peoples as inferior and uncivilized. Liberal discourses portrayed them as unproductive workers.
8 The term *mestizo* is used in contemporary Mexico to designate descendants of mixed Indian-white parentage and generally refers to the population which does not identify as indigenous.
9 Church base communities date back to the 1970s during the influence of liberation theology, a form of Christian socialism which emerged after the Second Vatican Council as a progressive sector of the Catholic Church that combined Catholic theology with political activism, inspired by Marxist ideas (Gutierrez 1973).
10 La Joya, Xuchiayo, Apetzco, San Antonio Xalcuayo, Chichimixtitla, Tierra Blanca, El Cristiano, Cruztitla, Ixtacamel, Peña Blanca, Xilosuchico, El Sabino, Petatillo, Plan de Júarez, El Canyon de Tlamaya, San Antonio Huitzcuilico.
11 Miramar, Coronel del Castillo, Poxtla, Portrerillos, Ahuacatlan, Xilitlilla, Pilateno.
12 Joya de las Vacas, El Chalahuite, La Trinidad, Ollita del Pino, La Victoria, Amayo de Zaragoza, El Cuartillo, Tlaletla

Chapter 12

'We'll never give in to the Indians'

Opposition to restitution in New York State

Brian Blancke

Abstract

The title of this chapter comes from a song sung by local property owners in the Cayuga land claim area (New York, US) to express their anger about that claim and about the attempts to restore land to the Cayuga Nation for a reservation. Numerous attempts to settle the Cayuga land claim through negotiation have failed over the decades, including a settlement reached in 1979, which was never implemented because of public opposition. This chapter looks at the sources of the public's anger which underlies the opposition, and suggests from a conflict resolution perspective what might be done to address it. Until this anger is dealt with, local landowners will continue to express 'reservations about reservations', demand 'No Nation within a Nation' and, as they have for over 20 years, block any negotiated settlement of the claim.

Introduction

'We'll Never Give in to the Indians and We'll Never Give Up Our Deeds' is a verse of a song that local property owners in the Cayuga land claim area (New York, US) used to sing. It reveals the anger that many residents of South Seneca County felt (and continue to feel) about the claim and the attempts to restore land to the Cayuga Nation for a reservation. Numerous attempts to settle the Cayuga land claim through negotiation have failed over the decades, despite the best efforts of nationally renowned mediators and the wishes of the litigating parties.

As a mediator myself, I am curious as to why land claims negotiations fail. What are the obstacles to settlement and how can they be overcome? After all, prior to the filing of the Cayuga claim (to 64,015 acres) in 1980, a negotiated settlement was reached, but never implemented. The settlement would have transferred a state park and some federal land to create a reservation for the now landless Cayuga Nation, a member of the Iroquois Confederacy. But many landowners did not want the Cayuga as neighbours. The settlement, which did not involve the local landowners, sparked a 'Not In My Backyard' (or NIMBY) backlash that ultimately scuttled the agreement. What are the sources of the public's anger and what, from a conflict resolution perspective, might be done about it?

Evolving international law (for example, the United Nations Declaration on the Rights of Indigenous Peoples) supports the restoration of land to indigenous peoples. One way of doing this is through negotiation (what Fay and James refer to as the 'transfer' stage, see Chapter 1, in this book). However, what are the practical problems of transfer? The present chapter explores this question, with a particular focus on how the costs of transfer are distributed. How these costs are distributed directly relates to public opposition to land claim settlements, as will be shown below.

What follows is a brief overview of the legal and historical basis of the Cayuga land claim, and of how land claims like the Cayuga's have been resolved – the context necessary to understand the angry public response to the 1979 Cayuga land claim settlement. After reviewing the public's response, I analyse its underlying causes in order to shed light on why such land transfers often fail, at least in the US. The conclusion will suggest an alternative method of conflict resolution that addresses and acknowledges these sources of anger, and offers a more productive approach for resolving disputes that arise over land transfers.

Indian land claims (in the eastern US)

The Cayuga Nation land claim to their original reservation of 64,015 acres (see Figure 12.1) is based on the Indian Trade and Intercourse Act (ITIA) adopted by the first Congress in 1790, which states:

> No sale of lands made by any Indians, or any nation or Nation of Indians within the United States, shall be valid to any person or persons, or to any state, whether having the right of pre-emption to such lands or not, unless the same shall be made and duly executed at some public treaty, held under the authority of the United States.[1]

Despite the law, New York State, which felt it had the right to negotiate with the Iroquois Confederacy anyway, acquired the entire Cayuga reservation in two state treaties – one in 1795 and the other in 1807 (New York, State Legislature 1889). Within two decades (1789–1809), the Cayuga Nation had lost all of its aboriginal and reservation territory.[2]

The Cayuga Nation asserts, and the federal district court agreed, that the federal government never approved the state treaties, as the ITIA requires (730 F Supp 485 [1990]). The Nation sought the return of its reservation (that is, the ejectment of thousands of current landowners) and hundreds of millions of dollars in trespass damages. Prior to 1974, nobody took ITIA land claims like the Cayuga's seriously. Federal courts dismissed them because

'We'll never give in to the Indians' 237

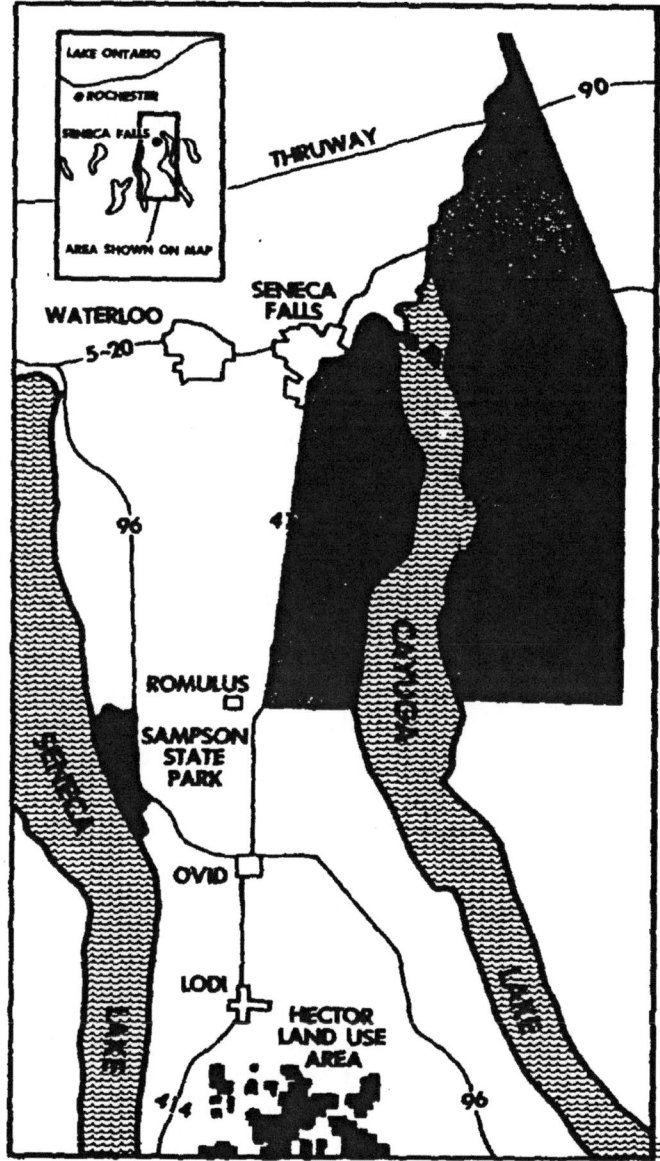

Map indicates areas involved in Cayuga claim. Shaded portion in upper right is original 100 square mile reservation. Cayugas would get Sampson State Park and Hector Land Use Area if compromise is adopted.

Figure 12.1 Map of original and proposed Cayuga Reservations.

Source: 'Patching Up History', The Cayuga Claim, *Democrat and Chronicle*, Rochester, New York, 17 August 1980.

they were legal actions of ejectment, which were state, not federal, matters (Shattuck 1991). But in 1974, the US Supreme Court overturned decades of precedent and swung open the doors of the courthouse (414 US 661). ITIA land claims then arose all along the eastern seaboard of the US, from Maine to Florida, in relation to cases in which a state, city or private party had negotiated with the Indians to acquire their land without the approval of the federal government (Campisi 1985; Jones 1979; Walke 1999).

Three approaches have been tried to resolve ITIA land claims: litigation, unilateral Congressional legislation and negotiated out-of-court settlements (Jones 1979). About half have settled out of court while the rest were litigated. While there were many attempts to settle the land claims through unilateral legislation, the bills never made it out of committee. Those that have settled usually involved the return of land (or money to purchase land), money (for services and economic development), jurisdictional arrangements, government services and federal recognition (for Nations that did not already have it) (Sutton 2000).

The return of land, however, especially to create or expand an Indian reservation, is a very touchy subject for landowners, neighbours of a reservation, local towns and counties in Upstate New York. The Federal, State of New York and tribal governments saw a negotiated settlement as the means for addressing an historical injustice while avoiding displacing the current landowners and disrupting local economies. In this sense, they were adopting an approach to restitution similar to that employed in several other cases discussed in this book (see Chapters 2, Fay, 5, Nadasdy, 10, Nuijten and Lorenzo). But many residents did not and do not accept that an injustice had been done to the Cayuga, or that using scarce public land to create a reservation in their midst was the solution, as the next section explores.

Public reaction to the 1979 Cayuga land claim settlement

After the Department of Justice announced in July 1977 that it, as the legal trustee of the Nation, would pursue the Cayuga Nation's claim, Congressman William Walsh called on President Jimmy Carter to appoint a mediator to resolve it. In December, New York State and Federal officials agreed to open negotiations, concluding that 'an out-of-court settlement would be better'.[3] A Cayuga Work Group was set up, which consisted of tribal, state and federal representatives. After 18 months of negotiation, the Working Group reached a Joint Memorandum of Understanding settling the Cayuga land claim. Under the settlement, the Cayuga were to receive, in exchange for extinguishing all their land claims: (1) 5,481 acres of land for a reservation (the 1,852 acre Sampson State Park and 3,629 acres of the Forest Service's Hector Land Use Area); (2) $8 million ($2.5 million of which could be used to purchase additional land to block up the two parcels);[4] (3) government services; (4) jurisdiction (the lands were to be subject to 25 US 232 and 233, provided that the Nation reserved the right to establish its own tribal court system and police department); and (5) a tribal member roll.[5]

Public reaction to the settlement was at best mixed. The Cayuga-Seneca Property Owners Association (CSPOA), made up mostly of the current day landowners in the claim area, supported the settlement because it would have cleared the title to their properties. (Compare locations of the new versus the old reservation in Figure 12.1). CSPOA was formed shortly after the land claim was announced in 1977 to protect their interests. Besides seeking safe, harmless legislation, CSPOA advocated a quick negotiated settlement:

> For us the ideal solution would be negotiation rather than litigation. A lawsuit of this magnitude may last 10 to 15 years. In the interim the property owners would be left holding the bag as they could not sell their real estate or get credit because it was involved in litigation.[6]

CSPOA called on its members to attend the public hearing in early September on the settlement: 'Whether or not the settlement is approved by Congress greatly depends upon how well or poorly it is received in Central New York. If a large body of people appears in favor of the settlement, without doubt, it will ultimately be approved by Congress'.[7]

While CSPOA supported the settlement because it promised to resolve ambiguities relating to their ownership of property, future neighbours – residents and local town and county officials – of the Cayuga Nation reservation were strongly opposed to it. They formed the Seneca County Liberation Organization (SCLO) to fight the settlement. The founder of SCLO said:

> I think the time has come to act. We must be together. I am therefore, making a motion from the floor, whereas the town of Romulus has now suffered the grievances set forth in this meeting because of the actions of agencies of the Federal and State of New York governments, in their production of the so-called settlement of claims of the Cayuga Nation . . . and whereas these secret negotiations and disregard of the due process of law are but one of many acts of bureaucratic tyranny to which Romulus and other towns and municipalities in Seneca County have been subjected, and whereas a common resistance to these tyrannies must be made by the citizens of Seneca County, united in defense if we are to begin to move toward liberation from such acts of bureaucratic tyranny. I therefore, move, that the Romulus Town Board recognize the floor vote on this motion as the act which organizes our grass roots general resistance here tonight under the proud title, Seneca County Liberation Organization, the SCLO [applause] to assist in any way, and to join forces with any who will help in the cause of freedom for Romulus and for Seneca County.[8]

SCLO stood for 'public use of public lands and waters in perpetuity, due process of law and responsible government'.[9] It hoped to 'organize the people of Seneca County because we are the townspeople who will be affected' by the agreement 'we are the ones who will have to live with whatever the effects of the proposal are'.[10]

The first formal opportunity for public comment on the settlement came at the public hearings held on 11 and 12 September 1979, at Eisenhower College in Seneca Falls, New York and South Seneca Central School in Ovid, New York, respectively. An estimated 1,000–1,500 people attended the first evening. Prior to the start of the meeting, members of SCLO and CSPOA were handing out literature, signs and ribbons to denote either support for or opposition to the settlement.[11]

After explaining the background of the land claim and the proposed settlement, Tim Vollmann, chair of the Cayuga Land Claim Work Group, opened the hearing up for public comment. The air was charged and the 'audience was unruly at times, interrupting speakers with applause, boos, jeers and catcalls'.[12] Not surprisingly, Seneca County representatives, including Ray Zajac, and SCLO, were stridently opposed to it, the 'giveaway', while Cayuga County representatives and CSPOA supported it. The former complained about the secret negotiations and the potential economic impact of settlement on the County, while the latter said that it was 'the best solution for private property owners'.[13] Seneca County residents retorted that Cayuga County residents would have a different attitude if the reservation had been located there instead.

Work Group members did try to address, during the public hearing, the substantive concerns raised by county officials, including increased welfare costs, tax base erosion, declining tourism, environmental impact and the closure of Samson State Park, among others. While some residents of Cayuga County thought the Work Group had fielded the questions well, residents from Seneca County thought that it was a farce: 'the issues have already been decided. We've been invited as a last-minute formality. The work group is not even listening to us'.[14]

The public hearing on 12 September was attended by fewer people and was calmer than that on the previous evening. Still, a number of questions were asked, and not all were answered. Topics included: the status of highway 96-A through the proposed reservation, road maintenance, ratification of any changes to the agreement, other settlement alternatives, law enforcement concerns, legal representation (if the government represents the Indians, who represents us?), finality (what about future claims?), the location of reservation (why only land in Seneca County?), additional land purchases (to connect the two parcels), the legal status of the Memorandum of Understanding, the recording (or lack thereof) of the public comments and commercial fishing by the Indians, among others. Work Group members tried to reassure the audience that 'in all questions of law enforcement, highway jurisdiction, water and fishing rights, the Indians would be subject to New York State laws'.[15] Also, Tim

Vollmann noted that the agreement could be amended, just as the Rhode Island land claim settlement was, to address their concerns.

The September public hearings did not slow down or satisfy SCLO who saw themselves as 'the Palestinians of this whole shenanigan'.[16] At the end of the second hearing, Wisner Kinne promised: 'We intend to fight you; we're opening a case in court as soon as we can find a way to do it'.[17] SCLO decided to join forces with the Finger Lakes Land Protection Association (FLLPA), a group formed to preserve public access to public lands.[18] Together, they filed a suit in the state supreme court to stop the transfer of Sampson State Park.[19] They argued that the governor did not have the authority to sign the Memorandum of Understanding of 20 August and that he could not transfer state parkland without the approval of the State Legislature.[20]

One of the primary objections local residents and county officials had about the settlement was that they were not included in the negotiation process even though they were the ones most directly affected by it. An opportunity to address this common complaint came in early October. Congressman Gary Lee asked that the Work Group reconvene and evaluate the settlement in the light of Attorney General Griffin Bell's June 1978 letter, about which he had just learned.[21] The congressman also made a request to include two members representing residents from Cayuga and Seneca Counties, a request also supported by CSPOA.[22] But the Working Group decided against it. They did agree, however, to the request to allow county representatives to review the draft implementation bill and suggest amendments.[23] After the Work Group reconvened and affirmed the settlement, Congressman Gary Lee reluctantly endorsed it too, commenting however that: 'this perplexing "twilight zone" saga tries the intellectual, spiritual and moral fabric of each of us'.[24]

When Ray Zajac, a Seneca County Supervisor, saw a draft of the bill in January 1980, he said that it was a slap in the face because the September public comments meant nothing to the Working Group. The changes to the bill were only minor, with none of the changes suggested by Seneca County having been made. This prompted the chair of the Seneca County Board of Supervisors to say: 'It looks like it [the public hearings] was a waste of everybody's time ... they're going to do what they want to do and the hell with you'.[25] SCLO likewise denounced the bill, accusing the Work Group and the federal government of trying to shove the settlement down their throats. Wisner Kinne, the head of SCLO, was not surprised that there were no changes: 'This is the same type of bureaucratic tyranny and the same treatment we've had all along ... what must happen now is that we must stand and pledge our fortunes and our lives to the defense of Seneca County'.[26]

As promised in October, Seneca and Cayuga County officials met in late February with legislators and their staff to review the bill and to discuss possible changes. At the meeting, Seneca County representatives proposed a number of amendments, including: (1) a cap on the amount of land the Nation could purchase, and a statement that all such land would be kept on the county's tax roll; (2) a payment to the county by the federal government to cover the Nation's use of the county sewer district ($300,000); (3) a reimbursement of $3.75 million for anticipated loss of employment, tourist trade and future tax base erosion; (4) a clear delineation of the Nations' hunting and fishing rights; and (5) protection of all highway rights of way.[27] Congressman Gary Lee promised to take them up with Congressman Mo Udall who had introduced the bill on behalf of the Carter Administration.

The last opportunity for public input came during the House hearing on HR 6631, the settlement implementation bill. Wisner Kinne organized a trip to Washington DC of SCLO members to protest the settlement. He, along with Walter Foulke from CSPOA and Ray Zajac, was allowed to testify before the House Committee, convened in Washington, DC. The same lines as before were drawn between the two counties, and the same substantive, procedural and ideological arguments for and against were rehashed.[28] Afterwards, Ray Zajac felt that SCLO members, including himself, had been mistreated by Congressman Udall. Wisner Kinne said that Congressman Udall spent 'all his time intimidating those who spoke against the settlement'.[29] SCLO was denied the two things that they stood for – representation and due process. Nevertheless, SCLO members were, in Wisner Kinne's words, the 'heroes . . . the real hockey players'.[30]

Congressman Udall was, however, sympathetic to the concerns that Seneca County had about tax-base erosion, and was willing to add a land cap amendment to the bill, if it could be mutually agreed upon.[31] However, the Seneca County Board of Supervisors rejected a proposed cap of 10,000 acres.[32] In two resolutions, the Board denied, repudiated and rejected HR 6631 and all its amendments 'which have as their object the permanent alienation of lands', and opposed the 'RAPE of Seneca County by President Carter and his administration in the handling of this Indian Land Claim Settlement' (capitals in original).[33]

The bill, which was expected to pass anyway even without the cap, was brought up for a vote under the suspension of the rules on 18 March 1980. But Congressman Gary Lee voted against it, and the bill – largely out of congressional courtesy – was defeated. Not surprisingly, SCLO was delighted. Ray Zajac called it 'a major victory for democracy'.[34] SCLO promised to stay active to fight for ratification and to pass bills in the State Legislature that would ensure title insurance and pay for legal fees for property owners who were to be sued. Walter Foulke of CSPOA was, however, angry. As a result of Lee's vote, it was likely that CSPOA members would be sued, which indeed they were.

Sources of public anger

Unfortunately, residents and government officials in Seneca County saw only the potential and feared costs of a reservation, ignoring any possible benefits. This unwanted change – the loss of public land to (re)create an Indian reservation, a community with its own rules and laws that had not existed for 180 years – sparked a NIMBY reaction in South Seneca County. One negotiator summed it up this way:

> Oh, it all blew up because people were saying, 'We're not going to give up our own lands. We don't want this. We don't want that.' And the main objection was the establishment of a Cayuga reservation. The underlying objection. You could put whipped cream over it. You could put cherries on top. You could put chocolate syrup all over it. But the underlying objection was the establishment of an Indian reservation in their backyard. The attitude basically was 'not in my backyard'.[35]

However, as dispute resolution experts Susskind and Field ask, 'wouldn't you be angry if you had been hurt, misled or threatened?' (1996: 1). Susskind and Field identify six sources of public anger: hurt, risk, beliefs, weakness, lies and show. To understand the sources of public anger in the Cayuga claim area, I break down the analysis into three sub-headings – hurt and risk, core beliefs and values, and weakness and lies. After that, I will explore how the Work Group responded to the public's anger. Their response was inadequate and ineffective, and ultimately unsuccessful.

Hurt and risk

Anger is 'a defensive response to pain or the threat of pain, real or perceived' (Susskind and Field 1996: 16). Anger is likely to arise, Susskind and Field argue, when either people have been hurt or when 'they feel threatened by risks not of their own making' (1996: 16–17), such as the siting of nuclear power plant in their backyard or, I would add, an Indian reservation, at least in the minds of South Seneca County residents.

Many property owners were afraid that, as reservation land was removed from the county tax base, they would lose their homes because of correspondingly increased taxes, which in turn would force them to sell their properties. Besides losing their homes, local residents and officials raised a number of other concerns/costs they associated with the settlement, including the eventual disappearance of entire towns (as lands were bought up by the Nation), tax-base erosion, additional governmental expenses for the counties, the closure of Sampson State Park and of some highways, economic instability (resulting from the creation of a reservation) and law enforcement problems, among others. They saw, in a reservation, only unwanted change to their communities, change in which they had no say.

Members of the Work Group tried to reassure the public that the risks of settlement were minimal at best, but local residents dismissed the Work Group's report, which was released when the bill was sent to Congress.[36] Work Group members had no credibility because they had neither listened nor responded to the public's concerns. Local stakeholders, having had no hand in the gathering of the facts about the (minimal) impact, did not believe them.

Core beliefs and values

Another source of anger is when core beliefs and values are threatened. The public gets angry because 'basic notions of self worth are at stake' (Susskind and Field 1996: 155). Citing Moore (1986), Susskind and Field note that 'value disputes focus on such issues of guilt and innocence, what norms should prevail in a social relationship, what facts should be considered valid, what beliefs are correct, who merits what or what principles should guide decision-making' (Susskind and Field 1996: 154). Comments like 'the Twilight Zone' reveal a view that the land claims, including the settlements, were outside many of the public's 'scope of justice,' or beliefs about who is entitled to fair treatment and outcomes (Deutsch 2000; Opotow 1990).[37] At most, the Cayuga were entitled to some money and no reservation. At the least, they were entitled to nothing at all. Why?

The blame game – there are no guilty parties

Blaming is about who is at fault because whoever is at fault has to pay (to redress the harm). Parties in a dispute put forward different accounts or theories of responsibility about who did what to whom and why (Cobb 1994). These accounts 'show (one person) as an agent, an action, and (the other) as recipient of that action, as well as a causal link between the action of the agent and the harm the (other) has suffered' (Cobb 1994: 165). Generally speaking, parties are held responsible when their actions were intentional (exhibiting control over their own actions) and they were aware of the consequences of those actions (Cobb 1994). They can contest the accusations against them, that is, mitigate the responsibility they have, through excuse, justification or denial (Cobb 1994). Denial entails refuting either the agency ascribed to the actors or the actions taken, whereas with excuses and justifications, the actors own the actions but deny the intent to harm (Cobb 1994).

Applying this model to the Cayuga case reveals the following: the Cayuga accuse the states, counties, municipalities and landowners (the agents) of taking their land in violation of the ITIA (the action), and as a result the Nations lost their reservations, their lands (the harm suffered). However, the property owners point out that *they themselves* did not take the land. They deny that they are responsible because they were not even alive when it happened! They did nothing wrong, so why were they being made to pay – either by losing their land or having a reservation forced upon them?

The purpose of the ITIA was to protect against unscrupulous purchases or transfers of Indian land. There were legitimate and illegitimate ways of acquiring land. These are matters of procedural justice or 'the procedures that determine the [fairness of] outcomes' (Deutsch 2000: 44). International law historically recognizes five ways of legally acquiring title to land: conquest, cession, accretion, discovery (of empty land) and occupation (Akehurst 1987). The ITIA itself reflects one of these principles: Indian land could only be acquired through cession, with the federal government's approval, under the ITIA. The property owners argued that the Cayuga had been paid at least three times already in three different agreements, cessions. Others argued that the Cayuga had lost title through conquest when in 1783 the American colonies defeated the English and their Indian allies, including the Cayuga, in the Revolutionary War. Either way, title to the land had been acquired legitimately.

Moreover, many landowners wondered why the passage of time, as embodied in a statute of limitations, did not bar these claims from being litigated in the first place. Roy Ike from Interlaken, New York, made this point in a letter to the Governor of New York: 'rob a bank and get away with it for seven years and according to the Statute of Limitations, [you] get away scot-free'.[38] So then, he implied, should the landowners after 200 years.

A CSPOA leader said shortly after the land claim was first announced, 'the sins of the past cannot be visited upon the property owners'.[39] Congressman William Walsh of New York said at the time, '[it is] time we attempt to call a halt to the *mea culpa* attitude of the United States government with respect to Indian nations. No doubt crimes were committed against Indians, but to proceed would be a crime against innocent citizens'.[40] 'Two wrongs don't make a right' was a common refrain.

There were limits to these property owners and politicians' sense of the scope of justice. To the extent that this scope of justice included any consideration for redress, it was usually limited to money and not land (see the next subsection below). Money could buy private land, but that land should, to the greatest extent possible, remain under state jurisdiction; that is, it should not become a fully-fledged Indian reservation.

Whose land is it anyway?

Local residents asked; if we give land back, then whose?[41] Early on in the Cayuga Work Group negotiations, the parties agreed to only consider public land; no private property would be involved, and this was supposed to allay the fears of the landowners in the claim area. Unfortunately, there were few tracts of state or federally owned land in the Cayuga Nation's aboriginal territory.

Of the public lands considered, Sampson State Park and the Hector Land Use Area (HLUA) were chosen by the Cayuga Nation because of their relative size, quality and proximity.[42] The Cayuga wanted a large enough land base to establish a viable reservation (Wilbur Smith and associates 1978). That meant large tracts of decent land that were relatively close to each other. This need for a significant land base, in turn, ruled out what some people had suggested as an alternative: the purchase of a lot of small, private and non-contiguous parcels of land.

Under the settlement, the status of Sampson State Park and all of HLUA in Seneca County (3,629 acres out of 13,259 acres) would have changed from public use to an Indian reservation, with the exception of a portion of Sampson that would have remained open as park, if it were economically viable, through 1988. The immediate land use changes were modest, according to the Work Group Report, and the impacts were minimal (United States Congress 1980).

This analysis did not, however, ease the anger that many Seneca County residents and officials felt about the settlement. For them, it represented salt in the wound. Not only were they innocent, not only were they going to suffer economically from a reservation in their midst, but – from the way they saw it – they were also going to lose their only parks in the process. They were responding out of a sense of ownership of Sampson and Hector. Many people opposed giving up Sampson State Park because the state had invested millions of dollars in improving it, turning it into productive land:

> The deed to Sampson State Park cedes the land to the people of New York to be used 'forever' for recreational purposes. At the Seneca Falls meeting [11 September 1979], we were told that if New York did not give up the land voluntarily it would be taken by the Federal government. Over 4 million dollars have been invested in improving this area. Your tax dollars paid for these improvements! The park serves over 140 thousand visitors annually, bringing over three million tourist dollars to the Finger Lakes region, dollars that are vital to our economic viability.[43]

Rather than emphasizing simply the economic loss, some residents emphasized a sense of entitlement to the land, and as such argued that the deal was unfair:

> Our tax money has built and run Sampson State Park. Now the Indians are to get it free and clear. They are to keep it open to the public for five years and if the Park doesn't show a profit they have the right to close it. It will certainly not show a profit and will be lost. That is not fair to all of us who have invested so much. Let's add an amendment saying that if the Reservation doesn't show improvement and is a tax burden on Seneca County it can also be closed![44]

The land was valuable because it was profitable. More importantly, it was thought to have value – which drew tourists to it – because the residents, through their tax dollars, had improved it. This reflects a Lockean concept of property ownership. One acquires title to land by mixing one's labour with it (see the Introduction to this book).[45] Labour imparts value to the land.[46] By enclosing and cultivating land, one gains title to it. In this case, the residents of Seneca County (through the state) had acquired ownership over Sampson because the state had built buildings, a marina, a sewer etc. on the property. They, not the Cayuga, had improved it. Local landowners resented and were angry about losing what they owned, about what they had put value into. The Indians were trespassing on their lands, and violating their sense of ownership in the process. When asked about returning land to the Indians, Wisner Kinne of SCLO replied '... give them "Nothing. Nothing! New York State was developed by people like my family. They did all the things the Indians didn't" '.[47]

Reservations about reservations

'No Nation within a Nation' was an often-heard refrain in the claim area. On reservations, Indian nations exercise their inherent sovereignty as 'domestic, dependent nations'.[48] This struck many citizens and politicians as unfair. Why did Indians have 'special rights' when other Americans did not?[49]

In America, argued SCLO, we are 'one nation under God', and therefore we should all live under the same law. Treating Indians separately was seen by many as a form of legal segregation. This argument came up frequently in letters from Seneca County residents to their elected officials:

- 'Under this settlement, the Cayuga Indians will be a sovereign nation whose people do not have to live in accordance to all the state and Federal rules and regulations that all other United States citizens must abide by. When on the reservation they are protected from prosecution if they commit a crime outside the reservation – this is just one example of the problems that will ramify out of this whole set up. They will be legally deemed a separate entity unto themselves with us paying for everything. I do not understand – when has the government decided to promote segregation of races within its own country? What happened to America as being the "melting pot" where all races can live harmoniously together.'[50]
- 'Reservations are the most archaic form of segregation that we have. In this twenty-first century the Indians should be integrated into society, not segregated. Let them buy their homes, become a part of the community and accept the responsibility of a true citizen.'[51]
- '... We had better stop treating each Indian Nation as a separate nation within the United States or we will have an Iran situation here. We are all Americans, black, white, or red, whether we came from Germany, Ireland, or England or worship as Catholics, Methodist, Jewish, or Presbyterians, so Indians would be much better off as Americans.'[52]

Reservations were, in the minds of these property owners, simply racist hangovers from a previous age. The federal government, in its role as guardian, had adopted a policy of reservations for Indians from the 1850s to the 1890s in order to protect them from harmful contact with whites (O'Brien 1989). But by the late 1880s:

> Game depletion and tribal relocation to unproductive regions had forced radical changes in life-style, accompanied, in many instances, by profound poverty, suffering and even starvation. Many reservations resembled prison camps, surrounded by barbwire.
>
> (O'Brien 1989: 75)

Wisner Kinne, president of SCLO, said 'anybody in his right mind knows the worst thing you can do with any human being is [to] put him in a segregated situation, no matter how you rationalize it ... on a reservation the only opportunity you have is to get out'.[53]

Segregation of Indians on reservations was, in their minds, morally wrong. The 1960s civil rights movement was about establishing equality for all races, not treating them differently and unequally. SCLO argued that the settlements were recreating racial inequality by establishing or expanding reservations: 'If we proposed isolating blacks on a reservation, no one in government would support it'.[54] Therefore, their opposition to a reservation was not racist, as many (especially federal officials) maintained, but the contrary: 'Americans have never chosen to live neighborly with the racial segregation and racial discrimination which the establishment of an Indian reservation inevitably creates'.[55]

But if Indians are a nationality, not (just) a race, then eliminating their sovereignty, the rights to govern themselves as a distinct people on their own lands (that is, their reservations), forces them to integrate, that is, assimilate, into the American body politic against their will. Assimilation was the policy that replaced reservations (O'Brien 1989). Prior to the civil rights and the red power movements of the 1960s, the federal government had adopted the assimilationist policy of termination through which the special relationship between some Indian tribes and the federal government was ended. The government aimed to relinquish responsibility for Indian nations.

Unfortunately, the confounding of the meanings of Indian (as race and nationality) allows racism to come across as tolerance, equality and fair mindedness. The issue of race and the charge of racism were deeply sensitive matters. Property owners were concerned that their substantive concerns about a reservation were being dismissed because their opponents, the proponents of the settlement, were labelling them as racists. Walter Foulke, the head of CSPOA, did not want CSPOA to be seen as 'anti-Indian' as SCLO was. Their concern at being labelled in this way, however, did not mean that many of the landowners and politicians were *not* racists or at least had some racist attitudes: attitudes that were often cloaked by talk of rights.[56]

Weakness and lies

To the charge of racism, the Seneca County Liberation Organization responded:

> Seneca County resistance arises not from racial prejudice but from the fact that affected Seneca County citizens have had no voice in the negotiations and other actions which have produced a Congressional bill. The issue is expropriation and imposition without representation.[57]

This was the critique most commonly levelled against the settlement. Those most affected by it had no say in it. The residents of Seneca and Cayuga Counties, whether they lived in the claim area or near the proposed reservation, had not been invited to sit at the negotiating table. As a result, their concerns, interests and fears were left out of the process, at least until the post-negotiation/ implementation stage. Not surprisingly, 'those who have been left out . . . are likely to try to block an agreement's implementation' (Bingham 1986: 96). SCLO became a spoiler, and a successful one at that. CSPOA, on the other had, did not become a spoiler because the agreement met their basic interests, and they had, at least indirectly, been involved from the beginning when they had met with the Work Group in March of 1978 to air their concerns.[58]

The broader public, however, had been in the dark about the negotiations. The Work Group decided early on that: 'we are going to have to keep the details of the negotiations confidential. We aren't going to meet our schedule if we try and work out the whole thing completely in public'.[59] Ironically, that decision guaranteed the Work Group would never make its schedule, since SCLO and others had no confidence in the process or its outcome.

In a complaint to Congressman Gary Lee, Frank Kulesze of Romulus wrote:

> I feel all our Federal and state legislative representatives of Seneca County let us down. You let us down because you did not request the chairman of the study group to include Seneca County Board of Supervisors in finalizing of the memorandum of understanding before it was signed. It is not appropriate procedure to request input *after* an agreement has been signed.
> (Emphasis in original)[60]

Ray Zajac, the supervisor from Romulus, echoed SCLO's charge:

> I believe that the tentative agreement put forth by your panel exhibits the fact that the Citizens of the Town of Romulus, County of Seneca, State of New York, along with all the Citizens of the United States of America, have been misrepresented by our United States Government Department of Interior in that agency's failure to follow the Due Process of Law guaranteed by the United States Constitution. The secret negotiations performed

in reaching the proposed settlement was a distinct exclusion of local government and residents and certainly has to be considered unconstitutional when acknowledging the detrimental impact such a settlement would definitively have upon the area.[61]

At the heart of this critique is the issue of procedural justice – the fairness of the procedures that determine outcomes (Deutsch 2000). Research has found that 'people feel affirmed if the procedures to which they are subjected treat them with the respect and dignity they feel is their due; if so treated, it is easier for them to accept a disappointing outcome' (Deutsch 2000: 45). Senecah (2004) argues that effective participatory processes are based on building and maintaining trust. Three practices – access, standing and influence – form what she calls 'the Trinity of Voice' which is the basis for trust (Senecah 2004: 22–3). Access means the public has sufficient and appropriate opportunities to express their choices and opinions. Standing means the public's opinions have 'civic legitimacy,' that is, respect and esteem. Influence means that said opinions are respectfully considered, and representatives of the public (and all key stakeholders) have a part in the process that determines the decision criteria and the alternatives that are measured against those criteria.

Accusations that the negotiations were secret and that the public only had a voice after a decision was already made reflect the fact that the public, especially neighbours of the future reservation, had little or no access to the negotiations. Congressman Gary Lee's request to allow representatives onto the Work Group in October 1979 was denied. Instead, county representatives were allowed to review the implementation bill, but not – as the case turned out – really to amend it. Access for South Seneca County residents was limited to the September public hearings and the House Committee Hearing on HR 6631. Indeed, few of the signposts of access – an attitude of collaboration, convenient times and places, readily available information and education, diverse opportunities to access information and education, technical assistance, adequate and widely disseminated notice, early public involvement and ongoing opportunities for participation (Senecah 2004) – were present in the Cayuga negotiations.

Worse still, though, was the situation in which, although access to the settlement was provided through public and legislative hearings, the gap or disparity between the two created such anger, scepticism and distrust as to prevent 'standing' – that is, opportunities for dialogue and deliberation, active listening, courtesy, clear expectations about authority in the decision-making process, collaborative room arrangements and genuine empathy (Senecah 2004). Unfortunately, public hearings, the most common form of public participation in the US, are notoriously bad at providing such standing. While public hearings provide the public with opportunities to state their opinions (opposition, support, concerns, etc.), government officials (that is, the negotiators), while they may address those concerns, are neither obliged to incorporate the public's concerns or suggestions into their decisions, nor to repudiate or revise their decisions (that is, the settlement) even if citizen opposition is strong (Senecah 2004).

In general, public hearings provide some access, but little standing and even less influence since the decisions have already been made, and the public knows this (Senecah 2004). Unfortunately, the Cayuga public hearings were no different. With the theatre-style question and answer format which allowed speakers a very limited amount of time to give testimony, there was no opportunity for dialogue, learning or problem-solving – just venting and grandstanding. Senecah (2004) notes that when people feel that they have no access or standing, and therefore no influence, they find ways to make others pay attention to them, such as lawsuits, escalating the conflict in the process.

The Cayuga Work Group's response to the public opposition

While surprised by the degree of vehemence, Work Group members were not surprised that there was opposition:

> I think everybody knew that from day one, of the working group, everybody said this will be very difficult to sell to those people most directly involved, because they were well organized and they were very emotional. And I think everybody knew that it was going to be hard to sell it to them, but I think the working group said we have to get this settled and it's going to be best for the State of New York, it's going to be best for the people that were involved.[62]

The attorney for the Cayuga Nation commented along similar lines, 'the real problem ... is getting past the political pressures being brought against a settlement'.[63] The question was how to overcome this political pressure. Work Group members tried a number of strategies to sell the settlement to the public, two of which are explored below – rational cost–benefit arguments, and promises of public discussion and input through the public hearing process.

The Work Group, and its government allies, tried to minimize the cost of settlement to the public while highlighting its benefits in the hopes that, assuming people were rational, the benefits would outweigh the costs. They hoped, that is, that the risks of economic disruption and litigation expenses incurred in failing to settle would outweigh the risks of settling. They did this through letters, public hearings and reports. For example, in responses to the letters from concerned citizens, New York State officials used the following logic to explain why the state was negotiating:

> In addition [to the legal strength of the claim], we considered the potentially devastating impact of litigation – regardless of the outcome. We have

seen the effect the mere presence of the claim has had on the real estate market in Cayuga County. The impact of the litigation would not be restricted to the claim zone; the entire State would suffer.[64]

The impact of the litigation on the towns and counties was starkly outlined in terms of the possible loss of land area, real estate values, population displacement and government revenues.[65] Settlement would avoid all of this negative impact.

When residents and local officials of Seneca County raised concerns about the costs of settlement, the Work Group parried with the potential benefits. The settlement would serve to clear property title; protect access to public recreation spots (by keeping the Sampson State Park open, and by selectively choosing Hector lands that were not recreational); bring employment to an economically depressed county through federal programmes for Indians; protect the tax base through a land cap; provide additional government services to augment or offset county services; guarantee all existing rights of way; compensate for public projects by providing money to cover the sewer system; and provide finality by forestalling all further Cayuga land claims, among others.

But this approach did not work. While the benefits may have outweighed the costs and risks of settling may have outweighed the risks of litigation, local residents did not believe Work Group members or federal or state officials because those officials had no credibility. This was because the negotiators had not given the Seneca County residents real access, standing or influence. They had not listened to the residents, and the residents in turn did not trust them.

Another means through which the negotiators tried to persuade area residents to accept the settlement was by arguing that their concerns ultimately *would* be heard at and through the public hearing process. But this attempt to include them after the fact backfired. First, from the residents' point of view, the government only wanted their input for show because the deal was already done. After all, they had been intentionally excluded from the negotiations – that is, from access. Second, no record or transcript was taken of the public hearings, which was another sign of the government's bad faith. The federal government was not taking their concerns seriously – that is, it was not giving them standing. Third, the implementation bill (HR 6631) was not substantially amended, despite the hearings in September 1979, and March 1980 – that is, they had no influence. Unfortunately, 'the less the public thinks it's being taken seriously, the louder it becomes' (Susskind and Field 1996: 183).

In the end, none of the strategies worked. Much of the public in Seneca County could not be persuaded to accept the settlement. Why? The problem was that the Work Group had adopted a 'decide-announce-defend' (DAD) public relations approach to dealing with an angry public (Susskind and

Field 1996). Under this approach, a deal is made behind closed doors, and then sold to the public. The decision-makers then rely on a number of strategies to overcome the inevitable public backlash against the deal, including the stone wall (that is, keeping silent), the whitewash (that is, minimizing the risk), the smokescreen (that is, creating doubt), the false front, the block-and-blame and the slash-and-burn (Susskind and Field 1996). The Work Group, whether intentionally or not, ended up whitewashing the concerns, fears and needs of South Seneca County residents. This, in turn, fuelled public opposition to the settlement and built up political pressure against it, creating and stoking the very obstacle the Work Group members were trying to overcome.

Conclusion

The Cayuga Work Group, through the DAD approach to public relations, failed effectively to deal with the public's anger about the settlement. Alternative approaches ought to have been tried, approaches that would provide the public with access, standing and influence. Failure to try these will leave negotiators facing continued public opposition to the negotiated settlement of Indian land claims.

One such alternative to the DAD model is the Mutual Gains Approach (MGA) (Susskind and Field 1996). Based on years of experience with environmental and public policy disputes, Susskind and Field suggest six steps negotiators should take to deal with an angry public: (1) acknowledge the concerns of the other side; (2) encourage joint fact-finding; (3) offer contingent commitments to minimize impacts if they do occur and promise to compensate knowable but unintended impacts; (4) accept responsibility, admit mistakes and share power; (5) act in a trustworthy fashion at all times; (6) focus on building long-term relationships (Susskind and Field 1996: 37–8).

In the Cayuga case, federal, state and Indian negotiators could take these steps in order to minimize risk from – and create further opportunities for – a settlement. Landowners, reservation neighbours and county officials have a number of issue-specific concerns about the impact of a reservation on their communities. By acknowledging these concerns and the anger and fear behind them, by admitting that they erred by excluding the public from participating in the negotiations in the first place, by sharing power with local residents and officials and by addressing their concerns through joint fact-finding and contingent commitments, such as payments-in-lieu-of-taxes (PILOTs), public opposition to settlement might be overcome.

While there is no empirical evidence yet about the efficacy of the MGA in land claim cases, the DAD approach is a known failure. The MGA calls for and works hand in hand with consensus building processes (CBP) – 'collaborative decision-making techniques in which a third-party neutral such as a facilitator or mediator assists diverse or competing interest groups to reach an agreement' (Emerson et al. 2003: 10) – which would guarantee that all key stakeholders, including the public, have a role in the negotiations (Susskind et al. 1999). Collectively, all the stakeholders would determine what the risks and costs of settlement are, and how they should be distributed. They would also determine what steps might be taken to mitigate the risks or compensate for any losses. As Susskind and Field point out:

> when the party who caused the harm [or risk] tries to decide on its own what the appropriate response should be, the wronged parties are likely to balk [as they did here]. Only when compensation [and mitigation] is seen as appropriate and fair in the eyes of those who feel harm [or at risk] will the need for further bloodletting subside'.
> (Susskind and Field 1996: 103)

The MGA and CBP offer the best hope of resolving land claims disputes. Such disputes have been termed 'nested conflicts' (Dugan 1996), that is, issue-specific disputes over land, money, government services and jurisdiction, which are nested or embedded in deeper relationship conflicts (for example, the guardian/ward trust relationship), in structural inequalities and in profound differences of world-view (Docherty 2001). These, put differently, are the 'ruptures in the social fabric' discussed in the Introduction to this book. Such claims are not and will not be easily resolved, and the stakes – the survival of indigenous nations, the futures of entire counties and states, the conscience of the American people and the upholding of international law – are high.[66] All the more reason why we, in analysing land restitution, need to understand the nature of public opposition to negotiated settlement of indigenous land claims.

References

Akehurst, M (1987) *A Modern Introduction to International Law*, London: Unwin Hyman.
Arneil, B (1996) 'The Wild Indian's Venison: Locke's Theory of Property in English Colonialism in America', *Political Studies* XLIV: 60–74.
Bingham, G (1986) *Resolving Environmental Disputes: A Decade of Experience*, Washington, DC: The Conservation Foundation.
Blancke, B (2005) 'Rebuilding the Longhouse: Obstacles to and Opportunities for Settling the Cayuga Indian Nation Land Claim through Negotiation', unpublished thesis, Syracuse University.
Campisi, J (1985) 'The Trade and Intercourse Acts: Land Claims on the Eastern Seaboard', in I Sutton (ed.) *Irredeemable America: the Indians' Estate and Land Claims*, Albuquerque: University of New Mexico Press.
Cobb, S (1994) 'Theories of Responsibility: The Social Construction of Intentions in Mediation', *Discourse Processes* 188: 164–86.
Deutsch, M (2000) 'Justice and Conflict', in M Deutsch and P Coleman (eds.) *The Handbook of Conflict Resolution*, San Francisco, CA: Jossey-Bass Publishers.

Docherty, J (2001) *Learning Lessons from Waco: When the Parties Bring Their Gods to the Negotiation Table*, Syracuse, NY: Syracuse University Press.

Dugan, M (1996) 'A Nested Theory of Conflict', *A Leadership Journal: Women in Leadership – Sharing the Vision*, 1: 9–20.

Emerson, Kirk et al. (2003) 'The Challenges of Environmental Conflict Resolution', in R O'Leary and L Bingham (eds.) *The Promise and Performance of Environmental Conflict Resolution*, Washington, DC: Resources for the Future.

Halftown, C (1998) 'The Haudenosaunee Cayuga Nation Land Claim: Cayuga Nation v New York', *Buffalo Law Review* 46(3): 1091–5.

Jones, R (1979) *Indians: Land Claims by Eastern Tribe*, Washington, DC: Congressional Research Service.

Lavin, C (1988) 'Responses to the Cayuga Land Claim', in C Vecsey and W Starna (eds) *Iroquois Land Claims*, Syracuse, NY: Syracuse University Press.

Mackey, E (2005) 'Universal Rights in Conflict: "Backlash" and "Benevolent Resistance" to Indigenous Land Rights', *Anthropology Today* 21: 14–20.

Moore, C (1986) *The Mediation Process: Practical Strategies for Resolving Conflict*, San Francisco, CA: Jossey-Bass Publishers.

New York, State Legislature (1889) *Report of Special Committee to Investigate the Indian Problem of the State of New York (Whipple Report)*, Albany, NY: New York State Legislature, Assembly.

O'Brien, S (1989) *American Indian Tribal Governments*, Normon, OK: University of Oklahoma Press.

Opotow, S (1990) 'Moral Exclusion and Injustice: an Introduction', *Journal of Social Issues* 46: 1–20.

Prucha, FP (1962) *American Indian Policy in the Formative Years: the Indian Trade and Intercourse Acts 1790–1834*, Lincoln, NE: University of Nebraska Press.

Senecah, S (2004) 'The Trinity of Voice: the Role of Practical Theory in Planning and Evaluating the Effectiveness of Environmental Participatory Processes', in D Stephen, J Delicath, MF Aepli Elsenbeer (eds) *Communication and Public Participation in Environmental Decision Making*, Albany, NY: State University of New York Press.

Shattuck, G (1991) *The Oneida Land Claims: a Legal History*, Syracuse, NY: Syracuse University Press.

Susskind, L and P Field (1996) *Dealing with an Angry Public: the Mutual Gains Approach to Resolving Disputes*, New York: The Free Press.

Susskind, L, S McKearnan and J Thomas-Larmer (eds) (1999) *The Consensus Building Handbook: a Comprehensive Guide to Reaching Agreement*, Thousand Oaks, CA: Sage Publications.

Sutton, I (2000) 'The Continuing Saga of Indian Land Claims', *American Indian Culture and Research Journal* 24: 129–62.

United States Congress, House of Representatives, Committee on Interior and Insular Affairs (1980) *Settlement of the Cayuga Indian Nation Land Claims in the State of New York (HR 6631)*, Washington, DC: United States Congress.

Vernon, H (1980) 'The Cayuga Claims: a Background Study', *American Indian Culture and Research Journal* 4(3): 21–35.

Walke, R (1999) *Cayuga, Oneida, and other Eastern Indian Land Claims*, Washington, DC: Congressional Research Service.

Wilbur Smith and Associates (1978) *Proposed Land Settlement: Cayuga Nation Claim*, Columbia, SC: Wilbur Smith Associates.

Notes

1. 1 Stat 37, reenacted in 1793, 1796, 1799, 1802 and 1834. It is now 25 USC 177. For a detailed history of the ITIAs, see Prucha (1962).
2. For more information on the Cayuga land claim, see Blancke (2005), Halftown (1998), Lavin (1988) and Vernon (1980).
3. Walter Rewald, 'Officials to meet Cayugas, Mohawks', *Citizen*, 30 January 1978.
4. By a private understanding, an additional $12 million would be made available through the Forest Economic Development programme for economic development. From an interview with a Cayuga negotiator, 5 January 2001.
5. Joint Memorandum of Understanding Concerning Settlement of the Land Claims of the Cayuga Indian Nation, 20 August 1979. Freedom of Information Act request, the Department of the Interior.
6. Sheila Tucker, 'Association Officers Discuss Indian Suit', 25 September 1977; 'Indian Land Claims Target of Lombardi Legislation', 4 December 1977, *Citizen*, Auburn, New York. At the time, only one of 14 insurance companies continued to offer title insurance, and banks required title insurance for mortgages.
7. Letter to Members of the Cayuga Seneca Property Owners Association and their Friends from Walter Foulke, Morton Kahn, John Reorh and Richard Hamilton, 23 August 1979, the Indian Land Claims File, the Romulus Townhouse, Willard, New York (hereinafter, 'Romulus Indian Land Claims File').
8. From a transcript of the 29 August 1979 Public Meeting to discuss the settlement, Romulus Townhouse, Willard New York. The transcript is on file with the author. SCLO modelled its name after the Palestinian Liberation Organization.
9. Sonni Sampson, 'Indian Agreement Meeting Set', *Finger Lakes Times* (hereinafter, *FLT*), 27 August 1979.
10. Ibid.
11. Rudy Elder, 'Bitter Feelings Erupt', *FLT*, 12 September 1979.
12. Ibid.
13. Ibid.
14. Bill Lancaster, 'Hearing Draws Mixed Reaction', *FLT*, 12 September 1979.
15. Alice Larsen, 'Residents Ask Pertinent Questions at Sept. 12 Hearing', *Ovid Gazette* (hereinafter, *OG*), 19 September 1979.
16. Walter Rewald, 'Counties Split on Indian Land Issue', *Citizen*, 12 September 1979. This was a year after the Camp David Peace Accords between Israel and Egypt were signed, accords which left unaddressed the Palestinian question.
17. Alice Larsen, 'Residents Ask Pertinent Questions at Sept. 12 Hearing', *OG*, 19 September 1979.
18. 'No action should be taken by any group or any governmental body which affects the public access and enjoyment of public land area without full public disclosure and without the support and involvement of the taxpayers and residents of the area': 'Options in Cayuga Land Case to be Listed', *FLT*, 1 June 1979.
19. Bill Lancaster, 'Opposition Plans Strategies', *FLT*, 7 September 1979.
20. 'Hearing Date Set on Indian Claims', *Citizen*, 20 December 1979. On 1 March 1980, the judge declined to grant a temporary injunction.
21. The Attorney General stated among other things that the Department of Justice would not sue private landowners in New York, and that the landowners should be made aware of his decision as soon as possible. Letter to Cecil Andrus, Secretary of the Interior from Griffin Bell, Attorney General of the United States, re: Ancient Eastern Indian Claims, 30 June 1978, NLC-1002-A-261, Indian Land Claims – Maine Key Memos, 01/1977–06/1979, Counsel's Office (Robert J Lipshutz). Box(es) 19, Jimmy Carter Library, Atlanta, Georgia.
22. Helen Casey, 'Lee Won't Ask for New Accord', *FLT*, 29 September 1979; George

Clay, 'Work Group to Meet on Cayuga Land-Claim Settlement', *Ithaca Journal* (hereinafter, *IJ*), 2 October 1979.
23 Helen Casey, 'Indian Pact Will Become Legislation', *Citizen*, 6 October 1979.
24 Gary A Lee, Indian Land Claims before the Seneca County Republican Dinner, 25 October 1979, Waterloo, New York, Jacob K Javits Collection: Series 4 Committees, Subseries 4 Governmental Affairs (1951–80), Box 10 (Cayuga Negotiations), State University of New York at Stony Brook (hereinafter, 'Javits's Cayuga Negotiations file'). The *Twilight Zone* was a television series that aired on CBS from 1959–64. The author of the series, Rod Sterling, described the series in an ad in the *New York Times* as 'the land that lies between science and superstition, between the pit of man's fears and the summit of his knowledge. You will find the bizarre, but the believable; the different, the shocking that is yet understandable. Its tales must be shown; they cannot be told. And each carries with it its own special surprise'. The Fifth Dimension, www.thetzsite.com/pages/premiere.html (accessed 26 August 2003).
25 Sonni Sampson, 'Land Claim Legislation Angers Seneca Officials', *FLT*, 14 January 1980.
26 Sonni Sampson, 'SCLO Head Blasts Settlement Bill', *FLT*, 8 February 1980.
27 Sonni Sampson, 'Cayuga Claim Legislation Introduced in House', *FLT*, 27 February 1980.
28 United States Congress, Committee on Interior and Insular Affairs, Hearings on HR 6631, 3 March 1980.
29 Sonni Sampson, 'SCLO Members Felt Slighted in D.C.', *FLT*, 5 March 1980.
30 Ibid. A few days prior, the United States Olympic hockey team, the underdogs, pulled off an upset victory over the Soviet Union in the semi-finals, an outcome that was described at the time as a miracle. Little did Wisner Kinne know how apt this metaphor would be, for everyone at the time thought that the bill would pass.
31 'Bill May Limit Cayugas' Land Purchases', *FLT*, 13 March 1980.
32 Sonni Sampson, 'No Limit on Indian Land Buys; House Votes Today on Settlement', *FLT*, 18 March 1980.
33 Board of Supervisors, Seneca County: Resolution No. 86, 'Supervisors – Deny, Repudiate and Reject Alleged Cayuga Indian Land Claim', and Resolution No. 88, 'Supervisors – Oppose Rape by President Carter', adopted 17 March 1980, Javits's Cayuga Negotiations file. Attached to Resolution No. 86 is an Economic Impact Statement of the 10,000 acre cap.
34 'Views Mixed, Surprise Universal', *FLT*, 19 March 1980.
35 From an interview with a Cayuga negotiator, 5 January 2001.
36 The report addressed the concerns, questions, and issues that were raised in the September public hearings and explained why no real substantive amendments were made. In general, the report concluded that the impact of the settlement was minimal. See United States Congress (1980), pp 96–102.
37 In the history of the US, Blacks, women, Jews, children, the disabled, gays and Indians, among others, have suffered to some degree from moral exclusion. As a result of moral exclusion, they have (and in some cases still are) treated in ways that would be considered immoral if members of the community were so treated (for example, lynching, employment discrimination, sexual exploitation, scapegoating, etc.) (Deutsch 2000).
38 Letter to Robert Morgado, Secretary to the Governor from Roy C Ike, 26 November 1979, Governor Hugh Carey Records, 1979–82, Subject Files, Reel #65, New York State Archives, Albany (hereinafter, 'Carey Subject Files').
39 Walter Rewald, 'Powwow Draws Crowd', *Citizen*, 5 August 1977.

40 'Amendment Halting Funds in Indian Claim Defeated', *Citizen*, 12 June 1977.
41 From the Indian perspective, this had always been their land – or land with which they had been entrusted.
42 Sonni Sampson, 'Agreement Clause Would Let Indians Close Sampson Park in 1983', *FLT*, 25 August 1979.
43 SCLO Fact Sheet, no date. Cayuga Land Claim Clippings File, *FLT*, Geneva, New York.
44 Letter to Governor Hugh Carey from Wanda Gaul, Thomas Gaul, Dorothy Gaul and Karin Highley, 1 October 1979 Carey Subject Files.
45 'The criterion Locke develops for the origin of private property is, of course, labour ... the two elements which characterize land that has been laboured on for both Locke in his chapter on property and the ethical and economic defenders of the American plantation, are cultivation and enclosure ... it is these two elements which distinguish aboriginal use of the land from that of the English' (Arneil 1996: 62, 63).
46 Locke argued that '... labour not only creates property, but is the source of all value in it. As he comments: "tis Labour then which puts the greatest part of Value upon Land without which it would scarcely be worth anything" ' (Arneil 1996: 70).
47 Dan Olmsted, 'Patching Up History', *Democrat and Chronicle* (hereinafter, *D&C*), 17 August 1980.
48 For a discussion of Indian sovereignty see O'Brien (1989).
49 SCLO Fact Sheet, 2nd Statement – February 1980, Javits's Cayuga Negotiations file.
50 Letter to Congressman Gary Lee from Linn Lahr, 12 September 1979, Carey Subject Files.
51 Letter to Governor Hugh Carey from Wanda Gaul et al., 1 October 1979, Carey Subject Files.
52 Letter to Governor Hugh Carey from Shirley Lawatsch, 22 January 1980, Carey Subject Files.
53 Carol Ritter, 'Lodi Will Give $5,000 to Fight Indian Land Claim', *D&C*, 22 September 1979.
54 George Clay, 'Reservations Called Racist', *IJ*, 12 October 1979.
55 Letter to Concerned Citizen from Stanley Van Vlett, Wisner Kinne and George Souhan, 21 January 1980, Javits's Cayuga Negotiations file.
56 See Mackey (2005) for a discussion of competing rights talk and the limitations of clothing land claims in human rights language.
57 Letter to Concerned Citizens from the Seneca County Liberation Organization, 21 January 1980, Javits's Cayuga Negotiations file.
58 And that meeting came about in an attempt, unsuccessful, by CSPOA to get a representative on the Work Group.
59 Laurie Bennett, 'Congress May Get Cayuga Indian Claim Proposal by Spring', *FLT*, 2 March 1978.
60 Letter to the Honorable Gary A Lee from FJ Kulesze, 15 September 1979, Carey Subject Files.
61 Letter to Tim Vollman from Raymond Zajac, 11 September 1979, Javits's Cayuga Negotiations file.
62 Interview with a negotiator for Congressman Gary Lee, 5 January 2001.
63 George Clay, 'Negotiations Near Critical Period on Cayuga Claims', *IJ*, 21 April 1979.
64 Letter to Mr Peter Borzilleri, President, New York State Wine Grape Growers, Inc. from Michael DelGiudice, 29 May 1979, Carey Subject Files.
65 Financial Impact Statement: Cayuga Nation Land Claim Area, July 1980, Cayuga Indian Land Claim Clippings File, *FLT*, Geneva, New York.
66 Although certain changes have occurred in the interim, the stakes remain as high as ever. In June of 2005, the Federal Court of Appeal overturned the District Court's

judgment in favour of the Cayuga for $247 million because of a 2005 Supreme Court decision (*City of Sherrill v Oneida Indian Nation*, S. Ct. 1478), which 'dramatically altered the legal landscape' (413 F 3d 273). The Appeal Court ruled, as a result, that the Cayuga's land claim was time barred by the Equitable Doctrine of Laches (413 F 3d 266). The Supreme Court denied review of the Appeal Court's decision. The land claim has since morphed into a trust application dispute. The Cayuga, following the advice of the Supreme Court in Sherrill, have petitioned the federal government to take land the Cayuga have bought in the meantime from willing sellers into trust in accordance with federal regulations (25 CFR 151.10). This process, however, opens up the decision to protect native lands to even more political influence (by the settler population) because these regulations: '... are sensitive to the complex interjurisdictional concerns that arise when a tribe seeks to regain sovereign control over territory. Before approving the acquisition, the Secretary [of the Interior] must consider, among other things, the tribe's need for additional land; "[t]he purpose for which the land will be used"; "the impact on the State [of New York] and its political subdivisions resulting from the removal of land form the tax rolls"; and "jurisdictional problems and potential conflicts in land use which may arise" ' (125 S Ct 1478, 1499). The claim lives on, but now in a new form.

Index

aboriginal
  image 72
  land claim agreements 85
  right 75–6, 81–2
aboriginal claims 86
Aboriginal Land Rights (Northern Territory) Act 1976 100
aboriginality 68–9, 82, 210
  colonised 118
academic debate 203, 205
access 8, 12, 25–27, 29, 34, 36–9, 43–5, 47, 50–51, 58–59, 85, 105, 121–2, 128–9, 133–4, 137, 149, 175, 189, 207, 214, 220, 226, 229, 241, 250–3, 256
accommodationism 76–8, 81–2
'accommodationist' and 'exclusivist' strategies 76
acta de posesión y deslinde 216
activists 8, 19, 124, 131–2, 139, 211–3, 230
adaptability 14, 17, 81–2
administration 27, 42, 78, 146, 193, 195, 242
  local 45
  provincial 71
adultery 189, 198
affirmation 144, 153
'African'
  official race category (SA) 142
Africans 12, 31, 143, 147–8, 158, 173
agenda
  nationalist 204
  political 104, 198, 203, 205
  productionist 166
  revolutionary 198
Agrarian Law 215–7
agrarian programmes 209, 224
agrarian reform 125
  Law of 1964 (Mexico) 202
  Mexico 209–10, 224, 229
  Peru 190, 192, 198
agreements
  Canadian 85
  shaping of 87
Agricultural Research Council (ARC) 176
agriculture 51
  commercial 167
  subsistence 211, 213, 222
Agriculture
  Department of 28, 40, 166, 169, 176
agri-village 168–9, 170–1, 177, 180
Alaska 86, 92–3, 97
Alaska Native Claims Settlement Act (1971) 86
alcaldes 187
alcohol 57
  ban on 103
alienation 149, 154, 159
  from *rom* 116
  of land 95, 187, 202, 227, 242
Alliance for Progress 125
Alligator River II land claim 8
ALRA 100–3, 107, 116–8, 121–2
aluminium smelter 167
Amatole District Municipality 27, 34
Ambrose Dlamini 174
Ambrose Makhoba 172
American Indian Movement 3
Amit
  Vered 145
ANC 28, 38, 167 175
ancestral
  aspects of land 111, 113–5, 119, 121, 127–9, 163, 165–8, 171–3, 175, 178–80, 185–7, 193, 204

ancestry
  mixed 73, 82
  native 17
Anchorage 86
Andean
  peasantry 203. *See* highlands, Peruvian
Anderson
  Benedict 145
anexos de altura 187
anthropologists 2, 11, 23, 64, 104, 107, 127, 139, 222
anthropology 2, 21–2, 26, 145, 163, 193, 205
apartheid 3, 6, 8, 17, 31, 41–2, 142, 145–7, 162–4, 173–4, 177–9, 181–2
Apolônio 123, 124, 127
apprehensiveness 155, 157, 159
appropriation 45, 163, 172, 216
arable 34, 47, 130, 176–8
Arctic 68, 76, 85, 96
arena
  the 105
Argesel River 46
army 199, 200–1
Arnhem Land 8, 99–101, 118–120
Arnhem Land Aboriginal Reserve 100
arrimadismo. *See* land, settlement of, by incomers
Article 4 (Mexico) 228–9
Article 27 (Mexico) 224, 229
articulation
  shifting 163, 165
asemblea 221, 225
aspiration 29, 34, 128, 136, 140–1, 145–7, 154–6, 159–160
  suburban 155
assets 44–5, 193
  public 16
  taxable 56–7
assimilation 214, 218–9, 223, 248
  in Canada 17, 69, 79–81
  in Mexico 214–9, 223
  in the US 247–8
Association. *See* Labrador Inuit Association (LIA), Labrador Metis Association (LMA), Naskapi-Montagnais Innu (NMIA), The Cayuga-Seneca Property Owners Association
Agrarian, of Social Interest 185
Communal Property (CPA) 179.
  See CPA

associations
  farmers' 165
  native 73
  quilombo 131, 135–6
Athapaskan 92
attacks 167, 199, 200, 204
Australia 6, 8–9, 15, 99–102, 104, 112–3, 118–21
authenticity 79, 82
authorities 37, 42, 174
autonomy 2–3, 13, 19, 34, 39, 50, 69, 71, 76–7, 82, 119, 164, 172, 181, 188, 210–11, 214, 216–21, 224, 226, 228–9
Ayacucho 198, 205

backlands 124–5, 136–7
Bahia 129
'balance'
  in land selection 94
balanda 115–16
bankruptcy 197
barbarian savagery 190
bargaining power 78, 180
Barth
  Fredrik 145
'becoming black' 136
Belhar extension 13, 158
belief
  in community 135
  in government 132
beliefs
  Andean 193
  local 228
  Nahua 222
  Yolngu 114
'beliefs'
  in negotiation 243–4
Bell
  Griffin, Attorney General 241, 256
beneficiaries 4, 16, 101, 144, 162–3, 165, 168–70, 172, 175–80, 191
  increase in numbers 175
  of restitution 165
benefit 43, 45, 57, 60, 71, 77–8, 81, 181, 195, 198, 242
  cost- 251
  material 43, 57–9, 196
  of government 125
  of local communities 31
  of loyalty 133

of restitution 27, 29, 35
of settlement 251–2
relation to private property 43–4
relation to rights 35, 38
social 46, 80, 156
symbolic 59
betrayal 197
'betterment' 37
'beyond restitution' 10
bill
  Congressional 249
black
  American, civil rights movement 70
  Americans 247
  homelands 27
  identities 127
  landholding 164
  or Indian, assumption of identity 136
  residents 135
  rural, community. See quilombo
  slaves 137
'black spot' 12, 173
blacks
  expulsion of 143
blacks
  'wild', in Australia 100
blame 17, 52, 173, 214
'blame
  block-and-' 253
'blame'
  in negotiation 244
bloodlines 68, 72, 74
Blue Mud Bay 9, 15, 99–104, 108, 111, 113, 116, 119, 121–2
Blue Mud Bay case 103–4, 122
Bolivia 138, 203, 205, 212, 228
border
  problems 194
boundaries 15, 29, 32, 88, 157, 226
  conflict over 224
  membership 82
  urban 226
Bourassa 6, 16, 18–9, 75
Brazilian government 123
Brazilian Northeast 4, 10, 12–3, 16, 120, 123–7, 132, 136–7, 139
bribery 53–4
British Columbia 15, 75, 83, 86, 95–6
broker 178
bureaucracy 1, 19, 46–7, 74

bureaucratic
  process 11, 32, 47, 87, 92, 198, 239, 241
  tyranny 239
business. See white business and administration
  interests 77
businesses 80
bylaws 135, 168–9

cabildo 214
caciques 215, 217
Cahuide 191, 199
Calder case 75
Calder v Attorney General of British Columbia 86
campesinado 212
campesino 4, 199, 217, 224
campesinos
  indigenous 221, 223
Canada 3, 7, 17–9, 21, 68–76, 81–7, 89, 95–6
  Government of 3, 75, 86
Canadian land claims process 14
Cape Flats 142–4, 150, 154, 158
Cape Times 148
Cape Town 9, 19–20, 22, 30, 40–1, 141–3, 146–7, 160–2, 181–2
capitalism 1, 2–4, 19–20, 206, 220
Cárdenas 216–7, 219–20
cargos 189
carts
  horse 54–5, 57
Carter
  President Jimmy 238, 242
casa ejidal 221
catch-22 80
categories
  social 172
categorization
  changing 213
  racial 202–3
cattle 42, 99, 124–5, 127, 130–1, 166, 169–1, 173, 187, 189–90, 192, 195, 226
Cayuga
  land claim area 235
Cayuga Land Claim Work Group 240
Cayuga Nation 235–6, 238–9, 245, 251, 255, 258
CEBs. See communities, church based
Cedara 169, 181
ceremonial ground 111–2

ceremonies 9, 190. *See* initiation, ritual
Cerro de Pasco Corporation 187, 190, 194–5, 207
cession 85–6, 91, 95, 245
Chalhuas 197, 202, 207
Chaseling 103
cheap labour force 52, 59
Chelcea 50–1, 60, 63–5
Chiapas 224, 228, 230–1
Chief Makhoba 172, 178
chiefs 21, 26, 36–7, 174, 232
chiefship 47, 56–7, 106, 108, 167, 174–5, 177–9, 181
   erosion of 173
   traditionalist 178
children
   as future dwellers on reclaimed land 153
Christmas 90–1
church
   Catholic 124–7, 135–6, 139, 233
   estates 214
   Shembe 166–8, 171
churches 27, 156, 189
Ciskei 143, 174
citizens
   full, of Canada 82
citizenship 2–3, 5, 12–14, 19, 21, 143–4, 146, 148, 160, 203, 210–4, 229–0
   differentiated 147, 228–30
   full 2, 128
   national 13
   privileged status 148
civil rights. *See* movement, civil rights.
civilization 1, 202, 214
clăcași 47
claim
   to land 12, 68, 77, 209
claimant community 174
claimant groups 8, 68, 117, 163–4, 175, 178
claimants 1, 2, 7–11, 13, 15–17, 19, 25–7, 29, 32–8, 42, 67–9, 79, 82–3, 105, 107–8, 117, 121, 141–60, 162, 165, 168–9, 172–81, 183, 215
   diversity of 27, 147–9
   legitimate 1
claims
   movement from mobilization to settling of 141–60
   comprehensive 75

class
   consciousness 203
   differences, influence of 147
   diversity, apprehensions about 159
   lowest 54
   middle- 156
   of entrepreneurs 163, 178
   second-, status 3, 13
   working 148
   working- 160
clause
   extinguishment. *See* title, treaty
   on abrogation 79. *See* abrogation
   on 'balance' 93
   relating to connection to area 102
   quilombo. *See* Quilombo Clause
clientelism 133
clothing 178, 181
CNC 215
Code of Forestry.
   See Law 26/1996 Romania
Cold War 3, 70
collaboration 199
   attitude of 250
collective
   landholding 13, 131
   ownership 49, 75, 129, 131–4, 178, 210, 221, 228
collectivization 47
colonial 99, 102
   administrators 186
   courts 186
   dimensions of domination 187
   dispossession. *See* dispossession, colonial
   encounter 99
   exploitative practices. *See* exploitative practices, colonial
   influences 74
   land titles. *See* land titles, colonial
   period 186, 202, 210, 214
   power 101–2
   racial hierarchies. *See* racial hierarchies, colonial
   regime. *See* regime, colonial
   rule 214
   times 129
colonialism 1, 19
colonization 102–4, 117
   historical effects of 102
   in relation to encapsulation 99–117

Index

coloured 9, 142, 146–9, 152, 154, 158, 160–2
'Coloureds'
   official race category (SA) 142–3, 148, 162
Coloured Labour Preference Policy 148
commensurability
   'enforced' 110
Commission of Inquiry 101
Commission on Restitution of Land Rights (CRLR) 165, 172
Committee on Traditional Affairs 178
commodities
   tradable 49
commoditization 164–5, 179
commodity chain 57
   analysis 57
commodity-relationships 12
common law 102, 117
Commonwealth statutes 100
communal
   pastures 54
Communal Land Rights Act (2004) 37
communal tenure 169, 178–9
communist
   agitators 197
   category of 190
communities
   Andean 205
   church based 212, 225
   highland 185–7, 190, 192–3, 198, 202–4
   indigenous 186–9, 204, 213–4, 228, 233
   Labrador Innu 81–2
community 2, 4, 8–13, 19, 21, 23, 26–9, 31, 34, 36–40, 50, 54, 71–2, 80–1, 83, 123–4, 128–37, 140–6, 149–51, 153–7, 159–60, 163–4, 166–9, 171–8, 180–1, 186, 188–90, 192–8, 200, 204–6, 210–13, 216, 220–3, 227–8, 243, 247, 257
contestations over 9
   diasporic 143
   imagined 8, 13, 28
   leader 174, 178
   regulations 189
   revival of the old 151
community resource management 16
'community' 9, 27–9, 34, 123, 133, 135, 141–6, 149–1, 153–60
   'will-to- 141, 146–7, 159–60
company 195, 197, 199
   joint-stock 201–12

North American 187
owners 225
comparative study 3, 11
   of protected areas 31
compensation 34, 47, 50, 71, 85, 127, 143–4, 146, 148–9, 164, 172, 174, 176, 188, 191, 210, 254
   lack of 126
competing
   claims 117
   conceptions of balance 93
   discourses 164
   identities 69
   interest groups 253
   organizations 73
   over resources 129
competition 73, 78, 83, 133, 148
comuneros 188–201, 197, 225
comunidad campesina 193
comunidad indígena 193, 210
comunidades 135, 187–90, 193, 199, 202, 204–5, 210, 215, 219, 221, 226, 230
comunidades indígenas 188, 219, 221, 226, 230
comunidades madres 187–8
comunidades socias 193
conflict resolution 235–6
conflicts 51, 73, 79, 127, 175, 179, 188, 198–9, 203, 224, 254, 259
Congress
   1790 (Canada) 236
   United States 86, 239, 243
Conne River M'kmaq 73
conquest 6, 103, 245
Cónsac 189, 190, 194, 195, 199, 200
Cónsac hacienda 190, 194
consensus building processes (CBP) 253
conservation 16, 23, 25–6, 30–1, 33–4, 38–9, 40–1, 82, 169
   international bodies 31
   discourses of 26
   shifting justification for 29–30
constitution
   1988 (Brazil) 124, 128–9
   Mexican 224
   Peruvian 188, 190
   post-apartheid 7
   United States 249
contestation 3, 5, 137, 139, 146, 164, 172, 186, 230
   of interpretations 169

contestations 124
context 15
  historical 136, 148
  of native title 109, 116
  of restitution 145, 204
  of the court 104, 110, 112, 115
  policy 7
  political 3
  political and legal 3
  post-removals 150
  post-socialist 44, 59
  socio-legal 5, 18, 141
contexts
  of restitution 4–5
contradictions 195
contras 133–4, 136
cooperative 201
  agricultural, formation of 212
  coffee 213
  dairy sales 132
  farming 191, 196
corrupt
  government 70
  practices 216
corvée 47, 63
cosmopolitan 146, 178
Costeşti 46–7, 53, 55, 58, 64
costs of a reservation 242
councils
  municipal 147
court
  cases 19, 74
  form and structure of the 104
  of law 70
  proceedings 106
courtroom 99, 105, 111
CPA. *See* Association, Communal Property
creolization 82
CRLR. *See* Commission on Restitution of Land Rights
CSPOA 239–42, 245, 248–9
cultural
  particularity 123
culture 8, 16, 69, 157, 173
  Andean 203
  as impediment 123
  city 54
  clash of 158
  hybrid 69
  indigenous 193
  recognition of 131

Culture
  Ministry of 129
custom 10, 110, 178, 180, 225
'custom' 181
Czechoslovakia 17

D6BRT 144–6, 159. *See* District Six Beneficiary and Redevelopment Trust
D6M 143–5, 154. *See* District Six Museum
Dacia 51
DAD
  approach to public relations 253
dam
  projects 125–7, 139
damages 236
dams 132, 139
Davis Inlet 81, 84
Dawes Act 10, 20
'Day of the Indian' 193
  'Peasant' 193
de Castro
  Dom José Brandão 125–7, 132, 139
de Oliveira
  João Pacheco 127
death 121, 131, 149, 189, 216
debt 192, 194, 197–8, 207
decency
  ethos of 157
deeds 15, 34, 49, 101, 108
deforestation 43, 49, 50–2, 55, 57, 59–0
  illegal 55
dehumanization 150
delegado 196
democracy 146, 179, 242
  consultative 71
  political 124
  'tribal' 218–9
demonstration 108
Dene 75–7
Department of Agriculture 28, 40, 166, 169, 176
Department of Bantu Administration 167
Department of Economic Affairs and Tourism (DEAT) 33
Department of Land Affairs (DLA) 33, 36, 39, 174, 180, 182
  See DLA
Department of Marine and Coastal Management 36
Department of Sea Fisheries 31

Department of Water Affairs and Forestry (DWAF) 33
dependency 8
  economic 220
descent 25, 27
  as basis for claims 27
  as basis for ownership 15, 29
  group 8
  indigenous 214
desires 80, 140–1, 145–6
development 1, 4, 7, 9, 13, 16–7, 20, 22, 29, 33–5, 37, 40–1, 43, 68, 70–1, 73–6, 78–9, 80, 82, 86, 96–7, 118, 123, 125–6, 132, 138–40, 143, 146, 163–6, 168, 174–6, 178–9, 181–3, 201, 226, 238, 256
  agricultural 126, 178
  critique of 132
  language of 164
  pitfalls of 127
  plans 34, 37
Development
  Department of Community 142
  Integrated Rural, Programme 176
  Integrated, Planning 37
  Mandlazini, Committee 166–7
  National Office of Cooperative 195
  Reconstruction and, Programme 177
developmentalism 8, 34, 163, 165, 172, 176, 178, 180
Devil's Peak 142
Dhuwa 113, 121
difference 146
  commentary on 110
  ethno-racial 137
  insistence on 114–5
differences 77, 142, 147, 149, 254
  cultural and ethnic 217–8
  cultural, historical and economic 28
  social 135, 141
  social and cultural 218
differentiation 54, 142–3, 147, 155
social/racial 147–9
  gender 111
  generational 158, 116
  social 1, 144, 147
disconnect 91
discourse
  'communalist' 13
  moral 1
discovery
  of America 4
  of empty land 245
  of indigenous identities 127
discrimination 27, 71, 202, 204, 219, 226, 248, 257
disenfranchisement 14, 83, 148
disjuncture
  social 4
disorder 149, 159
displacement 127, 144, 150, 160
dispossession 1, 6, 9–10, 12, 15, 17–9, 27, 36, 38, 67–8, 85, 99, 101–2, 129, 164, 166, 173–4, 178, 194
  effective 101
dispute 133–5
  over leadership 174
  resolution 243
dissolution
  of SAIS, demands for 198
District Six 9–10, 13–4, 19, 141–62
District Six Beneficiary and Redevelopment Trust (D6BRT) 143
District Six Beneficiary Trust 14
distrust 250
diversity
  racial 142
division 175
divisions 190
  internal 73
DLA *See* Department of Land Affairs
Dobyns 188, 202, 205, 207
dominio pleno 226
Dominy
  Michelle 16, 18, 20
Dona Maria 134
Dona Rosa 134
Dragomireşti 46–7, 49–50, 52, 57, 59, 64
drought 28, 34, 125
dueños de todo y de nada 192
duties
  relation to rights 25–6, 32–3, 44–5, 47, 49, 189
Dwesa-Cwebe 9, 15, 20–1, 23, 25–42
Dwesa-Cwebe Land Trust 29, 34, 37–9, 41
Dye
  Arthur 31

Eastern Cape 25–6, 28, 31–3, 38–9, 42, 143, 173–5, 182–3
Eastern Cape Nature Conservation 25–6, 28, 31, 42
Eastern Cape Province 25, 182

Eastern Cape Regional Land Claims
    Commission 173, 175, 182
ECDC
    (Eastern Cape Development
        Corporation) 34
ECNC 28, 30–4, 38, 42
ecological
    adaptation 16
    identity 229
    niche 50
    -political system 30
    resources 69
economic
    opportunity 80
    policies 177
    problems 193
    restructuring 212–3
economy
    littoral 69
ecotourism 35
ECPB (Eastern Cape Parks Board) 38
Ecuador 203, 205, 228
education 12, 28, 77, 105, 123, 126, 147,
    174, 189, 250
effectiveness
    of access 50
    of participatory processes 250
    of property 44
    of rights 19, 35, 36, 39. *See* rights
    of titling 213. *See* title
egalitarianism 13, 147, 154–6, 199
ejidatarios 211–2, 217, 219–20, 223–7,
    229
ejido 10, 13, 210–1, 215–6, 219–27,
    229–30, 233
Elcho Island (Galiwin'ku) 100
elections
    democratic 164, 166
eligibility
    for land endowment 186
    for membership 72
    for restitution 15–17
elite 43, 53–4, 57–9, 63, 80, 155, 178, 216,
    220, 224
Elliotdale 27–8, 33
employment 28, 35–6, 64, 126, 149, 166,
    242, 252, 257
encapsulation. *See* colonization
endowment
    as against restitution 185–6
    land 31, 185–6, 190–1, 193–4, 204,
        209–10, 223

energy
    needs 75
    sources of 74
    wealth 86
entitlement 13, 50, 134–5, 142–4, 147–8,
    186, 195, 244
    narratives of 157
environment 7, 17, 59, 124, 140, 164, 179,
    210
    built 156
environmental
    conservation 16
    degradation 31, 164
    discourse 16, 29–32
    disputes 253
    impact 75, 240
    regulations 34
    status of claims 7
    sustainability 168
Environmental Impact
    Federal, Review Process 76
environmentally noble savage 16
environments
    institutional 181
equality 13, 83, 214, 248
eSikhawini 167, 171
ethnic
    awareness 70
    categorization 202–3. *See*
        categorization, by ethnicity
    credibility 77
    difference 1, 221
    entitlement 205
    exclusivity 68
    group 43, 46, 50, 58, 63, 228
    identification 69
    identities 44, 69, 83, 210, 223,
        229
    identity 70, 72–4, 82
    inter-, relationships 46
    land claims 210, 217, 224
    land distribution 204
    movements 210, 212
    organisations 81–2
    permanence 83
    purity 81
    sovereignty 2
    spaces 209, 223
    symbolism 72
ethnicity 2, 7–8, 61, 145, 159
    markers of 222
ethnicization 123

Index

ethno
  -ecological identities 222–3
  -ecological stereotypes 218
  -nationalist 148
  -political 69, 70, 73–4, 77
  -politics 72, 79, 81–2
ethos 2, 147, 152–4, 156–8
Euro-Australian 100, 103, 111–5, 117–8
Europe
  Eastern 7, 18, 43, 49, 61–2
European law
  power of the 107
eviction 6
evidence 108, 111–2
  about *rom* 104, 115
  in land claims 1, 6, 8–9, 15–6, 32, 75, 102, 106, 117, 119, 151, 185
  rules of 106–7
exchange 45–6, 51, 131, 133, 238
exclusion 15, 19, 28–9, 31, 40, 74, 76, 135, 142, 160, 169, 204, 250, 257
exclusionary aspects
  of restitution 1, 7
exclusivist
  strategies 12–3, 76–7, 79, 81–2, 135
expert knowledge
  contestation of 172, 181
expert witness 105
'experts' 176
exploitation 49, 60, 86, 171, 194, 198, 203–4
  commercial 30, 82
  forest 57, 59, 65
  labour 226
  of forest 47
  of natural resources 30, 43–4
expropriation 6, 18, 47, 133, 186, 188, 190–5, 204, 215, 226, 249
extinguishment
  future acts of. *See* title, extinguishment of

'facts'
  in law 106
faenas 189, 190, 227
family feuds 123, 130
farmers
  commercial 176, 193
  small 225
  white 172, 177
farming 163, 165, 168, 172–3, 176–7, 179–81, 220, 224–5 *See* subsistence, agriculture

  commercial 164–6, 176, 180–1
farms 13, 16, 18, 32
Federal Court
  of Australia 102
Federal government 246
federal moneys 71, 77
fee
  payment of 189
fence-cutting 39
feudal
  relationships 194
fines 51, 54, 64–5, 201
First Nations 85–93, 95–7
fish 36, 68, 86, 90–2, 117
fishery 68, 77
fishing 36, 73, 79, 86, 240, 242. *See* subsistence
  commercial 68, 240
  rights 240, 242
flag. *See* Union Jack
  Brazilian 13, 128
  national 13
FLLPA (Finger Lakes Land Protection Association) 241
Florida 238
foetal alcohol syndrome 81. *See* alcohol
food 51, 57, 91, 132, 171, 196, 199, 213
  supply of 171
  traditional Indian 91, 222
forced recruitment 199
forefathers 173, 192
forest
  access 39. *See* access
  commercial value of 30
  guards, 43, 45, 47, 51–3, 55–6, 64.
  loss 55
  privately owned 53
  products 25–6, 28, 38
  restituted 52–3, 58
  restitution of 43–50
  sale of 56
forests 27, 40
Forjando Patria 218, 230
formal rights 44. *See* rights
Foulke
  Walter 242, 248, 256
fragmentation 171, 175, 181
Frazer (Liberal-Country Party) Coalition 101
frontage
  lake and highway 93–5

frustration 79, 106, 143, 197
fundo legal 214

Gamio 218–9, 223, 230
gamonales 198
Gänganbuy
    claim area 111
Garcia, Alan 198
genealogy 8
General Direction of Land Reform and Rural settlement 195
gift 53, 91, 192
    of native food 90–1
'gift'
    of land 186, 191
giveaway 240
Glasnost 78
goals
    common 29, 195
goats 171
Goose Bay Airbase 70, 72, 78
Gove case 101–3, 107
Gove Peninsula 100
governance 1, 3, 11–2, 87, 116, 165–6, 190
government 3–4, 7, 11, 25–30, 33, 35, 37–9, 42, 45, 47, 50, 56, 59, 71, 76–82, 85–95, 101–2, 118, 124–5, 127, 130–3, 135, 139, 142–3, 147, 164, 167, 169, 175–7, 180, 188, 192–3, 198–9, 211–2, 215–7, 219–0, 223, 228, 238, 240, 242, 247–8, 250–2, 254
    Commonwealth 100, 118
    federal 7, 70, 75–8, 85–9, 91–2, 95, 97, 236, 238, 241–2, 245, 247–8, 252, 259
    federal and territorial 88, 90, 95
    leasing of land 92
    local 37–8, 43
    local officials of 46–9, 53–7, 63, 65
    negotiations 93
    negotiators 87–95
    Northern Territory and Commonwealth (Australia) 105
    of Brazil 123, 125
    of Canada 87
    of South Africa 174
    of US 86, 245
    or third party interests 93
    policy 92–3
    rights to land 91
    self- 42, 90

Whitlam Labor (Australia) 101
Yukon 89
grants 25–6, 29, 34, 59, 130–1, 138, 174, 215
graves 15, 167, 173
grazing 16, 25–8, 34, 38, 51, 53–4, 92, 97, 166, 169, 171, 176, 178, 183, 189, 201
Greenhaven 158
Greenland 68, 77
grievances 4, 38–9, 164, 167, 188, 215, 239
Guatemala 203, 212, 232
Guguletu 150, 158
Gumatj clan 100

hacendados 186–8, 192
haciendas 165, 186–95, 200, 214–6, 220, 227, 232
Handelman 188, 205
Hanover Park 150, 158
harbour
    deep sea 166–7
harvest 127, 132
Haven Hotel 25, 27, 33–5
headman 42, 167, 174–5
headmen 33, 37
healing 157
hearings
    public 240–1, 250–2, 257
Hector Land Use Area 238, 245
Henkel
    Caesar C. 30, 40
herding 171, 187
heritage
    French–Indian 74
    national 31
heroes
    national 191
Heroínas Toledo 191, 199
heterogeneity 73, 122, 143, 145, 175, 179
hierarchy 105, 187, 202
High Court 101, 104, 116–7
highland villages 187
highlands 187–8, 198, 203–7
    Peruvian 190
historical
    and geographical circumstance 68
histories 1, 4, 18, 20, 72–3, 83, 178, 217
history 5, 7, 15, 27–8, 43, 50, 125, 130, 136, 147, 164, 179, 205, 210, 217, 229, 245

consciousness of 123
culture 193
experience of 70
memorialization of 143
of dispossession 173
of marginalization 227
of native white relations 85
of restitution 212
of Romanian jurisprudence 19
of segregation 149
social 146
HLUA. *See* Hector Land Use Area
home 6, 9, 22, 54, 97, 125–8, 150–2, 155, 166, 228
homeland
  'Coloured' 148
homelands 27, 29, 36–7, 42, 76–7, 82, 84, 111, 118, 143, 148, 173–7, 183
hope 8, 19, 25, 33, 81, 120, 150–6, 172, 188, 216, 254
horse carts 54
horses 53, 55, 92
housing
  provision of 28, 42, 49–54, 59, 64–5, 81, 131, 143, 155, 157, 159, 162, 166, 169, 170–1, 177–8, 226, 232
huacchis 195, 200–1
huaccho 195
Huanca 187
human rights 205. *See* rights
  discourse 4, 205
  law 76
humanity
  reinstatement of 151
humour 91
Hungary 17, 61
hunters 77
hunting 71, 73, 77–9, 86, 92, 242
'hurt'
  in negotiation 243
hybrid
  Canadians 17
  culture 69
  discourses 26
  group 81
  legal document. *See* witness statement
hybridity 143–5
hydroelectric 68, 71, 75, 86, 126

identification
  associational, flexible 141, 145
  self- 123–37, 131, 149

identities 1, 12, 63, 119, 123–5, 136–7, 171, 179–81, 212–3, 221, 223, 229
identity 1, 4, 13, 17, 22–3, 36, 67–9, 74, 82, 116–7, 123–7, 130, 132, 136, 142, 145–6, 148–9, 156, 168, 175, 178, 182, 193, 203, 206, 212, 218, 223, 229
  contingent and fluid character of 124
  indigenous 16, 127, 190, 214
  lack of 202–3
  national 193
  politics 67
  social 44–5
  social and economic 50
ideology 63, 138, 145, 178, 193, 218
illness 149, 151
imposition 103, 107, 139–40, 148, 175–6, 180, 190, 197, 204
Inca 191
inclusivity 14, 29
incommensurability 99, 108–10, 114, 116
independence 4, 13, 17, 42, 50, 73, 80, 162, 167, 185, 187–8, 204, 212, 220–1
  Peruvian 186–7
Indian
  Act 3, 70–1, 77
  nations 14, 245, 247–8
  reservations 7, 238, 243–9
  'return of the' 203
  Statute (1973) 127
  Trade and Intercourse Act (ITIA) (Canada) 236
Indian Ocean 27, 166
Indianness 84, 91, 127, 185, 203
  removal of 185–205
Indians 10, 14, 75, 83, 92–7, 123–8, 139, 186–7, 190–1, 193, 202–4, 223, 235–6, 238, 240, 245–8, 252, 254–8
  conversion of into peasants 193, 202–3, 212, 215, 218, 221
  Coeur d'Alene 10
  'the problem of the' 187–8
  'Indians'
    official race category (SA) 143
indigeneity 4, 7, 12, 16, 36, 69, 83, 203, 210, 213
indigenous 69, 71
  community 189
    change into 'peasant community' 185–6, 193–205
  difference to aboriginal 69

indigenous – *Contd.*
    organisation as 224
    people 83, 99, 139, 193, 205, 209–19,
        221, 223, 225, 228–30, 233, 236
    political institutions 227
    republics 214, 218–19, 230
    responses 209, 229
    'return of' 203
    population 193, 212, 214, 223–4
individual
    farming 189
    landholding 132
individualism 17, 81, 132, 147, 157,
        229
industrial
    development 86
    enclaves 86
'influence'
    in negotiation 250–3
initiation ceremonies 113
injustice 1–4, 19, 43, 150, 173, 204,
        238
Inkatha 167
'Innu 68–9, 72, 76–81
    Minister of Foreign Affairs' 79
institution
    continuity of structure of 195
    organized and disciplined 189
interests. *See* rights, state
    native 92–3
    non-state 165
    preexisting 92
    third party 92–3
interfaces 163–4, 174, 178–82
interim period
    in restitution 3, 6, 50
intermediaries 212
International Convention on the
        Protection of Biodiversity 31
International Union for the Conservation
        of Nature (IUCN) 32
intertidal zone 101, 116–7
Inuit 68–9, 72, 76–7, 81–4
investment 35, 86, 214, 226, 246
IPS (Integrated Planning Services) 169,
        172
Iroquois Confederacy 235–6
irrigation
    projects 125, 132
ITC 72, 76–8
Iturbide
    Agustín de 214

izlaz 51. See land, communal

James Bay 75–6, 84
    Agreement 76
James Bay Cree 75
Jesus Christ 50
joke 90–1
judge
    the 104–7, 111–2, 121–2, 256
Junín 188, 191, 201, 206–7
justice 1, 8, 11, 17, 135, 146, 150–1, 159,
        167, 185, 189, 194, 203, 244–5,
        250
    informal 167
    restorative 149, 159, 194
    social 18, 101, 156
    as incompatible with practicality 8
    restorative 149
Justice
    Department of (US) 238

KFN 14, 85, 87–97
killing 43, 52, 100, 197, 199, 200, 202
Kinne
    Wisner 241–2, 247–8, 257–8
kinship 45, 72, 109, 113, 120, 122, 135, 174
Kluane
    First Nation 8, 14, 85. *See* KFN
    Game Sanctuary 90
    Lake 92–3
Kruger National Park 35
KwaZulu-Natal Provincial Department of
        Agriculture 169

labour
    for landowners 189
labourers *see* landless, day labourers
    farm 177
Labrador Inuit Development Corporation
        (LIDC) 77
Labrador Metis 14, 68–9, 73–4, 79–80,
        82–3, 145
Labrador Settlers 69
Lahn
    Julie 102
Lake Mzingazi 167, 169
land
    allocation of 51, 189
    acquisition of 244–5
    alienable 216
    as nature park 245–7
    cession 85, 87

land – *Contd.*
  claim agreement 29, 85–6
  communal 13, 186, 188, 204, 209–10, 219
  corporate ownership of 216
  crown 88–9
  distribution of 198–9
    inequalities of 185
  entitlement to 9, 13, 246
  invasion of 16, 125, 185–8, 190, 194–5, 197, 201
  material significance of 1, 3, 5
  multiple meanings of 129–32, 163
  occupation of 26, 29
  payment for 192, 204
  privatization of 209
  purchase of 241. *See* purchase
  'quantum' 88–9, 96
  re-articulation of 164, 179
  redistribution of 204, 216–17.
    See redistribution
  restoration of 201, 210, 238
  rightful possession of 195, 197
  rights 8, 19–21, 26, 28, 39, 71, 74, 87, 92, 101–2, 107, 116, 163–5, 172, 178–80, 186, 203, 205, 210, 228.
    See rights
  sale of 34, 130, 210, 226
  'selections' 88, 91–4, 96–7
  settlement of, by incomers 27, 125, 215, 227–8
  stolen 185
  symbolic/spiritual aspects of 1, 5, 213, 223, 229
  'to the tiller' 202
  unequal distribution of 188, 214
  use 1, 13, 16, 25–6, 33, 67, 70, 75, 76–9, 92, 131–2, 164–6, 177, 180–1, 232, 246, 259
    change of 54
    continuity of 132
  'vacant' (*tierras baldías*) 216
  violent expulsion from 125
land claims 6–10, 14–8, 23, 25–9, 31, 33, 35–9, 41–2, 67, 69, 70–1, 74–80, 82, 85–9, 91, 94–7, 120, 144, 168, 175, 178–9, 180, 182, 193, 200, 210, 222, 235–6, 238–41, 244–5, 252–4, 256–9
  extinguishment of 238
  federal 77
  federal, office 75
  opposition to 235–54
  process 146
Land Claims
  Commission 15, 32–3, 39, 42, 143, 146, 165, 172–6, 182–3
  Commissioner, Regional 31, 42
  Court 32
Land Commissioner 8, 101–2
land reform 4, 16, 21, 28–9, 42, 45, 47, 58, 130–1, 140, 161, 174–5, 179, 181, 185, 188, 190–3, 204, 215, 219, 225
  demand for 188
  Mexican 186
  Peruvian 186, 190, 204–5
land restitution *See* restitution
landholding
  'Africanisation' of 176
landless 51, 125, 188, 209–11, 215–6, 227, 232, 235
  day labourers 51, 123
  peasants 210, 216
  people 51, 125, 131, 188, 209
landlessness 50, 188, 209, 215
landowners 127
  large 188, 191, 210, 216, 225
lands
  clan 101, 103
  communal 186, 214, 220, 225, 232
  Crown 101
  public 240–1, 245
landscape 16, 46, 59, 69–70, 86, 103, 166–8, 171–2, 259
Langa 158
language 8, 82, 212, 221
  of development. *See* development, language of
  of indigeneity 203
  of kinship 45
  of ownership 49
  of production 165. *See* production, language of
  of property 14–5, 87, 147
  of rights 159, 164, 205
  translation of 109
  Yolngu 100, 108, 115
latifundistas 188, 214
Latin America 4, 23, 205–6, 209–10, 212, 229, 231–2
Lavender Hill 150
la venganza de la Empresa 227

274 Index

law 18–19, 44–5, 51, 106, 187. *See* courts, European law, evidence, 'facts', human rights, state, white
  aboriginal 9
  and order 13
  and society 2
  Australian 101, 111, 114, 117–8, 122
  Brazilian land 134
  customary 110, 116–17, 178
  disputed meaning of 115
  enactment of 104
  Euro-Australian 114
  European 104, 107, 117–8
  incommensurable concepts of 115–16, 118
  incommensurable conceptualizations of 5
  international 75, 236, 254
  national 187
  native title 99, 107, 116
  overlooking of 47
  untried 133
  Yolngu 100, 107, 113–4
Law
  18 of 1991 (Romania) 47
  26/1996 (Romania) 47
  Lerdo 214, 216
laws 46–9, 99, 102, 104, 106, 110, 114, 117, 146, 187–8, 190, 215, 218, 228, 232, 240, 243
  new 123–4
'laws and customs' 99, 104, 106, 110, 117–8
lawsuits 86, 189, 194, 197, 201, 239, 251
lawyers 23, 108–11, 117, 128–9, 135, 139
leadership 29, 37, 39, 80, 146, 167, 173–4, 179, 214
lease
  of lands 18, 25, 33–7, 92, 97, 101, 103
Lee
  Congressman Gary 241–2, 249–50, 258
legal
  categories 137
  connotation, of 'indigenous' 204
  entity 175
  force 104
  form
    hybrid 179
  mechanisms 85, 187
  pluralism 228
  process 14, 23, 143, 146, 165
  struggles 186
  theory 85, 89, 91
Legal Resources Centre 32
legend 50
legislation 27, 100–2, 164, 168, 182, 188, 215–6, 225, 228, 238–9
  Congressional (Canada) 238
  environmental 228
legitimacy 1, 15, 78, 103, 110, 250
LIA 72–81, 84
liability 3, 10–11, 57
liberalism
  nineteenth-century 209, 212, 214
liberation theology 126, 128, 135, 233
Lima 198, 205–6
litigation 8, 102, 238–9, 251–2
Little Arm 92
livelihoods 1–2, 4, 19, 27, 33, 35, 41, 127, 149, 167, 171, 176, 180–3, 220
  sustainable 165, 173, 176, 178
livestock 166, 169, 177, 199
LMA 73–4, 79–80, 82
lobola 173
loss 1, 3–4, 6–10, 14–5, 19–20, 70–1, 80, 103, 141–2, 146, 148–9, 150, 159, 164, 227, 242, 246, 252
low water mark. *See* intertidal zone
low-income 142–3

Mabo 101, 104
Mackenzie Valley 73, 75–6, 83
  Pipeline 76
maize 15, 51, 169, 211–2
Makhoba 164, 172–82
Makhoba Community Trust 168, 172, 174, 177, 179
Makuleke
  land claim 22–3, 35, 41
  management 28–5, 37–40, 47, 60, 71, 82, 165, 169, 176, 179, 180, 195, 198, 204
  resource 220
  rights. *See* rights
Mandlazini 164, 166–9, 171–2, 180–2
Mandlazini Community Trust (MCT) 168
Manenberg 150
Mantaro 187–8, 205
  Valley 187
Mantziaris and Martin 104, 110

Maoists 199. *See* movements
Maori 16, 19
mapa y plano definitivo 216
marginality 70, 160
marginalization 14, 50, 67, 128, 202, 205, 214, 219–20, 227
Mariátegui 193, 206
Marine Protected Area
  Dwesa-Cwebe 36
Maripaulo 124
Mariscal Castilla 191, 199
market 2, 4, 6, 10–1, 19, 44, 47, 49, 51, 56–7, 81, 86, 101, 118, 213
  -based enterprise 17
  constraints 36
  forces 10–11, 214
  free 209, 225
  global 224–6
  labour 148
  -oriented production 213
  property 151
  real estate 252
  relations 12
  transactions 7
  value 59
Mawalan 103
Mayer
  Philip and Iona 27
Mbashe River 27
Mbeki
  President Thabo 172
MDC 167–9, 171
meaning. *See* land, multiple meanings of
  co-production of 180
  social 91
media 79, 81
medicinal plants 27, 38
member
  peasant communities 198
membership 16, 26–7, 72–4, 80, 82, 113, 131, 134–5, 194, 216
memories 1, 20, 141–2, 149–51, 154, 160, 168, 216
memory 4, 6, 9, 19–20, 151, 153, 157, 202, 217
Meriam 101
mestizo/s 187, 191, 202, 205, 214, 217–8, 220–3, 227, 232–3
Methodist missions 100
Metis 67–83
Metisness 74
Metroplan 169, 182

Mexico 4, 8, 10, 21, 118, 203, 206, 209–230
Mi'kmaq 72
migrants
  labour 27, 209
migration 28, 73, 219, 226
Milingimbi 100
militarization 67, 76–80
military 7, 17, 68, 70, 78–80, 124, 127, 139, 190, 193, 199–200, 202, 232
mine 86, 103, 121
mineral
  rights 34
  wealth 86
mines 28, 86, 174
minifundismo 220
mining 67, 68, 70–1, 97, 100, 103, 139, 187
miscegenation 68–9, 82, 218
misunderstanding
  wilful, in court 107
Mito 188–9
Mocambo 124–5, 127–40
moderation 80
modern
  and traditional lifestyles, blend of 171
modernity 1, 139, 159, 163–4, 171–2, 179, 181–2
  alternative 125, 133
modernization 70, 139, 164, 191, 193, 216
Camacho
  Moises 197, 202
Mokami Project Group (MPG) 80
moral
  claim 78
  equivalence 18
  grounds 32, 74
  weight 4, 17
Morelos 214, 232
Moscow 47
moşneni 47
mosques 156
movements
  civil rights 70
  communist. *See* communist
  land-seizure 190
  Maoist 198, 204
  outstation 103
  peasant 125
  resource rights 213
  social 7, 126, 188
Mposa Hill 166, 167

Mthiyane 166–8, 181
  Inkosi 167, 168
Mulkay and Gilbert 91
multiculturalism 4, 138, 146, 205, 209–12, 228–30
municipios 211, 213, 221, 226
muskeg 93
Muslims 142, 146, 148, 150, 152, 154, 158, 160–2
Myers
  Fred 8–9, 15, 21, 23

NAFTA 224–5
Nahuas 209, 211–32
Nahuatl 211, 217
Nain 72, 77, 83–4
Nancy Williams 103, 107, 112
NANL 72
nation
  -building 1, 209, 214, 217, 230
  'no, within a nation' 235, 247
national
  interest 7, 17
National Department of the Forest (NDF) 47
national heritage 29
nationalisation 47, 50, 58
nationalism 209–10, 212–13, 218, 229
nationalist
  agenda 204
  discourses 26, 217
  ideologies 217
  logic 204
nationality 218, 248
nationhood 2, 13
native 3, 5, 12, 16–17, 20–1, 67, 69, 70–5, 78–81, 83, 85, 91, 99, 101–7, 109–11, 113, 116–9, 121–2, 178, 205, 210, 259
  activist 3
  discourses 12
  organizations 16, 67, 72, 74–5, 78–81, 83
  peoples 3, 74, 85, 210
  'return of the' 12, 203
  status 12, 16
Native
  Agreements 77
  Alaska, Claims Settlement Act (1971) 86
  American movement 127
  Association of Newfoundland and Labrador 72

National, Title Tribunal 102
  South African, Trust 177
  Title Act 1993 100–1
nativeness 74
Natuashish 81, 84
natural resources 29, 34, 40–1, 43–4, 49–50, 59–60
negotiation 8, 18, 33, 39, 55, 77–80, 82, 84–9, 91, 96–7, 124, 164, 167–8, 174–5, 179, 228, 235–6, 238–9, 241, 249, 251
negotiations 7–8, 11, 14, 28–9, 33, 35, 38, 75–7, 79, 81, 84–96, 167–8, 172, 235, 238–40, 245, 249–50, 252–4
negotiators 8, 85, 87–9, 91–5, 97, 250, 252–3
neoliberal
  Commonwealth government 118
  master narrative 179
neoliberalism 18, 224
networks 32, 45, 129, 179
New Makhoba Location 173
New York State 7, 9–10, 14, 16, 235–54
New Zealand 16, 18–19
Newfoundland 68, 70–3, 77, 80, 84
Newfoundland–Canada Agreements 72
ngapaki 103–4, 116
NGOs 1–2, 8, 15, 28, 37, 42, 124, 161, 212
Nhulunbuy 103, 113
NIMBY 235, 243
Nisga'a 75–6
Nitassinan 77, 82, 84
NMIA 72, 77–8, 80
'non-evidence' 111
non-racial 158
non-state
  interests 165
North Atlantic Treaty Organization (NATO) 70
Northern Pipeline Act (NPA) 89
nostalgia 1, 6, 149, 151–2, 159
'notations' 92
NTA 100–2, 104, 109, 121
Ntambanana 166–8
Nunatsiavut Government 72, 81
Nunavut 76

obligations 13–14, 25–6, 33–4, 38, 44, 49–50, 96, 227. *See* duties
occupancy 36, 69, 75–8

occupation 6, 15, 26–7, 29, 50, 56, 69, 75, 99, 116, 148, 186, 245
oil fields 86
Olney
  Mr Justice 116
Operating Company 177
opposition 9–10, 14, 28, 80–2, 126, 133–4, 142, 181, 202, 227, 235–6, 240, 248, 250–1, 253–4
oppression 193
Oroya 187, 194
Our Footprints are Everywhere 76, 83
overgrazing 168
overlapping
  claims 67
  identities 69
owners
  property 91, 157, 235, 239–40, 242–45, 247–8
ownership 1, 3–5, 9–10, 13–15, 25–6, 29, 33–7, 42, 44, 46–7, 49–51, 53–4, 64, 67, 85–86, 107, 129–31, 133–4, 147, 162, 165, 171, 177–8, 181, 186, 192, 195, 198, 200, 204, 239, 246–7
  certainty of 86
  full 226
  Lockean concept of property 1, 14–15, 246
  private 43, 50, 189
  proof of 186
  property 11, 246

Pachacayo 195
Pachacutec 191, 201
padurari 47
Paerregaard 189, 198, 202–3, 206–7
Palestinians 241, 256
Palmares Cultural Foundation 129, 134
Panama 228
pan-Canadian
  Indian movement 78
Pan-Canadianness 69
Parliamentary Inquiry 101
participation 87, 103, 164, 195, 250
  as basis for land allocation 189
  community 180
  democratic 37
  in land claims 12, 14
  in market-oriented production. *See* market-oriented production
  in struggle 25–6
  past 29

political 38
  public 250
partnerships 175–6
past focus vs. forward looking approach 163–81, 186. *See* tension
pastoral leases 101
paternalism 3, 8, 10, 37, 89, 148, 195, 214
patronage 43–5, 51, 53, 56–7, 62, 65, 220
  political 133
Paulo Afonso 126
pe picioare 55
peasant
  confederations 198
Peasant Leagues 125
peasantry 127
  Andean 204
  campesinado 212
  highland 188
peasants 4, 6, 64, 124, 140, 165, 190, 193, 195, 198–206, 210–13, 216–18, 221, 223, 229
pensions 131–2, 174
performance, of *rom* 110–1
'permission'
  in translation 109
permits 47, 88
Pernambuco 125
persuasion 107, 122, 145
  politics of 112
Peru 8–9, 23, 165, 185, 187, 193, 198, 202–7, 212, 218, 222, 228
  highlands of 185
  Mayende
  Peter 31, 42
petition 77, 100–1
petitions 187–8, 197, 215
Pienaar
  Gerry 32
pilot case 176
Pimentel
  Francisco de 214
pipeline 83, 86, 92
Pitesti 46, 65
place 6, 15, 29, 32, 74, 107, 111, 124, 135, 149–50, 152, 155–6, 158, 167, 214, 227
  marginal 181
planning 4, 18, 22, 35, 37, 92, 143, 155, 164–6, 168–9, 176, 179–81, 183

278 Index

plot size
  historical 177
plots
  pegging of 169
  re-allocation of 189
  sub-division of 170
police 43, 46, 48, 51–2, 54–7, 64, 100, 156, 199, 200–1, 239
political
  /racial category 136. *See* categorization, race
  act of reconciliation 163
  activist 217
  activity 80
  agency 5, 139
  agents 145
  aims 69
  allies 77
  analysis 203
  and ideological implications of land 186
  arena, contested 230
  aspiration 160
  autonomy 13
  background of land invasions 190
  changes 43
  conditions of restitution 6
  conservative, groups 190
  demand for land 7
  destruction of tribe 10
  function of land 181
  indigenous institutions 227
  inequalities 85, 95
  influence 71, 259
  institutions 87
  integrity 81
  jurisdiction 187
  life, opening up of 124
  macro-, ideological clashes 136
  micro-, conflicts 136
  mobilization 145, 154, 188
  movements 203
  objectives 176
  organization 70
  party
    membership of 56
  platform 69, 76
  position 44
  power 45, 77, 168, 201
  power relations 114
  practice 142
  pressures 251
  process 136, 141, 143
  programmes 203
  significance 56, 147
  situation 103
  skills 196
  sovereignty 104
  space 75, 167
  status of claims 7
  strategies 16, 67, 78
  structure 78
  struggle 167
  support, electoral 133
  system 44
  transformation 19
  unrest 200
population
  Andean 202
  beneficiary 176–7
  civil 190
  claimant 167
  'Coloured' 148
  concentration of 214
  density 216, 220
  displacement 252
  growth 219
  Indian 186–7, 203
  mestizo 187
  Mexican 212
  Peruvian 202
  protection of 200
  rural 164, 198, 203, 213, 215
populations
  subordinate 204
Porfiriato 215–6, 232
possession
  immemorial 194
post-apartheid 7, 163, 174, 181
'post-restitution' 10
post-revolutionary
  nationalism 212
  reconstruction 209
post-socialism 3, 44, 61, 63
post-socialist 46
  countries 45
  Romania 22, 41, 43–4, 59
  state 43, 46–7, 58, 63
  villages 45
post-transfer 9–10
poverty 19, 41, 51, 53–4, 81, 124–5, 140, 163, 180, 222, 248
power 3–4, 8, 22, 37, 44–5, 48, 50, 56, 59–60, 71, 84, 87, 91, 100–3, 107,

110, 112, 114–5, 118, 124, 128,
    134–5, 140–1, 159, 174–5, 180–1,
    187, 196, 204, 206, 243, 248, 253
  differential 91
  disparity 87
  inequalities of 89
  lack of 150, 187
  relations 103, 110, 114, 135
power relations 141
  unequal 8, 87, 110
Powley case 82
Poxtla
  Ejido 220
pragmatism 11, 147, 152, 175, 194
prejudice 142, 149, 158, 249
PROCEDE 209–10, 224–32
Procuraduría Agraria 224–6, 232
production 1, 6, 10, 13, 16, 19, 35, 64–5,
    106, 159, 163–5, 171, 176–7, 179,
    181, 193–5, 205, 209, 212–3, 219,
    227, 239
  collective 132
  crop 131, 166
  language of 163, 165
  market-oriented 213, 227
  means of 54, 223
  regimes 165
productivity 16, 164, 168, 176, 179–80,
    187, 209
products
  caribou 81
  cheap 196
  forest 47
  sale of 51
professionals 196
Programme of Certification of Individual
    Rights to Farm Plots, Common
    Land and Urban Lots. *See*
    PROCEDE
'progress' 179–181
Project Steering Committee 176
proof
  of connection to area 102
propaganda 199
property
  anthropology of 2
  definition of 33, 44–5
  differentiated ideas of 15
  division of 198
  'fuzzy' 13
  institutionalization of 14–15
  landed 3

  language of 14–15
  materiality of 11, 15
  neo-liberal notions of 2
  private 12, 43–4, 49, 60, 91, 96, 188,
      240, 245, 258
  regimes 5, 47, 194
  relations 3, 5, 21, 47, 101, 157
  rights 6, 10, 35, 43–4, 47, 49, 57–9,
      91, 95–7, 102, 147, 157, 182, 189,
      218
  sale of 243
protest 3, 14, 28–9, 32, 39, 79, 190, 242
protests 14, 26, 39, 79, 95, 124, 212
Provision of Certain Land for Settlement
    Act 168
public 47, 65, 105, 117, 121, 188, 235–6,
    239–41, 243–6, 250–6
  anger 242–3, 252
  attention 79
  hearings 241
  image 74
  input 242
  land 216, 238, 242, 245, 256
  opposition 235–36, 253–4
  projects 252
  servants 56
  support 73, 78
Purcell
  Frank 107
purchase
  of cattle feed 169
  of land 12, 18, 49–50, 128, 169, 190,
      238, 240–1, 244, 246. *See* land,
      purchase
  of wood 55–6

Quebec
  Superior Court 75
Quechua 187
questions
  in court 106
quilombo 124, 129–6, 139
  remanescente de 129
Quilombo Clause 13, 124, 129, 132,
    139
quilombolas 124–5, 127, 133, 137,
    140

race 8, 141, 145, 158
  and class 149
  cosmic 218
  divide 214

race – *Contd.*
  essentialist discourses on 159
  integration 247–8
  mixed- 17, 123–4, 127
  prejudice 144
  segregation 247
rachiu 51
racial
  exclusion 143
    residual 142
  /ethnic identities, refashioning of 123–37
  inequality 248
racially differentiated experience of restitution 147–9
racialization
  of society 18, 187
racism 30, 193, 204, 247–8
  charges of 249
  fight against 202, 214
  refutation of 248
Radcliffe-Brown, A.R. 9
Rainbow Nation 172
Rámon Castilla 191
rangga 107
răritură 47
rebellion
  agrarian 215
  indigenous 215
  rural 188
rebels 199
reciprocity 45, 91, 190
recognition 4, 9, 12, 20, 22, 29, 32–3, 71, 73, 75–6, 80–4, 101, 103, 116–7, 119, 122–4, 126–9, 131–4, 136, 139, 144, 152–3, 155, 186–9, 191, 203–5, 207, 217, 223, 229, 238
reconciliation 165, 167, 172, 174, 180
  of old and new 152–4
  repudiation of 155–7
'red agents' 190
'red bishop' 126
redevelopment 143, 156, 158
redistribution
  of land 4, 44, 163–5, 185–6, 201, 204, 210, 215–17, 227–30. *See* land, redistribution
redress 1–4, 19, 141, 156–7, 163–5, 186, 244–5
reform
  constitutional 228–9

Reforma
  La 214
regeneration
  of 'community' ethos 153
regime
  changes 7
  communist 47, 51. *See* communist labour 177, 180
  land rights 101
regulations 177–8, 247
relational
  notion of place 30, 44. *See* place
religion 119, 161, 167, 172
removals
  apartheid 30, 143, 147–50, 155, 157, 159
  forced 27, 142, 150–1, 166
rent
  high 144
  payment of 177
rental income 25–6
renting
  of land 50, 170, 210, 216, 224
  of land, prohibition of 216
representation
  democratic 175
  lack of 249
  legal 240
  political 59, 165, 174, 228
representations
  of communities 175, 178
  of society 175
representatives 16, 31–2, 93, 147, 196–97, 258
reservations 6, 14, 235, 239–240, 244, 247–8, 253. *See* Indian reservations
  Cayuga 236, 243
resettlement
  as policy 146, 175–7
  choice of 148–9, 151, 154, 169
  concentrated 180
  narrative 164, 172
  of land 165, 179
  of people 10, 141, 144, 147, 163, 167, 169, 173–4, 179
  opposition to 10
  paradigm 173
  plans 127
resistance 4, 21, 77, 79, 83, 116, 173, 206, 228–9, 239, 249
resources 31, 36–8, 42, 45, 47, 57, 64, 67, 69–70, 73, 76, 87, 122, 133, 137,

139, 169, 174, 187, 192, 209, 219, 225
  genetic 31
  marine 31
  natural. *See* natural resources
respectability 189
responsibility 17, 77, 165, 227, 247, 248
  for development 13, 34
  of citizens 212
  of government 188
  professional 32
'responsibility'
  in negotiation 244, 253
restitution
  and reconciliation
    grand narrative of 180
  as bifurcated intervention strategy 166–181
  antithesis of 85–6
  circumscribing of 5, 7, 12, 17, 32, 38–9
  conditions of 6, 26, 35
  emergent properties of 178–80
  end of 10, 209–10, 224
  exclusionary aspects of 1–2, 8, 18
  laws 47
  of land 11, 47, 85, 100, 141, 175, 202, 215
  policies 3–4, 6
  process 141, 163, 171, 215
  programmes 10, 143
  reframing 85, 95
  stages of 6–11, 141, 165, 178
  temporal and spatial aspects 6, 100, 145, 146, 157
Restitution Act (1994) 27, 167
Restitution Commissioner 174
restitutive approach
  change from, to a distributive approach 185
restoration 1, 6, 11, 146, 174, 194
  of land 3, 39, 143, 167, 173, 215, 236
  of traditional leadership 173
'return' 124, 142, 144, 148–50, 152–3, 155, 159
revenge 199
revenues 30, 76, 252
revival
  cultural 156
revolution
  Cuban 125
  Mexican 215
revolutionaries 199

revolutionary
  caciques 215
  nation-state 217
  post-, land reform 217, 224
  post-, reform 225
  struggle 212
  war 218, 245
revolutionary war 245
rhetoric 92, 176, 193, 229
Rhode Island
  land claim 241
Rhylands 158
rice 124, 127
Richards Bay 166–9, 182–3
Richards Bay Transitional Local Council (RBTLC) 167
Riel
  Louis 69
right
  exclusive 117
  in land 151
  preexisting 92
  to fish 117
rightful
  possession 186, 192, 194
rightful owners 85, 195, 197
rights 90, 104
  aboriginal 71, 75, 86, 96
  African 164
  agrarian 224
  ancestral 185, 193, 204
  and interests 102, 110
  and privileges 70
  and responsibilities 13, 34, 229
  arable 33–4
  bundle of 33–4, 38, 45, 102
  'ceding' 7
  certification of 224
  citizenship 82, 128. *See* citizenship
  claiming of 39, 74, 141, 157, 209
  claims, compatibility with communitarian rememberings 159
  collective 210, 212, 230
  cultural 228
  discourse about 104
  distinct from abilities 45
  equal 227
  exclusive 118
  grazing 201
  human 75
  inalienable 216
  indigenous 4, 10, 16, 202, 205, 228, 230

rights – *Contd.*
 individual 159
 land 22, 34, 74, 81, 92, 100–1, 165, 200, 210
  transfer of 10, 25–7, 32–3, 35, 37, 50, 96, 139, 165, 176, 195, 197, 200–1, 216, 235
 land and other 91
 legal 38, 92
 minority 148
 native 74
 of way 92, 242, 252
 property. *See* property rights
 property, claiming of 201
 relation to access 45
 restriction of 32
 settlement of 141
 special 13–4, 210, 212, 219, 247
 -talk as cloak for racism 248
 third party 91
 to forests 43
 to grazing 92
 to Labrador 77
 to leadership 179
 to resources 82
 to self-determination 76
 to speak 106
 transfer of 39
 unequal 147
 use 200, 216, 220, 232
 usufructary 195, 210
 water 34, 186
'rights' 103, 110, 118
Rirratjingu clan 103
risk 35, 79, 116, 197, 254
 in negotiation 243, 254
 minimizing of 253
 of childrens' inheritance 131
 relation to benefit 133, 252
rituals 105, 136, 171, 203. *See* ceremonies
rom 99, 104, 107, 110–12, 114–18, 122.
  See performance
Roma 46, 62–3
Romania 13, 18, 26, 43, 47, 51, 60, 63, 96
romanticism 172
Romulus 239, 249, 256
Roosevelt
 Theodore 125
rondas campesinas 200, 205
Rosebank 151
Rudari 45–7, 50–60, 63–5

rules 4, 26, 36, 47, 87, 102, 105–6, 121, 177–8, 189–90, 197, 220, 242–43, 247
rural poor
 the 124–5, 133, 215, 219–20

sacred
 objects 107
 past 204
 power 110
 sites 95, 167, 228
SAIS 185, 190–2, 198, 200, 204, 206–7
samba de coco 127, 136
'same car, different driver' 165, 176
Sampson State Park 238, 240–1, 243, 245–6, 252
San José de Quero 188
San Juan de Ondores 201, 207
Santa Claus 89–91
São Francisco River 125, 127, 139–40
Sarhili
 Chief 28
scientific
 discourses 26
 knowledge 30
 research 30
sea country
 rights to 103, 116–17, 121–2
self
 broken 149–52, 159
 -determination 19, 39, 82, 219
 rights to. *See* rights
Selway
 Mr Justice 104, 116–18
sendero luminoso 198–9, 200–1, 204.
  See Shining Path
Sergipe 123–6, 139–40
services
 access to 137
 demand for 79
 flow of 45
 municipal 177
 native 71
 promise of 133
 provision of 54, 70, 77, 87, 132, 147, 167, 169, 195, 238, 252
 social, responsibility for 13
 support 166
settlement 33–4, 37, 51, 64, 75, 77, 97, 111, 131, 139, 147–8, 156, 162–3, 165–6, 168–71, 175–6, 179, 181–3
 alternatives 240

settlement – *Contd.*
  'celebration' 172, 176
  concentrated 131, 177
  costs of 252
  funds 34
  in land negotiations 76–78
  'land acquisition grant'. *See* SLAG
  land claims 25, 33–4, 37, 75, 172, 174–5
    opposition to 235–6, 238–43,
      246–54, 256–7
  monetary 143
  negotiated 179, 235, 238–9, 253–4
  Norse 68
  on communal grazing lands 51
  orderly 168
  out-of-court 238
  'post-', phase of restitution 163, 165
  pre-colonial 210
  process 170
  proponents of 248, 251
  residential 177
  Rudari 55, 64
Settlement
  Land (Yukon) 93
settlements 103, 111, 124, 170
  land restitution 163
settler
  Australian parlance 100
  citizens 7
  -native, origins 17
  occupation 99
  society 99
settlers 16, 69, 85
  Spanish 186
Settlers 69
  Labrador 20, 73
sharecroppers 124–5, 127–8, 131–2
shared imaginary 178, 180
shepherds 195, 198
Shining Path 4, 185, 198, 203
Shipton
  Parker 1, 23
Siegfried
  Roy 30
Sierra Madre 211
singing and dancing 172
'situational analysis' 176
slave/s
  black 137
  category 133
  community 129
  fugitive, descendants 13, 16, 123–4

slavery
  abolition of 124
  end of 214
smallholders 46–7
Smallwood
  Joey 70, 71
social
  differences
    denial of 141
  exclusion
    class-based 141
  justice 18, 101, 156
  malaise 81
  mobility 144, 147, 152, 156–7, 159, 174
  order 3, 155, 198
  turmoil 3
solicitud 216
solidarity 28, 135, 154
Sonderwater 172, 176
song. *See* singing and dancing
  of property owners 235
  popular, Kluane 92
South Seneca County 235, 243, 250, 253
sovereignty 2, 4, 13, 69, 75, 77, 99, 102–4,
    110, 112–4, 116, 118, 228, 247–8
  ceding of 103
  enactment 99–118. *See* performance
  'radical assumption of' 102
space
  'coloured' 148
  public 105
  restricted 105, 121
  ritual 104–5, 111
Spanish 186–7, 191, 202, 204, 207, 214
'speak, ability to' 105–8
St John's 68, 79, 83–4
stakeholders 8, 27, 32–3, 143, 166, 176,
    244, 250, 253–4
  secondary 25–6, 33
Stanner
  WEH 107, 120
state 2, 4–5, 7, 9–14, 16–3, 19, 26, 28, 30,
    32, 34, 36, 39–40, 42–53, 57, 59, 64,
    83, 87, 99–100, 103–4, 118, 130–2,
    139, 146–7, 164, 172, 174, 182–3,
    186, 190–2, 194, 197–8, 200, 204,
    206–7, 210, 212–13, 216, 228–30,
    236, 241, 246–7, 251, 254
  actors 179
  agencies 8, 33, 38, 45, 58, 124, 163–4
  agrarian programmes 229
  apartheid 181

state – *Contd.*
  assets 16, 18
  benevolent 178
  bureaucracy 19
  colonial 28
  control 8, 48
  development 34
  discourse 203
  employees 51–2, 174
  expropriation 215
  grants 186
  impact of, economic restructuring 213
  institutions 8, 10, 195, 216
  interests 165
  intervention 38, 225
  jurisdiction 245
  land titling 213
  Latin American 185
  Mexican 217, 224
  laws 218
  legislation 165
  Mexican 213
  modern 3, 179
  nation 191, 212, 229, 230
  national 48
  negotiators 253
  officers 176, 226
  officials 37, 50, 54, 56, 59, 87, 166, 185, 252
  -owned land 216, 245
  parks 14, 16, 235, 241
  Peruvian 187, 191, 193, 197, 203–4
  planning 8, 10
  policies 213, 221, 229–30
  politics 175, 229
  post-colonial 7
  -projected nationalism 213
  projects 212, 218–9, 222, 228
  protectionism 214
  regulations 49
  relative inefficiency of 213
  representatives 8, 46–7, 238, 249
  role of, in restitution 8, 26, 28, 175
  -run enterprise 198
  settler 99–100
  -society relations 229
  subsidies 219–20
  supreme court 241
  treaties 236
  weak 46, 48, 173
State of New York
  Legislature 236, 241–2, 255

'statistical ethnocide' 222
stereotype 28, 202, 218, 222
stratification 54, 175
struggle 5, 20, 25–6, 28–9, 36–9, 84, 124, 130–1, 133–7, 139, 144, 147, 149, 157, 160, 166–7, 188, 192, 195, 203–4, 206, 213, 217, 227
  class 203
struggles 5, 82, 124–5, 127, 130, 132, 136, 174, 179, 181, 190, 203, 206, 215, 217, 227, 229, 232
Subarctic 21, 85
subjection
  civic 37
  new forms of 2, 25–6, 36–7
subjects 2, 100, 102, 117
  of their own destiny 140
  or citizens 13, 36
  traditionalist 171
subsidies 162, 169
subsistence 166, 170
  agriculture 167, 211, 218, 227
  economies 195, 210
  exploitation 82
  farming 165, 176, 212–3. *See* farming
  fishing 86. *See* fishing
  harvesting 31
Superintendency of Studies and Works against the Effects of Droughts 125
support
  popular 168, 178
Supreme Court 75, 83, 86–7, 101, 238, 259
symbolism 1, 5, 11, 19, 56, 59, 105, 136, 142, 144–5, 148, 157, 160, 163, 166, 172, 182, 191, 220–3, 229
  of court. *See* court
  of land 129 *See* land, multiple meanings
symbols 45, 121, 172

Table Mountain 142
Tanner 76, 78, 84
tapadas 195
tax 241
  base 14, 240, 242–3, 252
  erosion 240, 242–3
  dollars 16, 246
  evasion of 53–54
temporal/social
  discontinuity 173

temporal/spatial aspects of restitution. *See* restitution
tenants 6, 155
　relation to owners 9, 12, 143, 147, 170
tension
　between desire and expectation 141
　between historical redress and present-oriented production 163–81
　between theory and practice of SAIS structure 196–7
territory
　Innu 78
　surrender of 77
Territory
　Northern 99–101, 105, 116, 118–22
　Yukon 85, 87
'terrorists' 200
tierra para el que la trabaja, la 202
theatre 164, 251
theft 45, 50, 52–3, 56, 59, 173, 192, 198
theory
　contrast to practice 85–95, 196, 199, 214
threat 30, 32, 56, 59, 74, 140, 173, 187, 199, 224–5, 227, 243
Thule 68
țigani 46, 63
time
　better, nostalgia for 6
　effect of 157
　immemorial 69, 75, 186, 189, 204
　of disintegration 10
　of removals 143
　of *sendero* 199
　of the indigenous republics 218
　of forefathers 189
　passage of, in restitution 6
title 10, 134, 136
　alienable 131
　extinguishment of 77, 102
　fee simple 88, 91–2, 96, 101, 117
　inalienable. *See* inalienability
　native 99, 101–7, 109–11, 113, 116–19, 121–2
　untreatied 75
titles
　ancient 186

titling 211, 224, 226, 227–8
　individual 209, 212, 227
Torres Strait 100–1, 119
tourism 7, 26–7, 29, 33–7, 240
trade 51
　free 225
　fur 69
　tourist 242
traders
　former 143–4, 147
tradition
　cultural 148
　reinvention of 174
'tradition' 10, 178, 181
traditional
　authorities. *See* authorities
　clothes 168
　crafts 77
　crops 222
　culture 127
　farming 176
　hacienda 192
　institutions 175
　lands 101
　law. *See* law
　laws 102
　leader 167, 173–4
　leadership 173
　lifestyle 12, 15, 37, 42, 56, 76, 93–4, 97, 101–3, 110, 117, 127, 167–8, 171–6, 179, 192, 204, 222
　neo-, forms of subjection. *See* subjection
　occupation 56
　owners 101, 103, 117
　rights 15
　territory 93–4, 97
　values. *See* values, traditional
Traditional
　Territory 88, 93
traditionalist
　lifestyle 171
　narratives 175
Tralso 28–9, 37, 41–2
transition 136
　gradual 3
　rapid 3
　social 2
　to democracy 146
Transitional Rural Councils 33
translation
　problems of 108–110

Transkei 27–8, 30–2, 35–6, 40–2, 143, 173, 177
transportation
 of wood 54–5
trapping 71, 73, 79, 92
traps 92
treaties 7, 75–7
 as marginalizing 225
 extinguishment of title by 86.
  See title
 in Australia 99
 in Canada 68, 70–1, 75, 86
 in US 236
 state 236
Treaties 8 and 11 (Canada) 76
tree-cutting
 illegal 52
trespass 51, 57, 79, 236, 247
tribal
 ritual 178
Tribal Authorities 26, 33, 37, 42
tribal strife 173
trucks 53–5, 57, 199
Trudeau 3, 70–1, 74
trust 10, 252
 guardian/ward, relationship 254
 landowning 26–7
 maintenance of 250
Trust
 land 165–166
Truth and Reconciliation Commission 17
Túpac Amaru SAIS 185, 191, 193–9, 200–1, 204. *See* SAIS
turtle
 catching of 106, 115

Udall
 Congressman Morris 242
Umbrella Final Agreement (UFA) 88
UN. *See* United Nations
underdevelopment 19, 70
'understanding'
 in native law 108
unequal
 distribution 188
 land distribution 164, 190, 204
 treatment 248
unfair
 treatment 14, 133, 192–3, 246–7
Unidad de Producción Cónsac 194
Union Jack 99

unionization 125
United Nations 32, 205, 236
 Convention on Biological Diversity 32
 Declaration on the Rights of Indigenous Peoples 236
 Universal Declaration on Human Rights 205
United States 236, 245–7, 249, 255–7
unity 9, 29, 74, 82, 135, 147, 159, 175
universalism 137
University of Transkei 31, 42
 of Zululand 166
upward mobility 151, 157
urban/rural
 blend of 171
use
 future 92
Usibamba 185, 188–90, 193–5, 198–1, 206–7
Usibambinos 188–9, 195, 197

Vâlceni 46–7, 64
Valhalla Park 151
validation
 of land claims 17, 174–5
value 164
 disputes 244
 land 246
 of difference 115
 of diversity 137
 of forest 30, 49, 59
 of labour 246
 of land 5, 93, 194
 of land claim 75, 143
 of legal procedure 190
 of package 147
 of reserve 31
 of resources 93
 of restitution 129, 174
 political 166, 220
 scientific 29, 30
 symbolic 220
 'things' of 44
values 157
 contestation of 164
 cultural 168, 212
 democratization 178
 development 175
 in negotiation 244
 land 226
 national 13

real estate 252
  traditional 168
vegetable gardens 166, 170–1
Velasco 190, 192–3
Verdery
  Katherine 2–4, 7, 11, 13, 16–9, 22, 26,
    35–6, 41, 44–5, 57, 61–3, 87, 96,
    146, 157, 162
victims 17, 166
Vietnam
  anti-, protest 3
'view'
  as distinct from evidence 112
Village Conservation Committee 28
villagization 37
violence 22, 140, 150, 154, 167, 173, 190,
    197–9, 200, 206, 221
voice
  in negotiations 250
  lack of 150, 249
  of indigenous people 230
  political, lack of 73
  pro-development 80
voices
  multiplicity of 212
  plurality of 144
volition 145, 147, 153, 159
Vollmann
  Tim 240–1
vulnerability 7–8, 18, 36, 73, 78, 80, 140,
    214

wages 171
Waitangi Tribunal 18
Walsh
  Congressman William 238, 245
war 50, 63, 65, 103, 199, 205
Washington DC 242
waters
  rights in 100–1, 103, 116–17, 119, 240
way of life 8, 15–7, 68–9, 72–4, 76, 82,
    173, 223, 229
weakness
  in negotiation 243, 249
  of communities 8
welfare
  costs 240
  grants 174
  social 59
white
  Americans 247
  area 148, 151

business and administration 78
  dominance 148
  farmers. *See* farmers, white
  law 103
  native-, relations 85
  neighbours 176
  neither, nor African 142
  officials 173
  -owned farms 32
  people 28, 115, 146
  'people's things', *izinto zabelungu* 28
  suburbs 169
  Zimbabwean farmers 18
White Paper on Indian Affairs 71, 74
Whitehorse 86, 96
whiteness 202
whites 27, 30, 124, 248
  -only 142
Wild Coast Spatial Development Initiative
    (SDI) 33
Wildlife Protection and Conservation
    Society of South Africa 30
Willowvale 27
Winkler
  Harald 33
'winning'
  in court 107
witness statements 106, 108–10
women
  role of 50, 79, 110–111, 149, 171, 178,
    209, 221–2, 257
wood
  cutting, illegal 45–60
woodcutters 30, 45, 53, 56
Woodstock 158, 161
Woodward
  Mr Justice 101–2
workers 192, 195
  farm 6
  government 135
  laid off 51
  rural 123–5, 127, 128
World Bank 139, 181, 224

Xilitla 211, 213, 215–17, 219–21, 224–6,
    230
Xocó 123–30, 133, 136, 139–40

Yarmirr 116, 118, 122
Yellowknife 86
Yilpara 111
Yirritja moiety 111, 121

Yirrkala 100, 103, 105, 120
Yolngu 99–118
youth
   role of 6, 81, 171
YTG 88, 89
Yukon Umbrella Final Agreement 93

Zajac
   Ray 240–2, 249

Zapata
   Emiliano 217
Zapatistas 230
Zimbabwe 16, 21, 60, 182
Žižek 9
zoologist 31
Zulu 168, 171
Zuma
   Jacob 9